Business Economics

Theory and application

Neil Harris

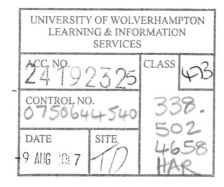

BUTTERWORTH HEINEMANN

OXFORD   AUCKLAND   BOSTON   JOHANNESBURG   MELBOURNE   NEW DELHI

Butterworth-Heinemann
Linacre House, Jordan Hill, Oxford OX2 8DP
225 Wildwood Avenue, Woburn, MA 01801-2041
A division of Reed Educational and Professional Publishing Ltd

℞ A member of the Reed Elsevier plc group

First published 2001

British Library Cataloguing in Publication Data
Harris, Neil
    Business Economics: theory and application
    1.   Managerial economics
    I.   Title
    338.5′024658

ISBN 0 7506 4454 0

Every effort has been made to contact Copyright holders requesting
permission to reproduce their material in this book. Any omissions
will be rectified in subsequent printings if notice is given to the Publisher.

Typeset by Florence Production Ltd, Stoodleigh, Devon
Printed and bound in Great Britain by MPG Books Ltd, Bodmin, Cornwall

Contents

List of figures   ix
List of tables   xi
List of abbreviations   xiii
Acknowledgements   xv
Introduction   xvii

Chapter 1.   What is business economics? An overview   **1**
    1.1   What business economics is and why it is needed –
          how it differs from economics   1
    1.2   Types of business organisation, profitability,
          industrial sectors, domestic ownership and
          foreign direct investment   12
    1.3   A brief introduction to price determination;
          demand and supply; types of market structure   20
    1.4   The business economic environment and how
          businesses appraise it; key macroeconomic
          variables; economic policies   27
    1.5   BskyB's attempted acquisition of
          Manchester United   37
    1.6   Summary of chapter   41
    1.7   Further questions   42
    1.8   Further reading   43

Chapter 2.   How businesses produce   **44**
    2.1   Competing theories of the business: profitability
          and other motives   44
    2.2   Porter's value chain. Formulating a strategy to
          meet business objectives   49

2.3	SWOT analysis; anticipating production – market research and forecasting	55
2.4	Flexible management systems; TQM and lean production; just in case and just in time production; Japanisation	63
2.5	Nissan car plant, Sunderland: a case study of Japanisation	68
2.6	Summary of chapter	70
2.7	Further questions	70
2.8	Further reading	71

Chapter 3. Producing for profit   **73**

3.1	The short term production process: developing cost theory	73
3.2	The impact of the long term: economies of scale	81
3.3	Calculating business revenues	87
3.4	Profitability; optimum production levels	90
3.5	The global car industry: seeking profitability through rationalisation	100
3.6	Summary of chapter	104
3.7	Further questions	104
3.8	Further reading	105

Chapter 4. Marketing the product   **106**

4.1	Marketing characteristics	106
4.2	Segmenting markets, targeting and positioning	110
4.3	The marketing mix; the product life cycle; pricing theories	114
4.4	Developing a marketing strategy	131
4.5	The decline of the fine fragrance industry	135
4.6	Summary of chapter	138
4.7	Further questions	138
4.8	Further reading	139

Chapter 5. Market forces   **140**

5.1	How markets function; consumer sovereignty. The collapse of non-market economies in Central and Eastern Europe	140
5.2	Market demand	146
5.3	Market supply	151
5.4	Determining market prices	155
5.5	The rise of the grey market	162
5.6	Summary of chapter	167
5.7	Further questions	167
5.8	Further reading	168

Chapter 6.	**Markets in the real world**	**169**
6.1	Elasticity of demand	169
6.2	Elasticity of supply	180
6.3	Market failure	184
6.4	Input markets	192
6.5	The minimum wage	197
6.6	Summary of chapter	202
6.7	Further questions	203
6.8	Further reading	203
Chapter 7.	**Competition and competitive strategy**	**204**
7.1	Business strategies: the structure–conduct–performance paradigm. Porter's five forces model	204
7.2	Oligopolies; competition and collusion strategies. Porter's generic strategies for gaining competitive advantage	211
7.3	Monopolistic competition; how firms compete	221
7.4	Other market structures: monopolies; perfect competition as the template	224
7.5	Competition for British retailing	230
7.6	Summary of chapter	232
7.7	Further questions	233
7.8	Further reading	233
Chapter 8.	**Regulating market power**	**235**
8.1	How and why firms grow. Mergers and acquisitions. Diversification as a competitive strategy	235
8.2	The need for legislation – monopolies, oligopolies and market failure	243
8.3	UK policy – the Office of Fair Trading and the Competition Commission. Regulating privatised industries	245
8.4	The role of the EU – policies; state aid and subsidies; public procurement	251
8.5	Scottish Widows carried off by Lloyds–TSB	258
8.6	Summary of chapter	261
8.7	Further questions	261
8.8	Further reading	262
Chapter 9.	**The macroeconomy and its impact on business: I**	**263**
9.1	Defining national income	263
9.2	Ways to measure real gross domestic product	267
9.3	The components of real GDP	272

9.4   Inflation – causes and costs of; money supply
        and monetary policy   280
9.5   The 1999 Budget   295
9.6   Summary of chapter   299
9.7   Further questions   299
9.8   Further reading   299

Chapter 10. The macroeconomy and its impact on business: II   301
10.1 Unemployment – types, causes and remedies   301
10.2 The inflation–unemployment relationship and
        its effect on business   309
10.3 The business cycle – causes and trends   313
10.4 Economic growth – theories, causes and costs   325
10.5 The role of economic briefings for business   330
10.6 Summary of chapter   333
10.7 Further questions   333
10.8 Further reading   333

Chapter 11. International trade and finance   335
11.1 International trade: theories, gains and
        implications. The terms of trade   335
11.2 The balance of payments accounts. Problems and
        remedies. The impact of capital flows   345
11.3 Managing exchange rates as a policy tool.
        Implications of exchange rate fluctuations for
        trade and businesses   350
11.4 Different exchange rate regimes   359
11.5 Economic and monetary union; the implications
        of the single currency for European business   362
11.6 Summary of chapter   368
11.7 Further questions   369
11.8 Further reading   369

Index   371

List of figures

1.1	A diagram of business economics.	4
1.2	The influences on business economics.	11
1.3	Types of market structure.	24
2.1	The break-even chart.	47
2.2	The total quality management model.	65
3.1	Total revenue and total cost curves of Sounds 'R' Us.	77
3.2	Average and marginal costs of Sounds 'R' Us.	79
3.3	Long term average costs: economies and diseconomies of scale.	85
3.4	Marginal and average revenue and cost curves and profits made by Sounds 'R' Us.	89
3.5	A blow-up section of Figure 3.4, where MC = MR.	95
4.1	The product life cycle.	123
4.2	Ansoff's product/market matrix.	132
4.3	The Boston Consulting Group's (BCG) product portfolio matrix.	133
5.1	A demand curve for audio cassettes of novels.	148
5.2	Demand curves for complementary goods.	149
5.3	A supply curve for audio cassettes of novels.	152
5.4	Effect of a change in the price of inputs on a business's supply curve.	154
5.5	Demand and supply curves for audio cassettes of novels.	156
5.6	The market for yo-yos.	157
5.7	Price controls and the black market.	159
6.1	An inelastic demand curve.	171
6.2	Other types of price elasticity.	174
6.3	The effects of advertising on the demand for Microsoft Office.	177
6.4	Income demand curves illustrating different income elasticities of demand.	179

6.5	Inelastic and elastic supply curves.	180
6.6	Perfectly elastic and inelastic supply curves.	181
6.7	Marginal private and social benefits and marginal private costs.	188
6.8	The marginal revenue product and marginal cost of labour curves.	192
6.9	The introduction of a minimum wage.	199
7.1	The structure–conduct–performance model.	207
7.2	The kinked demand curve.	219
7.3	(a) Monopolistically competitive firm making supernormal profits in the short term. (b) Monopolistically competitive firm making normal profits in the long term.	222
7.4	Discriminating monopoly.	227
7.5	Equilibrium conditions for the industry and the firm under perfect competition.	229
8.1	The effects of a subsidy on the demand for a good.	256
9.1	The circular flow of income.	275
9.2	Aggregate demand and aggregate supply curves.	278
9.3	A production possibility curve.	279
10.1	The short term Phillips curve.	310
10.2	The expectations–augmented Phillips curve.	311
10.3	The UK business cycle, 1990–1998.	314
11.1	The effects of protectionist import tariffs.	345
11.2	Demand and supply curves for sterling against the US dollar.	354

List of tables

1.1	Top ten British companies, 2000.	13
1.2	UK industrial sectors by size of workforce employed, 1998–1999.	16
1.3	FDI in the UK, 1996.	19
1.4	UK retail price increases, 1990–1999.	32
1.5	UK unemployment, 1990–1999.	33
1.6	UK balance of payments, current account, 1990–1998.	35
2.1	Market research and forecasting.	59
3.1	Total variable, total fixed and total costs of operating Sounds 'R' Us.	76
3.2	Average and marginal costs incurred by Sounds 'R' Us.	79
3.3	Potential revenue of Sounds 'R' Us.	88
3.4	Summary of consolidated profit and loss account for year ended 31 December 1998, Halifax Plc.	91
3.5	Total costs, total revenue and profit figures for Sounds 'R' Us.	95
3.6	Average and marginal costs and revenues for Sounds 'R' Us.	96
3.7	International Ownership of Marques, April 2000.	102
4.1	Socio-economic groupings.	112
4.2	Adopter categories.	128
5.1	A demand schedule for audio cassettes of novels.	147
5.2	A supply schedule for audio cassettes of novels.	152
5.3	Demand and supply schedules for audio cassettes of novels.	155
6.1	Demand schedule for the use of a local swimming pool.	172
6.2	Top ten UK polluters, 1998.	184
6.3	Top five trade unions by membership, 1995.	196
7.1	A dominant strategy pay-off matrix.	217
8.1	Purchase of UK businesses by foreign investors, 1995–1997.	240
9.1	Comparison of leading countries' GDP, $ billion, 1998.	271

9.2   Final consumption expenditure, £ billion, 1995 prices.   272
9.3   UK investment: percentage of GDP, 1995–1998.   273
9.4   UK household savings ratio, 1990–1998.   274
9.5   Components of UK aggregate demand, 1998.   277
9.6   Main measures of UK money supply.   285
9.7   Money supply increases, 1990–1999.   286
9.8   Changes in UK base rate, 1997–2000.   290
10.1   The accelerator principle.   318
11.1   Main UK trading partners, 1996.   338
11.2   Pre-specialisation production.   339
11.3   Post-specialisation production.   340
11.4   Post-trade situation.   340
11.5   The UK's balance of payments on current account,
        1996–1998 (second quarter) £m.   348
11.6   Sterling spot and forward rates at close of business.   352
11.7   Sterling/deutschmark and sterling/dollar exchange rates,
        1997–2000.   357

List of abbreviations

AC	Average Costs
AD	Aggregate Demand
AFC	Average Fixed Costs
AGM	Annual General Meeting
AS	Aggregate Supply
AVC	Average Variable Costs
BAe	British Aerospace
BCG	Boston Consulting Group
BL	British Leyland
BSkyB	British Sky Broadcasting
CBI	Confederation of British Industry
ERM	Exchange Rate Mechanism
EU	European Union
FDI	Foreign Direct Investment
FOREX	Foreign Exchange
FTSE100	Financial Times/Stock Exchange Leading 100 shares index
GDP	Gross Domestic Product
GNP	Gross National Product
ILO	International Labour Office
IMF	International Monetary Fund
ISA	Individual Savings Account
JIT	Just in Time
LRAC	Long Run Average Cost
MC	Marginal Cost
MMC	Monopolies and Mergers Commission
MPC	Monetary Policy Committee
MPI	Marginal Propensity to Import
MPS	Marginal Propensity to Save
MPT	Marginal Propensity to Tax
MR	Marginal Revenue

MSB	Marginal Social Benefits
MSC	Marginal Social Costs
M&S	Marks and Spencer
NE	National Expenditure
NI	National Income
NP	National Product
OFT	Office of Fair Trading
ONS	Office of National Statistics
OPEC	Organisation of Petroleum Exporting Countries
(The 4) Ps	Product, Price, Promotion, Place
PESTLE	Political, Economic, Social, Technological, Legal, Environmental/Ethical
PLC	Public Limited Company
PPC	Production Possibility Curve
PSNCR	Public Sector Net Cash Requirement
PSDR	Public Sector Debt Repayment
R&D	Research and Development
RPI	Retail Price Index
RPIX	Retail Price Index Excluding mortgage interest payments
SME	Small and Medium Sized Enterprise
SWOT	Strengths, Weaknesses, Opportunities, Threats
TFC	Total Fixed Costs
TQM	Total Quality Management
TSB	Trustee Savings Bank
TVC	Total Variable Costs
WTO	World Trade Organisation

Acknowledgements

The author would like to thank the following colleagues of Southampton Business School for their help and critical comments in the writing of this book: Charles Caplen, Edward Little, Jutta Manser, Geoff Settatree and Ian Stephenson.

Thanks also go to postgraduate student Josh Simons for his help with data collection. Particular thanks go to Ian Taylor who has produced the diagrams for this book without ever complaining about the frequent changes which were made.

The author also gratefully acknowledges the help of the editorial staff of Butterworth-Heinemann and the anonymous reviewers used by the company.

The author and publishers also wish to thank the following for their kind permission to reproduce copyright material: artnet.com for the advertisement on p. 142; the Environmental Agency for Table 6.2; Halifax Plc for Table 3.4; Microsoft Corporation for the advertisement on p. 177; the OECD for Table 9.1; the Office of National Statistics for Tables 1.3, 6.3, 9.2, 11.1 and 11.5; NTC Publications Ltd for Table 4.1; Posh Windows for the advertisement on p. 221; Saga Group Ltd for the advertisement on p. 110; Sunday Business Publishing Ltd for Table 1.1; and Volvo Car UK Ltd for the advertisement on p. 116.

Introduction

Economics is exciting – or it should be! It's about the real world today. It affects each and everyone of us – you reading these words; your family and friends, your work colleagues and fellow students; and me, even as I write this. The pace of life is changing; things happen faster, giving less time for reflection and response. Most importantly, in recent years, there has been a re-emphasis of the belief that maximising profitability is what businesses are all about. Whether this is achieved by developing new products and services, improving quality or cutting costs – usually labour – or merging with, or acquiring competitors. Creating wealth creates jobs and improves living standards. Therefore, understanding how businesses operate, their impact on the economies within which they are based, and on the consumers who buy their products, and the effects of the economy – national and global – on these businesses, is clearly important. Indeed, this tighter focus is the essential difference between business economics and economics.

Why another economics textbook?

There are many economics books available for today's student. Similarly, there are a number of books on business economics, so this poses the question 'why another one?' This is a valid question which deserves a good answer from the viewpoint both of the student and of the tutor. However, this author believes that there are common issues which apply equally when responding to both these groups.

Firstly, business economics is often studied on business related courses – HNDs and degrees such as Business Studies or Business Management – rather than pure economics courses and, most commonly, in the first year, although not always so. Sometimes the business economics course, or module leads into another economics type course in a subsequent year – for example European Business, as at the author's place of work, or managerial economics. Sometimes, economics education stops with the completion of the business economics course. In a sense, however, economics has been its own worst enemy, causing it to suffer a bad press in recent years. It is perceived by many students as mathematical, esoteric and driven by abstract theories, unrelated to the real world. Hence it confuses rather than explains. This is shown in the subject's declining popularity at 'A' level examinations, although subjects perceived as more exciting – some might say 'softer' subjects – have also proved more popular, particularly business studies.

Ironically, economics plays a key role in other subjects which, on higher education courses, are now preferred to it. Marketing and strategy both fall into this category, with economics providing much theoretical underpinning for both these intellectual disciplines. Similarly other subjects, such as the business environment, human resource management, international business and environmental studies, also draw heavily on economics. Therefore, economics, and for business related courses, business economics, plays a key role in providing a theoretical foundation. This book therefore draws on theories used in operational management, marketing and strategy, to better inform the business economist and to demonstrate the links between these different disciplines.

Further, economic literacy is essential for the well informed citizen. Merely to read one of the broadsheets or quality newspapers, or to follow the debates on television between interviewers and politicians, requires an understanding of how economies work and what policies governments might employ to address such problems as inflation and unemployment. Similarly, when a car producer lays off several thousand workers, or when the US government takes legal action against Bill Gates' Microsoft corporation for the alleged abuse of its monopoly powers, it is necessary to explore the economic reasons underlying this, to try and understand the reasoning behind the decisions.

Again, many economic events occur which impact upon UK citizens, whether they like it or not. The South East Asian economic crisis of 1997–1998 had an effect upon the economies and businesses of most countries. The advent of the single currency within the European Union; the globalisation of businesses which formerly operated within national boundaries; the growing importance of communication and information technologies – all of these and more have had major repercussions for individual citizens, for the businesses for which they work, and for the countries in which they live. Therefore, business economics is clearly a subject which needs to be studied if today's student is to have an understanding of how businesses operate and the environment within which they operate.

Addressing the student

However, many business economics books lose students, as do economics books in general. Their approach is to hit the student with large amounts of theory and, if there is the time, look only briefly at an example or two to see how relevant the theory actually is. I believe that this is the wrong approach. Having worked as an academic, a teacher and a researcher for many years, I believe that learning needs to be based on existing know-ledge and experience, i.e. the cognitive theories of learning where current knowledge is linked back to past knowledge and thus a new body of know-ledge, individual to each student, is developed. It is more important to look at the real world and examine the problems which occur. From these we can then seek to explain why events happen, how businesses might react in different ways to these, what policies governments might pursue in response to these problems and the implications these policies have for businesses. Quite simply then this book seeks to turn the conventional study of business economics on its head. From the real life issues we develop the theories which economists rely on and see how effective these are in explaining economic life and its problems. To myself, this approach seems more relevant to life, without losing the intellectual rigour necessary for studying this subject and for meeting threshold academic standards.

Linked to this is the use of what may be termed problem based learning. This has a long and honourable tradition in many US and other universi-ties, such as Harvard and the University of Maastricht in the Netherlands. Simply, it is the idea that economics is only of value if it can be used to solve economic problems, so problem solving is an effective way to learn. There is limited value in studying theory for its own sake. As discussed above, problems are the vehicle for developing a knowledge, understanding and application of business economics. I very much hope that the reader will be happy to work with this approach and will find it intellectually stim-ulating and rewarding – after success in course work and examinations which is, in the end, the key test of the usefulness of a book.

Addressing the tutor

This section has been written very much to address the student reader. However, I recognise the importance of fellow professionals. Research has suggested that many academics want a book with a more pragmatic approach. I have attempted to address this issue by the use of relevant applied case studies with supporting questions and answers, as well as an instructor's manual.

How to study business economics

There is not time or space in a brief introduction to explore in depth theo-ries of learning. All one can do is to provide a few pointers for student readers.

1 Do attend classes. There is a high positive correlation between class attendance and success in examinations and course work.

2 Use classes, especially tutorials or seminars, to ask questions and make sure that you understand what is being advanced, and why.

3 Read the relevant and appropriate sections of this book. Then make brief notes, combining them with lecture notes or other material from classes to produce one definitive set of notes which you understand.

4 Do not read for too long or your mind will wander and your understanding will decline. Take a ten minute break per hour to make a cup of coffee or whatever.

5 Do not make notes or write things which you do not understand. Explaining to yourself aloud a particular argument is a good way of testing your understanding. This is most important and will help your learning. Do not just try to learn things 'parrot-fashion'. This produces poor quality learning and understanding is often lacking. How many parrots understand what 'who's a pretty boy then?' actually means?

6 Cut out relevant newspaper articles and keep them in a folder or wallet. Try to link them to your notes; giving up to date and relevant examples looks good when writing assignments and in examinations and may well gain you extra marks.

7 Go through the questions in this book to test your understanding. If something is not clear ask your tutor.

Keeping up to date

Almost as important as reading this book is keeping up to date with the latest developments in business economics and in the economy as a whole. The most obvious way of doing this is to make use of the broadsheet or quality newspapers, television and radio, and the Internet.

If you haven't read one of the quality newspapers, now is the time to start. By the 'qualities' or 'broadsheets', we mean the *Financial Times*, *The Guardian*, the *Independent*, *The Times* and *The Daily Telegraph*. These have sections which deal with business and economics and give a breadth of coverage and depth of analysis which the tabloids fail to provide. Ask at your university or college newsagent as the broadsheets often provide a major discount for students (and staff). Do not forget that your college or university library may well have back copies of these on stand-alone CD-ROMs or on the student Intranet. If at first you have trouble coping with this on a daily basis, try one of the quality Sunday newspapers. Another magazine with a quality reputation is *The Economist*; check out your university or college library for this. All newspapers have websites; the main ones are:

The *Financial Times*: http://www.FT.com
The Guardian: http://www.guardian.co.uk
The Daily Telegraph: http://www.telegraph.co.uk
The Times: http://www.the-times.co.uk

In terms of the broadcast media, Radio 4 provides a good range of programmes which discuss the economy and the business world. Again, on television there are a variety of good programmes, including Channel 4's Monday to Friday 7 pm news programme, BBC2's *Newsnight* and the main BBC and ITN nightly news bulletins. BBC2's *The Money Programme* on Sunday is also well worth watching. For students who get up very early (not many from my personal memories of being a student, or from my experiences in teaching students!), the BBC breakfast programme has a good business news section from 6.30 am each morning – but recommending this may be wishful thinking on my part.

There are many excellent websites with which a student of business economics needs to be familiar. Search engines will help with finding much relevant information, but of course the problem with the Internet is the feeling of being overwhelmed with so much information. Focusing on the sites listed here will help save valuable time spent searching or, as I find, getting side-tracked into totally irrelevant areas. The main ones, at the time of writing, are:

> The Bank of England: http://www.bankofengland.co.uk
> Business Education: http://www.bized.ac.uk
> The Department of Trade and Industry: http:/www.dti.gov.uk
> The European Bank for Reconstruction and Development:
>   http://www. ebrd.com
> The European Commission: http://www.cec.org.uk
> The European Investment Bank: http://www.eib.org/over.htm
> The International Monetary Fund: http://www.imf.org
> The Organisation for Economic Cooperation and Development:
>   http:www.oecd.org
> The Office of National Statistics: http://www.ons.gov.uk
> The Treasury: http://www.hm-treasury.gov.uk
> The White House Briefing Room: http://www.whitehouse.gov/
>   WH/html/briefroom.html
> The World Bank: http://www. worldbank.org.

Good luck with your studies. I hope that you find this book both useful and interesting. Let me know what you think – I really would appreciate the feedback. Letters to me, care of Butterworth-Heinemann, will be personally acknowledged.

Neil Harris
Associate Dean (Enhancement)
Southampton Business School
Southampton Institute

Note: In all cases when used throughout this book, the term 'billion' should be taken to mean 'a thousand million'.

Chapter 1

What is business economics? An overview

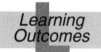

Learning Outcomes

After completing this chapter the reader will be able to:
- understand what business economics is and why it is needed;
- gain a broad overview of the main topics developed in the book;
- utilise a framework, acquired through case studies, for studying business economics.

1.1 What business economics is and why it is needed – how it differs from economics

The fall of the house of Yardley

Synopsis

This case study explores the decline of the perfume manufacturer, Yardley. It identifies a number of key characteristics if a business is to grow. These are:

1 to make profits to survive;
2 to continually update its products, targeting growth sectors of the market, and to support this with effective marketing campaigns;
3 to acquire other businesses, or merge with them, to boost potential profits.

Yardley, the toiletries and perfume manufacturer, has a long and distinguished history dating back to 1770 when King Charles I granted the company a concession to manufacture lavender soap in London. At the beginning of the twentieth century the Yardley family gained control of the business and in 1921 Yardley was granted its first royal warrant, with others following subsequently. These related to Yardley's famous soaps and eau-de-colognes, including English Fine Cologne, Sandalwood, Lily of the Valley and Yardley English Lavender. They enabled Yardley to declare on its product packaging, advertising and letters 'by appointment to. . . .' followed by the name of a particular member of the royal family. In 1996 it was the Prince of Wales.

In the 1960s the company launched the Yardley Y range of toiletries for men but was then taken over by British American Tobacco (BAT). They launched new products such as White Satin, Yardley Lace for women and Yardley Gold and Blazer for men. They also sponsored the McLaren Formula One racing team. In 1981, the pharmaceuticals company, Beecham, bought Yardley from BAT, but after merging with SmithKline to form SmithKline Beecham, sold Yardley in 1990 for £110 million to Old Bond Street, the American based business. This was 88 per cent owned by Wasserstein Perells, the American fund management company.

In spite of previous advertising campaigns, featuring actress Helena Bonham Carter, between 1993 and 1996 and, from 1996, top model Linda Evangelista, to promote its products such as the perfumes Panache, Satin and Tweed, in August 1998 Yardley was threatened with liquidation and the loss of 300 jobs, unless the receivers KPMG could find another buyer. The company found itself with secured debts of £126 million, in spite of annual sales of £60 million; unsecured debtors were told that there were no funds to repay them.

So why did such a well established business run into such problems? A number of reasons can be identified, all within the broad sphere of business economics. Most importantly, insufficient money was invested in the company to permit the development of new products and new production methods, in part a reflection of the regular changes of ownership. This resulted in the company acquiring an image of being old-fashioned and with older consumers, although this had created a loyal customer base. Although there is nothing wrong with targeting the over-50s, as the holiday company Saga has demonstrated, for perfumes, cosmetics and clothes it is the end of the market with younger consumers that is the most profitable in terms of growth and expenditure. In contrast, Yardley's competitors such as Chanel, Dior and Estée Lauder, all high quality existing brand names offering strong competition, have invested more and developed new brands. Additionally, products must be priced competitively if they are to sell, something which Yardley needed to reflect on.

In late 1998, Yardley's Bath Luxuries division, which accounted for 25 per cent of Yardley's sales, was sold to Cosmopolitan Cosmetics, a subsidiary of Wella, the German hair care and cosmetics group, to be run by a newly established subsidiary of Cosmopolitan Cosmetics, called Yardley of London. The remainder of Yardley's business, relating to perfumes such as Tweed and Panache, proved less popular, but in April 1999 was sold by the receivers to IWP International.

What does this case study say about business economics?

The above illustrates a number of issues fundamental to business economics, namely:

- A business must use its resources as efficiently as possible since they are limited in supply and there are costs in acquiring and using them. These include employees (known as labour), machinery and buildings (known as capital), and the land on which the buildings stand. Businesses also have the expertise of their top managers (known as entrepreneurs) who put the labour, capital and land together to produce the finished products most efficiently. Their purpose, amongst other things, is to ensure the business is profitable and grows; if losses are made over time the business will close. Hence, entrepreneurs must think about what and how the business produces, and its long term direction.
- Investing money (known as working capital) in new capital, products and ways to produce them is important if a business is to make maximum profits and grow. Clearly, insufficient was invested in Yardley to enable it to keep up with its competitors.
- Products must be priced competitively, be of good quality, imaginatively designed, marketed effectively and distributed as efficiently and cheaply as possible if customers are to demand them.
- A business must have long term plans to achieve its objectives. With Yardley, the objectives might be to remain as competitive as possible by investing more in the business, and launching new products which target younger consumers who spend more, helping it shed its older person image. Maximising profits will also be a long term objective.
- To promote the business' objectives and respond to challenges from competitors and from the business environment in which they operate. Cosmopolitan Cosmetics will have developed such strategies to gain a greater market share for the products it acquired from Yardley's Bath Luxuries division.
- Although it is less obvious in the above case study, developments in the economy will impact significantly on a business's operations. In 1997 and 1998, increasing uncertainly, caused in part by the Asian economic crisis,

caused consumers to cut back on spending, including toiletries and per-fume. This reduced expenditure was reinforced by a high interest rate policy pursued by the Bank of England, from May 1997 until late 1998, after it was given autonomy to set the base rate. All other interest rates, such as credit card, overdraft and personal loan rates are based on this base rate, hence its name. These high interest rates discouraged consumer borrowing and spending. Consumers seeking to economise will buy cheaper cosmetics and bath products in the local supermarket rather than more expensive Yardley products. Other perfume manufacturers, in a stronger position economically, were not so affected by this.

● Business is increasingly global in its nature and larger organisations look across national boundaries to secure economic advantage. This was shown by the last two owners of Yardley, the company with products having a quintessentially English image, being American and German.

Basic economics concepts

Figure 1.1 shows, in simplified form, the relationship between the three main parties in an economy: businesses, households and the government. Businesses produce goods and services; they sell these to the government (e.g. warships) and to households (e.g. perfumes). Businesses and house-holds pay taxes to the government and, in return, businesses may receive

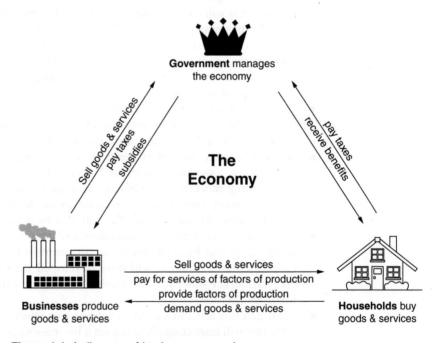

Figure 1.1 A diagram of business economics.

subsidies whilst households receive benefits such as unemployment benefits, state pensions etc. Households provide factors of production, such as labour, to businesses and in return are paid wages etc. They use this money to buy goods and services from businesses.

Of course this diagram does not show the full complexities of the economy. Later in this book we shall explore issues such as inflation, unemployment and economic growth, which affect businesses and households, and the government's use of economic policies to influence these issues. Neither does Figure 1.1 show external forces such as foreign businesses which compete with domestic producers to sell goods to British households, which are imports from the UK's viewpoint. In turn, British businesses sell goods abroad to foreign businesses and households, i.e. the UK's exports. Additionally, the European Union has a significant impact on the British economy, as does the influence of the increasingly global economy whose behaviour affects the value of Sterling, share prices in the London Stock Exchange, economic growth and so on.

Defining economics

Economics is, therefore, the study of how the resources land, labour, capital and enterprise are used or allocated by a country to meet its demands for goods, services and ideas, now and in the future. The resources are employed by businesses or firms and are also known as inputs to the production process, or factors of production.

Business outputs

Goods

Businesses, also known as producers, manufacture goods and services. Goods are classified by economists under two main headings, consumer goods and producer goods. Examples of consumer goods include cars, chocolate bars, Levis, compact discs, a video or disk of the latest movie, and personal computers if used at home for personal or leisure use. The people who buy them are consumers, or customers and they live in households.

In contrast, producer goods, as their name suggests, are used to produce other goods. Examples of producer goods include robots used on assembly lines to manufacture cars, personal computers used in offices for work purposes, cement mixers on building sites, jet engines for airliners and prefabricated factories which can be easily assembled. Many businesses are, therefore, the customers of other businesses which buy their output.

Some goods are also used in the act of consumption – food, drink or disposable products such as toilet paper or nappies for example – but other goods, known as consumer durables, clearly are not. It would be horribly expensive, for example, if we had to buy a new television set every time we turned it off at night.

Services

Services consist of the provision of non-physical items. The list is endless and includes using a cash dispenser at your local bank (although the cash dispenser is a producer good), attending a home game of your local football team, listening to a live band, working out at your local gym, staying in a hotel, watching a video of the latest movie (as opposed to the video as a physical object), making a plane journey, and so on. In each case, consumers are using or consuming a particular service which gives it a distinctive character compared with a good. A service is used up in the act of consumption although it may live on in our memory such as the fond remembrance of a foreign holiday.

Businesses also provide services to other businesses and, in that sense, the latter are consumers of the former's products. For example cleaning agencies employ staff to clean offices in the evening or early morning when the work force are not there. In Chapter 2, Section 2.4, the possibility of one part of a business being the customer of another part of the same business and using its goods or services will be explored under TQM (total quality management).

Ideas

An idea is intellectual property which can also be bought and sold. Examples include the ideas in a novel or computer software. Of course, the book and floppy disk containing the ideas are goods.

Externalities

The production process of a business also creates another type of output which accrues to society as a whole but whose effect may not be reflected in a company's accounts, whereas the wages of the workforce, for example, will be. This type of output is called an externality and may be a benefit to society or a cost. It occurs as a consequence of either production by businesses or consumption by an individual or household. Pollution caused by a factory is the obvious example of an externality and it imposes a cost on society which is not borne by the producer, although the business may be fined by a court for polluting the environment. The effects of traffic congestion and vehicle exhaust fumes are other examples of an external cost of production. Conversely there may be external benefits, e.g. enjoying a neighbour's garden full of flowers in summer.

Society, rather than the business producing it, bears the costs of pollution, for example, in increased illness and hospitalisation, reduced life expectancy and so on. Chapter 6, Section 6.3 discusses externalities in more detail, as part of market failure.

Resources

The production process is when a business uses its resources, also known as inputs or factors of production, to produce outputs of goods, services and ideas; it may also produce externalities.

These consist of:

- **Land** – This includes not just what its name suggests but also what is found on it and in it – forests and the timber obtained from them, minerals such as crude oil, natural gas and diamonds, and even the fish in the sea. The cost to be paid by employing land, defined in its widest sense, in the production process, is known as rent.
- **Labour** – This is that part of the population who work. Approximately half the UK's population are too young or too old to work, ill and so unable to work, unemployed, or not wishing to work for various reasons such as being a homemaker, to use the American term. How the work force is determined, and how the number of unemployed is calculated, are discussed elsewhere in Chapter 10, Section 10.1. Those who work receive wages.
- **Capital** – This word is used for machinery, factories, computers, office blocks and information technology. Capital loses its value over time as buildings suffer wear and tear, and so need maintenance, whilst computers become technologically obsolete. So businesses have to set money aside to replace capital as it wears out or becomes technologically obsolete; this is known as depreciation. The term capital is also used to mean money; accountants talk of liquid capital to distinguish money from machinery. This money may be used to finance a new office block or a new factory. Alternatively it may be used to purchase shares in existing companies. Interest is the return earned from making capital available to a business. Finally, working capital is the term used to describe stocks of components and raw materials waiting to be converted into finished goods, and the finished goods themselves, held in warehouses, for example, waiting to be delivered to retailers for sale.
- **Enterprise** – or entrepreneurship, is the resource provided by the entrepreneur. It is the expertise he/she provides to combine the other resources most efficiently to produce the output of goods or services. It requires managerial, financial, inter-personal and strategic abilities if the business is to succeed. Famous examples of entrepreneurs are Richard Branson, chairman of the Virgin Group, Anita Roddick of Body Shop, Rupert Murdoch, chairman of the News Corporation which owns publishing and broadcasting businesses around the world, and Bill Gates who co-founded Microsoft.

Scarcity of resources

There is a limited supply of resources, i.e. they are scarce or finite, whereas the demand for goods and services produced from them is virtually infinite. This means resources have to be used by businesses and government as efficiently as possible to enable society to best supply what is needed to meet its own needs and demands. Every time a resource is used in one way it means that it cannot be used in other ways. Land used to build a by-pass cannot be used for housing, or as an industrial site, or left alone for the wildlife who live there. An economy therefore seeks to achieve allocative efficiency. This means that it wants to use its resources so efficiently that none are wasted. If it were to make any changes to their use no one could be better off except at the cost of someone else being worse off.

The costs of using resources

Each tutor at your university or college who teaches you is paid a salary or, if employed part time, a wage of between £15 and £30 per hour. This is a cost for the university or college, called the historic cost. Similar costs apply to the use of other resources, as discussed above.

For the economist, there is also a second cost to be taken into account, known as the opportunity cost. This is defined as the next best alternative foregone. For example, your university or college regularly buys computers for you to word process your assignments and to use spreadsheets. The opportunity cost is the next best alternative use for that money, for example extending the student canteen.

For your tutor, because he/she has chosen to work in education, the next best use of his/her abilities – say working as a manager for a local marketing agency – is foregone. For society as a whole, therefore, the total cost of working as a tutor is the income as a tutor, i.e. the historic cost of his/her wage, plus the economic value of what he/she would have contributed to the economy had he/she managed the marketing agency, i.e. the opportunity cost.

Economic theory assumes that people behave rationally. So why does your tutor teach when he/she could earn more money in business? The answer is that there are non-monetary returns, such as job-satisfaction, that provide sufficient benefit as to offer the best total return i.e. monetary and non-monetary.

At this stage it is also useful to tell the reader that the study of economics is divided into two broad sub-categories, microeconomics and macro-economics.

Microeconomics and macroeconomics

Microeconomics

Micro means small, so microeconomics looks at an individual business and how it behaves – a business such as British Telecom, or the chain of HMV record stores or a small and medium sized enterprise (SME) – the name given to a business which employs less than 500 people. It also looks at individual industries – the car industry or the television industry – and how businesses within them behave, although these industries can be European Union-wide or global. The focus of microeconomics is on issues such as: the demand by consumers for goods and services; the supply of such goods and services by businesses; the determination of prices by the interaction of demand and supply in a market; the costs which firms incur in producing and the implications for the level of production and the pricing of their output; and how businesses behave in an industry, depending on how it is structured, especially the number of firms in it.

Let us look for example at the US plane manufacturers Boeing and McDonnell Douglas which merged in 1997. This created serious implications for the European plane manufacturing consortium Airbus in terms of its ability to compete effectively against such a large corporation, since the new US company and Airbus account for most of the world's civil aircraft production. This was aggravated by McDonnell Douglas receiving large amounts of money in defence contracts from the US Department of Defense, money which could be used to cross-subsidise its civilian plane manufacture. Both the US government and the European Commission investigated these implications, drawing in part on economic theory which explains the behaviour of firms including how they might misuse their economic muscle. The EU only agreed to the merger when safeguards for Airbus had been clearly established.

Macroeconomics

Macro means large and macroeconomics analyses the economy as a whole, both nationally and internationally. This includes the exploration of key variables or concepts such as inflation, unemployment, economic growth, trade flows, rates of exchange and the balance of payments, and their impact on each other and on the economy as a whole. It also examines the role of government, and its policies to influence these variables and, hence, the performance of the economy as a whole.

These policies include fiscal policy, which relates to government taxation and expenditure, and monetary policy, which is concerned with influencing the economy through varying interest rates. Both of these types of policy seek to manage the level of demand for goods and services in the economy. Also used by governments are supply side policies which, as the name suggests, seek to influence how the economy supplies its goods and services – for example by improving education and training provision to enable the workforce to acquire more skills and thus be more flexible in its work patterns; or by reducing the power of trade unions to obstruct more flexible working and reducing the power of businesses to restrict competition or keep their prices high. Supply side policies were the centre of much debate between the UK and the rest of the European Union in the mid 1990s.

Although international trade has been included here as part of macroeconomics, with more advanced textbooks it is classified separately. When international trade and all external links are ignored to simplify economic analysis, the economy is known as a closed one. When the effects of international trade and other external factors are allowed, the economy is known as an open one. The UK is a classic example of an open economy since it depends so heavily on foreign trade with the rest of the world.

Business economics – how it differs from economics

Business economics uses largely the same concepts and terminology as economics and addresses many of the same issues. The reader might therefore ask how and why a distinction is made between the two. This author would argue that business economics is worthy of being distinguished and studied separately for a number of reasons.

First and foremost, business economics specifically seeks to investigate and analyse how and why businesses behave as they do, and what the implications of their actions are for the industry in which they operate, and for the economy as a whole. Businesses are constrained in their operations by many factors, both internal to them and external. The internal factors include: the types of resources businesses use, their availability, and how they are combined together in the production process; the nature and levels of the costs businesses incur in producing their goods or services; and the extent to which growth can be achieved internally as opposed to by acquisitions or mergers.

Externally, businesses face constraints from the types of market in which they operate: how competitive are they, for example, and hence how easy to enter or leave; what is the level of demand for the products they produce, and the trends in this demand over time. Other constraints are from policies imposed by the government or the European Union, in relation to competition, minimum wages paid and so on. Additionally, businesses have to work within the constraints imposed on them by the economy. In times of economic recession, for instance, falling consumer demand due to reduced incomes and rising unemployment may limit the ability of businesses to launch new products, diversify into new markets or even survive. Therefore, business economics seeks to analyse these constraints which face businesses,

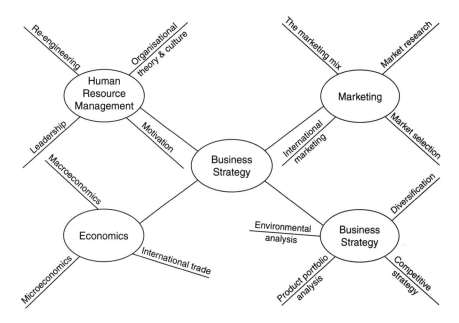

Figure 1.2 The influences on business economics.

draw conclusions as to how and why businesses behave as they do, and analyse the implications of such behaviour.

Business economics also draws on a wide range of different theories from a variety of different disciplines of which economics is just one, albeit the main one. Economics has had a major impact on the development of other intellectual disciplines such as business strategy, organisational behaviour, human resource management and marketing. All of these have drawn on it for parts of their theoretical content and, in turn, business economics draws on developments in these other areas. For example, Michael Porter's work on competitive advantage, which is regarded as business strategy, has been highly influential and is explored in Chapter 7, Sections 7.1 and 7.2 as part of the broad framework of business economics as defined in this book. Marketing theories, which include the pricing strategies which businesses use for their products, are explored in Chapter 4. This drawing on other disciplines again gives a wider perspective to the analysis with which business economics is concerned and, in particular, the constraints within which businesses work. Using a spider diagram, Figure 1.2 illustrates these connections.

Business economics therefore focuses on the issues directly relevant to a business and its operations, and to the business environment. This means, for example, that economic policy issues are not explored except in so far as they impact on a business's operations, i.e. running the business in the short term, and its strategy, i.e. its long term plans and how to achieve them.

What business economics and more general economics do share is the use of theories to try and explain how the economy works and impacts on businesses and households, and also how businesses work. A theory is defined by the Concise Oxford Dictionary as 'a system of ideas explaining something, especially one based on general principles independent of the facts, phenomena etc to be explained'. So the theory of evolution, for example, seeks to explain how man developed from lower life forms over millions of years. The competing theory, of creation, argues that God created the earth and all life forms relatively quickly.

Theories are important because they can be used to explain how to solve similar problems which occur at different times and in different circumstances. In other words, we don't have to keep reinventing the wheel. They can also be tested to see whether or not they are valid – if they are not then they are rejected and new theories must be put forward which better explain the facts. However, as can be seen in the example above, it is sometimes a problem when competing theories are advanced which cannot easily be tested. We shall encounter a significant number of economic theories during the course of this book.

1.2 Types of business organisation, profitability, industrial sectors, domestic ownership and foreign direct investment

Types of business organisation

Limited liability companies

The main type of business organisation in modern economies is the firm. It is owned by its shareholders who, in the UK, are largely institutional investors such as pension funds, insurance companies and banks. These financial institutions collect money from their depositors and contributors and invest it in company shares and government bonds to increase its value. Other shareholders are households and the number of private individuals holding shares has grown significantly in the last twenty years since the Thatcher government began the privatisation of state assets such as gas, electricity and water. Internet share trading has recently boosted private share dealing considerably.

Shareholders have limited liability, which means that if the business becomes bankrupt they will lose some or all of the money they have put into the business by buying its shares. However, their other assets, e.g. home and income, will be safe.

Table 1.1 Top ten British companies, 2000.

Ranking	Company	Sector	Market capitalisation £bn
1	Vodafone	Telecoms	226
2	BP Amoco	Oil	108
3	British Telecom	Telecoms	88
4	HSBC Holdings	Finance	60
5	Glaxo Wellcome	Pharmaceuticals	59
6	Shell Transport	Oil	48
7	Astrazeneca	Pharmaceuticals	44
8	Smithkline Beecham	Pharmaceuticals	42
9	Cable & Wireless	Telecoms	37
10	BSkyB	Media	37

Source: Courtesy Sunday Business Publishing Limited

Companies are either public limited liability, as in Freeserve Plc, or private limited liability, as in C&A Ltd. A public limited company (Plc) has its shares sold on the London stock market, which is also called the stock exchange, and may also be quoted, i.e. have its shares sold on other stock markets such as New York. In contrast, with a private limited company, the other shareholders have to give their permission if one share-holder wishes to sell some or all of his/her shares. So a company owned by members of a family – such as C&A Ltd – might use private limited liability to prevent loss of control of the business by excluding outsiders from becoming shareholders.

A public limited company, however, can always be taken over if a buyer is willing to pay a sufficiently high price to the shareholders to gain control of 51 per cent of the shares, giving it a voting majority at the annual general meeting (AGM) of the company, and hence control. A Plc has the advantage of being able to issue new shares to raise more funds to expand, for example by building new factories, developing new products or diversifying into new markets, rather than relying on undistributed (retained) profits, or bank borrowing which are the main options for a private limited company.

A business employing 500 employees or fewer is known as a SME, a small and medium sized enterprise. These are distinguished in their own right because they are seen as a major creator of jobs and an engine of economic growth. Hence both the UK government and the EU have sought to provide help to enable them to be established and to flourish. In contrast, large companies have sought for many years to reduce employment as a means to grow, substituting capital for labour – for example, automation of assembly lines. A SME may be a private or a public limited company.

Sole trader

If companies carry the greatest economic weight in terms of size, the largest sector by number is the sole trader. This is the business run by one person, although more than one person might be employed. The building industry has large numbers of sole traders or one man businesses as they are often known, e.g. plumbers, electricians, carpenters etc. The retail trade is also dominated by sole traders such as butchers and bakers although increasingly these have been replaced in recent years by the supermarket chains which are public limited companies.

Although many sole traders argue that there are real benefits in terms of independence, suiting oneself when one works etc., in reality this type of business can be characterised by low financial returns, long working hours and uncertainty. Most importantly it has unlimited liability, i.e. in the event of the business failing the sole trader is liable for the business's debts to the value of all his/her personal assets – house, car and so forth.

The partnership

This is the other main type of business organisation in the UK. Partnerships are most typically found in the professions such as law, accountancy, and architecture. Some partnerships have limited liability but many are unlimited. The problems of a partnership arise from decision making through the need to get agreement from all partners for business decisions; the difficulties posed when a partner wishes to retire (he/she has to be bought out); and for some partnerships unlimited liability. These are the least common type of business organisation.

Profitability

In general, businesses exist to make a profit, i.e. when the revenue from selling their goods and/or services exceeds the costs of producing that output. In economic theory, the assumption made is that a private sector business will seek to maximise its profits. Profitability can be expressed in a number of different ways, such as a lump sum, as a rate of return on turnover, or as a rate of return on capital invested. For the purposes of this book it will be assumed that firms seek to maximise profits. The ways in which profits are calculated, and the differences in how profits are defined by economists, accountants and marketers are explored in Chapter 2.

Industrial sectors

The economy of a country, and hence its businesses, are classified into three main categories: primary, secondary and tertiary.

Primary sector

The primary sector covers such industries as agriculture, forestry, fishing, mining for coal, tin etc. and the extraction of other raw materials such as oil from the North Sea. In other words, it is concerned with the production and extraction of raw materials, which are classified as the resource land. Examples of such businesses, listed on the London Stock Exchange under Mining, include De Beers (diamonds), English China Clay, Rio Tinto (mining) and Zambia Copper. Other relevant stock market categories include oil & gas and water.

This sector has progressively declined in importance over time both in terms of its output as a percentage of Gross Domestic Product (GDP), which is the value of goods and services produced in a country during a time period (usually a year), and as a source of employment. The only exception was the impact of the large scale extraction of North Sea oil in the 1970s and 1980s, but this has now contracted.

Secondary sector

The secondary sector relates to manufacturing, the provision of energy and the construction industry; so it processes the output of the primary sector. The manufacturing sector of an economy has traditionally been perceived as the major creator of wealth and jobs, as illustrated by the economic strength of Germany, Japan and increasingly PR China (the Peoples' Republic of China), all based significantly on manufacturing.

The UK's manufacturing sector has declined substantially in importance since World War II and particularly since 1973. This experience has been termed 'deindustrialisation' and, it is argued, is symptomatic of mature industrialised countries. If the reader looks at the share price listings in any of the broadsheets he/she will see a range of headings which encompass the secondary sector including alcoholic beverages, chemicals, construction, electricity, food manufacturers, pharmaceuticals and transport.

Tertiary sector

The tertiary sector of the economy relates to the provision of services and is the fastest growing sector in many mature economies. It covers a wide range of activities from hairdressing to the services provided by a top

Table 1.2 UK industrial sectors by size of workforce employed, 1998–1999.

Year	Primary sector 000	Manufacturing 000	Services 000
1998(1)	527	4202	17 923
1998(2)	520	4196	17 973
1998(3)	518	4180	18 131
1998(4)	514	4122	18 236
1999(1)	528	4084	18 312
1999(2)	536	4049	18 382
1999(3)	517	4019	18 526
1999(4)	508	4005	18 586

computer software author. Enterprise is another example and is often marketed under the heading of management consultancy, through major accountancy firms. The tertiary sector is the major provider of employment, a considerable amount of which is part time, and the major contributor to GDP. In the stock market listings, businesses providing services are grouped under such headings as banks, insurance, investment trusts, health care, media, retailers, support services, and telecommunications. The growth sector is 'dot com' companies.

Table 1.2 provides the employment data for the three sectors for 1998–1999.

Domestic ownership and foreign direct investment

Foreign direct investment – the dominance of American televised sport by News Corporation

Synopsis

This case study demonstrates the impact of foreign direct investment on an industry, namely the US sports industry. The key characteristics it identifies are:

1 that categorising industries into neat compartments is not always appropriate – here broadcasting and sports overlap substantially;
2 News Corporation has a long term strategy of dominating US sports broadcasting to boost potential profits. It does this by acquiring part ownership in major teams, a strategy it is also seeking to apply to the UK Premier League.

Case Study

News Corporation is a multinational communications organisation with control of many television stations in Australia (the birthplace of its chairman, the entrepreneur Rupert Murdoch), America, where Murdoch is now resident and for which he holds a passport, and the UK, through part ownership of BSkyB. It also is a partner in satellite communications in Asia.

Between 1994 and 1998, Rupert Murdoch undertook major expenditure in the US to make sports broadcasting the centrepiece of his American television activity. He already owns Twentieth Century Fox and Fox Television. At a cost of £2.75 billion he outbid all his rivals to secure control of the NFL (National Football League) broadcasting rights from CBS (Columbia Broadcasting System); in 1998 this was renewed for another seven years for £11 billion.

In March 1998, Fox TV successfully bid £190 million for the Los Angeles Dodgers baseball team. One month later it acquired 40 per cent of a new indoor sports stadium in Central LA. This deal brought under the Fox umbrella the Lakers basketball team, whilst Fox also acquired a stake in the ice hockey team the LA Kings.

Fox Sports has also made two key deals for regional sports coverage. Firstly, it has entered into a 50:50 joint venture (where each partner owns half the business) with the giant Denver based cable company Tele-Communications. This gives Fox Sports, and hence its parent company News Corporation, shared control of most US regional cable sports networks. Secondly, it has entered into a deal with Cablevision Systems Corp. Fox Sports has acquired a 20 per cent interest in Madison Square Garden, the famous New York venue, and the two teams who play there – the New York Knicks basketball team, and the Rangers, an ice hockey team.

As a consequence, Rupert Murdoch now owns the rights to every league team in New York that appears on cable television. This includes the Yankees and the Mets, the only baseball teams to rival the Dodgers for name recognition.

The reader will find this case study developed further later in Chapter 1.

It has been implicitly assumed so far that a country's assets are owned by its nationals. In practice, this is often not the case. Many office blocks and shopping malls in Sydney, Melbourne and Perth are owned by the Japanese. Many houses in Hampstead, London NW3, one of the most expensive residential parts of the capital, are owned by Arabs. More typically, companies will often invest in other countries. Examples include Générale des Eaux, the French conglomerate which controls such

UK businesses as the rail company Connex South Central; volume car producers Ford; and General Motors (Vauxhall) in the UK. Alternatively, foreign businesses may license production under a brand name such as McDonalds in the UK, or Bodyshop in the US. The main reason for this is that the investing companies anticipate being able to increase their profits.

Therefore, foreign direct investment (FDI) occurs when businesses invest in other countries. It is defined as an investment undertaken for the purpose of creating a lasting financial relationship between the donor and the recipient companies, which will result in the former exerting significant influence over the latter; this is classified as ownership of at least 10 per cent of the equity.

The FDI may result in the foreign company owning the new investment 100 per cent, or it may involve a joint venture where a domestic firm and the foreign firm share between them the costs of setting up and operating the business, and the profits. A foreign firm may even acquire shares in an existing firm, which is known as portfolio investment. If the amount of shares acquired is sufficiently large this will give the new investor control over the firm whose shares it has acquired. BMW's acquisition of Rover cars is an example of portfolio investment whilst its more recent sale is an example of disinvestment. In contrast, Nissan's plant in Sunderland, built from scratch, illustrates FDI. Central and Eastern Europe have offered considerable investment opportunities for American and Western European businesses since the fall of Communism in 1990, whilst for many years both America and Japan have seen Western Europe as offering a number of important markets with profitable investment opportunities.

To the host or recipient country one concern of receiving foreign direct investment is that a significant proportion of the profits – over 40 per cent in the case of Japanese firms investing in the UK – are repatriated to the donor country. This removes income from the host country and reduces the economic benefits of the new investment. Another concern is that potential domestic firms may not be established because of the competition they face from foreign investors. However, for the UK car industry, Japanese foreign direct investment has resurrected an industry which had virtually ceased to exist. Another benefit of Japanese investment in consumer electronics production has been to help regenerate areas in South Wales that had suffered high levels of unemployment and economic deprivation, after the disappearance of coal mining and steel production.

In practice, economic theory, as has already been indicated, suggests that resources should be allowed to move to where they can best be used i.e. achieving allocative efficiency. Nonetheless, the free movement of large amounts of money internationally can have a severely destabilising effect on the exchange rates both of the country losing the money and of that gaining it, and hence their economic stability. This is because changes in exchange rates impact on the price of a country's exports and hence its ability to sell them, and on the price it pays for its imports. In turn this affects its balance of payments, which is the record of its trade and other transactions with the rest of the world. This is more of a problem with movements of speculative funds, called 'hot' money, than with FDI, since hot money is moved from country to country in anticipation of short term profits, rather than for long term investment. It is, therefore, very desta-bilising. Portfolio investment may be an example of hot money but more commonly hot money is placed on deposit in money markets or used to purchase government bonds, to earn interest.

There is also the concern with FDI that foreign investors will gain control of the domestic economy and France has policies in place specifically to limit foreign ownership of its major businesses. In practice, however, this has not generally happened and indeed seems an ill-founded fear since the global economy is increasingly inter-dependent. In other words, the recip-ient country is just as likely to also have foreign direct investments in the donor country – unless it is a poor, developing nation.

On the positive side, FDI generates extra income and jobs by providing resources which the domestic country may not be able or willing to free up. Exports sales of the products the foreign donor produces will contribute to the host country's balance of payments and, of course, the capital inflows from Japan are an input to the host country's balance of payments (see Chapter 11, Section 11.2). Britain has also benefited significantly from acquiring Japanese production quality assurance methods (see Chapter 2, Section 2.4).

It should be noted that FDI will also impact on the donor country. For example, Japanese cars produced in the UK have been exported back to Japan to compete with Japanese domestically produced cars, with the impli-cations that has for Japanese employment etc.

Table 1.3 gives flows of FDI into and out of the UK for 1996, listing the major donors. It should also be noted that these need to be interpreted

Table 1.3 FDI in the UK, 1996.

Country	FDI into the UK £m	FDI received from the UK £m
France	356	2235
Germany	74	1277
Ireland	185	680
Italy	(171)	343
Japan	390	324
Netherlands	2677	6423
US	6994	2044

Source: National Statistics – the official UK statistics website, The Office of National Statistics. © Crown Copyright 2000

with care, since the figures may fluctuate considerably due to single large transactions.

Self testing questions

1 Under which factor of production would you classify the following: (a) A software programmer? (b) The New Forest? (c) A personal computer? (d) Sir Paul McCartney? (e) The new Severn Bridge?

2 List, in order of priority, the three best jobs you could be doing if you were not a student, and attach a wage to each. What is the total cost of what you are now doing?

3 Why do you think agriculture has declined so much in importance in the UK economy since 1900?

4 What are the advantages and disadvantages of a business being registered as a public limited company?

5 Is the large inflow of foreign direct investment into the UK in recent years a benefit or a disadvantage to the UK? Explain your answer.

1.3 A brief introduction to price determination; demand and supply; types of market structure

Determining a market price – Ford Fiesta for sale

Synopsis

This case study, taken from the small ads of a local newspaper, demonstrates that although economic theory predicts one market price for each type of good, in fact producers differentiate the products they sell. This in turn causes prices to differ between broadly similar products.

- Ford Fiesta XR2i. New shape, 90G, full service history, 88 000 miles, black, sunroof, stereo, long MOT/tax, very good condition. (**No price given**).
- Ford Fiesta 1.1L MK 3. F-reg-89, white, 81k, radio, f/sh, very reliable, MOT and tax, June. **£1175**.
- Ford Fiesta XR2. 1985/B-reg, Red, MOT September '99, tax, sunroof, alloys, r/cassette, vgc. P/X welcome, finance available. **£595**.

- Ford Fiesta XR2i. 1990, white, alloys, s/r, MOT, tax, 86 000 miles, f/s/h, excellent condition. **£3000 o.n.o.**

Most countries in the world are now market economies. This means that the prices of goods and services bought and sold are broadly determined by the market forces of supply and demand. A market is a location where potential buyers and sellers meet. It may be a physical location, for example a local fruit and vegetable market in your town; it may be through a printed medium such as the advertisements for second-hand cars in your local newspaper; or it may exist electronically, e.g. trading on the foreign exchange market where foreign currencies are bought and sold, or through the Internet. With the latter the market has no physical existence. Economic theory suggests that, in a market, only one price will exist for a particular good or service and for the moment that is assumed to be so. In practice, the real world shows that several quite different prices can exist for very similar outputs as the case study above shows; the reasons for this will be explored in Chapter 4.

The exception to market economies are centrally planned economies such as North Korea and Cuba where the government owns the majority, if not all, of the economic resources and decides what is produced, how and at what price it is sold. Often, this price bears little relation to the price that would prevail if it were determined by market forces. Centrally planned economies are discussed more fully in Chapter 5, Section 5.1.

The demand for goods and services

The above shows that society and individual households and businesses must make choices about the best use of scarce resources to meet their demands. In a market, the demand for goods and services may come from businesses or households. Businesses, such as British Aerospace or British Telecom, demand raw materials to manufacture goods or provide services, whilst households demand goods and services from businesses such as Boots the chemists or a local public house.

Households demand consumer goods and services because they obtain satisfaction or utility from consuming or using them. Because consumers have only limited incomes they arrange their expenditures in order of preference so that they buy more of the products that give them most satisfaction. For example, they may prefer to buy more fish, fresh vegetables and wholemeal bread, and less burgers, tinned vegetables and white sliced bread (depending on individual preferences, this may be reversed!)

Demand is used in a precise way, meaning here, that those demanding goods and services, at a particular price, also have the ability to pay for them. Otherwise the demand remains an unsatisfied want. Needs, in contrast, are what people must have; food and water, drugs if ill or addicted, and so forth. Most are purchased through one's income so become demand, but may be supplied by the state at less than the cost of purchasing them, or at zero cost, such as compulsory education to the age of 16. The government believes people should consume these merit goods, as they are known, but this may not happen sufficiently in a market economy. The fact that the government has to intervene in some way to ensure sufficient consumption of these goods and services indicates what economists call market failure (i.e. the market is not allocating its resources most efficiently). One form of government intervention to redress this was shown in Figure 1.1, i.e. using taxes. Chapter 6, Section 6.3 discusses this in more detail.

Savings are deferred demand

Consumers may choose to save some of their income, for example, in a building society account. Or, there may be compulsory savings in the form of contributions to state pension schemes. Savings are, in effect, consumption which is postponed or deferred to the future, when the savings are spent, rather than being undertaken now. They also give consumers satisfaction in the knowledge there is a safety margin for a rainy day, or they would not save. How consumers allocate their income between savings and consumption will vary depending on factors such as income, age, preferences etc.; however, the desire to maximise their satisfaction or utility will still apply as they seek a balance between current consumption and savings.

The supply of goods and services

Businesses supply goods and services which consumers demand. Business economics theory distinguishes between supply in the short term, when only certain factors of production such as labour and raw materials may be varied in quantity, and in the long term, when all inputs can be changed, such as a new factory being built, or a top executive hired from the US. The longer the time span allowed the more output can be changed. Price is the key determinant of how much of a product a business will supply; the higher the price, the more is supplied, since the business seeks to increase its profits. In reality, this may not occur if production costs rise too much as output is increased. Whether consumers demand the same amount as businesses supply is another matter, which is discussed later.

The interaction between demand and supply

This is fundamental to how economies function; it determines, to a considerable extent, the price at which the good or service is sold in the market. Economic theory argues that there will be a high demand for a product if its price is relatively low; yet a business will be reluctant to supply much since a low price means low profits. Conversely, if the market price is high, the business will wish to supply as much as possible yet consumers will not pay the high price, so demand is low. Somewhere between the low and high prices there is a price where demand and supply are equal, known as the equilibrium price; a free market will automatically move to this point.

Of course this is theory and a key feature of this book is to look at how things happen in reality, which is not always the same. Markets move to equilibrium positions, which is a fundamental characteristic of market economies. However, not every market is able to function freely and there is not always just one price for a product. There may be a band within which prices in a market may fall; the second-hand car market is illustrative of this. Similarly, the market for new cars is an example of one not functioning freely. There was much concern in the UK in the late 1990s over the fact that new car prices were up to 50 per cent higher than in Continental Europe, even for models produced in the UK. It was alleged that manufacturers force up car prices to 'rip off' UK consumers, an issue subsequently investigated by the Competition Commission. Additionally, if new car prices are kept high then second-hand car prices will also be high.

It should also be noted that the assumption made above is that consumers demand products and producers meet these demands. In reality, goods and services are usually supplied by businesses who seek to generate demand from consumers previously unaware that they had this demand. Usually, this is done by marketing the product or service in anticipation of supplying it. The ever changing specification of personal computers is one example of a producer generated demand rather than a consumer generated one, whilst the constant design and style changes to automobiles is another. Chapter 4 discusses marketing in more depth.

Types of markets structure

This section has talked of markets bringing together buyers and sellers. Business economics identifies a number of different types of market each with its own structure. In part, each market is distinguished by the number of businesses operating in it; Figure 1.3 identifies these.

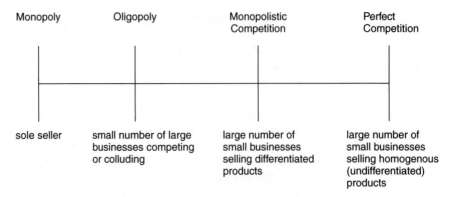

Figure 1.3 Types of market structure.

A few large businesses who dominate an industry

One type of market structure is where the market is dominated by a small number of large firms. High street banks such as Barclays, Halifax, HSBC, Lloyds–TSB, and NatWest are one example of this type of market structure, whilst filling stations such as BP, Esso, Mobil, Shell, and Texaco are another. It is quite possible that some small businesses, e.g. a family run filling station, will also exist in the market; however they will have little economic influence over such factors as the price of petrol, or the long term plans of the big companies. The technical name for this type of market is an oligopoly. Its importance to business economics is that whatever any one big business does will have an impact on the others, encouraging them to respond in a similar fashion. They may compete vigorously or they may collude to stifle competition, exclude newcomers and hence maximise profits. Both the UK and the European Union (EU) have passed legislation to control the behaviour of businesses in oligopolistic markets. Chapter 7, Section 7.2 discusses this.

Many small businesses selling slightly different products and services

At the other end of the scale from oligopoly is a market structure with many small businesses, known as monopolistic competition. They offer broadly the same products but compete by differentiating these through advertising and branding to make consumers perceive them as slightly different. As such, they are local monopolies since they dominate a local area but compete with other similar businesses close by. Newsagents are one example, whilst Chinese takeaways are another. It is relatively low cost to enter this type of market whilst the expertise needed is also limited;

economists call these low entry barriers facing newcomers. Similarly, it is relatively easy to leave the industry, i.e. exit barriers are low.

One business controls the entire market

This is the most extreme case of concentration of economic power and is known as a monopoly. Typically monopolies have been state-owned through the fear that they would abuse their power by charging high prices and blocking entrants, to make greater than normal, i.e. monopoly, profits. Former state owned public utilities such as gas, electricity and water were examples of this and were known as natural monopolies because it would not make economic sense to have more than one supplier (three different companies' gas pipes all going to the same house would waste resources).

In the last twenty years, in the UK and other countries, many state owned industries have been privatised. This has merely transferred monopolies from the state or public sector to the private sector. To ensure that these businesses do not abuse their power, the UK government has created regulators such as OFWAT (to regulate the water companies), OFTEL (to regulate telecommunications companies, particularly BT), and OFGEN (to regulate the gas and electricity industries). Those companies who control the distribution networks are now also obliged to allow other companies to use their networks, for example gas companies can supply electricity to a domestic residence. Chapter 8, Sections 8.3 and 8.4 explore more fully the issue of legislating against the abuse of monopoly power.

It should also be noted that a small group of large businesses who collude very closely will also act, in effect, as a monopoly, since they will charge the same price, restrict new businesses from entering the market etc.

Many small businesses selling very similar products and services

This last type of market structure is largely theoretical and is known as perfect competition. Its main difference from monopolistic competition is that the goods and services the very many businesses sell are not differentiated in any way. So, for example, consumers will have no preference between one tin of baked beans and another. There is no Heinz, Cross & Blackwell or Sainsbury's brand, nor any advertising, therefore. There are also very many buyers in the market, so neither any business selling the products, nor any consumer buying them, is economically powerful enough to influence the market price. It is determined solely by market forces, whereas the monopolist, or firms colluding very closely in an oligopoly, can easily influence prices. It is also assumed that everyone has a perfect knowledge of who is selling what, where and at what price, so there will only be one price in the market.

The reader may say at this point 'why bother with such an unrealistic situation? It doesn't relate to the real world, which business economics should be all about.' The answer to this is that a perfectly competitive market structure gives an ideal of how markets should work. The other three market structures all interfere with the free working of the market in some ways: through advertising and branding to influence consumer preferences; through restrictions on new businesses entering a market; charging excessively high prices; making excessive profits etc. In essence, the economy's scarce resources are not being used most efficiently, which is wasteful, i.e. allocative efficiency is not being achieved. It may not be realistic, or even desirable, to try and force all markets to be perfectly competitive. For example, since there are so many businesses in a perfectly competitive market, they will not be big enough to compete globally against American and Japanese businesses or multinational enterprises (MNEs) operating in several different continents. Nonetheless, economists and legislators use perfect competition as a template to judge other markets to see to what extent they fall short, and hence what should be done to rectify this.

Self testing questions

1 Give an example of a good or service for which only one price exists. Why is this so?

2 List as many reasons as you can why the Ford Fiestas listed at the beginning of this section have different prices. Assuming the owner of the first car did not forget to include the price in his/her advertisement what do you think the motives for this omission might have been?

3 The amount of disposable income (i.e. after tax and other deductions) which households save (do not spend currently on goods and services) has varied over the years, from 4 per cent to 12 per cent of their income. What factors do you think influence a person to save rather than spend all his/her disposable income currently?

4 Give three examples, other than those cited earlier, of goods and services where changes in demand are obviously generated by the businesses producing them, rather than by changing consumer tastes. Can this be justified on any grounds?

5 Give examples of: (a) an industry which is an oligopoly; (b) an industry which is a monopoly. How easy would it be for a newcomer to start up a business in either of your examples? Explain your answer.

1.4 The business economic environment and how businesses appraise it; key macro-economic variables; economic policies

The business economic environment and how businesses appraise it

The environment within which businesses operate is constantly changing, which will affect how they perform. This changing environment therefore forces businesses to regularly review their operations and their strategies for achieving their defined objectives. This will mean a business examining a wide range of different issues. Some, but not an exhaustive list, are given here as an illustration.

1 **Product portfolio**
   - The range of products it produces, called its product portfolio, whether these need to be changed and, if so, to what extent.
   - How well each product or brand is doing – in other words, whereabouts it is in its life cycle (see Chapter 4, Section 4.3). Are sales of some older products slowing down and, if so, can the products be revitalised or should they be allowed to die?
   - Which new products competitors are bringing to the market and how they compare with this business's own products.

2 **New markets**
   - The markets supplied and whether these need changing, e.g. with the implementation of the euro should the business expand into other European Union markets, or should it look to the US more, rather than just supplying to the UK?

3 **Investment**
   - Is sufficient being spent on research and development (R&D) of new products, compared with competitors? Are sufficient new products (or brands) being brought to the market quickly enough to replace declining ones?
   - Should the business seek to reduce its operating costs by reducing labour and substituting capital? Can it afford a new investment programme?

4 **New partners**
   - Can the business continue as at present or should it seek to grow by ploughing back retained earnings and/or borrowing from its bank and/or issuing new shares.

● Should it be looking for mergers and acquisitions as means to grow? If it is a pharmaceuticals firm, for example, a merger with a rival will enable it to secure a wider portfolio of products and share the very expensive R&D costs.

Appraising the environment

If a business does not remain alert to its changing environment then it will be left behind by other competing businesses which do regularly monitor it. The resultant loss of competitive advantage, in other words its ability to compete effectively with its business rivals, will lead to reduced profits or worse. Businesses need to review a number of areas which might affect their short term operations (running the business from day to day) and their long term strategy (where the business intends to be in three years, for instance, and how it will get there). Such an appraisal of its business environment may be undertaken under a number of headings which, together, are known as PESTLE, an acronym for Political, Economic, Social, Technological, Legal and Environmental/Ethical. These are variables or factors which can affect a business.

Political

Political changes may have a major impact on a business. After a general election, for example, a newly elected party will usually want to introduce a different tax structure or other policies which impact on business. Businesses based in Scotland will watch with some trepidation to see whether the Scottish electorate votes for independence, with some Scottish based businesses talking of moving their head offices to England if such an event occurs. Again, London based businesses will watch the election of an American style mayor for London to see how far he uses the tax gathering powers allocated to the office, whether anything can be done about traffic congestion etc.

Economic

There are many economic issues which can affect a business environment. For example, the rate of inflation and the level of the exchange rate against other main trading partners, especially the US and the reminder of the EU, can have a major impact on the competitiveness of UK exports and the extent to which foreign imports penetrate the domestic market. Large businesses will undertake their own forecasts; smaller ones will rely on buying in specialist agencies' forecasts to plan ahead and assess the impact on their pricing strategies and production costs. Similarly, the collapse of Asian export markets in 1997 and 1998, and the world economic slowdown, had implications for British businesses in terms of lost sales opportunities.

Social

The impact of EU social policy has had a major effect on businesses. Regulations have been introduced forbidding a business from requiring its workforce to work more than forty eight hours per week, unless they wish to do so. Another regulation requires both parents to be allowed three months leave after the birth or adoption of a child and the right to return to work with no loss of seniority. Both of these impose costs on a business and explain why the previous Conservative government of John Major opposed the UK signing the social charter which introduced these and other regulations.

Taking social in a wider sense, the nature of the workforce has changed, with the growth of part time work for women at the expense of full time jobs for men. Additionally, women are now securing more senior posts in business. As well as simple issues, such as the need for businesses to provide more crèches for the children of women staff, there are much wider issues in terms of the range of products and services businesses seek to sell to women, marketing policies aimed at women, and a whole range of other complex issues which pose businesses very different problems from those say twenty years ago when fewer women worked, and in much lower level jobs.

Technological

For the last decade the world has been experiencing a technological revolution so profound as to change the very nature of how we live and work. Obviously this has enormous implications for businesses. The rapid growth of e-mail and Internet-based voice telecommunications, increasingly supported by computer based cameras, has real implications in terms of lost revenue for traditional postal services and telephone companies.

E-commerce (electronic commerce) is growing rapidly, led by such companies as Amazon books (http://www.Amazon.co.uk). This also has implications for business workforces; they are increasingly likely to work from home, whilst consumers are increasingly likely to shop from home. US analysts have predicted that companies will have to get involved in minute-by-minute price wars as consumers use specialist search engines to compare the prices of similar goods across different outlets and countries. The reader might like to compare this with the assumption of perfect knowledge in the theoretical case of perfect competition discussed earlier.

Computer animation is now used more in television, for example, the image of American actor Steve McQueen in scenes from the film *Bullitt*, fifteen years after his death, to advertise the Ford Puma; or Dennis Hopper driving a Ford along a US highway in 1999 and meeting himself from the late 1960s riding a Harley Davidson motor cycle in the film *Easy Rider*. In the cinema, it has been used in the crowd scenes in the film *Titanic*. All these illustrate the creative as well as the commercial effects of communication and information technologies (CIT).

Microsoft is currently working on voice activated computers in vehicles and electronic books. By the time this book is published new developments will have occurred, such is the pace of change. Without putting communication and information technologies central to their business strategies businesses will soon be left behind.

Legal

Legislation changes and impacts directly on businesses, whether it be drafted in the UK or in the EU. The new Competition Act, introduced by the Labour Government and discussed in Chapter 8, Section 8.3, is one such example, whilst EU social legislation, discussed above, is another.

Similarly, as a consequence of a previous Budget and its resulting legislation, the 1999 replacement of PEPs (personal equity plans) and TESSAs (Tax Exempt Special Savings Accounts) by ISAs (Independent Savings Accounts) had implications for financial services providers, such as banks and building societies.

Environmental/ethical

Environmental issues and ethical ones may, at times, overlap. Hence E is used here to denote both.

Companies which, by their actions, cause harm to the environment, or their workforce, must understand the impact it will have on their sales and their corporate image when consumers become aware of this, as well as the legal penalties. Good companies will have a health and safety strategy, which betters legal requirements, and will be aware of what their competitors are doing.

Intensive farming methods are another example of environmental harm. The use of phospho-organic compounds such as fertilisers and pesticides have not only caused concerns about their impact on the health of the consumers of farm produce; they have also harmed the habitat of birds and mammals once common to the countryside but now in danger of extinction in some cases. The effect of CJD, or mad cow disease, and genetically modified foodstuffs, the so-called Frankenstein foods, is further illustration of environmental issues.

Ethical issues are of limited but growing importance to British businesses. Senior executives of a company awarding themselves large pay increases, often unwarranted by company performance, has been one example. Companies which exploit child labour in developing nations as some sports shoe manufacturing companies are alleged to have done, and companies which harm rainforests by felling hardwood trees for furniture production, are other examples of how businesses are increasingly being monitored by consumer agencies and pressure groups. Consequently, businesses have to be alert to changing consumer values and ensure that they conform to these.

Key macroeconomic variables

The impact of key factors or variables on the economic performance of a business have already been alluded to in this chapter and Chapters 9 to 11 discuss them in more depth. Here they are very briefly reviewed so that the reader will have a framework within which to' build his/her understanding of them.

Inflation

Inflation may be defined as a sustained rise in average prices over time. Usually, it is taken to be rising prices of consumer goods and services in the shops, although changes in the cost of mortgages may or may not be included, depending on the measure of inflation used. Other measures of inflation, also called indices, may relate to the prices of raw materials or producer goods, so are particularly relevant to businesses.

Table 1.4 gives changes in the UK retail price index, the main measure of inflation, for the 1990s. The headline rate of inflation, often quoted in the media, is the rate of change of the Retail Prices Index (RPI) and includes mortgage interest rates. The underlying rate of inflation, which excludes mortgage interest payments is denoted RPIX; it is targeted by the Bank of England. As can be seen, inflation fell in the early 1990s, then rose to a lesser extent before falling back again.

Inflation is perceived to be harmful to an economy since, as it increases, it causes employees to seek higher wages. These costs are passed on by businesses, as higher prices for goods sold in shops which in turn will push up wage demands the next year. Additionally, goods become less competitive in foreign markets so sales fall and increase the risk of firms reducing labour to cut costs and keep price rises lower. Savings may also fall in value after deducting the effects of inflation, discouraging people from saving and particularly affecting retired people relying on interest from their savings for income.

One distinction to make at this stage is between nominal and real values. Nominal Value minus the Rate of Inflation = Real Value. Suppose a group of employees receive a 5 per cent pay increase (nominal value); if inflation is running at 6 per cent the real value of their pay increase, after removing the effects of inflation, is minus 1 per cent (5% – 6%). In other words, they are 1 per cent worse off compared with previously.

Table 1.4 UK retail price increases, 1990–1999.

Year	RPI %	RPIX %
1990	9.5	8.1
1991	5.9	6.7
1992	3.7	4.7
1993	1.6	3.0
1994	2.4	2.3
1995	3.5	2.9
1996	2.4	3.0
1997	3.1	2.8
1998	3.4	2.6
1999	1.5	2.3

Source: HM Treasury

Unemployment

There are a number of definitions of unemployment, which will be explored more fully in Chapter 10, Section 10.1. In this overview chapter it may be described simply as the number of people in the working population of a country who are not working yet, who could and would wish to be. The working population therefore excludes, for example, those too young to work, the retired, and those in full time education although, in practice, many students do work. Within the working population some may not be seeking work, e.g. a parent staying home to look after the children. Of those of working age who are seeking work, the ones unable to secure a job, for whatever reason, are classified as unemployed. Also classified as unemployed are some who ostensibly seek work but, in practice, may prefer not to, but prefer to draw unemployment benefit.

Unemployment is undesirable because when people do not work then potential output of a country is lost and will never be recovered. To link to earlier theory, the lost output is the opportunity cost of not working.

Statistical or empirical data collected over time has suggested, at times, a link, or to be more precise an inverse relationship, between unemployment and inflation. So the lower the level of unemployment the higher the rate of inflation. Why do you think this might be so? The inverse relationship between unemployment and inflation suggests that the cost of having high employment is high inflation; conversely to keep inflation low the UK has to accept high unemployment. In reality, high unemployment and high inflation are both unacceptable, so a government may seek some tradeoff between the two, i.e. it may have to accept inflation at a higher

Table 1.5 UK unemployment, 1990–1999.

Year	ILO unemployment		Claimant benefit	
	Level thousands	% change	Level thousands	% change
1990	2005	6.9	1661	5.8
1991	2445	8.4	2286	8.0
1992	2830	9.9	2765	9.7
1993	2996	10.5	2901	10.3
1994	2796	9.8	2619	9.3
1995	2516	8.8	2306	8.0
1996	2394	8.3	2103	7.3
1997	2093	7.3	1586	5.5
1998	1824	6.3	1347	4.7
1999	1769	6.0	1363	4.4

Source: HM Treasury

level than it would otherwise wish, in order to prevent very high unemployment.

In the UK at the turn of the century, however, there is a historically low rate of inflation and relatively low unemployment, so the simple relationship suggested above does not always hold. We shall explore this more in Chapter 10, Section 10.2. Table 1.5 shows UK unemployment for 1990 to 1999, by two measures, the International Labour Office (ILO) and Claimant Benefit methods. These are discussed more fully in Chapter 10, Section 10.1. As can be seen, unemployment rose to a peak in the early 1990s but since then, has slipped back.

Economic growth

This may be defined as the increase in the output of goods and services produced in a country over a period of time, usually a year. So Ireland, with one of the fastest growth rates in the EU in the 1990s, achieved real, as opposed to nominal, growth rates of 9 per cent a year. Economic growth is therefore desirable and high unemployment will limit it.

The output of goods and services may be calculated in a number of ways but two definitions are explained here. Gross Domestic Product (GDP) is the total value of goods and services, measured in money, produced in a country during a period of time, usually one year; it also does not matter whether nationals or foreign companies own the factories. In contrast, Gross National Product (GNP) is defined as GDP plus net property income from abroad. For example profits made by Japanese companies in the UK are repatriated to Tokyo; these need to be deducted. Conversely, money enters the UK from investments overseas by British companies and residents. This will need to be added. The difference between the two income flows is known as net property income from abroad.

Sustainable economic growth

The only other qualification to make at this stage is that economic growth may create externalities, as mentioned previously. Sustainable growth is used to denote economic growth with the minimum depletion of non-renewable resources such as oil and coal, and with reductions in such externalities as greenhouse gases and other pollutants.

The business cycle

The economic growth of a modern economy will vary over a time span of approximately five years and is known as a business cycle. This consists of four distinct phases: boom, which is the peak of the cycle; the downturn when economic growth slows down; the slump or trough, when the economy is in recession and economic growth is low, zero or negative; and the upturn, (when the economy recovers. This is discussed in depth in Chapter 10, Section 10.3, and the UK's business cycle is illustrated in Figure 10.3 for the period 1990 to 1998.

Fiscal and monetary policy are used to try and iron out these fluctuations since steady economic growth over time with full employment is much more desirable than booms and slumps.

The balance of payments

This is a record of a country's trade with the rest of the world. As well as trade in goods and services the balance of payments also records flows of capital (money) between countries (the foreign direct investment discussed above), dividend and interest payments and profits earned on such investments, money repatriated by those working abroad to families in other countries, loans and gifts between countries, and so on. Nonetheless, trade in primary goods and manufactures (known as visible trade) and in services (invisible trade) are the major items in the media. Together, they constitute the balance of payments on current account. Table 1.6 shows this for the UK in the 1990s, with a more detailed table provided in Chapter 11. Brackets denote a negative value or trade deficit; as can be seen the UK's current account has been mainly in deficit in the 1990s.

Table 1.6 UK balance of payments on current account, 1990–1998.

Year	Current account balance £bn
1990	(19.5)
1991	(8.4)
1992	(10.1)
1993	(10.6)
1994	(1.5)
1995	(3.7)
1996	(0.6)
1997	6.6
1998	0.1

Source: HM Treasury

Economic policy weapons

The government has a number of policies to control the economy, which will be discussed more fully in Chapters 9 and 10. These may be used to reduce inflation, boost employment and growth, combat a trade deficit and make sterling cheaper to boost British exports. For the moment, three are distinguished: fiscal policy, monetary policy and exchange rate policy.

Fiscal policy

Fiscal policy is the use of government expenditure, which puts money into the economy, and taxation, which takes money out of the economy and into the government's coffers, to influence the level of economic activity and key variables such as those defined above. Of course, government tax revenues are subsequently spent so they re-enter the economy but not necessarily immediately, nor to the same parties as they were taken from. If the government feels that the economy is growing too fast, and so may overheat, causing inflation, it can reduce its expenditure. For example, a new road is not built and the men who would have constructed it are not employed, nor do they earn money and spend it. At the same time, it can raise taxes to remove income from citizens to reduce spending. The cumulative effect will reduce economic activity and slow down economic growth. However, taxes are usually only varied at Budget time (March) whilst the fiscal policy takes time to have an effect, so it is essentially longer term.

Monetary policy

In contrast, monetary policy will have a much quicker effect once implemented and so can be used for 'fine tuning the economy.' The most important instrument of monetary policy is interest rates. In the UK, these are set by the Monetary Policy Committee of the Bank of England, whilst in that part of the European Union already committed to the single currency, known as the Eurozone, the European Central Bank sets the interest rate for its eleven members. In the US the Federal Reserve Bank in Washington, DC, undertakes the task.

If the economy grows too fast, total or aggregate demand from consumers and businesses in the UK, and from overseas for UK exports, is growing faster than British businesses can produce the goods and services, the latter being known as total or aggregate supply. The Bank of England will therefore need to slow the economy. By raising interest rates, it raises the cost of borrowing from banks for consumers, who wish to buy consumer goods, and for businesses, who may wish to invest in machinery, buildings etc. This discourages demand for bank credit and hence the goods and services it buys; this will slow down economic activity. People respond more quickly to changes in monetary policy than fiscal policy. This is especially so in the UK where nearly 70 per cent of households are owner-occupiers, and hence very sensitive to increasing interest and mortgage rates.

To help economic recovery from a recession, interest rates can be cut.

Exchange rate policy

An exchange rate is the amount of domestic currency given up to buy foreign currency. Hence, for one pound Sterling (£) one can buy $1.60 or 3.20 Deutschmarks (DM 3.20) or 10 French Francs (FF 10.00) or whatever the market price (the exchange rate) is for each currency. These prices will vary according to demand and supply in the foreign exchange markets where currencies are bought and sold. The factors influencing the levels of demand and supply of currencies are discussed in Chapter 11, Section 11.3.

By influencing exchange rates a government can influence the domestic economy. For example, if the government can cause the exchange rate to rise from $1.60 = £1 to $2.00 = £1, sterling is more expensive (dollars are cheaper), so imports from the US will be cheaper. Previously, for £1 one could buy $1.60 of American goods, now one gets $2.00 worth. If the UK suffers from inflation and the exchange rate can be raised, then imports become cheaper. If these are raw materials they will be used to manufacture goods which can also be sold more cheaply, hence reducing prices more.

Self testing questions

1 Why might a government worry about its country having high inflation?

2 Should a government always strive to achieve the highest possible economic growth for its citizens? Explain your answer.

3 Summarise the difference between fiscal and monetary policy. When were interest rates last changed by the Monetary Policy Committee of the Bank of England, and what reasons were given for this?

4 Look up the rate of exchange of Sterling against the US dollar, the euro and the yen. Compare these rates with those of one week and two weeks before. How far have they changed? Think of three main reasons why exchange rates change over time and explain these in a sentence each.

5 Find up to date figures of the UK's balance of payments position. How are we doing? Why do you think we have a large deficit on the current account?

1.5 BskyB's attempted acquisition of Manchester United

Synopsis

This case study explores the failed attempt of BSkyB to acquire Manchester United football club. It therefore links to the earlier case study of News Corporation seeking to secure part ownership of many US sports businesses. It examines as key characteristics of a business:

1 The diversification of Manchester United into areas linked to its main activity, football.
2 Why BSkyB wanted to acquire ownership of Manchester United to protect its exclusive rights to screen football live, a key revenue source.
3 Why the British government was unable to allow the acquisition to occur.

Manchester United Plc

Manchester United Plc, commonly known as Man Utd or Man U, is the most prosperous sports club in the world; in early 2000 it was valued at £1 billion.

It had a revenue of £88 million in 1997, a rise of 65 per cent on the previous year, when it made a pre-tax profit of £27.5 million. This is despite the highest wage bill in the Premiership. It makes £1 million profit from every game its first team play at home and, through a £30 million extension, has raised ground capacity from 55 000 to 67 400. Man U have an estimated 100 million fans yet only one million have actually seen the first team play at home. Nonetheless, the official fanzine sells more than 118 000 copies in over 30 countries. There are more than 200 branches of the supporters club in 24 countries and 17 000 unofficial websites devoted to United. Its own website gets 8 million hits per month. As a result, the name Manchester United is one of the world's most famous brand names. To capitalise on this, in late 1998, the company started its own satellite television channel, a joint venture with Granada Television and BSkyB, so that subscribers anywhere in the world can watch its games. According to marketing experts, the potential revenue for the channel is incalculable.

In 1996/97, its main sources of revenue were: gate receipts and programmes (£30.1 million); merchandising (shirts and souvenirs), of which more is sold than any other club's (£28.7 million); television (£12.6 million); sponsorship (£11.1 million); and conferences and catering (£5.5 million). Currently it makes £22 million per year from broadcasting rights.

Manchester Utd changed from being a private to a public limited company in 1991, when it was valued at £47 million, whilst in the 1980s it had been for sale for £10 million. It also has cash reserves of £16.5 million and assets of £72.4 million, including a museum and a four star hotel with over 100 rooms. Its financial success has been helped enormously by its sporting success in nurturing its own talent such as Ryan Giggs, David Beckham, Paul Scholes, and Nicky Butt.

BskyB

BSkyB is a Plc whose main shareholders are News Corporation (the parent company of *The Times*, *The Sun*, *The News of the World* etc.) with a 40 per cent stake; Granada; and Chargeurs, the French transport and communications group. Rupert Murdoch is chairman and chief executive of News Corporation. BSkyB has revolutionised football coverage in the UK with its satellite sports channel showing live games since winning exclusive rights to show FA Carling Premiership matches live. As Manchester United's manager Alex Ferguson has argued 'Sky has created a profile for players. In the Sixties it was Albert Finney, Richard Burton and Tom Courtney who were idols of the screen but they have been replaced by footballers.'

However, at £30 per month the cost of the total BSkyB package, i.e. sport, movies, Discovery channel etc., it is too expensive for some. In late 1998 BSkyB launched a multiple channel digital broadcasting system.

The proposed take-over

In September 1998, BSkyB made a bid of £625 million to buy Manchester United, which was strongly opposed by supporters' clubs in spite of the extra buying power it would bring to the club. BSkyB's rationale was as an insurance policy to protect its exclusive live football in case it lost a case, initiated by the Office of Fair Trading (OFT), that opened in the Restrictive Practices Court in January 1999. The Court considered whether the Premier League was an illegal cartel that could not collectively negotiate television rights. If it concluded that it was, then it had the power to strike out the existing television rights deals between BSkyB, the BBC and the Premier League, on the grounds that collective bargaining for television rights by the league is against the public interest.

In fact, in July 1999, the Restrictive Practices Court dismissed the OFT's challenge to the £743 million deal that the Premier League have with BSkyB and the BBC. This was the OFT's first loss of a case in the Restrictive Practices Court for some time; as a result the deal was allowed to continue until the 2001 expiry date, when its renewal is expected to be worth £1500 million. The judge who made the ruling argued that the benefits arising from the deal, in terms of reinvestment of money back into the game, and the fact that smaller clubs received some of the money, offset any potential anti-competitive aspects.

Additionally, for BSkyB, with its deal to show FA Carling Premiership games exclusively expiring in 2001, and with 200 digital TV channels coming on stream, football clubs could launch their own channels, including electronic pay-per-view season tickets. By owning United, BSkyB would be guaranteed some of the most attractive games; deals could also be done with other clubs. Other Premiership clubs did not object to the take-over on the grounds that, whoever owned Manchester Utd would still have only one voice out of twenty on issues affecting the Premiership. There were, however, concerns over a conflict of interests.

The Premiership

The Premiership, in which Manchester United plays, was established in 1992 as a means to secure greater income for the top twenty football clubs in England. It has been argued that this is an oligopoly of 20 top clubs regulated by the Football League (see Section 1.3).

Similarly, there was nothing in the FA Premier League rules that would block the BSkyB take-over of Man U. Keith Wiseman, the Football Association chairman, said the governing body would not get involved in any take-over. FA rules essentially deal with football matters. In fact, as it subsequently turned out, the FA Premier League did object to the Monopolies and Mergers Commission (MMC) on the grounds that, if BSkyB did acquire Manchester Utd, it would be privy to confidential information regarding rival bids for television rights from other broadcasters, which would give it a significant advantage. Matters of company law and so on would be for the Stock Exchange and Office of Fair Trading to resolve.

Implications of the proposed take-over

It was initially suggested that other broadcasters might be tempted to take out their own insurance policies and buy one of the larger publicly quoted football clubs such as Newcastle or Aston Villa, and this was soon demonstrated by the attempt of NTL, the American cable broadcaster, to buy Newcastle Utd. Both were perceived as having good regional franchises, being heavily involved in the Premier League talks on pay-per-view, and on the peripheries of the European Super League. There is also the worry that BSkyB might one day have a dominant hold over sports and the broadcasting of them, as is starting to happen in the US (see Section 1.2). This resulted in objections to the take-over from the BBC, ITV, OnDigital, Cable & Wireless Communications and Telewest Communications. ITN argued, for example, that if BSkyB became stronger it could block highlights of games being shown on news bulletins.

As noted above, the Office of Fair Trading investigated the proposed take-over and had to decide whether or not to recommend that the Secretary of State for Trade and Industry should refer the deal for a full investigation by the Monopolies and Mergers Commission. This recommendation was made.

The outcome

In April 1999, Stephen Byers, the Trade & Industry Secretary, supported the recommendations of the Monopolies & Mergers Commission (MMC) which blocked BSkyB's proposed acquisition of Manchester Utd. Byers argued that the proposed acquisition would not be in the public's interest, and accepted the views of the MMC that if the proposed take-over were to occur, it would reduce competition for the broadcasting rights to top matches; 'in turn, this would feed through into reduced competition in the wider pay TV market.' Byers and the MMC also believed that, if BSkyB did buy Manchester Utd, the gap between the richer and poorer clubs would become still wider which would not be in football's best interests, since it would damage competition in the sport. It also had concerns that if BSkyB acquired Man U this would trigger other media take-overs of other football clubs, lessening competition still further.

On learning of the failure of its bid, BSkyB argued that this decision would disadvantage British clubs against Continental European clubs which are backed by powerful media companies, whilst supporters' clubs called for the resignation of Manchester Utd chairman Martin Edwards, who was strongly associated with the bid. The City reacted by falls in the price of Manchester Utd shares, by 32.5p to 186p, and those of other football clubs which are public limited companies (Plcs). NTL also abandoned its attempt to buy Newcastle United.

The European Super League

There has been talk, intermittently, about a European Super League including teams such as Juventus and Inter-Milan of Italy, Barcelona and Real Madrid of Spain, Bayern Munich of Germany and Manchester United. The companies most linked to this have been Italian marketing company Media Partners, and Electra Fleming, the venture capitalist. If this came into being it would tear apart national soccer leagues. Certainly this continues to lurk in the background and is another reason why BSkyB had hoped to acquire Manchester United.

BSkyB's alternative strategy

If BSkyB owned Man U, it would be guaranteed some of the most attractive games; additionally, deals could still be done with other clubs. With its failure to acquire Manchester Utd, BSkyB embarked on a strategy of acquiring minority shares of other clubs, following similar deals between other media companies and football clubs. BSkyB's investments include acquiring 9.9 per cent of Manchester City for £5.5 million, and also shares in Chelsea, Leeds and Sunderland. The rationale for this is that many large clubs intend to establish individual television deals with broadcasters when BSkyB's contract with the Premier League expires in 2002; BSkyB therefore sought to protect its negotiating position by acquiring a share in a number of leading clubs. However, the regulators have argued that BSkyB will not be allowed to have boardroom representation.

1.6 Summary of chapter

This chapter highlights a number of important business economics issues; they are discussed in broad terms in order to provide an overview. The last case study emphasises the importance of profit maximisation, both for Manchester United and for BSkyB. The role of the entrepreneur is clearly illustrated in the activities of Rupert Murdoch, who has been the driving force in News Corporation, the parent company. It also illustrates the global nature of modern business since Murdoch is an Australian who adopted an American nationality in order to gain a strong presence in the US market;

his company also has a strong position in the UK market. It further illustrates the crucial importance of communication and information technologies in the 21st century, part of the tertiary sector of modern market economies. The attempted acquisition of Manchester United by News Corporation is also a good illustration of foreign direct investment.

The growth of a business through acquisitions and mergers, as opposed to organic growth through expansion, is clearly demonstrated here; this is of increasing importance in the European Union and globally. However, as businesses grow they stifle competition. The role of the Restrictive Practices Court, the Office of Fair Trading and the Competition Commission are a clear illustration of this. Had Manchester United been acquired by News Corporation this could have affected the prices charged at Old Trafford (Manchester United's ground) and, more importantly, the prices viewers pay for watching sport on satellite and cable television. There could also have been long term effects on other television companies and their ability to supply sports events; the BBC has already been priced out of many sports events which it has traditionally shown through having to rely largely on income from licence fees and hence being unable to compete with BSkyB.

The chapter also shows that clear and neat separation of economics into discrete topics does not work; there is considerable overlap. The case study also illustrates the importance of economic data. Without looking at the profitability of Manchester United, its crowd attendance and its revenue sources it is hard to gain an accurate picture of how a business is performing. In the same way, looking at a country's rates of inflation and unemployment, its balance of payments, deficit or surplus and so on, paint a picture in figures of how its economy is performing.

Most importantly of all it is very much hoped that the reader will see that business economics is not just abstract and irrelevant theories. Rather it is about explaining how and why events occur in the real world and what their implications are. The questions below seek to develop some of these issues.

1.7 Further questions

These questions will need more research. You should use your library to access quality newspapers, CD-ROMs, including back copies of newspapers, and websites on the Internet.

Don't forget that most clubs have a website and also that many newspapers, national and regional, are on the Internet. Ask your library staff and economics tutor if you need further help.

Further Questions

1 Imagine you were working for News Corporation at the time the possibility of acquiring Manchester United was being debated in the boardroom. Undertake, for Rupert Murdoch, a PESTLE analysis of the UK sports/television sector of the economy to provide background information for him as to whether the bid should go ahead.

2 If unemployment were to rise substantially in the UK what effects, if any, would this have on demand for the television services BSkyB provides? Explain your answer.

3 Would your analysis change if unemployment were low but inflation was high (say more than 5 per cent per annum)?

4 Identify the benefits and costs of having a European Super League for soccer and recommend whether such a league should be implemented.

5 In no more than one side of A4, and in your own words, summarise what business economics is about and what benefits knowledge of it can bring.

1.8 Further reading

Artis, M. (1996). *The UK Economy,* 14th edition. Oxford: Oxford University Press.

Bank of England. *Bank Briefing series.*

Griffiths, A. and Wall, S. (1999). *Applied Economics,* 8th edition. Harlow: Longman Group.

Harris, N. (1999). *European Business*, 2nd edition. Basingstoke: Macmillan Business.

The *Financial Times*

The Office of National Statistics: Labour Market Trends

The Daily Telegraph

The Times

Amazon booksellers. http://www.Amazon.co.uk

BSkyB website. http://www.sky.com./home/Generalindex.html

Competition Commission. http://www.competition-commission.gov.uk

Manchester United. http://www.manutd.com

The Office of National Statistics. http://www.ons.gov.uk

The Treasury. http://www.hm-treasury.gov.uk

Chapter 2

How businesses produce

Learning Outcomes

After completing this chapter the reader will be able to:
- understand and evaluate competing targets for business operations;
- understand competitive advantage and its relationship to Porter's value chain, and how to formulate a strategy to meet business objectives;
- analyse the role of SWOT analysis and market research and forecasting in determining what businesses produce;
- evaluate Japanese production philosophies such as TQM.

2.1 Competing theories of the business: profitability and other motives

The decline of Marks and Spencer

Synopsis

This case study explores the decline in profitability and market share of Marks and Spencer (M&S), especially in clothing, due to dated and unimaginative designs. The case study discusses the effects of this on:

1 other areas of M&S sales;
2 its suppliers;
3 its share price.

Case Study

Marks and Spencer (M&S), one of the UK's leading retailers, has experienced declining profits since 1998, through falling demand for its products. Although renowned for good quality, its clothes had become increasingly dated in their style and designs; in turn this meant fewer people were coming into their shops for groceries and other products. The reputation of the company was further harmed as a boardroom power struggle developed and the price of M&S shares on the London stock market fell from over 500p each in 1998 to a low of 232p in early 2000.

The downturn in its sales had a major impact on its suppliers, who often had an exclusive contract to supply M&S. It cut orders with them and, to restore profitability, moved some production to low labour cost countries such as Sri Lanka. In turn, the UK suppliers suffered lower profits and had to sack staff, for example William Baird, M&S's fourth largest clothing supplier, which led to the closure of five factories. Similarly, Coates Viyella, M&S's second largest supplier, closed a factory in Alloa, Scotland, which made women's underwear, causing 200 job losses.

In March 1999 M&S suffered a further blow to its reputation when Moody's Investors Services reduced its credit rating from the coveted AAA status to the lower AA1. This was because the weakening of the company's competitive position in the UK retail market was harming its business position and its financial flexibility. In September 1999, M&S launched its new autumn collection of clothes, but this did not sell as well as anticipated; this downward trend was further emphasised by continuing falling sales over the Christmas 1999 period as rivals slashed their prices. In December 1999, with M&S shares at 273p, rumours spread of a possible take-over bid by Philip Green, a retail entrepreneur, although subsequently this did not materialise. To address its continuing weaknesses M&S split the group into seven business units, to improve its focus on customers, each charged with being fully profit-accountable, so that no underperforming part of the business might hide behind the results of the group as a whole. However, hopes of a speedy recovery currently look slim with continuing low sales and share price.

Profitability

As can be seen from this case study, increasing profits are essential to corporate survival. Without this, confidence declines, sales fall, jobs are lost and, ultimately, the business may cease trading.

Profit was defined in Chapter 1 as the excess of total revenue earned by a business over its total costs; conversely if total costs exceed total revenue a business makes a loss. Total revenue is estimated by the price of each good produced multiplied by the quantity sold. The business's production costs are incurred by using its four factors of production or inputs. Exactly how total costs are calculated is discussed in Chapter 3, Section 3.1.

Business profitability can be expressed in a number of different ways, such as a lump sum, e.g. £50 million. It can also be expressed as a rate of return (R/R) on turnover. The rate of return is the net profit of the business, i.e. after deducting money which it sets aside each year towards replacing capital equipment as it wears out, i.e. depreciation. Turnover is the total sales revenue of the business. So if net profit is £10 million, and turnover is £100 million, then the R/R is 10 per cent. Alternatively, profit can be expressed as a rate of return on investment (ROI). So, if net profit is £10 million and investment is £40 million, then the ROI is 25 per cent. For investors, businesses are more likely to couch their profits in terms of the ROI, which is more important to investors, than the absolute level of profits.

This view of costs does not reflect that each of the business's resources might have been employed in alternative uses; unlike the accountant, the economist has also to allow for the opportunity cost. Therefore, although both the accountant and the economist measure the revenue from business activities in the same way, the economist estimates the opportunity cost of resources as well as the historic cost. Since the economist's costs are higher, the estimation of profits will be lower (see also Chapter 1, Section 1.1).

After using its revenue to cover its costs, and setting aside enough to meet the demands of the Inland Revenue (businesses pay corporation tax, amongst others), part of a business's profits will be distributed as dividends to shareholders, assuming the business has them, as their financial reward for investing their money in it. The remainder is retained by the business, known as undistributed profits or retained earnings, to finance future capital expenditure, or as working capital to ease any cash flow problems it faces. These can be caused by its customers delaying payments for several months meaning that the business, in turn, might not be able to pay its bills. Alternatively it might hold reserves for a 'rainy day' to cover any losses it might make later.

Other targets for business operations

Breaking even

From 1945 until 1979, when Margaret Thatcher's government came to power, the UK had many publicly owned or nationalised industries, including the electricity industry, British Telecom, British Gas, the National Coal Board, British Steel, and British Airways. They were not required to make a profit but rather to break even, taking one year with another.

This did not encourage efficiency in production, nor did it ensure allocative efficiency. In 1961, to address this, the financial responsibilities

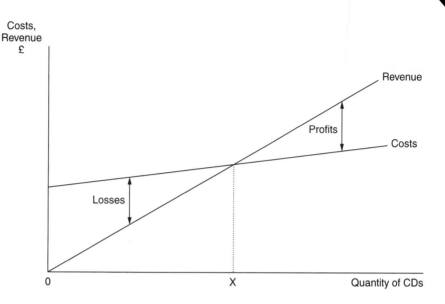

Figure 2.1 The break-even chart.

of nationalised industries were tightened, although in 1967, the government recognised that they could provide loss-making services if they benefited the community, i.e. that the social benefits of the services were greater than their social costs, as with subsidised bus services in rural areas. In 1978, in trying to bring state owned industries closer to the private sector, nationalised industries were required when undertaking new investment, to achieve a 5 per cent real rate of return, i.e. after allowing for inflation. The issue was subsequently eliminated when the Thatcher governments began a programme of privatising state owned industries. As a result these industries, now owned by shareholders, had to maximise profits. In contrast, when state owned, some 11 per cent of UK industry had no such objectives.

Figure 2.1 provides an example of a break-even chart, plotting revenues against costs. The more output a business produces the more revenue it earns but also the higher the costs of producing this output. Where the revenue and cost lines cross, at output X, gives the break-even point where revenues equal costs. Output less than X shows losses; output greater than X shows profits. For the business economist more useful information is needed; this is explored in Chapter 3, Section 3.1.

Sales revenue maximisation

Rather than profit maximisation, businesses may seek sales revenue maximisation because a manager's rewards may be linked to company sales rather than its profitability. So a company achieving sales revenue growth each year rewards its managers with bigger bonuses. This will encourage managers to focus on sales rather than profit maximisation. Consequently the costs of producing the output may be higher than if profit maximisation were the motive.

Pursuing management interests

In modern businesses there has been a separation between its ownership, i.e. the shareholders, and its control, namely the management. Since shareholders have no detailed knowledge of the business except for information published in the annual accounts and disseminated at the Annual General Meeting (AGM) they must, of necessity, delegate responsibility for daily running and longer term strategic direction to management. In turn this frees the latter to pursue other objectives which may suit their own interests, such as increasing the number of employees, or the size of the business. These may benefit them through bonuses or share options, size and type of company car, free membership of better health clubs etc.

Satisfactory profit

Another theory is that business managers will seek satisfactory rather than maximum profits, i.e. they will be profit satisficers rather than profit maximisers. In this case a suitable target profit level will be defined rather than the maximum. Shareholders will be content since they won't know the gap between the target or satisfactory profits and potential or maximum profits. In return, the managers can have a quiet and easier working life.

Others

It may be that businesses seek objectives other than profitability, such as maximising growth, achieving a target percentage for market share or merely surviving when there is a downturn in the business cycle. It may be that a business is guided primarily by ethical considerations such as not investing in countries which have repressive regimes, even if potential profits are reduced.

In contrast, public sector businesses such as health authorities or the civil aviation authority, operate to other targets. These include: working within allocated budgets; achieving bed occupancy and patient throughput targets, and minimising operation waiting times for hospitals; and handling more flights without extra staff and with no diminution of safety standards, in the case of the Civil Aviation Authority. In these examples cost minimisation rather than profit maximisation is a success criterion.

In the former centrally planned economies of Central and Eastern Europe most businesses were, before the fall of communism, in the public sector.

They worked to production levels to be met by each business over five year periods, the normal length for each national economic plan. Usually the business was the industry since only one producer was allowed, competition being actively discouraged.

Conclusions

The above are known as sales and managerial theories of the business. One way to combat the problems they pose is to link managers' rewards directly to company profitability. For example, the higher the profitability, the bigger the bonuses paid, or the greater the number of shares in the business they can acquire at a reduced price, known as share options. This addresses the separation of ownership and control which is a major problem underlying the various targets for business operations.

If business managers do not seek profit maximisation, competitors will overtake them. The business's share value will fall making it more vulnerable to a take-over bid. Mergers and acquisitions or take-overs normally result in redundancy programmes, which will, therefore, put pressure on managers to maximise profits.

It has been argued by marketers that, rather than considering the above theories as competing alternatives, it should be recognised that a business might operate with a variety of objectives. It will have a profit objective, although this may not be to maximise profits. It will also, for example, have objectives relating to its market share and how fast it wishes to grow, and these may all exist and be worked towards at the same time. The economist's counter-argument is that profit is the all encompassing motive. If there is not profit maximisation, market share will not be as great, nor will growth. So the other motives are subsumed in profit maximisation.

In reality, research also suggests that profit maximisation is a realistic motive for us to assume that businesses work to. It explains how businesses operate, and is an effective predictor of their behaviour.

2.2 Porter's value chain. Formulating a strategy to meet business objectives

Porter's value chain

The bigger the profits a business makes the more successful it is compared to its competitors. Underlying the costs and revenues which determine profits are the economic activities the business undertakes.

Porter (1985), argued that a business can have two types of advantage over rivals. It may undertake its economic activities more cheaply, i.e. there is a cost advantage, and it may be able to differentiate them from other businesses' activities, by branding, advertising, after sales service, the high quality of its products etc. Differentiation is discussed more fully in Chapter 4, Section 4.3. If a business produces more cheaply or differentiates its products, these are its two types of competitive advantage over its rivals. Its economic activities consist of many distinct activities from designing the products, through manufacturing and distributing them, to their sales. To explore the impact of these activities on the two types of competitive advantage, cost advantage and differentiation, Porter developed a theoretical concept or tool, the 'value chain,' which breaks down a business's operations into the distinct activities identified above.

The value chain displays the total value created in a business's economic activity. It consists of:

1   Value activities – these are physically or technologically distinct activities which use purchased inputs such as raw materials, human resources, i.e. the workforce and management, technology and information. They are described by Porter as the building blocks on which a firm creates a product which is valuable to consumers, making them want to buy it. In so doing the business creates competitive advantage over other firms.

2   The margin – this is the total value of production minus the cost of performing the value activities, i.e. the surplus created by the productive process. The reader should compare this with the definition of profit above.

A value chain is therefore a linkage of inter-dependent activities. Linkages are relationships between the way one value activity is performed and the cost or performance of another, e.g. between warehousing car components and the cost of assembling the cars; or between advertising and promoting white goods, such as washing machines or freezers, and the subsequent after-sales service. More precisely, argues Porter, each value chain consists of nine categories of activities linked together in characteristic ways to each other. Since a value chain can extend beyond the physical confines of a firm, to the activities of the business's suppliers of raw materials and components, the channels of distribution and its buyers, there is created, in effect, an extended or vertical value chain for that business.

The nine categories of activities are classified as primary and secondary. The primary ones are:

1   Inbound logistics – warehousing, inventory control etc.
2   Operations – manufacturing, assembly, testing and packaging
3   Outbound logistics – physically distributing goods to buyers
4   Marketing and sales – advertising, promotion etc.
5   Service – after sales service, installation and repairs.

The secondary ones are:

A Purchasing inputs – for example, raw materials
B Human resources – the work force and developing its appropriate skills through training
C Technology – including robotic production, assembly lines and CIT
D Firm-wide functions – general management, planning, finance, legal etc.

The linkages in the value chain can lead to a business gaining competitive advantage over its rivals in two ways – optimisation and co-ordination.

Optimisation

This means the best option available, e.g. a more costly product design may, in practice, result in reduced service costs after it is sold. This will make it more attractive compared with competitors' products which may need more frequent servicing – a car needing a service every 12 000 miles, compared to one needing a service every 6000 miles, for example.

Co-ordination

With the other way to gain competitive advantage, better co-ordination may lead to a reduced need for inventories throughout the firm. Just in Time production, discussed in Section 2.4, illustrates this.

Therefore, if a business is to maximise profits, or to maximise its margin, as Porter terms it, it must manipulate its value chain to gain competitive advantage over its rivals in the industry in which it operates. This involves formulating a strategy.

Formulating a strategy to meet business objectives

The mission

Many organisations have a mission or mission statement. This is a short phrase or sentence which encapsulates the underlying rationale of the organisation – its work activities or why it exists, in other words. For example the author's employer has as its mission 'Courses for Careers, Research for Results.' However, by itself, it is merely a general statement and lacks detailed content. As such, it would be hard to direct the future progress of the higher education institution merely on that basis. A mission statement also needs to be customer oriented rather than product oriented; in other words, how does it meet the consumer's needs rather than its own interests?

Strategy

Strategy is concerned with the purpose and goals of a business's activities and matching these goals to its resources, and to the environment in which it operates. The business's strategy will also be affected by the values and expectations of those who manage it, and the decisions they make will be complex and will affect the long term direction of the business (Johnson and Scholes, 1999). Strategy is therefore concerned with defining, in broad terms, the long term goals of a business and determining the courses of action necessary to achieve these goals, subject to the business's resource constraints. The business's strategy will not be frequently revised.

Strategy may encompass a variety of different aspects such as the mix of products and markets which the business chooses; this is discussed under marketing strategy in Chapter 4, Section 4.4. It may be concerned with the business's policy towards acquisitions of, or merger with, competitors (Chapter 8, Section 8.1). Strategy may also be concerned with a major new investment programme such as Disney Corporation's decision to build a second theme park alongside the existing one at Disneyland, Paris.

To achieve its strategic goals a business needs to define its objectives, i.e. what it wants to achieve, how and by when. These objectives are statements of intent, set in a strategic context and preferably quantified. They provide the business with a focus for future actions, encourage it to put in place plans to achieve these objectives and provide a means for exercising control over the business to determine whether the objectives are met. This is why it is important to be able to quantify them. They therefore encompass the relationship between a business and its environment, which was discussed in Chapter 1, Section 1.4, and they may cover a period of 3–5 years. They have to address such issues as:

- the business itself – its ownership, size, structure, product mix and technology;
- the industry in which it operates – its structure, its economic situation, the strength of existing competition, the likelihood of new entrants, domestic or foreign; the impact of government or EU policies;
- how the business is currently performing – its profitability; whether it is growing or contracting; whether it is undertaking new investment programmes; whether it is at risk of being taken over or is intending to acquire other businesses; its labour relations; whether some products are reaching the end of their life in terms of consumer demand.

Sony – implementing a strategy to challenge Microsoft and Intel

Synopsis

This case study provides a simple example of the strategy pursued by a business, in this case Sony. The case study examines:

1 the competition between Sony and Sega in the electronic games market;
2 the strategy of Sony to diversify into markets dominated by Intel and Microsoft to meet all the electronic entertainment needs of households;
3 the collaboration with Toyota to develop Playstation II.

Case Study

In 1999, the Japanese entertainment group Sony announced the launch of Playstation II, its new games consol; this was intended to be a follow up to Playstation, which had recently sold its 50 millionth unit, making it the most successful consumer electronic product in the world. Playstation II, Sony stated, was to be launched in Japan by March 2000 and in the US and the EU by Christmas 2000.

Sony is a very integrated entertainment company. As well as manufacturing videos and televisions, stereo systems, games machines and the games to use on them, Sony also owns the record company CBS and an American film studio.

At first glance it might seem that Sony was developing a new product to challenge Sega, its main rival in the electronic games market. Sega had launched a new product, Dreamcast, in Autumn 1998 which had, within six months, sold over half a million units. However, Sony also has other strategic objectives. Nobuyuki Idei, Sony's president argued that the next generation of Playstation would be a challenge to Intel and Microsoft. Using a cpu (central processing unit) named the Emotion Engine, which it developed with Toyota at a cost of £100 million, Sony would be able to ensure its Playstation II had cinema quality computer graphics.

Toyota brings laptop and desktop computer manufacturing expertise, which Sony does not currently have.

The Emotion Engine is some 300 per cent more powerful than the Pentium III, which Intel launched in early 1999, and incorporates DVD which is replacing CD-ROMs and video for information storage and showing films. By also providing Internet access and a digital music system Playstation II has the potential to take over and provide all the electronic entertainment needs of households, although Sony argues that it is a new type of domestic entertainment system, not a replacement of existing ones.

Just as the mission is a brief general statement about the strategic direction of a business so our assumption of profit maximisation, if viewed as a strategic objective rather than just an operating philosophy, is also too brief. Strategic objective means an objective of the business set within the strategic context. In reality, a business has a number of stakeholders and it is likely that strategic objectives will need to be set for the business to meet, which will reflect the interests of each group. The stakeholders will include the business's shareholders, the management, the work force, suppliers of components and raw materials, and customers of the business. It has been argued that the interests of the first three groups are often perceived as objectives whilst the interests of suppliers and customers are constraints on the business.

However, ethical models of business behaviour, such as the stakeholder model, argue that all interested parties have claims on a business when decisions are made. For example, as discussed earlier, Marks and Spencer has, until recently, bought many of its goods from British suppliers to whom it has been the sole customer. Where a supplier is the main source of employment in a locality, Marks and Spencer cancelling its orders causes the community severe harm. The stakeholder model would argue that the interests of the supplier should also, in some way, be taken into account when Marks and Spencer sets its objectives. Continental European business organisations are more likely to recognise the importance of all stakeholders to a business; this is reflected, for example, in having the banks, which loan the business money, and raw material/component suppliers, sitting on the board of directors of the company.

Whether stakeholders are taken just as management and workforce or in the broader sense, the business must identify its strategic objectives. These cover a range of different areas and relate to issues already discussed such as long run profitability targets, whether to merge with or acquire another business, whether to diversify into other products or markets, and whether to move much more into e-commerce (electronic commerce).

Operations

To complete this brief picture a business also needs to be concerned with the short term operational side of its activities. These relate to the business's day to day operations or activities and, for manufacturing, include minimising waste in terms of rejects produced on a weekly basis, assembly line downtime and overtime to keep within the labour costs budget. Without controlling these short term aspects of the business, for example, the long term strategic objective of profit maximisation will not be met.

Self testing questions

1 Is profit maximisation the best way of summarising the rationale for the existence of a business? Explain your answer.

2 Should Marks and Spencer provide some form of financial compensation to its suppliers for the effect its reduced sales are having on them?

3 Argue the case for or against the separation of ownership and control in a modern business.

4 What are the two types of competitive advantage that Porter says a business can have over others? How far do these apply to Sony's Playstation II?

5 From the case study provided, discuss the main strategic objectives which Sony appears to have. Why do you think it has these?

2.3 SWOT analysis; anticipating production – market research and forecasting

SWOT analysis

For a business to identify realistic, appropriate and achievable strategic objectives, it must have a clear knowledge and understanding of the environment within which it is operating and its own internal resources. It therefore needs to undertake an audit of these to know where it stands.

SWOT analysis appraises the external environment within which the business operates, in terms of the opportunities it offers and the threats it poses. It also analyses the business's internal resources in terms of its strengths and weaknesses. This is known as a SWOT analysis, where SWOT stands for strengths, weaknesses, opportunities, threats.

The external environment factors affecting a business

These include political, economic, social, technological, legal, environmental and ethical (PESTLE) factors, as discussed in Chapter 1, Section 1.4. Arising from these are opportunities and threats.

Business environment opportunities

These enable a business to seize commercial or economic openings and gain a significant market share of a new product or become the market leader. This may be through the business environment changing rapidly, or research and development leading to new products or services, the development of new production technology and methods, or a medium term decline in a country's exchange rate offering new opportunities for exporters.

Examples of opportunities arising in recent years which have been seized by innovative and dynamic companies include the growth of mobile telephones, the development of the Internet and e-commerce, and the development of low cost air travel by companies such as Ryanair and Easyjet.

Business environment threats

External threats are likely to harm a business's operations and may, in extreme cases, force it into liquidation. Forecasting and analysing the threats a business faces is, therefore, as important as identifying the opportunities.

The SE Asian economic crisis of 1997–98 was a potential danger to British businesses because it threatened their export markets. With the collapse of many businesses, job losses and hence falling demand for UK products, which were now also more expensive because of the fall in the value of the Asian currencies, businesses which were substantial exporters to SE Asia suddenly lost key markets. Similarly the arrival of the euro is likely, in the longer term, to cause greater instability for Sterling when measured against it (see Chapter 11, Section 11.3); this will cause the value of exports to and imports from the Eurozone to vary more and this will make business costs and revenues less certain and predictable. In the same way the single currency is likely to accelerate the completion of the single market and accelerate still further mergers and acquisitions in EU businesses. This will put greater pressure on UK businesses and the UK government to respond accordingly.

The internal resources of a business

These will include such factors as: the size, quality and productivity of the business's labour force; its capital stock including the age of machinery and how up to date it is technologically; the amount of land it owns, its suitability for expansion of premises, and its nearness to main transport links; and the capability and innovation of its entrepreneurs/managers. In other words the four factors of production discussed in Chapter 1. Other resources of a business in a broader sense include: its stocks of completed goods ready for sale; stock of semi-manufactures and raw materials; its goodwill which is a money valuation of its business reputation and how customers perceive its products and image; its R&D programme and its marketing capability.

Business strengths

The strengths of a business are its capabilities to employ its resources as effectively as possible to supply products to the market. For example, a pharmaceuticals company such as Zeneca, or Glaxo Wellcome has a large R&D programme. One of its main strengths is its ability to develop and market new products to fight AIDS, senile dementia or cancer, despite the very high development costs incurred. The Virgin Group has a very dynamic, high profile and popular entrepreneur in Richard Branson. His face is probably more valuable to the businesses than the Virgin logo and is used as much as possible to promote new ventures. A business needs, therefore, to identify its strengths and build on them.

Business weaknesses

Conversely, a company with internal weaknesses needs to recognise and address these if it is to continue in business and prosper. In the mid 1990s, British Gas suffered very bad publicity because it closed down its High Street showrooms with consequent job losses whilst its Chief Executive, Cedric Brown, was paid a 75 per cent salary increase. Similarly, whilst Richard Branson may be a popular man, Virgin Trains, which runs one of the UK's rail services, suffers customer complaints about lateness or cancelled trains.

Conclusions

A business needs, therefore, to undertake an audit of its external environment and internal factors together and determine to what extent, and how effectively, it can use its resources and capabilities to meet the external challenges it faces.

Anticipating production: market research and forecasting

Market research investigates the nature of the markets within which a business operates. It is undertaken, therefore, as the opportunities and threats part of the SWOT analysis discussed above. It investigates such issues as: the current size of markets and their growth potential; the characteristics of markets and how they are, and might be, segmented, e.g. business and household uses of the same personal computers making them separate market segments; information on actual and potential customers including their needs and wants; and competitors and their actual and potential strategies and actions. Therefore, forecasting is an integral part of market research.

A book of this nature does not have the space to discuss market research in any depth. What this section will do is to explain briefly why market research is undertaken, the process employed, and give examples of the application of market research. The reader wishing to pursue this further is referred to the reading section at the end of this chapter.

Why market research is undertaken

Market research is undertaken to provide a business with as much relevant and useful information as possible to enable it to make informed decisions which will give it a competitive advantage over its rivals. It may be undertaken by the business itself, if it is large enough to employ specialist staff, or, if a small business, it will employ an outside agency as necessary.

If a market is going to grow in size through increasing consumer demand, for example the mobile phone market, then the businesses first entering it will be able to charge high prices for their products since customers anxious to be first to own them will pay a premium. This will enable the business to make the biggest profits. To have that knowledge means having to forecast such developments before they occur. Of course, forecasts can be wrong so, on occasion, money, energy and time are allocated to market research which does not pay off subsequently in terms of sales, customer loyalty etc. As an illustration, when supermarkets such as Sainsbury and Tesco launched their postal banking services, they failed to forecast the high initial demand for them. Consequently, customers who sent in cheques as the first deposit to open their new accounts had to wait for over a month before they were open through insufficient staff being employed to handle the flood of applications. Similarly when, in 1999, McDonalds launched its ' buy a burger, get one free' promotion it found it had seriously underestimated demand and had to suspend the campaign as restaurants were running out of food. Had it been able to estimate more accurately, this would not have happened.

The process employed

The market research process employed needs to be distinguished as a number of different stages. These are shown in Table 2.1.

1   Before market research is undertaken, it is important that the researchers understand what they are seeking to achieve. The research needs to be focused and address a particular problem rather than being all encompassing; there also needs to be a realistic time scale for completion. For example, when market research was undertaken to assess the demand for 'alcopops' – fruit flavoured alcoholic drinks aimed at young people – it would have been futile to investigate demand for all alcoholic drinks since some, e.g. gin and tonic, are not a young person's drink. Rather,

Table 2.1 Market research and forecasting.

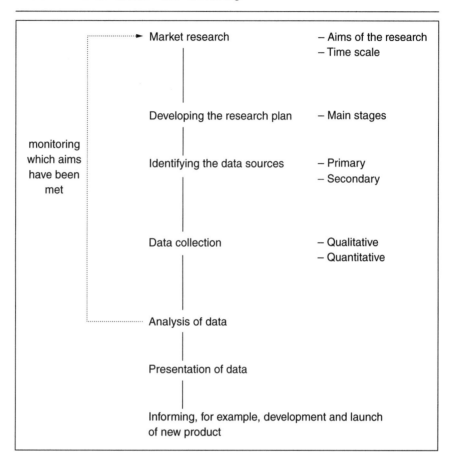

the market had to be segmented and demand for existing products, aimed at young consumers, had to be compared against forecast demands for the new alcoholic drinks (see Chapter 4, Section 4.2). For example, will demand for the new products be additional to or will it detract from demand for existing company products? The aims of the research must also be written down so that there is a clear understanding by every relevant person in the business of what is being undertaken.

2 The research plan then has be developed. This will identify all the main stages to be completed from the initial definition of the project to final writing up of results.

3 The sources of data to be employed need to be identified. These will be primary and/or secondary data. Primary data is original data collected by researchers for the business, for example, by interviewing potential customers. It is likely to be of direct relevance to the research project but can be expensive to collect. Secondary data is that collected by others, both within the business and externally, usually for different

purposes; if external it will have been published in newspapers, journals, trade papers, government and EU statistical publications etc. It is much cheaper to access than primary data but may not be specifically relevant. There may also be a great deal of it, so sorting and collating takes time and effort.

4   Data may be collected in a number of different ways but broadly they may be distinguished as qualitative and quantitative.

- Qualitative methods will include the use of: telephone and mail questionnaires; personal surveys, e.g. where people are stopped in the street and asked questions; in-depth interviews, where an individual agrees to discuss in depth his/her consumer preferences; panel research, where a group of consumers meet regularly to discuss their preferences for and perceptions of different products and services; and observational research, e.g. watching though closed circuit cameras, customers' shopping patterns in a supermarket. When questioning consumers, by whatever method, there is always a danger of bias, for example that questions will inadvertently be phrased in such a way as to lead the respondent to what he/she thinks should be said rather than giving a totally honest answer. Qualitative research methods usually collect primary data. Mintel, for example, publishes regular surveys of industry sectors and analyses of companies and brands which are an important information source.

- Quantitative research methods collect numbers rather than statements. For example, a qualitative questionnaire or interview might ask consumers why they prefer Mars ice cream to Snickers ice cream. A quantitative questionnaire will, for example, ask people to rate a product on an attitude scale of 1 to 5 (known as a Liekert scale); this ranges from liking a product very much (1) to disliking it a lot (5). The collection of data from secondary sources such as government and EU publications on the state of the economy are an important source but again are more likely to be general and relate to the economy as a whole, than to a specific problem the business needs addressing.

5   After collection the data is analysed. Forecasting techniques can be used to project past and current trends and forecast how a business's market might be in a year or two, the demand for its products etc.

6   Lastly the results of the market research are presented to the manager who has commissioned it, or to the business's board of directors. On the basis of this the business can then make decisions as to its future strategy, whether it can meet existing targets, and so on.

The reader should note the distinction between market research and marketing research. The latter includes market research but also relates to research into products, e.g. testing through consumer panels a product concept, such as a new savoury snack. It will also research pricing, such as testing how much demand changes in response to a change in the price of a product, known as elasticity of demand (Chapter 6, Section 6.1). Marketing research also encompasses marketing communications, e.g. investigating how effective a potential advertising campaign will be if undertaken, and distribution research such as how to improve distribution links between a business's warehouses and retail outlets. Although the discussion above relates to market research, since this is a book concerned with business economics rather than a marketing text, other aspects of marketing research are discussed elsewhere in this book, particularly pricing.

Local radio: Wave 105.2 FM

Synopsis

This case study examines the licensing of a new local radio station, and sets this in the context of its market and competitors.

The case study raises the issues of:

1   the need to maintain profitability;
2   forecasting to determine audience characteristics;
3   formulating a strategy to achieve the company's objectives.

Case Study

Having beaten 12 other competitors and secured its licence from the Independent Broadcasting Authority, Wave 105.2 FM began broadcasting in June 1998, for the licence which will last until 2008. Established as a private limited company, it is financed by a range of businesses including an existing commercial radio company. A number of its employees formerly worked for its nearby rival station, Ocean FM. Based in premises on an industrial estate near Fareham, Hampshire, its area of coverage is Hampshire, Dorset and the Isle of Wight, with an estimated population of 1 687 000 potential listeners. Its target audience is 25 to 54 year olds for whom it provides contemporary music, news and lifestyle features. In 1999 its weekly reach (audience) was 183 000.

Like all commercial radio stations it relies on advertising for its revenue and profits. Since it is relatively newly founded, it has the latest state of the art computer based technology and uses Windows NT to access all music played, which is stored on the main computer hard disk. This enables the disc jockey to work to very precise time schedules within each programme. News, business news and traffic reports are syndicated and bought in from external providers. A news team keeps up to date with all the local and national news and provides hourly bulletins. For special programmes, such as Budget day, a local expert commentator (for the 1999 Budget, this author) is brought in to provide analysis.

Wave 105.2 FM's main local commercial competitor in Central Southern England is located about half a mile away on the western part of the same industrial estate. Owned by the London based Capital Radio Group, this comprises Power FM, Ocean FM and Capital Gold. Ocean FM began broadcasting in December 1986. It covers Portsmouth, Southampton and Winchester and is aimed at 25 to 45 year olds for whom it provides chart and contemporary hits, entertainment and information. With an estimated population of 1 111 000, its weekly reach is 260 000. Power FM, which began broadcasting in 1998, provides the same music and covers the same catchment area as its sister station, and achieves a weekly reach of 315 000. The third station, Capital Gold, broadcasts pop music of the last 40 years and so is aimed more at a middle aged audience. It also provides fairly extensive sports coverage, predominantly soccer, targeted on listeners in the local region. It also broadcasts via the Internet.

On the boundaries of its territory, Wave FM also faces competition from other commercial competitors such as Isle of Wight Radio (with a weekly reach of 37 000), Spire FM (in Salisbury) and Bournemouth based 2CR (Two Counties Radio) which covers Dorset and West Hampshire. In late 1999 it also encountered competition from new very local commercial stations opening in Portsmouth, Victory FM, Southampton, SouthCity FM and Winchester Wind FM.

Its main local BBC competitor is the long established Radio Solent, based in Southampton and covering Portsmouth, Southampton, Winchester, West Dorset, parts of Wiltshire and the Isle of Wight. This is aimed at an older audience than Wave FM, mainly the over 50s, and relies heavily on local news and sport and many audience phone-in programmes. It emphasises the Radio Solent audience as a family although it does offer limited specialist programmes such as a weekly one hour jazz programme.

Wave 105.2 FM's audience composition will obviously vary during the day; for example those listening during the morning will be different to those listening during drivetime from 5.00 pm to 7.00 pm. Marketing research to determine the precise characteristics of each segment of its audience is, therefore, crucial, as is forecasting potential audience growth, and hence revenue growth. To differentiate itself from its competitors other than by its name, and to build up its audience base, its slogan is 'Great music, better talk.' A major advertising campaign relying on posters on the side of buses was used very successfully as was the use of Wave 105.2 FM car back window stickers. With the latter, motorists spotted with a sticker on their car can win a free tank of petrol.

In its two years, Wave FM certainly succeeded in developing strong audience figures; and a key long term strategic goal must be to gain and then maintain greater market share, and hence advertising revenue. However, this is a very competitive market and Wave 105.2 FM will need to work hard to build on its initial success.

2.4 Flexible management systems; TQM and lean production; just in case and just in time production; Japanisation

The problems of mass production

The reader may assume from the above case study that a business seeks to forecast potential demand and then produce sufficient to meet that demand. Until the 1970s that was certainly the case for British businesses. In fact, as forecasting demand is not totally accurate, firms tended to produce more than was anticipated in case demand subsequently exceeded forecasts. This later became known as 'just in case' production, i.e. production just in case there was a demand for its output.

Allied to this was the need to hold stocks of goods in warehouses to provide them quickly to retailers as the need arose, which incurs extra costs. There is also an opportunity cost attached to these stocks, namely the next best use of the money value of producing and holding them.

Another past business problem in Europe and the US, was the variable quality of what was produced. Although businesses sought to produce competently and profitably, for 25 years after World War II, consumer incomes and demand rose so that businesses could sell whatever they produced, even if it was not high quality. Additionally, profits were sufficiently high to cover the costs of any rejects, or repairs needed by goods after production; some western European car production was an example of this, particularly British Leyland and Fiat of Italy. They were infamous for the poor quality of their workmanship, body corrosion after very few years, mechanical unreliability and a lack of what are now taken as essentials, such as well upholstered seats, attractive dashboard, heated rear window and car radio-cassette player.

European car production was hit in the early 1970s by Japanese car imports such as Nissan (Datsun), Toyota and Honda. Although some early models, such as the Datsun Sunny, suffered corrosion problems they made major inroads into European car markets because of their mechanical reliability, the range of extras provided as standard, price competitiveness and their emphasis on quality. This soon gave them global domination.

Underlying Japanese car and other production, such as electrical consumer goods and electronics, shipbuilding, motorcycles etc., was the production philosophy known as TQM or total quality management. This put total quality, and hence cost reduction through minimal production faults, at the centre of any production process or service provision. Its impact was so substantial in terms of the competitive advantage it gave Japanese businesses that it has now become the underlying production philosophy of a substantial proportion of US and European companies. It is explored here.

Total quality management

TQM's origins lie in the work of American pioneers such as W. Edwards Deming and Joseph M. Juran, but it is most commonly associated with Japan because of the subsequent work of people such as Karou Ishikawa, known as 'the father of quality circles', and because Japan was the first country to implement TQM on a wide scale basis. It developed because, after World War II, Japan faced severe raw material shortages, as well as major social and production dislocations as a consequence of Allied bombings. Lacking indigenous natural resources, and the income to import all the resources it wished, Japanese industry needed to use what it had as efficiently as possible, with minimum waste. Linked to this was the concept of continuous improvement of production processes and goods to make Japanese goods more attractive to customers.

TQM is a business philosophy which enables a business to produce products without defects, as efficiently as possible and at minimum cost for maximum customer satisfaction. It encompasses a number of characteristics:

1 Zero Defects – production must use resources as efficiently as possible, with minimal waste. Zero defects gives the theoretical target for which each business should aim; continuous improvement is a way to achieve this. In other words, a business needs to get things right the first time.

2 Anticipation – problems should be anticipated before they occur so they may be prevented from happening. For example, if faults in the production of a new good are anticipated they do not have to be recalled subsequently with the attendant costs this imposes; or improvements to design of a good may eliminate later cost incurring modifications or repairs. Again, therefore, the key issue is getting it right the first time to avoid future problems.

3 Cost control – may be distinguished in three ways in a TQM context. First, there is cost of conformance. This covers the cost of establishing activities to prevent failure happening, for example, staff training programmes, and the cost of ensuring the business conforms to its quality standards. Secondly, there is the cost of non-conformance. This covers internal costs such as correcting/repairing goods and services which do not meet standards and which have been identified before they reach the customer; external costs, when the goods have reached the customer and have to be recalled for repair; and the cost of excess requirements, when unneeded information or services are provided. The implication here is that activities, which do not add value, must be removed from the production process. The reader should look back to Porter's value chain for comparison. The last type of cost is the cost of lost opportunities – the economist's opportunity cost in other words. This relates to potential customers deterred by poor quality, existing customers who don't come back a second time and the loss of potential business growth.

4   Ownership – for TQM to work there must be ownership of the quality philosophy and its implementation in the production process or service provision by all who work for the business. Although the business's managers are paid to manage production, everyone from the company's chairman to its cleaners must subscribe to and work towards achieving total quality in all aspects of the business. Teamwork is therefore an essential part of the quality philosophy. By working together as a team, and seeking to implement TQM, more can be achieved than if each individual on an assembly line, for example, is only concerned with his/her own efforts.

5   Internal customers – linked to ownership is the idea of internal customers. Everyone who works in the business is a customer of the person before them in the production process. This may be on the assembly line or it may be the services the information technology department provide to the rest of the organisation. The internal customers are entitled to as high a quality of work passed on to them to undertake their stage of the process as is the external customer who buys the completed product. This requires continuous monitoring of all business activities, not just the production processes, and of the level of quality achieved. TQM therefore empowers every member of the team to expect and work towards these objectives through self-management.

6   External customers – as suggested above, TQM seeks to give a business competitive advantage by ensuring maximum customer satisfaction with the product sold. This will lead to repeat purchase and customer loyalty as well as to other consumers becoming aware of the quality reputation, i.e. customer goodwill. This is the best form of advertising possible. It will also enable the business using TQM to maximise its profits.

7   Competitive benchmarking – to ensure that a business is actually meeting its quality standards it is necessary for it to compare how well it is performing against defined standards, to ensure that it is achieving them, and against its best competitors. Targets can then be established to enable the business to be better than its best competitor. The business

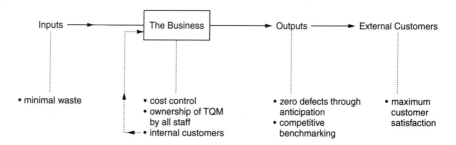

Figure 2.2 The total quality management model.

subsequently monitors its performance to ensure that it meets these best standards.

In Figure 2.2, the main characteristics of TQM are illustrated.

Just in time production

The idea of producing just in case of demand was discussed earlier, and the opportunity cost of holding stocks of raw materials, components or finished goods was identified. An alternative, which is part of the quality revolution, is just in time (JIT) production and stock control.

JIT occurs when a business produces goods or services just when they are needed by the customer. The two implications are that production does not occur until demand has been identified, for example by specific customer orders, implying that the production process has to be very flexible. With Japanese car producer Toyota, monthly forecasts of production are made, based on demand, then fine tuned on a daily basis as demand patterns change. This in turn avoids excess production or the holding of stocks of cars in case there is demand, and the financial and opportunity costs associated with that. Secondly, the business needs to manage its production runs so that the goods currently produced are those needed next by customers.

The idea of flexibility is important and is embodied in the production method of what is known as flexible specialisation or flexible management systems. The ability of a business to produce in small batches and to switch easily and quickly from product to product using the same assembly lines is a key characteristic of JIT, and flexible specialisation enables this to take place. JIT enables a business to: be quickly responsive to changing consumer demands and to changing pressures from competitors; maximise profits without seeking the long production runs necessary to achieve economies of scale (see Chapter 3, Section 3.2); avoids holding large stocks of unsold goods; and prevents employee boredom through greater variety of work. The economic benefits come from economies of scope, which are also discussed in Chapter 3, Section 3.2.

Linked to JIT production is JIT stock control. Producers, such as car plants, will require components manufacturers to supply them with just the amount of components they need at just the right time. For large car plants this can necessitate up to sixteen deliveries each day. This saves the car producer holding stocks of components and shifts the burden to the components supplier. It also integrates the components supplier into the car manufacturer's production process. The JIT system therefore stretches vertically backwards as far as necessary to enable the manufacturer to run this system. Similarly, raw materials will be supplied to a business just as they are needed for processing. Again, the emphasis is on minimising costs by avoiding waste and ensuring the best possible quality through tight control of the production process as in TQM. It also necessitates the suppliers being physically located close to the manufacturer, a point of particular importance with increasing traffic congestion. At the other end of the supply (or value) chain, JIT needs to continue vertically forwards into the sales department of a company. Lean production is the name of Toyota's JIT system.

JIT also requires simplified work flows. This is achieved by grouping together all the work force who make a particular product, known as output-based production, rather than grouping together all machines of a certain type, known as input-based or process-based production. As well as providing more focus for the workforce and creating a greater sense of ownership it helps avoid stock accumulating at the stages already identified, i.e. raw materials, components and finished goods, and hence enables working capital to be used more effectively elsewhere. It also makes it easier to exercise effective total quality control processes over this production and it reduces waste.

The spread of Japanisation

The influence of Japanese imported production methods such as TQM, JIT and flexible specialisation has had a major impact on European and American businesses in the last twenty years. Where these have been introduced by Japanese transplants such as Honda, Nissan and National Panasonic, i.e. Japanese businesses which have built plants in the UK, they have generally worked well albeit at times having to be adapted to meet the differences in the cultural conditions of the UK workforce compared with the Japanese, e.g. Western culture puts more emphasis on the individual, whereas the Japanese culture stresses teamwork much more. Nonetheless, human resource policies such as one union plants, or even no union plants, performance related pay, tight recruitment polices, and guaranteed long term employment in return for worker flexibility, including compulsory overtime, have also been implemented. However, this has also bred resentment of the control which Japanese firms exercise both over production processes and the workforce. In the early days of Japanese investments, companies had problems implementing JIT production, whilst JIT component and raw materials supplies can still pose problems. Nonetheless, this has not meant that the key elements of the Japanese production philosophy have had to be abandoned; in contrast, they have proved to be capable of successful implementation.

Where domestic companies have tried to copy Japanese production methods, although reasonably successful, they have not, overall, done as well as the Japanese transplants. Apart from the fact that the Japanese pioneered these methods and so might reasonably be expected to implement them most effectively in the UK, they have also benefited from locating plants in green field sites where high unemployment has meant recruiting new compliant labour, e.g. South Wales. In contrast, indigenous companies have either located in brown field sites, where existing buildings have had to be cleared or adapted, or applied Japanese methods to existing factories, and used existing labour which, in some case, has been reluctant to adopt radically new production methods and philosophies.

2.5 Nissan car plant, Sunderland: a case study of Japanisation

Synopsis

This case study explores the operations of the Japanese transplant car plant Nissan, which was constructed at Sunderland. It discusses:

1 why Nissan wished to locate in the UK;
2 the implications for the workforce of working in a Japanese owned plant with a quite different culture;
3 how successful the plant has been commercially.

Case Study

Nissan Motor Manufacturing (UK) Ltd is a classic example of inward Japanese investment. It was opened in 1984 on a greenfield site in Sunderland, Tyne and Wear. Sunderland was chosen in spite of the fact that it had no history of car manufacturing, its previous main employment source having been shipbuilding.

Nissan had wanted to locate in Europe because of developing moves to complete the single European market. The UK was chosen because it was Japan's biggest European customer and because Japanese businesses like to locate in English speaking countries. Sunderland had sold itself well to Nissan, presenting the region as a team, which is an important facet of the Japanese culture. The region's representatives also made the Japanese visitors from Nissan feel welcome, which Japanese people like. This was further reinforced by regional aid to the company and the existence of a transport infrastructure.

The Sunderland site occupies 3 053 000 m^2 and is the base for Nissan's passenger cars produced in Europe, with two models being built, the Micra and the Primera. It has nine plants on site and is a highly integrated production process. This has been made possible by Japanese inward investment of £1.25 billion.

The implications for the workforce
When building the factory Nissan wanted a flexible workforce able to move freely between jobs. This was in real contrast to UK factories where

demarcation disputes between unions had caused many strikes. Originally, it was envisaged that Japanese methods would be transplanted directly to the Sunderland factory. However, it was soon realised that, to be successful, what was needed was a mix of the best of Japanese and UK production cultures.

The factory was built in one year. Careful recruitment procedures were employed to hire the best staff. Over 11 000 people were interviewed for 240 production jobs. Over 90 per cent of those employed for the shop floor, e.g. building the cars, maintaining the equipment and moving materials, were local people. For the office workforce, which covers such functions as designers, cost analysts, buyers and human resource managers about 30 per cent were local. The reason why more were brought in from outside, particularly the West Midlands, was because people were needed with car experience.

Initially, it was also perceived, wrongly, that the Japanese workforce was single status and very democratic. In fact this was not so. Japanese workers are very status conscious, and highly stratified. They wear uniforms which may initially look similar but in fact carry insignia which denote their status. Status is also denoted by the size of one's desk, or whether one has a desk at all or shares one, whether one has a driver etc.

Teamwork is crucial to the Japanese workforce. The Japanese concept is that one is a member of a group working for the common good, so that the individual is suppressed. It is all about group accountability and responsibility. In contrast, in Western workforces, so long as one is doing one's job that is all that matters, even if one's colleagues are not doing well.

The success of Nissan, Sunderland

Nissan car plant in Sunderland has proved to be the most efficient car producer in Europe for each of the three years 1997–1999, according to a report published by the Economist Intelligence Unit. In 1998 it produced almost 288 838 cars, an average of 105 cars per employee, an increase from 98 per employee in 1997; this made it the tenth most efficient car plant in the world, compared with 160 cars per worker for the world's most efficient car plant in Japan, and a US most efficient plant figure of 87 per worker. In contrast, when Nissan UK first started up they were hoping to build up to 100 000 cars p.a.

Renault

Most recently the acquisition of a 36.8 per cent stake in Nissan by Renault for £3.3 billion has meant that a cost cutting and restructuring programme has been adopted, although this should not have a major effect on Sunderland because of its considerable efficiencies. The new partnership will involve a merging of many European finance and dealer functions of Nissan and Renault, shared joint purchasing, a common platform for a new small car and major cost cutting.

For Sunderland there will be investment of a further £200 million, which will enable it to build the Almera and increase the capacity of the plant from 310 000 cars to 350 000 cars p.a. However, the MD of Nissan UK, John Cushnaghan, declared that, for the year 2000, he would be looking for 6 per cent savings in labour productivity and 3 per cent savings in overheads and material costs to offset the adverse effects of sterling being so strong.

2.6 Summary of chapter

This chapter has considered different theories to explain business motives; as a working theory we have opted for profit maximisation. To achieve this, businesses seek competitive advantage over their rivals either by producing their products more cheaply or by differentiating them from those of their competitors, through advertising, branding, quality, after sales service and so on.

Production can be broken down into a number of stages stretching from the initial design of the product to after sales service, known as value activities. Additionally, the business anticipates that the value of the production undertaken will exceed its costs, known as the margin. Together, the value activities and the margin make up the value chain. Each business needs to be able to manipulate its value chain to gain the competitive advantage it seeks over its rivals.

Business strategy is about how a business seeks to achieve its long term or strategic objectives. Additionally, it will have operational objectives relating to its day to day or short term activities. Profit maximisation will underlie these. To decide on its short run and long run objectives a business needs a good knowledge of its current internal and external positions, which can be obtained through SWOT analysis. The business can then use market research, i.e. forecast market demands for its products, existing and new, and produce accordingly.

The influence of Japanisation on modern production methods was then analysed with the failure of traditional European and American mass production methods explored. Newer production philosophies such as TQM and JIT were discussed.

2.7 Further questions

Further Questions

1 Write a briefing paper (two sides of A4 maximum) arguing either for or against the need for all senior managers to have their salaries linked specifically to the profitability of their businesses to avoid them pursuing other motives.

2 Why have European businesses had to adopt Japanese production methods in the last 25 years?

3 Draw up a list of the advantages and disadvantages of TQM. How suitable is it for (a) a volume car producer; (b) a small scale specialist car producer; (c) a small scale family run business producing double glazing?

4 Are TQM and JIT value activities for creating competitive advantage for the businesses which adopt them? Explain your answer.

5 'All companies should adopt JIT production methods since, clearly, they work.' Discuss critically the validity of this statement.

6 Imagine you were employed by Wave 105.2 FM when they decided to bid for the local radio licence they subsequently secured. Given the information in the case study undertake a SWOT analysis of the proposed business.

7 How far might cultural differences between Japanese and Western workers pose problems for the implementation of Japanese production methods in the US and the EU?

2.8 Further reading

Bank, J. (1992). *The Essence of Total Quality Management*. Hemel Hempstead: Prentice Hall International (UK) Ltd.

Beckford, J. (1998). *Quality: A Critical Introduction*. London: Routledge.

BRAD Advertising Media, March 2000

Branson, R. (1998) *Losing My Virginity*. London: Virgin Publishing Ltd.

Cole, W. E. and Mogab, J. W. (1995). *The Economics of Total Quality Management. Clashing Paradigms in the Global Market*. Oxford: Basil Blackwell Ltd.

Fifield, P. (1992). *Marketing Strategy*. Oxford: Butterworth Heinemann Ltd.

Grieve Smith, J. (1990). *Business Strategy,* 2nd edition. Oxford: Basil Blackwell Ltd.

Harris, N. *European Business,* 2nd edition. Basingstoke: Macmillan Business.

Johnson, G. and Scholes, K. (1999). *Exploring Corporate Strategy: Text & Cases,* 5th ed. Hemel Hempstead: Prentice Hall.

Oliver, N. and Wilkinson, B. (1992). *The Japanisation of British Industry. New Developments in the 1990s,* 2nd edition. Oxford: Blackwell Publishers Ltd.

Porter, M. E. (1985). *Competitive Advantage. Creating and Sustaining Superior Performance*. New York: The Free Press.

Yamada, M. (1998). *Japan's Top Management From the Inside*. Basingstoke: Macmillan Press Ltd.

The Economist
The *Financial Times*
The Observer
The Daily Telegraph
The Times
BBC 2 TV (1992). *The Money Programme. Regions Apart.*
Department of Trade and Industry: http://www.dti.gov.uk/
Nissan website: http://www.nissan-europe.com/europ/eng/uk.html

Chapter 3

Producing for profit

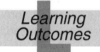
Learning Outcomes

After completing this chapter the reader will be able to:
- understand the nature and types of short term business costs and the effects of the law of diminishing returns;
- analyse the implications for business costs of the long term and the opportunity to achieve economies of scale and economies of scope;
- understand the determination of business revenues and profitability.

3.1 The short term production process: developing cost theory

British Airways: cost cutting to success?

Synopsis
This case study explores British Airways' strategy of cost cutting to gain competitive advantage in a market with over-capacity.

The key characteristics of the case study are:

1 Cost cutting involves large capital assets, i.e. aircraft, which takes time to achieve.
2 It can be expensive to replace older aircraft before the end of their economic lives.
3 Cost cutting needs to be accompanied by increased revenues.

In late 1999, British Airways (BA), like other airlines, experienced significant operational losses. The main reason was rising fuel costs as the price of crude oil increased from $10 to $25 per barrel in 1999, as a result of OPEC (the Organisation of Oil Exporting Countries) restricting supplies. Another problem arose from the 1998 SE Asian economic crisis. SE Asian passenger demand fell so airlines switched spare capacity to the Atlantic routes causing excess capacity to force down airfares. Airlines are also under pressure as congestion in the sky increases flight delays whilst passengers complain of being squeezed into small seats with little leg room.

One strategy airlines have adopted to combat over capacity is creating strategic alliances to share gates and landing slots at airports and keep rival alliances at bay. In contrast, BA's strategy has been to cut costs by reducing unused capacity. Large 401 seat under-occupied Boeing 747s are being replaced with smaller planes such as 272 seat Boeing 777s, which offer fewer economy seats, i.e. the ones not earning sufficient profit; but the same total number of BA seats is still offered. As a result more flights are offered, more seats are occupied, and yield per seat increases; BA figures have shown that yield per seat can increase by 28 per cent through these changes without increasing the number of premium, i.e. first class and club class passengers. This more than offsets the 11 per cent increase in costs through running the smaller aircraft with the same number of premium (first and club class) seats. This strategy is based on evidence from the North East of the US where frequent flights of smaller aircraft have built up passenger traffic.

However, replacing older larger aircraft with newer smaller ones is expensive and cannot be achieved short term. Some older planes have been retired sooner than originally intended whilst the money has had to be found for the newer aircraft. In so doing, BA is reversing its strategy of 1992–1999 when it increased its capacity by over 9 per cent per annum; now it seeks to reduce capacity by 12 per cent before March 2003 which will remove 25 per cent of the economy seats whose fares do not cover the costs of carrying the passengers (what economists call marginal costs).

Recap of Chapters 1 and 2

Chapter 1 introduced the idea of the inputs, which a business uses to produce goods and/or services, and the costs these incur. Chapter 2 showed the importance for a business to respond promptly to changing customer demands. This means it may need to quickly change the amount of resources it uses, although effective forecasting should, in theory, mean that it has anticipated change. However, some inputs are easier to change than others.

Factors of production

Raw materials may be quickly varied as may labour, by the use of over-time. In contrast, a top company executive may have to be head hunted which could take months. Similarly, acquiring land, whether green field, i.e. countryside or farmland, or brown field, i.e. land in cities already used for building, and the construction on it of a new office block may take years. The writing of new software to run a new computer system may take years, as with the new air traffic control centre at Swanwick, Hampshire, completed in the mid 1990s but, as a result of software problems, not ready to use until at least 2002.

It is necessary, therefore, to distinguish between inputs which can be altered in the short term, known as variable inputs or factors, i.e. labour, raw materials and components, and those which can only be altered in the long term, known as fixed factors or inputs, e.g. land, premises, machinery, and enterprise. The short term is any period of time that is less than the long term – a week, a month etc.

The short term

The use of variable inputs generates variable costs. If a factory manager asks his workforce to work more hours he will have to pay them more, say time and a half for evenings and double time for Saturdays and Sundays. Similarly with raw materials or components, the more goods that are produced the more raw materials (or components) that will be used, and the more costs incurred.

In contrast, the amount of fixed factors used cannot be changed in the short term and hence their costs will also be fixed. An entrepreneur's income may change from year to year, especially if it is linked to the business's profits, but is likely to be fixed in the short term, because the amount of him/her is fixed. Similarly, the business rates a company pays to its local council and contracts with a security firm for night staff are also likely to be fixed in the short term, because factory premises or a shop cannot be extended in the short term.

At this point a case study is developed to illustrate more fully what is being discussed here.

Sounds 'R' Us

Sounds 'R' Us is a factory situated on an industrial estate at the edge of a large UK city. It manufactures a wide range of CDs for different record labels and also other products such as videos and DVD discs. It is run by a small management team and a labour force, both full time and part time. The hours the part time staff work depend on how busy the factory is but they are normally fairly flexible if there is an urgent job to be completed. Deliveries of CDs are made by the factory through distributors to wholesalers daily, with payment made monthly through the business's accounts with the wholesalers. The factory has its own heating and lighting expenses, the exact costs depending on how many hours per week the factory operates. It also makes monthly rental payments on its ten year lease to the company who developed the estate, and pays business rates to the city council, its local authority. The production of CDs is directly related to the amount of time the factory is open, although there will, of course, be variations in production across different weeks as demand for CDs varies in shops across different times of the year.

Question

Which are the variable costs Sounds 'R' Us has to pay and which are the fixed costs?

Answer

The fixed factors, which generate fixed costs are the rent for the premises, the costs of repaying bank loans for machinery used to manufacture CDs including the depreciation costs, the salaries of the management team and the business rates. The variable factors, which generate variable costs are heating and lighting, the wages and overtime earnings of full time and part time staff, and the material costs of the CDs. By definition, the fixed costs are constant whereas the variable costs increase the more hours the factory is open, the more hours the work force is employed and hence the more CDs manufactured.

Table 3.1 Total variable, total fixed and total costs of operating Sounds 'R' Us.

Weekly production of CDs	Total variable costs of CDs (TVC) £	Total fixed costs (TFC) £	Total costs (TC = TVC + TFC) £
0	0	8500	8500
5000	7500	8500	16 000
10 000	11 000	8500	19 500
15 000	16 000	8500	24 500
20 000	22 000	8500	30 500
25 000	29 000	8500	37 500
30 000	44 500	8500	53 000
35 000	68 500	8500	77 000
40 000	98 500	8500	107 000

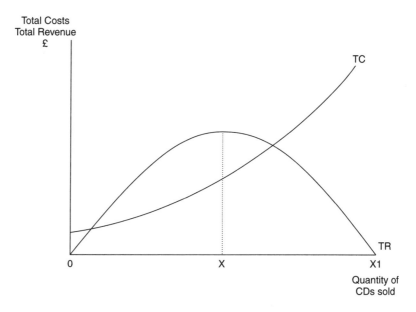

Figure 3.1 Total revenue and total cost curves of Sounds 'R' Us.

Sounds 'R' Us is currently facing pressure to work seven days per week, and for longer hours each day to meet extra demand for its services from record companies. The management team is unsure what the costs of this will be and undertakes the weekly estimates as in Table 3.1, grouping them into the factory's total fixed and total variable costs at different levels of CD sales. Adding fixed to variable costs gives the total costs of running the business.

The figures can be plotted on a graph with thousands of pounds on the vertical axis, and the number of CDs sold in thousands on the horizontal axis. Total costs are shown as TC on Figure 3.1. For the moment the reader should ignore the line marked TR.

If the reader wishes to draw TVC and TFC it will be seen that total fixed costs (TFC) are constant and hence a horizontal straight line. The total variable costs (TVC) have a more distinctive shape; initially the line rises less and less fast as more variable inputs are added to the fixed inputs. This may be because the workforce are using the machines which make CDs more intensively. However, beyond a certain point, as still more variable inputs are added, e.g. the workforce work longer hours, the TVC cost line becomes much steeper. This is because the workforce is getting more expensive as it is paid more and more overtime and it is producing progressively less. This is due to a phenomenon known as the law of diminishing returns which is discussed more fully below. Adding the TVC line to the TFC line gives the TC line in Figure 3.1.

However, economists are much more interested into two other types of cost, both of which can be obtained from the total cost figures of Sounds 'R' Us. These are average costs and marginal costs.

Average costs

Average costs show, in our example, the cost per CD manufactured by Sounds 'R' Us. Average cost (AC) can be estimated as:

$$\text{Average cost (AC)} = \frac{\text{Total cost}}{\text{Quantity of CDs manufactured}}$$

We could take this further and also calculate the average fixed costs (AFC), and the average variable costs (AVC) of each CD sold, just by putting total fixed costs or total variable costs in place of total costs in the above equation.

Question

Calculate the average fixed costs and the average variable costs of Sounds 'R' Us, for each level of sales.

You can then check your answers against Table 3.2 and against Figure 3.2 where the data is plotted as AVC and AFC curves.

Marginal costs

This cost is important to economists. It shows, in our example, the cost of manufacturing one extra CD. In reality, the marginal unit is likely to be more than just one extra CD produced. In Table 3.1, Sounds 'R' Us will only produce an extra 5000 CDs; it is not worth while producing only one more. For a volume house builder such as Barrett, the marginal unit might be an estate of 50 houses, whilst for a car producer it might be a batch of 1000 cars.

By comparing marginal cost against the price it receives for the last or marginal unit it produces a business can decide whether it is economically worthwhile producing that marginal unit – the five thousand more CDs, or one more car or house, or whatever is considered.

Strictly, when we talk about a marginal unit of 5000 CDs or 50 houses, the costs of these should be termed incremental costs rather than marginal costs since, in the example of Sounds 'R' Us, we are not looking at marginal units of one CD more or less made but rather increments of 5000 CDs extra or less. If we were to reduce the increments to 50 CDs, or 25, or 10 more or less then, at each reduction, the incremental cost would be a better approximation to the marginal cost. Having said that, this author intends

Table 3.2 Average and marginal costs incurred by Sounds 'R' Us.

Production of CDs	Average total costs (ATC) £	Marginal costs (MC) £	Average variable costs (AVC) £	Average fixed costs (AFC) £
0	0	0	0	
5000	3.2	1.5	1.5	1.7
10 000	1.95	0.7	1.1	0.85
15 000	1.63	1.0	1.07	0.57
20 000	1.53	1.1	1.1	0.43
25 000	1.5	1.7	1.16	0.34
30 000	1.77	3.1	1.48	0.28
35 000	2.2	4.8	1.96	0.24
40 000	2.68	6.0	2.46	0.21

to continue using the term marginal cost throughout this book since this is much more commonly employed; however the reader should remember the above qualification.

The principle of calculation for marginal cost and incremental cost are essentially the same:

$$\text{Marginal cost} = \text{total cost of } x \text{ units} - \text{total cost of } (x-1) \text{ units}$$

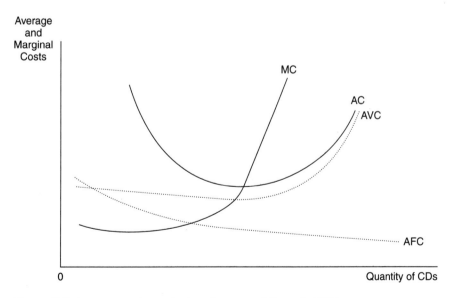

Figure 3.2 Average and marginal cost curves of Sounds 'R' Us.

So if x is 12 then the marginal unit is the 12th unit, or the last 5000 CDs made in Sounds 'R' Us, e.g. the total cost of 15 000 CDs minus the total cost of 10 000 CDs.

These figures are plotted as Figure 3.2 below. As can be seen from this figure, the average cost (AC) curve is typically U-shaped as is the marginal cost (MC) curve, and the average variable cost (AVC) curve. With each of these three curves, at first they fall as sales increase, then they reach minimum points; as sales continue to increase, each of the curves rises. It will also be noted that the marginal cost (MC) curve cuts both the AC and the AVC curves at their minimum points; this is always the case. The important thing to consider here is what exactly these mean. This necessitates considering an important economic law called the Law of Diminishing Returns.

The law of diminishing returns

This law states that when additional units of a variable input, say the Sounds 'R' Us employees' working hours in this case, are added to fixed inputs, e.g. the machinery, then at some point the output produced (CDs) by each extra unit of the variable input (each extra hour the employees work) will diminish. If one thinks about this it is fairly logical. If any of the factory workers in Sounds 'R' Us were made to work longer and longer hours each day his/her productivity would decline as he/she became more and more tired; when working, say eighteen hours per day, he/she would just want to sleep and output would fall to zero. The other side of the coin is that the longer the hours the employee works the more expensive he/she becomes, especially if he/she is being paid overtime after, say, eight hours.

If demand for Sounds 'R' Us CDs were to continue rising the part time employees could temporarily work full time, or more staff could be taken on. However, the fixed factor machinery cannot be increased except in the long term so, in the short term, variable costs will have to continue to rise as the factory works longer and longer hours, if CD output is to increase.

To explain why the average cost curve is U-shaped, first consider Table 3.1. Fixed costs (FC) are, by definition, always constant. However, as more CDs are made, then average fixed costs (AFC) must fall. The reader will recall that these are obtained by dividing total fixed costs by the number of CDs sold; effectively the same amount of fixed costs or overheads are being 'spread' over more and more CDs.

Variable costs (VC) will rise from zero when no CDs are made – the factory is closed – and will continue to rise the more that are made. If VC rise more slowly than the production of CDs, then average variable costs (AVC) will fall, as happens at low levels of production in our example. If VC rise faster than production of CDs, as happens at higher levels of output, then average variable costs (AVC) will rise.

Therefore, at low levels of output the falling AFC and the falling AVC together, cause AC to fall. However, at higher levels of output, i.e. beyond the minimum point of AC, rising AVC will more than offset the falling AFC and cause the average cost (AC) curve to rise. The minimum point of the AC curve shows the lowest average cost per thousand CDs produced. This is the best or optimum place for the business to be and is known as the minimum efficient scale of production (MES), where the words scale of production mean the amount of output produced, or CDs in our case study. Beyond the MES is when the law of diminishing returns sets in.

One other point to remind the reader is that, as yet, we have no information on the revenues which Sounds 'R' Us is earning, so cannot judge whether the business is profitable or not.

3.2 The impact of the long term: economies of scale

The long term

If the short term limits which inputs can be changed then, in the long term, all inputs, variable and fixed, can be altered. For Sounds 'R' Us an extension to the existing factory could be undertaken by buying the adjoining unit and knocking the two into one; or another premises could be purchased elsewhere; or a rival company could be acquired. Additionally, in the long term, the business can diversify into other activities, e.g. manufacturing video cassettes or DVD films, once existing staff have been sent on training courses. This gives much greater flexibility.

Increasing returns to scale

If, for a moment, we examine a Japanese company manufacturing saloon cars then, in the long term, as it expands production it can achieve increasing returns to scale, and thus economies of scale. Quite simply, if the business were to double all its inputs and output were to more than double, it would be experiencing increasing returns to scale. Costs per unit of output should, therefore, also fall, i.e. the business achieves economies of scale (also called scale economies).

Economies of scale

Economies of scale occur because of division of labour and specialisation. Some scale economies relate to the size of the plant, e.g. a factory, whilst others relate to the size of the business.

Plant related economies of scale

These include:

1 Division of labour occurs when a complex task is subdivided into a number of simpler tasks, most typically on an assembly line, for example, producing washing machines, or assembling cars.
2 Each worker then specialises on a particular task (specialisation). The argument is that, by constant repetition, each worker becomes highly skilled in his/her task and can work faster and better, e.g. one worker fits only wheels to each car.
3 Linked to this, production may be multi-stage, e.g. car component suppliers are increasingly linked closely to car manufacturers, sometimes operating under the same roof. On a large scale, this is very cost-effective.
4 Another factor contributing to economies of scale is the indivisibility of certain inputs, i.e. they have to be used on a large scale to make them economically viable. The cruise ship market is a growth sector of the holiday market. Very large cruise ships can carry many people, reducing costs per passenger; however one cannot only sail the front half of the ship if bookings are down.
5 Large machines are more efficient than smaller machines, e.g. a large earth mover such as a JCB, will shift more earth per man and machine than a small one from a tool hire centre.
6 Large scale production yields substantial amounts of commercially valuable waste products, e.g. large scale commercial trawling for fish yields more inedible fish which can be used for fertilisers, than a small fishing boat, which may throw the non edible fish back into the sea.

Business related scale economies

These include:

1 Marketing costs will not be much higher regardless of whether, in the example above, the cruise line has four ships or eight.
2 There may be financial economies: bigger businesses can negotiate more favourable discounts through bulk purchase or more favourable interest rates on loans secured from a bank, compared with a small business.
3 There may also be organisational economies; the computer software used will probably cost the same regardless of whether a company has a small or a large factory, or five factories; one licence will allow the business to use Microsoft Office whether there are fifty or one hundred personal computers.

The scale economies above are internal to the business.

External economies of scale

There are also external economies of scale which accrue to the businesses in an industry. The computer software firms in California's Silicon Valley, for example, will share external economies from their close proximity to each other. There is a pool of highly skilled staff which businesses can draw on. There will also be shared training programmes (and costs) between the businesses and with the University of California at its nearby campus which will benefit all. Additionally, where businesses group together there are likely to be better transport links, although at times the latter can promote the former, e.g. the UK's 'Silicon Valley' along the M4 with easy access to London, Bristol and the Midlands.

Diseconomies of scale

There is a limit to how big an organisation can become without the managers losing control of it. If a business keeps expanding coordination may be less effective, lines of communication break down and strikes occur as workers feel more remote from management; in turn this will disrupt production elsewhere in the factory. When this occurs, costs per unit produced will rise and the business experiences diseconomies of scale.

British Leyland – diseconomies of scale in action

Synopsis

This case study explores the existence of diseconomies of scale at British Leyland in the 1970s. In particular it examines:

1   potential causes of diseconomies of scale;
2   how Michael Edwardes sought to combat this problem;
3   the long term effects of diseconomies of scale for the British owned car industry.

Case Study

In the 1960s, the UK car producer British Leyland (BL) was created from several previous amalgamations of British car producers: Austin, Morris and MG, Rover and Land Rover, Standard and Triumph, Jaguar and Daimler, Pressed Steel, and Leyland Trucks, to give it a critical mass to achieve economies of scale and to enable it to compete effectively with European competitors. Many of these individual companies had been unprofitable and the creation of BL was seen as a way to redress this. In practice, because of limited investment programmes over long periods of time, the number of cars which could be built of each model was insufficient to achieve economies of scale. Ironically, BL also experienced diseconomies of scale through the inability of managers to manage effectively, resulting in poor communications between different sections of the very large business, the existence of a number of dominant and politically motivated militant unions who actively sought to dislocate production as well as feuding with each other, and a lack of effective quality assurance procedures resulting in the production of very poor quality cars. Most importantly, however, was the fact that existing models were dated whilst BL had failed to develop any new models. As a result, sales of BL cars fell and the government was forced to provide more and more subsidies to keep BL in production and ensure that jobs were retained.

It was only when the government brought in a tough entrepreneur, Michael Edwardes, to run BL that things began to improve. As well as taking a stance against strikes he split the monolithic BL back into a number of small separate companies – Austin–Morris, Rover and Leyland Trucks – to combat the diseconomies of scale. With reduced size, it was thought that the constituent elements would be able to compete more effectively with competitors. However, the historical lack of investment causing outdated machinery, inefficient working practices and, most importantly, Japanese competition with good quality products, meant that the British owned car industry was never able to recover. Consequently, there are no longer any British owned volume car producers.

Figure 3.3 illustrates the long run average cost curve (LRAC) of a business. Implicit in this curve are the assumptions that the business will seek to combine its resources in the most efficient manner (known as the least-cost combination of resources), that the prices of the inputs it uses are constant and that the state of technology does not change. As can be seen, the LRAC has broadly the same shape as the short term average cost curve examined in Figure 3.2, although it is flatter. As output expands in the long term, so long run or long term average costs fall and the business experiences economies of scale. There then comes a point, as production and the scale of the plant continues to expand, when the declining average costs start to level off; the business is now experiencing constant returns to scale. If it continues to expand production it will experience diseconomies of scale, i.e. average cost per unit of output will start to increase. As the case study of British Leyland indicates, the business may not realise, until it is too late, that this is happening.

It is also important to emphasise that the long term time period is a planning concept for a business. In reality, all firms always operate in the short term since there are always constraints facing the extent to which inputs can be varied. A business's long term cost curves are derived from a very large number of short term cost curves. At some point, the business will decide what its intended scale of production will be; in turn this will determine the particular technology which it will employ. Each level of technology from which the business can choose relates to a particular set

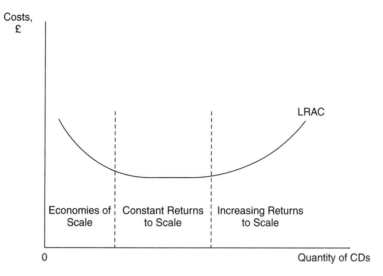

Figure 3.3 Long term average costs: economies and diseconomies of scale.

of short term average and marginal cost curves. Once the business implements that level of technology its factors of production will be fixed, and hence a technical reality.

Economies of scope

Clearly economies of scale are important to a business as a means of reducing its production costs. However, the assumption underlying economies of scale is that all of the units which are mass-produced can be sold. If not, the business will have unwanted goods in warehouses with the storage and opportunity costs implicit in holding these, and so forecasting, which was discussed in Chapter 2, Section 2.3, is important to estimate demand accurately. The other problem with mass production to achieve scale economies is that consumers increasingly want their goods, and especially large consumer goods like cars, to have individual characteristics. Producers, therefore, need to produce limited production runs, known as batch size, yet still secure the benefits of scale economies. An example of this would be a car aimed at summer buyers with a seasonal extra name, new paintwork on its sides and a sunshine roof as standard.

To achieve this, producers rely on flexible specialisation which enables them to secure economies of scope. Instead of assembly lines being set up to produce one car ad infinitum, i.e. a large batch size, they are set up to switch quickly and at low cost from one model to another, using standardised machines and multi-flexible machine tools. Downtime, when the assembly line is reset for a new product run, is therefore minimised whilst flexible trained staff, helped by the significant automation, can easily switch from product to product. This may well also be supported by just in time (JIT) production and components supply methods. The wide range of engines which Honda produces at its Swindon plant is an example of this.

Although it may seem that the benefits of economies of scale are lost by low batch sizes, the reduced downtime by setting up assembly lines more quickly, reduced stock holding costs through low production runs and lower raw material and component holding costs, if JIT production is used, result in cost savings known as economies of scope. These savings offset the lost cost benefits of not achieving economies of scale.

Economies of scope – Peugeot 106 Quicksilver; the drive of your life

Synopsis

This case study provides an example of a product, in this case a limited edition model of a car, which illustrates economies of scope. It is an advertisement for a limited edition Peugeot 106. The key characteristic which the case study identifies is that economies of scope, in this case, are achieved by reliance on a basic model of car, but with minor, yet effectively marketed, variations.

What the hard bits at the edge of the ocean are for?

This advertisement portrays a man in a wetsuit, gazing out to sea, by the surf, at sunset. His arm is round an upright surfboard rather than a woman, and alongside him is a Peugeot 106 Quicksilver:

'Eventually you'll return to dry land. And at least now there's a good reason to. The Peugeot 106 Quicksilver. Available for a limited period only, it comes in a three-door format with a 1.4 litre engine. Plus tinted glass, a sliding sunroof, short sport aerial and a platinum silver finish. Who said looks aren't everything? There's power steering too and (if only you had one on your board) a driver's airbag. A touch of refinement? How about electric front windows? And in case it all proves too tempting for some, we've added an immobiliser and plip central locking. Despite this, the Quicksilver is priced at only £9895. Well worth leaving the sea for.'

Self testing questions

Self Testing Questions

1 What are the essential differences between the short term and the long term in cost theory?

2 In your own words define:

- fixed costs
- variable costs
- average costs
- marginal costs
- why a firm will want to produce at the lowest point on its average cost curve.

3 Why is the law of diminishing returns significant to a business?

4 (a) Distinguish between economies of scale and economies of scope. How will a firm know if it is experiencing diseconomies of scale? (b) In the case study of the Peugeot 106 Quicksilver how do we know that this demonstrates the underlying economic concept of economies of scope?

5 Can you think of any disadvantages of a business requiring its assembly line workers to specialise to achieve economies of scale?

3.3 Calculating business revenues

As noted previously, a business's revenues may be defined, for each product it supplies, as the price of the product multiplied by the quantity of it sold, i.e.:

Total revenue = price × quantity

If a business wants to sell more of its product in the short term it will need to lower the price of it; people who previously could not afford to will then buy it for the first time, whilst people who previously bought only a certain quantity will now buy more (assuming it is a product that disappears in the act of consumption, such as food or services, rather than a consumer durable such as a freezer, where most households will only want one). The implication of this is that the total revenue curve will have the dome shape shown in Figure 3.1, and denoted TR; the figures are obtained from Table 3.3. In other words, it will rise from zero (when none is sold) to a maximum and then, if the price is lowered sufficiently, fall back to zero. Why does it have this shape? The answer is that as price is cut, demand for the product increases (the growth and maturity phases of the product life cycle if the price cuts happen over a long period of time, see Chapter 4, Section 4.3); then, to continue increasing demand price is cut still further. At this point

Table 3.3 Potential revenue of Sounds 'R' Us.

Price of a CD £	Quantity of CDs demanded	Total revenue (TR) £	Average revenue (AR) £	Marginal revenue (MR) £
5	5000	25 000	5	
4.5	10 000	45 000	4.5	4
4	15 000	60 000	4	3
3.5	20 000	70 000	3.5	2
3	25 000	75 000	3	1
2.5	30 000	75 000	2.5	0
2	35 000	70 000	2	[1]
1.5	40 000	60 000	1.5	[2]

it should be remembered that with any price cut, two effects are in operation. First, extra revenue is obtained from new purchases of the product. Secondly, however, revenue is also lost since the price is now reduced on all those units of the product which otherwise would have been sold at the previous (higher) price.

Therefore, in the earlier stages of price cuts, the first effect exceeds the second (this is when the total revenue curve is rising). As price cuts continue, however, the second effect exceeds the first (which is when the total revenue curve falls).

Table 3.3, columns 1 and 2 show forecasts of the potential demand if Sounds 'R' Us varies the price which it charges wholesalers for the CDs it produces. The third column gives the total revenue to be earned by Sounds 'R' Us from selling these CDs. Note that at outputs of 35 000 or above, marginal revenue is negative and is denoted by square brackets around the numbers.

In Figure 3.1, the reader should note that the total revenue curve shows the relationship between alternative levels of output and the revenue obtained at each of those levels of output, at a moment in time (which is, of course, the time when all factors or inputs are fixed). By varying the price it charges a business can decide where on the curve it wants to be (the final decision will need to be taken in conjunction with its cost curve – see Section 3.4).

The reader might also say that, in reality, there is not one price at which CDs are sold – rather there are a range of alternate prices. That is true so our assumption of one price is a simplifying one to make it easier to analyse the situation. In reality, different prices are charged to reflect the status of the recording artists and their current popularity; the CDs of top stars such as Celine Dion will be highly priced reflecting what the market will bear, i.e. what is known as ' skimming the cream'. In contrast, stars from the

1960s, for example Gerry & the Pacemakers or Billy J. Kramer & the Dakotas, will often have their records for sale at low prices because it is a long time since they were top stars. However, companies such as Naxos provide high quality recordings of classical music at low prices to compete effectively with the full price issues of the big labels. This is known as market segmentation where a company segments the market into segments or niches and focuses on one of these.

Average and marginal revenue

Recap

Earlier in this chapter, cost theory was developed relating to the short term and long term time spans within which a business operates. We distinguished between short term average and marginal costs, when only variable inputs could be altered, and long term average and marginal costs, when both fixed and variable inputs could be altered. In the same way we now distinguish average and marginal revenue.

Average revenue

This may be simply defined as:

$$\text{Average revenue} = \frac{\text{Total revenue}}{\text{Quantity of the product sold}}$$

(i.e. Total revenue is price × quantity of the product sold)

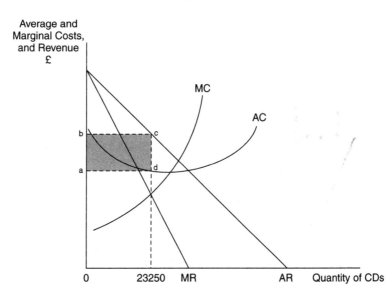

Figure 3.4
Marginal and average revenue and cost curves, and profits made by Sounds 'R' Us.

In other words, it is the total revenue earned from selling the product averaged out over all the units sold. A numerical example of this is given in Table 3.3, column 4. Since the quantities on the top and the bottom of the right hand side of the above equation cancel each other out, average revenue is equal to the product's price. This line will slope downwards to the right as in Figure 3.4, denoted by AR. Since the price has to be reduced the more is sold, and price equals average revenue, then average revenue also must fall. The average revenue curve is also the demand curve for the product which we discuss in Chapter 5, Section 5.2.

Marginal revenue

This may be defined as follows:

Marginal revenue = total revenue of x units – total revenue of $(x–1)$ units

So, if $x = 100$ units sold, then the marginal revenue is that obtained from the last/marginal unit manufactured and sold, i.e. the 100th, since x minus $(x – 1) = 100$ minus 99.

Marginal revenue is, therefore, the revenue earned from the last unit of the product sold. As with costs, batch size may be such that the marginal unit is the last 100 washing machines produced in a factory, or the last 1000 cars produced. A numerical example is provided in the last column of Table 3.3.

The marginal revenue curve (MR) always lies below the average revenue curve; again this is shown in Figure 3.4. Total revenue is the addition of all the marginal revenues earned. If the reader takes the first three lines of Table 3.3, for example, and adds together the marginal revenues, this will give the total revenue of line three.

For the moment, the reader should ignore the shaded area, abcd, in Figure 3.4.

3.4 Profitability; optimum production levels

This part of Chapter 3 brings together Sections 3.2 and 3.3, to examine how business chooses the optimum output for its products.

Profit has been defined as the excess of revenue over costs incurred by a business. In this sense we are merely looking at those costs and revenues included in a company's profit and loss account. The revenues and costs in a profit and loss account may be set out in more detail, and using different terms, to those which have been identified above because they are drafted to reflect accounting conventions and terminology rather than those of the economist; however, the principles remain the same.

For example, in abbreviated form the summary consolidated profit and loss account of Halifax Plc for the year ended 31 December 1998 is as Table 3.4. The figures for 1997 are shown in the far column for comparison with this year. It should be noted that figures in brackets denote a minus amount, i.e. an outgoing. The profit and loss account is, therefore, a statement of how Halifax Plc's incomings (revenue) and outgoings (costs) during the calendar year 1998 resulted in a pre-tax profit of £1705 million. This is obtained by:

Incomings (revenue) – outgoings (costs) = profit (before tax)

£3158 million – £(1180 + 148 + 96 + 29) = £1705 million

It will be noted that net interest income (£2366 million) is by far the biggest source of income and is the interest Halifax receives on money loaned as mortgages, minus what they pay to depositors as interest (hence the word net). Ongoing administrative expenses are the main cost the Halifax faces as well as the staff salaries, computer costs etc., i.e. the day to day expenses of running the business. The difference between incomings and outgoings gives

Table 3.4 Summary of consolidated profit and loss account for year ended 31 December 1998, Halifax Plc.

	1998 £ million	1997 £ million
Net interest income (b)	2366	2315
Other income and charges	792	642
Operating income	3158	2957
Administrative expenses		
Exceptional	–	(18)
Ongoing	(1180)	(1050)
Depreciation and amortization	(148)	(156)
Provisions for bad and doubtful debts	(96)	(102)
Provisions for contingent liabilities and commitments	(29)	–
Profit on ordinary activities before tax	1705	1631
Tax on profit on ordinary activities	(534)	(540)
Profit attributable to the shareholders of Halifax Plc	1171	1091
Dividends (d)	(489)	(441)
Profits retained for the financial year	682	650
Basic earnings per share	47.5p	43.5p
Diluted earnings per share	47.4p	43.4p
Directors' remuneration	3 509 782	3 989 004

profits before tax – since Halifax Plc has to pay corporation tax to the Inland Revenue on its profits. Once tax of £534 million (an outgoing) has been paid, the Halifax is left with net of tax profits of £1171 million.

Part of the post tax profits, £682 million, are retained by the company whilst the remainder, £489 million, are distributed to shareholders as dividends; the latter gives, in 1998, an earning per share held of 47.5p. Diluted earnings per share relates to the fact that a company may have the authority to issue more ordinary shares if it wishes to (to raise more money for a new investment programme, for example) but so far has not chosen to do so. Nonetheless, on the assumption that one day these will be issued, 'diluted earnings per share' take these into account; hence the earnings per share are slightly lower than basic earnings per share.

The other main financial statement of a company is the balance sheet – with the profit and loss account it makes up the company's accounts. The balance sheet is a statement of all the assets and liabilities (debts) of a company for the same financial period. Whereas the profit and loss account shows income flows (such as this author's monthly salary entering and leaving a bank account) the balance sheet gives a statement of the stock of assets and debts which a company has (comparable to the author's assets – house, car, computer etc. and his liabilities/debts – mortgage, car loan etc.). The main Halifax Plc asset is its loans and advances to its customers (£85.1 billion in 1998), whilst the main liability is the accounts of its customers (£85 billion in 1998). The Halifax's balance sheet is not shown here.

Two major differences between the accountant's and the economist's definitions of profit may be noted here. First, there is no reference in the accounts to any social costs or social benefits discussed previously – nor do we try to value these in monetary terms. Secondly, and even more importantly, there is no allowance for opportunity cost, which is a crucial cost for the economist. To present the economist's view of the profitability of Halifax Plc, the opportunity cost of its Administrative expenses, Depreciation and Amortisation, Provisions for bad and doubtful debts, and Provisions for contingent liabilities and commitments should be included, i.e. the amount lost by not employing this money in the next best uses. Since these are extra costs they would inevitably substantially reduce the 1998 figure of £1705 million for Profit on Ordinary Activities before Tax. So the economist's measure of total profits will, inevitably, be lower than the accountant's (in the same way the opportunity cost of the Halifax's assets would need to be included in the balance sheet). However, since accountants do not include opportunity cost in company accounts, then Table 3.4 stands.

Economists distinguish three main types of profits which we should briefly consider:

Normal profits

If normal profits are being earned in a business then they are sufficient to keep the existing businesses in that industry, i.e. they cannot make higher profits elsewhere. However, these profits are not so high as to tempt other businesses into the industry. In other words, the industry is in equilibrium.

This assumes that there is perfect knowledge so that every business in every industry knows what each other is earning, and that there are no barriers, including costs, preventing entry to or exit from an industry (part of the conditions of perfect competition, see Chapter 7, Section 7.4). Of course this does not reflect reality; rather these are limiting assumptions. More likely is the existence of imperfect knowledge so that businesses do not realise they could earn bigger profits by moving to another industry. Entry or exit barriers are also likely to exist; entry barriers will include the costs of buying new equipment, acquiring staff with the requisite skills or retraining existing staff, acquiring a new customer base in the face of competition from already established firms etc. Exit barriers will include the costs of a business selling its machinery and other equipment before it can leave the industry; if the equipment is very specialised and other businesses do not wish to enter this may cause high exit barriers. The exiting firm may, in the end, have to write off its production facilities, i.e. lose their value by selling them as scrap.

Supernormal profits

A business makes supernormal profits, sometimes called abnormal profits, when they exceed normal profits. Supernormal profits may be defined as the return a business could secure over and above the return it could obtain if it loaned its money elsewhere at the prevailing market interest rate.

It may be that Firm A makes supernormal profits, whilst Firms B and C in the same industry only make normal profits, because A is simply more efficient. It may have greater automation of production processes, it may have tighter cost control processes, it may be bigger and more able to achieve economies of scale or scope etc. In this case it may be able to sustain its supernormal profits long term and yet not attract other businesses into its industry because they know they cannot match its efficiency.

Suppose, however, that all the firms in the industry are making supernormal profits because of some external reason, e.g. an upsurge in demand for a new service or product which the industry provides such as was the case when video rental shops first appeared in the 1980s. In this case, businesses outside the industry will be tempted to enter to share the profits of those already inside. Consequently greater competition will drive down prices and, in time, supernormal profits will fall. Once they reach the level of normal profits there will be no incentive for new firms to enter the business and entry will cease. Profits will then stabilise at a level consistent with that of other industries, i.e. normal profits will again be made.

Monopoly profits

Whereas supernormal profits are essentially short term, which in time may well be competed away, monopoly profits, also confusingly called abnormal or even supernormal profits, are long term. The business making them will be able to maintain them because, typically, it operates entry barriers, preventing other businesses entering and competing away those of its profits above the normal profits level.

Most typically, a monopolist who is the sole seller of a good or service, or a group of firms acting as one, called a cartel, will be in a position to secure monopoly profits. Although such restrictions on the free entry of new firms into an industry are illegal, it may take years for these practices to be detected and proven in the courts. The US has seen court actions against Microsoft by the Justice Department and twenty states under the provisions of the 1894 Sherman Anti-Trust Act. The accusation is that Microsoft has, through its bundling of its Windows 95 and Windows 98 operating systems with Explorer, its Internet browser, sought to protect its operating systems monopoly (Windows is installed on 90 per cent of new PCs) and to establish one in the browser market. In other words it has undertaken predatory behaviour, seeking to harm its rivals, particularly Netscape, Microsoft's main Internet browser rival, in ways other than through competition. Microsoft's counter-argument is that the bundling of the operating system and the browser are legal because they are valuable to the consumer through helping with access to the Internet. It argues that any tying of consumers to products is legal, provided it can be shown to benefit the consumer.

This author will use the convention throughout this book that supernormal profits are those that will be competed away in the long term, whereas, due to entry barriers, monopoly profits will last long term.

Sounds 'R' Us: profitability

We now examine the profitability of Sounds 'R' Us, using the revenues and costs examined previously.

Table 3.5   Total costs, total revenue and profit figures for Sounds 'R' Us.

Price of CD £	Weekly sales	Total costs of selling CDs £	Total revenue earned £	Profit £
0	0	8500	0	[8500]
5	5000	8500	25 000	16 500
4.5	10 000	19 500	45 000	25 500
4	15 000	24 500	60 000	35 500
3.5	20 000	30 500	70 000	39 500
3	25 000	37 500	75 000	37 500
2.5	30 000	53 000	75 000	22 000
2	35 000	77 000	70 000	[7000]
1.5	40 000	107 000	60 000	[47 000]

Total costs and total revenue

Table 3.5 is a combination of parts of two previous tables, Tables 3.1 and
3.3. The final column of Table 3.5, profit, is obtained by subtracting column
3 (total costs of selling CDs) from column 4 (total revenue earned). This
is also the vertical distance between the TR and TC curves at any level of
output in Figure 3.1, multiplied by the number of CDs sold.

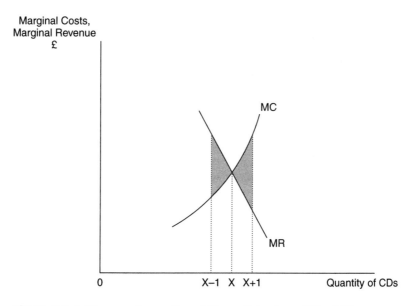

Figure 3.5 A blow-up of a section of Figure 3.4, where MC = MR.

The business has two concerns – to minimise its costs of producing CDs and to maximise its revenue, subject to demand. This will give it the maximum profits. The appropriate figures demonstrating these are shown in Table 3.5. The level of weekly sales which gives the greatest profits for Sounds 'R' Us is somewhere between 20 000 units and 25 000 CDs, since this is where revenue exceeds costs by the greatest amount. The reason this is not more precise is because these data only show variations of 5000 CDs; however, as we see in Figure 3.4, the optimum output is actually 23 250 CDs.

The reader should note that profit maximisation is not the same as revenue maximisation since this would involve sales of somewhere between 25 000 and 30 000 in Table 3.5, yet would also incur much higher costs. Additionally, total costs do not start at zero because some of the total costs are fixed, i.e. they exist even when nothing is being produced.

Marginal costs and marginal revenue

Profit maximisation may also be viewed from the viewpoint of a business's marginal costs and marginal revenues. These are presented in Table 3.6 and represented graphically in Figure 3.4.

Table 3.6 is obtained from Table 3.2 and Table 3.3.

The important point to note with marginal costs and marginal revenues (known as marginal analysis) is that they examine precisely the same things as total cost and total revenue but merely in a different way, namely how to determine the level of output which maximises profits for the business.

As Figure 3.4 shows, marginal revenue will always fall as the output produced, in this case CDs, rises since the more produced, the more price must fall to persuade people to purchase the output. Additionally, marginal

Table 3.6 Average and marginal costs and revenues of Sounds 'R' Us.

Quantity	Average total costs (ATC) £	Marginal costs (MC) £	Average revenue (AR) £	Marginal revenue (MR) £
5000	3.2	1.5	5	
10 000	1.95	0.7	4.5	4
15 000	1.63	1.0	4	3
20 000	1.53	1.1	3.5	2
25 000	1.50	1.7	3	1
30 000	1.77	3.1	2.5	0
35 000	2.2	4.8	2	[1]
40 000	2.68	6.0	1.5	[2]

revenue is less than the price of the last unit of the good, because the impact of the lower price on revenue earned from previous units of output must also be deducted.

If the reader focuses just on the marginal cost and marginal revenue curves, as sales increase by each 1000 CDs, the marginal revenue earned falls (since prices have to be cut to boost sales) whilst marginal costs rise (as extra staff are employed, the factory stays open longer etc.). Now consider where MC = MR. In Figure 3.5 this section of Figure 3.4 is blown up.

At this level of sales the revenue earned from the last or marginal CD sold will be equal to the cost of selling that CD. Suppose now Sounds 'R' Us sells one more CD, i.e. $x + 1$ CDs. Here the cost of the marginal unit (the +1 unit) is higher than the revenue it earns (the loss is shown by the shaded triangle to the right of output x); so there is little point in selling this last unit. Now let us consider selling one unit less than x, i.e. $x - 1$ CDs. Here, the marginal revenue is greater than the marginal cost. If Sounds 'R' Us had only sold one more CD (up to x) they could have earned the shaded area of profit which is to the left of x – it's worth having, so they will.

So x must be the level of output which maximises profits, i.e. where MC = MR.

The reader should also note that this level of output x is the same as the optimum level of output x in Figure 3.4 and is approximately 23 250 CDs.

Why bother with marginal costs and marginal revenues when we could make do with total costs and total revenue? The reason is that the marginal values give a better picture than totals. If a firm producing high quality furniture asks 'what if I manufacture one more suite – will it be profitable?' the picture is much clearer and more focused, looking at that last suite (the marginal unit) rather than at all the suites produced so far – which is irrelevant information.

Do businesses actually use marginal analysis?

So far we have assumed that the business we have been examining is a manufacturer. As such it can determine fairly precisely, albeit perhaps not to the nearest unit in our example, how much it needs to produce to maximise its profits. However, service industries, which increasingly account for the major section of the economy, do not produce physical output. So how does an Internet provider, or a marketing agency or a bank decide where its MC = MR is?

The simple answer is that such a business will not seek to work out its marginal costs or marginal revenue to the last customer served since this would not be appropriate or feasible. Marginal analysis, as used by the economist, seeks to approximate the decision making of businesses. It is certainly the case that businesses need to look at the revenues they will generate and the costs they will incur from undertaking an extra level of activities, such as processing an extra 20 000 customers for a telephone banking service, or the provision of an Internet banking service; however, the marginal cost and revenues of one more customer is not something a business could or would wish to calculate.

Therefore, the process of a business evaluating the extra costs and extra revenues of an increased level of activity are certainly correct – although this won't be called marginal analysis nor will the terms marginal revenue and marginal cost be used. Why then does the business economist use this analysis and these terms? The answer is that they enable the detailed analysis of business behaviour and decision making, and the ability to demonstrate and predict how businesses will behave and the outcomes of this behaviour; this is, in part, what business economics is all about. We can continue to use marginal analysis in the knowledge that it is an effective tool of analysis. It will also enable us to reach the same conclusions as business decisions, and to make meaningful predictions, even if by a slightly different route and using different terms.

Average costs and average revenue

Why do we bother with average costs and average revenue is the next question to ask. We can answer this in two ways. First, it is useful information to have. If I ask Ford, the car producers, what is the average cost of producing a Ford in Spain and in the UK, I may get the answer £6000 in Spain and £7000 in the UK (these are hypothetical figures). This is really useful since, if I were in charge of Ford's investment programme, I might conclude from this that it would be better to build a new plant in Spain since they can produce cars cheaper than at Hailwood in Liverpool. If I then learn, from forecasts, that a Ford car could be produced in Albania for £3000 I would have to think carefully about whether a new plant should be built there. Of course, many other factors than just average cost would need to be taken into account before making such a decision, such as political stability and the quality of output.

Average revenue, as noted before, is also the same as the price of the product. Just as the difference between total cost and total revenue is used to measure profits, so average costs and average revenue may also be used in the same way. We re-examine Figure 3.4. The profit maximising output (x) is, of course, determined by where MC = MR, at 23 250.

If we look at the relationship between average cost (AC) and average revenue (AR) at the output x, we find that AR > AC (the symbol > means greater than).

The excess revenue over costs is shown by the shaded area, abcd. These may be supernormal or monopoly profits as we discussed earlier (we cannot tell which since we know nothing else about the industry), i.e. profits in excess of normal profits. So if at output x (where MC = MR), AR > AC, there are supernormal or monopoly profits; and, depending on whether entry barriers exist or not, there may be a tendency for new firms to be attracted into the industry, i.e.:

Rule 1: If AR > AC, then the firm is making supernormal or monopoly profits.

In the case of Sounds 'R' Us, barriers to entry might be the fact that it is well established and any outside producer setting up would have to overcome the customer loyalty which Sounds 'R' Us has established. In the same way we can identify two other rules:

Rule 2: If AC > AR, then the firm is making losses. If these persist long term it may be forced to close down.

Rule 3: If AC = AR, the firm is making normal profits and will stay in the industry, but new firms will not be tempted in.

From rule 3, if AC = AR, then AC must include normal profits. In other words, AC is the sum of the average costs of production (wages + rent + interest) plus an extra amount as the reward for staying in this industry and producing whatever it does produce (profit). In this sense profit can be viewed not just as a reward to the entrepreneur but also as a cost of using his/her expertise to run the business.

Self testing questions

1 If profit = revenue minus costs, make a list, or draw a mind map of the ways in which a business might increase its profits.

2 Why do a business's average revenue (AR) and marginal revenue (MR) curves slope downwards to the right?

3 Using Figure 3.1, why would a business not maximise profits if it produced at the level where total revenue = total costs?

4 If a business is producing where AR > AC, what implications does this have for the number of firms in the industry staying constant?

5 Why can a business not produce in the long term at a point where AC > AR?

3.5 The global car industry: seeking profitability through rationalisation

Synopsis

This case study demonstrates the importance of economies of scale to modern businesses and how attempts to benefit further from these are being pursued by the strategy of rationalisation within the global car industry, through mergers and acquisitions. It examines, in particular, Ford's acquisition of Volvo and the reasons advanced by each party for the take-over. It also briefly reviews other mergers and acquisitions in the global car industry. The case study discusses:

1 Volvo's inability to secure economies of scale because of the small size of its main markets;
2 the benefits to Ford and Volvo from the acquisition of the latter by the former;
3 comparable rationales adopted by other car producers for merger activity.

 *Case Study*

In late January 1999, after fighting off potential competition from Volkswagen and Fiat, Ford agreed to buy Volvo's passenger car division for £3.9 billion. In 1998, Volvo's car business had sales of £7.6 billion on 400 000 vehicles. In contrast, US car manufacturer Ford, the second largest car producer in the world after Toyota, with a market capitalisation (share value) of $72 billion, sold 6.8 million cars.

The rationale which Swedish company Volvo advanced for the sale was that its car business needed to achieve economies of scale to survive long term. Yet, it felt too small to be able to invest the huge amounts of money needed to produce a new range of models and compete against the likes of Ford and General Motors. In other words, by being acquired by Ford, the two companies could share designers, components, distribution networks, marketing and so on, which would reduce costs significantly. Volvo's main markets for sales have been Sweden, the Netherlands and the UK, and of these the UK has by far the biggest population. Sales to other formerly important markets, such as the US, were static or declining as the once popular Volvo estate was displaced by four wheel drive vehicles such as the Land Rover Discovery, or people movers such as the Renault Éspace. For example, in the UK, Volvo car sales which were 38 283 in 1980 (2.53 per cent of the UK market) had risen to 80 427 in 1988 (3.63 per cent) but by 1998 had fallen back to 37 585 (1.67 per cent). Additionally, Volvo cars, renowned for their durability, reliability and safety characteristics, were not able to capitalise fully on the competitive advantage this gave them over their rivals. Additionally, because of their solid construction, they also were perceived as heavy in terms of fuel consumption.

Ford, in turn, argued that its previous acquisition of Jaguar cars, albeit at an inflated price, demonstrated that it could run a foreign subsidiary without affecting the identity and appeal of the acquired company. In other words, Volvo could still expect to continue as an independent marque (badge). Ford also argued that it wanted to boost its sales of luxury cars. In 1998 it sold 200 000 a year, but intended to increase this to 700 000 by the year 2000, and to 1 million soon after, again to achieve scale economies. Owning Volvo would help as the marque had a following among female and young buyers who could not afford Ford's other 'quality' (as opposed to volume) production cars, the Jaguar and the Lincoln. Additionally, Ford could develop its existing cars and the newly acquired Volvos jointly using common 'platforms' or characteristics to save money. Indeed, a main strategy of Ford in the 1990s was to volume produce a minimum number of engines and platforms to achieve economies of scale, and use these to produce a maximum number of different models across different marques – in effect, to achieve economies of scope. In time, therefore, the production of new Volvo cars will broaden Ford's range of products and enable it to fill the gap between its volume produced Ford cars and its top of the range Jaguars. The acquisition also gave Ford a global market share of 14 per cent.

Volvo, which retained its commercial vehicle activities, said that in future it would focus its activities on its buses and trucks, construction equipment, engines and aerospace. It subsequently sought to buy its Swedish truck producing rival Scania, in which it already had a 20 per cent share, for £4.7 billion, although the European Commission may block this. As the rationale for its acquisition of Scania, Volvo argued that 'only the largest and financially strongest players will be able to afford to invest in the future to the extent required'; this logic, it has been argued, applies equally to the car industry. Volvo also had a joint production venture in the Netherlands, with Japanese manufacturer Mitsubishi, which closed as a result of Ford's acquisition of Volvo.

The Volvo name continues to be used by both the companies, Ford for the cars and Volvo for its other activities, with a jointly owned company owning the Volvo brand and licensing it to Ford and Volvo. Ford distributes its and Volvo's cars jointly, generating significant cost savings.

Ford's acquisition of Volvo was a further step in the moves to rationalisation in the global car industry which have been prompted by manufacturing over-capacity pushing down prices, market saturation in mature economies resulting in severe competition, and the high development costs of new models. Further, in 1998–1999, the situation was exacerbated by the collapse of demand in emerging markets. At one time, German car manufacturer Volkswagen had also been rumoured to want the car division of Volvo whilst Italian car producer Fiat was reported to want all of Volvo. Ford's successful bid for Volvo also quashed rumours of a three way merger of Ford, BMW and Honda.

Table 3.7 International ownership of Marques, April 2000.

Vehicle manufacturer	Nationality	Other marques
BMW	Germany	Land Rover – sold to Ford*
		Mini
		MG
		Rolls-Royce (after 2001)
		Rover – sold to Phoenix Consortium*
DaimlerChrysler	Germany/US	Dodge
		Jeep
		Mercedes
		Plymouth
Daewoo	S Korea	Samsung
		Sangyong
Fiat	Italy	Alfa Romeo
		Ferrari
		Lancia
		Maserati
Ford	US	Aston Martin
		Jaguar
		Lincoln
		Mazda (33%)
		Volvo (car)
General Motors	US	Buick
		Cadillac
		Chevrolet
		Holden
		Isuzu (37.5%)
		Opel
		Pontiac
		Saab (50%)
		Saturn
		Suzuki (3.5%)
		Vauxhall
Hyundai	S Korea	Kia (51%)
PSA	France	Citroen
		Peugeot
Proton	Malaysia	Lotus (80%)
Toyota	Japan	Daihatsu (25%)
		Lexus
Volkswagen	Germany	Audi
		Bentley
		Bugatti
		Lamborghini
		SEAT
		Skoda
		Rolls-Royce (until 2001)

* In March 2000, due to ongoing heavy losses, BMW sold the Rover Group to John Towers' Phoenix Consortium. Following the takeover Rover was renamed MG Rover and a new company, Techtronic, was formed to run it. Surprisingly, it also agreed to sell the profitable Land Rover part of the business to the Ford Motor Company. The heavy scale of BMW's losses in the UK was making it vulnerable to a hostile bid from another business.

Figures in brackets after a marque indicate the percentage ownership by the main company; for example Toyota owns 25 per cent of Daihatsu.

Since the mid 1990s, the global car industry has seen major consolidation across national borders, and some analysts suggest that by 2005 there will probably be only six to seven volume car producers left. BMW acquired Rover but, in early 2000, sold this to John Towers' Phoenix Consortium. Ford bought Jaguar cars and also owns Aston Martin and has a large stake in Mazda; it also bought Land Rover from BMW as the latter pulled out of its loss making acquisition. Volkswagen purchased Bentley and Rolls-Royce (although BMW acquires use of the latter's marque after 2001), and there has been the purchase of Chrysler (US) by Daimler Benz (Germany), creating the giant DaimlerChrysler. Additionally, French company Renault, the world's ninth biggest car producer with sales of £2.1 million in 1998 and profits of £1 billion, acquired a 36.5 per cent stake in the troubled Japanese car producer Nissan, enabling the former, which is 45 per cent owned by the French state, to enter markets beyond Europe, particularly Asia and North America, without the traumas of a full-scale merger. Currently Renault is too dependent on the European market, making it vulnerable in times of European economic downturn.

Nissan had debts of at least $20 billion (£12.5 billion), and declining sales for its cars, the latter caused in part by the collapse of home demand following the worst economic recession Japan experienced since World War II. In 1998 alone, it lost $625 million. It needed external funding to help develop new products to update its range and make it more competitive, having already closed a main factory and sold its Tokyo headquarters. At one time DaimlerChrysler was also reported to be interested in acquiring a stake of up to 30 per cent in Nissan, at a cost of $2.6 billion (£1.6 billion), or 40 per cent of the heavy goods vehicle part, Nissan Diesel Motor. However, it subsequently decided not to pursue this purchase, deciding instead to focus its attentions on fully integrating the Daimler and Chrysler parts of the new business. If DaimlerChrysler had decided to pursue the partial acquisition, and had succeeded, there would have been the possibility of developing and producing new models, as well as the opportunity to expand into Asia.

Other possible mergers which were mooted included a three way link up of Honda with a market value of $65 billion, BMW ($23 billion) and Ford ($72 billion), whilst another initial rumour, subsequently dispelled by events, was a merger between Fiat, Volvo and Renault. In March 2000, there was further consolidation of the global car industry when Fiat and General Motors (GM) signed a strategic cross-share holding alliance, with GM acquiring a 20 per cent stake in Fiat Auto and Fiat, in turn, acquiring 5 per cent of GM. The two companies also agreed to form a joint venture involving car engines and components. GM currently has a European presence through Opel and Vauxhall.

The main reason for these car industry mergers has been the fact that only global car producers able to achieve economies of scale, and hence keep costs down, will be able to survive into the 21st Century. These businesses will need a wide range of models built with common platforms or characteristics also enabling economies of scope to be achieved, where appropriate. There may be room in the future for small scale niche producers such as Morgan cars, or TVR but not, some analysts suggest, for specialist producers of medium size such as Volvo; although the exception to the rule is Porsche which has an agreement to develop cars with VW. Similarly, to survive, it was argued that BMW, another medium sized producer, needed Rover cars, both as a volume producer and for specialist vehicles such as the Land Rover and Range Rover models, to give it a wide product portfolio. BMW's disinvestment of Rover prompted talks of a possible merger between it and VW, to enable it to survive long term.

3.6 Summary of chapter

This chapter began by re-examining fixed and variable inputs and the costs associated with each of these. Their relationship to the short term and the long term was examined and the calculation of short run and long run total, average and marginal costs was considered. The importance of the law of diminishing returns was examined in this context. In the long run, economies of scale and economies of scope were examined.

The same analysis was then applied to revenue with total, marginal and average revenues identified. With revenue no distinction is made between short and long runs. From this, costs and revenues were then examined in total to determine profits. Distinction was made between how economists and accountants measure profits. The differences between normal, supernormal and monopoly profits were also discussed.

The use of marginal analysis was then explored to determine the optimum level of output for a business, where MC = MR, as was the relationship between AC and AR, to identify whether a business was making normal or supernormal/monopoly profits. The chapter concluded with a case study of the global car industry to explore economies of scale and the means to secure these through rationalisation.

3.7 Further questions

You will need to use wider information sources for these, such as CD-ROMs of newspapers, the Internet or other information sources.

Further Questions

1 Discuss the relationship between average fixed costs, average variable costs, average total costs and marginal costs. Explain why a business economist needs to know about each of these in relation to the operations of a business.

2 What is the relationship between price, average revenue and marginal revenue?

3 Why might some businesses make normal profits, some supernormal profits and some monopoly profits? Which of these will last in the long term?

4 How important is market research to a business seeking to achieve (a) economies of scale and (b) economies of scope?

5 Discuss the reasons why the global car industry is seeking to rationalise. Is further contraction inevitable? Explain your answer.

3.8 Further reading

Baumol, W. J. (1959). *Business Behaviour, Value and Growth*. London/New York: Macmillan.

Begg, D., Fischer, S. and Dornbusch, R. (1997). *Economics,* 5th edition. Maidenhead: McGraw Hill.

Griffiths, A. and Wall, S. (1999). *Applied Economics,* 8th edition. Harlow: Longman Group.

Sloman, J. (1997). *Economics,* 3rd edition. Hemel Hempstead: Prentice Hall.

The Economist

The *Financial Times*

The Times

British Airways website: http://www.british-airways.com

Halifax Plc website: http://www.halifax.co.uk/fr_home.html

Microsoft website: http://biz.yahoo.com/p/m/msft.html
http://www.Microsoft.com

Volvo website: http://biz.yahoo.com/p/v/volvy.html

Chapter 4

Marketing the product

Learning Outcomes

After completing this chapter the reader will be able to:
- appreciate the relationship between marketing and business economics and the impact of marketing on profitability;
- understand and be able to apply basic marketing concepts;
- critically review marketing strategies developed by businesses.

4.1 Marketing characteristics

Marks and Spencer – the need for a marketing revolution

The impact of Marks and Spencer's (M&S) declining profits on its suppliers was examined in Chapter 2, Section 2.1. As part of the process to reverse this declining profitability, M&S has had to introduce a marketing revolution. In the past M&S relied on its reputation for quality, if unexciting, clothes, considerable customer loyalty and its stores, particulaly its flagship at Marble Arch, London and its new out-of-town developments. Therefore, it did not advertise, believing there was no need to, although some perceived this as arrogance. When forced to in December 1998, to clear excess stocks after it significantly overestimated autumn demand, this made headlines in many newspapers.

A new costly marketing strategy was therefore adopted, focusing firstly on merchandising within its stores, i.e. at the customer end of the business. This included such things as improved store layout, better presentation of clothes on the rail on which they hang, better labelling and lower pricing. New shop fronts were provided for its 297 stores along with updated uniforms for staff, carrier bags and clothing lines.

The second part of the strategy was to focus on a more effective marketing of M&S to the outside world, including a new designer label and a downgrading of the St Michael brand. St Michael was well known but peoples' perception of it needed to be changed. Therefore the logo was removed from its labels and replaced with a quality pledge, the St. Michael Promise. M&S marketing director Alan McWalter argued 'what we are showing is a refreshed, updated look, which will give a strong, coherent and consistent identity'.

New staff were recruited and a review of all types of potential advertising was undertaken, including television and the Internet. In October 1999 a series of M&S roadshows were mounted in circus tents around the country, containing fashion shows, celebrity chef 'master classes', etc. to show consumers that M&S could no longer be seen as old fashioned and out of touch. This effort is known as a turnaround strategy.

The main message which the initial promotional campaign sought to put across was that 'M&S has more to offer than people think', since many customers were not aware of the full range of products offered, e.g. furniture in some stores. Prices were cut on many products by about 3 per cent overall, but in some departments by up to 8–10 per cent. As noted in Chapter 2, Section 2.1, in order to reduce prices M&S had to look for lower production costs from its suppliers, necessitating switching from British, to lower cost Far Eastern suppliers. It also reduced jobs at head office and where there were overlaps between M&S staff and its suppliers, in terms of functions. However, the bottom line of the marketing strategy is that price cuts can only be justified if sales (demand for M&S products) increase.

Marketing the product – characteristics

In Chapter 2, Porter's value chain was explored as a means to break down a business's operations into distinct activities which display the total value created in a business's economic functions. These may be undertaken more cheaply than competitors or they may be differentiated from competitors' activities. Either can give a business competitive advantage over its rivals. This chapter focuses on the latter, looking at marketing in creating competitive advantage and on the relationship of marketing to business economics. The impact of marketing on business revenues, and hence profitability, is explored, as is the impact of price and non-price influences on demand.

Marketing, which draws heavily on economics among other disciplines, may be described as a profit oriented business philosophy which puts the customer at the centre of all the business's activities. This is known as the marketing concept. It is concerned with identifying who the potential customers are (the markets) and what their needs and wants are (the demand); in other words it recognises consumer sovereignty. It is then the responsibility of the business, using a set of management techniques, to meet that demand and the whole business organisation should be co-ordinated and focused on satisfying these customer requirements (the supply). Of course, it also has to compete in a dynamic business environment with rival businesses. These supply products which are similar to, or substitutes for, its products in the same geographical area.

Marketing is, therefore, a functional activity which converts consumer needs into specific corporate activities to meet the company's objectives. This has implications in terms of how the business is defined, for example, focusing on customer satisfaction rather than just the products supplied. It also encompasses the attitudes of management and the workforce through their need to accept the marketing focus and the operational systems for planning, gathering information, and decision making, with the implication of effective coordination of marketing activities through the whole business.

Marketing also requires the business to be proactive and constantly look for new products, i.e. goods, services or ideas, markets and opportunities. Therefore, market research and forecasting, which are known as market intelligence and which were discussed in Chapter 2, Section 2.2, are clearly of importance, as is research into products which, with market intelligence, is known as marketing research. In this sense, the above case study of Marks and Spencer is clearly informative in that it provides a classic example of a business which has neglected the marketing of its products, or relied on word of mouth as a communicative method and, consequently, suffered reduced profits.

Marketing strategy

Marketing is not, therefore, just about identifying consumer needs or market opportunities, producing the wanted good or service, and convincing the consumer that it is inherently superior to that of competitors, which is the rationale of a production oriented business and of business economics. It is also about the use of a range of marketing tools, known as the marketing mix, in a selected and researched target market – in other words developing a marketing strategy. These marketing tools include the product design, using the right people in the right ways, correctly pricing the product, the packaging used, how the product is promoted, using the correct distribution channels for it, and after-sales service. In this way, the business is totally focused on supplying goods, services and ideas to satisfy the needs of the specific customer; this is known as a marketing oriented business. As noted above, for this to be effective, it must permeate all aspects of a business from top to bottom.

Within its marketing strategy a business can influence its marketing mix. This encompasses a number of variables. They include:

1 the product – including developing new, modifying existing and eliminating failing products; branding and packaging of products;
2 its distribution channels (or place), e.g. finding optimal locations for retailers; relationships with retailers and dealers; minimising transport and distribution costs;
3 how the product is promoted, e.g. advertising, salesforce, free samples;
4 the price of the product – establishing appropriate pricing policies and evaluating them against those of competitors; deciding whether discounts should be given and to whom.

Some marketers include a fifth 'P' in the marketing mix, along with product, place, promotion and price, which are customarily known as the four 'P's. This is people and covers such aspects as the provision of service levels including customer handling, after-sales service and motivating marketing staff. Indeed, we shall see later, that we can also distinguish a seven 'P' model. The marketing mix is discussed more fully in Section 4.3.

In contrast, the business environment factors such as political, legal, economic etc., which were discussed in Chapter 1, Section 1.4, cannot so easily be influenced by businesses, if at all. However, these factors also influence the needs of potential customers. One part of marketing strategy is, therefore, identifying and analysing opportunities which arise for businesses, e.g. a sudden increase in demand for a new children's toy at Christmas.

Another part of marketing strategy is target markets where a business identifies a particular market and uses a marketing mix to meet the needs and preferences of the customers in that target market, e.g. the quality sandwich market, where suppliers have developed to meet city centre workers' lunchtime needs. To meet the precise needs of these customers, marketing managers in a business must use the marketing mix to satisfy customers' needs. In London, therefore, some sandwich firms deliver to offices to save workers having to leave their desks if they work through their lunch breaks, i.e. using the right distribution channels for the product, to give convenience. To maintain the right marketing mix, detailed information needs to be gathered on all marketing mix variables, as was discussed in Chapter 2, Section 2.3. For instance, looking at the product; in the case of sandwich sales, changing tastes for more sophisticated yet healthy sandwich fillings has had a big impact on what people will buy. Similarly, the moves in consumer preferences from instant coffee to cappuccino, double latté and other coffee types has created opportunities for a variety of specialist coffee houses and bars to develop in recent years.

The final element of marketing strategy is marketing management. This involves: planning marketing activities to meet the business's objectives consistently with its strategy; ensuring that marketing resources within the business are combined effectively; implementing the plans to ensure that the objectives are realised; and monitoring and controlling the processes as they occur.

Marketing strategy is discussed more fully in Section 4.4.

4.2 Segmenting markets, targeting and positioning

Case Study

The Saga tradition: I came back from my holiday two weeks older and ten years younger!

'Saga's holidays are exclusively for people aged 50 years and over. We are committed to providing the very highest quality of standards of service from the moment you book direct with us, right through every aspect of your holiday. We take care of all the details leaving you free to relax and enjoy yourself on your well-earned holiday.

Saga has 48 years experience of organising holidays for mature travellers through our companies in Britain, the USA and Australia.

We believe our success is due to our personal service, attention to detail, and our continued response to the comments and suggestions of our holidaymakers.'

The concept of markets was discussed in Chapter 1, Section 1.3 and is discussed again, more fully, in Chapter 5. We defined a market as a situation where buyers and sellers come together. Buyers may be households, businesses or public sector bodies such as local authorities, whilst demand must be backed by a willingness and ability to pay, otherwise it is just an unsatisfied want. Suppliers will seek to meet demands and the market may be a physical or non-physical location. Although economic theory argues that a perfect market will result in one price resulting from the interaction of demand and supply, in reality, there will be a range of prices for a product, since markets are not perfect.

Segmentation

From the viewpoint of businesses, they will select target markets which, if they enter them, will enhance their sales and profits.

Target markets

A target market is defined as one where businesses which enter it will develop a marketing mix which specifically matches the demands and preferences of the group of potential buyers who constitute it. A business's target market may be the total market facing it; this approach is known as the total or undifferentiated market approach. Alternatively a business may divide the total market into segments, each of which has its own characteristics; this is known as market segmentation.

Undifferentiated market approach

When a business adopts an undifferentiated market approach it assumes that all consumers in the market have broadly similar tastes and wants. It will therefore use its marketing mix to apply to everyone. This is only likely to be appropriate if there is a very limited variation in customer demands or needs and, if the business can maintain one marketing mix across the entire market; this can be very costly. Additionally, consumer tastes are becoming more sophisticated with them demanding a greater variety of products, therefore, market segmentation is likely to be much more appropriate in many cases.

Market segmentation

This involves a business distinguishing groups of customers with similar characteristics and product demands. These sub-markets can then be targeted by businesses to supply them with the most appropriate goods and services; these will be supplied at appropriate prices, supported by an appropriate promotional campaign and supplied through the most appropriate distribution channels (place) – this latter is known as positioning.

Customers can be grouped and markets segmented in many ways, as shown in Table 4.1. It is important to know as much about one's customers as possible, so that an appropriate marketing mix can be tailored to them. A variety of variables can be used by a business to segment consumer markets. These include the characteristics of consumers such as demographics – age, sex, race, religion etc.; socio-economic background – income, occupation, education etc.; and location – area of the UK, type of environment, e.g. semi-rural, type of house etc. The variables also include: how people behave in relation to the products they buy, e.g. the extent to which there is brand loyalty or whether people are price sensitive (is the demand for it elastic or inelastic – see Chapter 6, Section 6.1); moral values, e.g. more people are buying shares yet the importance of investing ethically is

Table 4.1 Socio-economic groupings.

Social group	Social status	Occupation
A	Upper middle class	Higher managerial, administrative or professional
B	Middle class	Intermediate managerial, administrative or professional
C1	Lower middle class	Supervisory or clerical, and junior managerial, administrative or professional
C2	Skilled working class	Skilled manual workers
D	Working class	Semi and unskilled manual workers
E	Lowest subsistence levels	State pensioners or widows (no other earner), casual or lowest grade workers

Source: Marketing Pocketbook 2000, NTC Publications Ltd

of growing importance; what benefits consumers seek from a product, e.g. Volvo is wanted essentially for its safety record whereas the Lotus is wanted for its sporty/stylish image.

To a business, the advantages of market segmentation, as a part of its marketing strategy, are that it can increase sales in existing markets, offer for sale new products in existing markets, offer existing products in new markets, and diversify into new markets with new products. For example, building on the case study above, Saga now offers financial services to its existing customer base, building on the knowledge that the over 50s are not just living longer but, in many cases, are increasingly the most prosperous sector of the population by age.

There are a number of benefits of market segmentation. The business is able to know its customers' characteristics better since the market is defined more tightly, and this also applies to the competitors it faces in the segmented markets. Segmentation is more cost effective than the undifferentiated market approach since a business's resources are scarce and the latter approach is very resource intensive. It also helps strategic marketing planning since plans can be tailored to the specific segment's characteristics.

To summarise the argument above, market segmentation consists of three stages:

1 segmentation
2 targeting
3 positioning.

Targeting strategies

As was said before, a target market is defined as one which businesses will enter to develop a marketing mix which specifically matches the demands and preferences of the group of potential buyers who constitute it. Targeting strategies, therefore, precede this. They are the process of making decisions about which of the market segments the business has identified it should focus on for its sales and marketing activities.

A business may operate a concentration strategy, whereby it concentrates on a single market segment, e.g. Club 18–30 holidays, or Rolls-Royce cars. Until its acquisition by BMW, Rolls-Royce Motor Company was always short of resources. However, by concentrating on the top of the range car market, it was able to establish a small niche market which volume car producers did not concentrate on at all, or only in a very limited way. Nonetheless, the business could encounter problems if that segment contracted, e.g. a downturn in the business cycle severely hit demand for Porsche cars in the early to mid 1990s.

The other option for a business is to pursue a multi-segment strategy where it focuses on more than one market segment. Since this will enable it to interface with more customers it should be a more profitable strategy; this will involve the use of more than one marketing mix, depending on the individual segments. For a production based company this may involve higher costs as production switches from one product to another. However, if production is efficient and uses automated lines, it may be feasible to achieve economies of scope to minimise costs (see Chapter 3, Section 3.2). Therefore, the extent of a business's resources is an essential factor in deciding whether to opt for a concentration or a multi-segment strategy; others include the extent of the business's expertise and what competitors are doing.

For market segmentation to be effective, there should be a different types of consumer demand for the product. Different market segments must also be measurable so that the economic worth of each can be compared against the others. Segmentation also requires that the segments be big and stable enough to merit the costs and time of developing their own distinctive marketing mixes.

Additionally, in deciding which marketing strategy to adopt and which segments to target, a business should also very carefully consider its competitors' strengths. It needs to have a distinctive or differential advantage over its competitors products which cannot be matched by them if it is to succeed long term. The marketing programme then needs to be geared to this. For example, in the recent battle for customers between the RAC and the AA, the former made much of giving priority to women drivers whose cars broke down when they were driving alone, pledging an average response time of 30 minutes. In contrast, the AA's positioning, and hence its differential advantage was to promote itself on a par with the police, fire and ambulance services – 'to our members we're the fourth emergency service.' In both cases the perception was that customers wanted quick responses and reassurance at a time of stress and insecurity, i.e. when one's car breaks down; however, the AA's differential advantage was the gravitas of its reputation, backed by its ability to deliver.

Positioning

Once a business has segmented its market and decided which one or more segments to target it then has to position its product, i.e. develop the product to meet the needs of the customers which make up the segment.

Positioning means creating a differentiated image and position for the product in the minds of its target consumers, compared with competitors' products. In other words, the customer must perceive the product to be different from and superior to competitors' products. The lager market illustrates this with Carlsberg, Carling Black Label and others seeking to position their products against those of similarly priced competitors.

The price a business charges for a product may, therefore, say something about the values associated with that product. So, a high price may be perceived as indicating a high quality, e.g. a Rolls-Royce selling for the price of a Ford would make people doubt that it was a 'real' Rolls. The phrase 'you only get what you pay for' is often used to justify this, yet consumer magazines such as 'Which' clearly demonstrate that this is not always so. For example, people going to the same foreign holiday resort at the same time may pay quite different prices; or two refrigerators may be priced £100 apart yet the cheaper one is better quality. For foreign goods the rate of inflation in the foreign country, and hence the rate of exchange of that country's currency against sterling, may cause price differences which bear no reflection of quality.

The marketing mix is, therefore, used to reinforce the positioning through pricing, packaging, branding (promotion) and distribution channels (place); distinctive product image is of major importance in this respect. However, since consumer perception is the crucial variable, then businesses can only partly control this through their actions. In-depth market research is therefore essential to determine how consumers perceive products, and promotion of the product is then essential to build on this perception.

4.3 The marketing mix; the product life cycle; pricing theories

The marketing mix

The marketing mix was discussed briefly in Section 4.2 and is now analysed more fully.

Since corporate strategy (Chapter 2, Section 2.2) and marketing strategy are interlinked by the fact that marketing should pervade all aspects of the business's activities, marketing tools need to be used to enable a business to achieve its corporate objectives. These are known as the marketing mix and, as noted before, consist of four Ps: product; price; promotion; and place. If the marketing relates to services rather than goods then three extra Ps are added to the standard four. These are: physical evidence; people; and processes. So the marketing mix is a set of variables which create the product's positioning. There should, therefore, be consistency between the elements of the mix.

Product

As noted above, this term covers a wide range of tangible and intangible benefits and disbenefits which a person receives from the purchase of a good, service or idea, i.e. it is acquired to satisfy the consumer's wants or needs. Economic theory tells us that a person consumes a product because he/she derives utility or satisfaction from it. However, marketing theory says the product may also yield disbenefits or disutility, such as post-purchase dissatisfaction from the poor mechanical reliability of a car, or its poor resale value. It will also cover such issues as: the range and type of products sold by a business; how they are differentiated from rival products by branding; their quality; how they are packaged and labelled; what sort of warranty or after-sales service is provided, and so on.

Products are branded to differentiate them from those of their competitors and to yield competitive advantage. This includes product name (e.g. Penguin, Kit Kat, Twix), packaging, labelling, and customer and after sales service. This means that the products in a business's portfolio must be constantly reviewed. In the case study in Chapter 4, Section 4.1, the St. Michael brand was recognised as denoting reasonably priced quality but staid design. The Virgin logo and branding is used to link the personality and entrepreneurship of Richard Branson to the products being sold. Reebok and Nike are brands denoting fashionable quality sports and leisure wear. The Lloyds Bank (now Lloyds–TSB) black horse image is another example of branding to distinguish one banking service from other similar ones.

How well a product sells depends on its position in its product life cycle. This concept is discussed more fully below. However, it should be noted here that the portfolio of products a business has, known as the product mix, needs to be reviewed on a regular basis. Some products will have reached the end of their life and should be discarded whilst others need to be marketed more vigorously to continue their life with higher sales. Additionally, new products need to come on stream to replace those which will soon be defunct. For example, Ford decided in the 1990s to cease production of its Sierra, in turn a replacement for the much loved Cortina which went through four distinct models, and to replace it with the Mondeo, to compete more effectively in the fleet and lease car markets; however, the Fiesta and the Escort were continued in production after major revamps.

In reviewing its product mix a business must also consider all other areas of the company, from finance to human resources, from information management systems to investment in production processes. It also needs to look at its balance between existing and new markets. This is where the BCG product portfolio matrix, discussed in Section 4.4, is helpful for making the right decisions.

The New Volvo S80. From £22 930.

The World's Most Exhilarating Safe Choice.
Whiplash is one of the most common in-car injuries.
Which is why the front seats in the Volvo S80 have been designed so that the G-forces created by a rear impact are reduced by 50 per cent.
Helping to save your neck and back.
It's a system that sets new standards.
And, as you'd expect from Volvo, it's standard equipment.

From this advertisement for the Volvo S80, in terms of the definition of a product, the reader should consider what are the full range of benefits this product might offer from first considering a purchase to having owned it for a year. Are there any disbenefits which should be considered?

Price

The price a business charges for its products determines how much of them it sells and, therefore, the revenue it earns, since revenue equals the price of the good multiplied by the quantity of it sold. The more revenue a business earns in relation to the costs of producing the goods, the more profit it makes.

To sell more, a business may have to, over time, lower its price, as market demand declines. At other times, and with other products, a business may be able to charge a high price for a new product for which people are willing to pay a premium, such as a top of the range new specification personal computer, or a new Jaguar car. This is known as the pricing strategy of 'skimming the cream' and is discussed below. This demonstrates that, rather than one specific price for a good, a business has a margin for price setting lying somewhere between a high price where demand will suffer if it is raised anymore and a low price where revenue will not cover costs. The exact point will depend on the business's strategic objectives and will link into such issues as the price in relation to competitors' prices, the market average, whether price discounting will be employed at any stage and whether the business will vary price regularly or seek stable prices. These strategies are discussed below under the heading pricing theories.

A business will also need to respond to price changes adopted by its competitors; the larger the number of competitors selling similar products, i.e. the market type known as monopolistic competition, the more impact such a price change will have. Conversely, for an oligopoly market structure, where there are a few large sellers, there is likely to be more price stability. This is because whatever one firm does will have an impact on the others, and hence provoke a response, which they will wish to avoid. Additionally, other factors in the business's external environment may change and this will impact on its pricing strategy, e.g. a merger between competitors, a new business entering the market, or contracting demand. Furthermore, businesses will differentiate their products through advertising and branding and these factors need to be considered in association with prices since they seek to tie in consumer loyalty and prevent customers switching brands as price rises and also incur further costs which must be covered.

The pricing part of the marketing mix therefore covers such areas as the prices charged for the business's goods and/or services *vis à vis* those of its competitors, the extent of price discounts and trade facilities, and pricing strategies which are discussed below. The level at which the price is initially set will depend on estimates of demand for the product and the sensitivity of demand to price changes. It will also depend on the category of consumer being targeted – see the five adopter categories below. Most importantly, however, pricing decisions are a part of the overall marketing objectives and strategy of a business. This includes, in particular, how pricing fits in with the rest of the marketing mix.

Promotion

Promotion relates to marketing communications. This is the process of the business communicating information to the target audience of consumers which promotes the exchange of goods, services and ideas, the last being known as intellectual property. Largely, but not exclusively, this seeks to persuade consumers to buy the business's products. In the marketing mix, promotional mix involves advertising, selling, public relations and publicity, and sales promotion. All non-media promotions are known as 'below-the-line-promotions.'

Advertising is the use of a non-personal message which is communicated through the mass media, e.g. as an advertisement on television, local radio or a newspaper/magazine, such as the Volvo advertisement above. Although potentially it has a wide audience, it is expensive and may take quite some time to be effective; the effectiveness of advertising is hard to measure.

Selling, as the name suggests, is undertaken on a personal basis and seeks to persuade the consumer to buy the product or service. The mis-selling of pensions by financial advisers in the 1980s is the most alarming example. People were persuaded to leave their employers' pension schemes and start new free standing schemes which made them worse off; however, the sales persons earned large commissions from this. Selling is expensive because of the labour costs of its sales force but is generally more effective than advertising because the personal interaction between the sales person and the customer is more likely to achieve a sale.

Public relations and publicity is distributed through the mass media to raise awareness of the company and its products and should be seen as an ongoing process. For example, your college/university might supply material to local newspaper and television stations if something newsworthy occurs which will boost its public image, e.g. a particular celebrity being awarded an honorary degree at the annual graduation ceremony. Finally, sales promotion will encompass such things as coupons and free gifts, for example a 'free' camera or watch with five litres of engine oil bought at your local garage; or, on TV, a simple quiz which enables you to win a holiday to Australia. However, the cost of the prize is more than recouped by the donor through a premium rate phone line.

Marketing theory distinguishes a range of consumers known as adopter categories. This ranges from the innovators at one end of the scale – those who are first to buy a new product when it appears and are willing to pay a high price to be the first to be seen with it – to the laggards at the other end of the scale. These are the last to buy the product when it is near the end of its commercial life and is soon to disappear or be replaced by an updated version, e.g. buying a 486 computer when most people had a Pentium. It is clearly important, in this case, to know who the target audience is, since different messages and pricing strategies will be needed for each of the two categories above. Adopter categories are discussed more fully later in this chapter.

Place

This covers a wide range of issues such as distribution channels, levels of stock held, delivery of goods to customers etc. It means that a business must ensure that its products are in the right place and at the right time for consumers, and at the right price.

Most typically distribution involves manufacturers selling to wholesalers who then sell to retailers, from whom households buy their products. However, manufacturers may sell directly to consumers, which is known as direct marketing. This applies from a low level such as farm shops to national networks such as Sony shops where the Japanese electrical goods manufacturer sells direct. More generally, however, they sell indirectly via intermediaries such as retail outlets. This is because the latter possess the distribution resources and skills which manufacturers do not have or, because they are located in the same country as the final consumers.

For example, products may need to be displayed, as with a car showroom, or a fitted kitchen centre in B&Q or Sainsbury's Homebase, which requires space and expertise to make the products look attractive. Additionally, since time is at a premium, many people want many goods together; hence the development of out of town superstores and hypermarkets at the expense of inner city high street shopping areas which require more time and effort to visit. Therefore, distribution channels are clearly an important part of the marketing mix for a business as well as a major source of employment and wealth creation for the economy as a whole.

The effectiveness of the marketing channel will be determined by a number of factors, of which the two most important are:

- Its length – a greater number of intermediary stages in the chain between manufacturer and consumer does not necessarily mean that the longer chain is less efficient than a shorter one, otherwise every business would sell direct.
- How members of the distribution channel relate to each other, including where power and decision making is based; this is known as channel relationships. The most conventional structure is one where the manufacturer, the wholesaler (who breaks down the bulk products supplied by the manufacturer) and retailers are discrete and independent businesses. Since each seeks to maximise profits it has its own agenda but also no significant control over the other parties. They function as an effective channel because they all benefit from trading or dealing with each other.

Distribution should be viewed as a part of production in the total sense because it enables the products to reach the consumer. It therefore has strategic implications since it is a crucial part of the marketing mix and, once locked into a distribution chain, it is expensive and time consuming for a business to change it. A business therefore needs to decide such issues as:

1 The length of the channel, including the types of intermediaries it needs to get the products to the consumer and what each of the intermediaries does. Generally, the shorter the channel the more control the business has over the distribution of its products.
2 How many intermediaries it needs in the channel and where they need to be located – the more intermediaries a business has, and the wider their distribution, the more effective distribution of the products to consumers should be. Since the 1960s, the clothing manufacturer Benetton has sought to expand into nearly every country in the world, including those with low incomes per head of the population, to ensure maximum coverage of its products.

3 Processes to ensure that the distribution channel functions with maximum efficiency, e.g. avoiding conflict between different types of retail outlet both selling the product, or between wholesaler and retailer. Benetton, for example, which operates a system of franchises for its retail outlets rather than owning then directly, has a strategy of encouraging several branches to operate in close proximity to each other to keep them on their toes, by competing with each other.

4 What marketing efforts are needed regarding the distribution channel, e.g. is the marketing strategy aimed at the trade, e.g. as with some builders' merchants, or at the consumer, as with B&Q. Depending on this, different marketing strategies will be needed.

Of course, in making such decisions, a business will also face a number of issues which it needs to consider, which may constrain its choice. It will need to consider the markets where it wants to sell its products and the nature of the consumers. For example, in launching its Independent Savings Accounts (ISAs) the government wanted particularly to encourage people with lower incomes, or those who do not regularly save, to do so. It therefore targeted supermarkets which it considered were more likely to reach these people than banks, the idea being that people could put some money into their ISA after paying their grocery bill. In practice, this has not happened.

The business will also need to consider the nature of its products. For example, flowers flown in from the Canary Isles will be chilled, yet have a very short life. They therefore need to be delivered to florists as quickly as possible. Artificial flowers will not face this problem, of course. There are other examples but the interested reader should consult the further reading section at the end of this chapter for more specialist texts.

The changing nature of distribution

In recent years the rapid growth of multiples such as Etam, Richard Shops and Debenhams have transformed distribution in the UK by offering standardised outlets, quality of service and certainty to consumers. In the same way, the development of supermarkets and hypermarkets, particularly out of town, has transformed shopping by hastening the decline of the traditional corner shop. The growth of mail order, e.g. via newspaper colour supplements, has shortened the length of the distribution chain in that goods bypass retailers' outlets and go direct from wholesalers to customers. The exponential growth of electronic commerce (e-commerce), where people buy goods and services via the Internet, has also drastically changed the nature of the distribution chain. Additionally, technology has impacted on the distribution chain through such issues as computerised stock control systems and bar codes and laser scanning at checkout tills. The reader should also consider the relevance of Porter's value chain in the context of the distribution chain and the changes identified here.

The three extra Ps for services

For the marketing of services, i.e. intangible products, three extra Ps need to be considered. They are very briefly reviewed here.

Physical evidence

This relates to anything that impacts on the customer's senses, e.g. uniforms, logo, smell, brochures, signs etc. The atmosphere and ambience of a store is such an example. The development of US style bookstores in the UK, where sofas are provided to sit and read books before buying them, whilst drinking a cup of coffee, clearly creates a much more attractive situation than a standard WH Smith store, for instance.

People

This will cover the personnel who work for the business and their contribution to the marketing mix. These are crucial in providing a service and securing return sales. DIY superstores are sometimes criticised for the lack of personnel to provide expert advice which used to be provided by ironmongers and other small specialist shops before they were wiped out by the DIY superstores. Indeed, B&Q operates a policy of employing over-50 year olds, with some stores completely run by these. Senior management argue that these people are more knowledgeable, conscientious and reliable than young staff.

Processes

This overlaps 'People', in part, and refers to such issues as information flows, ease of payment, lack of queuing, etc. Post Offices have a very bad reputation because they have very long queues at peak times. Having to wait ten minutes to be served is very frustrating. A supermarket which provides staff on extra checkout tills, when queues lengthen beyond a certain point, is clearly attractive to time pressed customers. Even better is telephone or Internet banking, which bypasses physical premises completely.

Conclusion

If the business is to achieve its corporate, including marketing, objectives then it must combine these main variables, or Ps, in such a way as to give it competitive advantage over its rivals. This means that there should be consistency between the various elements of the mix.

Choosing a particular marketing mix

In summary, the marketing mix has been defined as a set of policies by which a company can achieve its strategic objectives through some combination of these, relevant to the environment in which it operates. The marketing mix was defined as the four Ps – product, price, promotion and place. For the marketing of services three extra Ps were added – physical evidence, people and processes.

How a business varies its four Ps – in the case of products – will depend upon the particular organisation and the strategic objectives which it seeks to achieve. These will vary depending on whether the business is the market leader, or a follower of the leader, or is seeking to challenge the market leader to obtain that position for itself, or to establish a niche for itself. Its product can be influenced by innovation, e.g. curried baked beans in the 1980s; or it may be repositioned, e.g. the defunct weekly newspaper 'The European' which changed its format three times in six years. In its final incarnation, it sought to be a one section, tabloid shaped, European focused 'The Economist' rather than its initial more broadsheet sized three section newspaper, one of which was a colour supplement.

Clearly its pricing policy can vary from high initial price to secure maximum income quickly, to a lower price to secure maximum market share. This depends on the product. One option is price discounting – when a new version of a computer enters the market, e.g. one with a Pentium III processor, price discounting is used to clear the stock of machines with Pentium II processors.

Promotion of a product can use a variety of different means – advertising in the media, a sales promotion campaign, personal selling, e.g. the Prudential Insurance Co. offering to visit people at home or work to help them when they want a mortgage, rather than having to go to the bank or building society as with other financial services providers.

Place, and particularly distribution of products, again offers a variety of different options. The cross-over between filling stations and supermarkets is an interesting illustration of this. When supermarkets started selling petrol they hit garages hard. The latter retaliated by setting up mini-supermarkets, offering newspapers, groceries etc. Although one might not go to a garage for one's weekly shop, they still offer a convenience for the items one has forgotten and doesn't wish to queue for in a supermarket. Manufacturers not using garages as outlets for their products could, for example, consider this option.

In the end, however, in its efforts to maximise its profits, a business must choose the mix which is most appropriate to its strategies and needs.

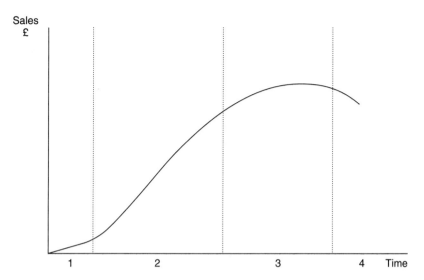

Figure 4.1 The product life cycle.

The product life cycle

In Chapter 3, Section 3.3, the total revenue curve was examined and it was noted that this shows the relationship between alternative levels of output and the revenue obtained at each of those levels of output, at a moment in time, which is the time when all factors or inputs are fixed. By varying the price it charges, a business can decide where on the curve it wants to be. In contrast, the product life cycle shows sales over time – which may be many years – rather than at a moment in time. Therefore, there might be a series of different total revenue curves relating to each point on the product life cycle curve. Additionally, inputs can be varied – so that at the growth and early maturity stages, more resources will be put into production and they will be worked more intensively.

Like human beings, products have a finite life; exactly how long will vary from product to product; some, such as Mars Bars or Guinness seem to have been around for ever, whilst others, like the 1970s Sinclair C5 electric vehicle or the infamous Strand cigarettes of the late 1950s/early 1960s, or womens' fashions, appear and are soon gone. In each case, although the life of the product may be quite different, its characteristics are very similar. Four main stages of the product life cycle have been identified and are illustrated in Figure 4.1. They are:

1   Introduction. The product has just entered the market at this stage, therefore, marketing will involve generating consumer awareness of the product, typically through advertising. It is likely that competition will be low, especially if the product is the first in its field. There will be

high promotional expenditure and continued R&D costs; this means high unit costs and limited sales. Additionally, the failure rates of new products is high, so the business is likely to incur net cash outflows at this stage.

2 Growth. As the product enters this stage of its life, new competing brands enter the market to challenge the pioneer product; this is known as a 'follow the leader' strategy. Therefore, the business has to promote its product by a marketing campaign aimed at reinforcing existing consumer knowledge which was already established at the introduction stage. The growth of 'alchopops' is a good example of this. As more consumers buy the product, sales increase and, hopefully, profits also appear. The other key feature of the marketing mix at this stage is place, i.e. the effective distribution of the product. Nothing is more deterring to consumer demand than looking for a product which is not on the shelves. The shortage of childrens' toys at Christmas, such as Cabbage Patch dolls, or teletubbies or furbies, illustrates this. Additionally, supermarkets carefully monitor sales and soon drop products which don't sell strongly, e.g. wholemeal spaghetti rather than white spaghetti, so the product's life may be very limited; hence the importance of continued promotion. Profits will peak by the end of the growth period and, as sales and profits then begin to slow, the product enters the maturity phase.

3 Maturity. This is the longest stage of the product life cycle and is where most products are. Sales continue growing but not as fast as at the growth phase. Businesses may cut their prices to retain market share, quite possibly causing profits to fall; they will only be able to grow at the expense of their competitors. Less efficient businesses will leave the industry as their profits fall below the levels necessary to keep them in their current activities. These are known as normal profits and are discussed more fully in Chapter 3, Section 3.4, although it is still possible that new low cost producers could enter the industry, especially if entry barriers are low. In using the marketing mix the main emphasis will be on promotion to encourage existing loyal consumers to buy more of the business's product as well as seeking to attract new customers from competitors. Regarding place, businesses will need to ensure they retain existing distributors or they will lose key outlets which they will not subsequently recover.

4 Decline. This is the final stage of the product life cycle and sales are now declining fast. Some producers will leave the industry whilst others will cut prices drastically to try and secure a greater market share. It may be possible for a business to survive in a niche market but it may not. However, some businesses will 'harvest', i.e. deliberately put up prices to exploit die-hard buyers. Although this will speed the demise of the product it will increase profits in the meantime, or cover the rising unit or average costs that go with falling sales.

Synopsis

This case study examines a product at the maturity stage of its life cycle. The case study demonstrates:

1 the importance of advertising in maintaining demand for a well-established product;
2 the role of supporting services such as design and planning in reinforcing the attractiveness of the physical good and its distinctiveness from other products.

The mature product – Portland Conservatories

Style, choice and the complete service. It can only be Portland.

Have a premium quality Portland hardwood conservatory built for Spring and you'll be amazed by the sheer choice of sizes and styles designed to suit your needs and your budget. As Britain's most experienced conservatory company we'll take care of everything, from design and planning through to construction and completion – even furnishings. For a limited period we'll even pay the equivalent of the VAT on your new Portland conservatory – and we'll fit your choice of Nairn flooring absolutely free! With Portland, creating a new lifestyle couldn't be easier.

Call to arrange a free no-obligation design survey and for details of the Portland Premier Selection Catalogue.

Conclusions

The duration of each stage of the product life cycle will vary considerably from product to product and can be very hard to identify. For the Sinclair C5 the life cycle barely progressed beyond the introduction stage, so unsuccessful was the product. In contrast, the Sony Walkman had a fairly rapid introduction and growth stages whilst its maturity stage has been of considerable duration. Now the portable CD player is replacing it. The same might be said of the Mars Bar but, of course, effective marketing campaigns have often boosted sales, and hence extended the maturity stage at times when, otherwise, the product might have entered its decline phase. In some cases a new product has effectively emerged from the old one, e.g. the emergence of biological washing powders from traditional soap powders in the 1980s. For most businesses, however, as one product enters its decline the next product should be entering its maturity phase to maintain corporate profitability. This implies that, whatever the duration of a product's life and of each phase, there should be a marketing strategy for each phase. There also needs to be a new product development strategy.

A final comment on the product life cycle is that it can become a self fulfilling prophecy whereby managers of a business expect the decline to occur and it therefore does, through lack of effort on their part!

Pricing strategies

Chapter 1 briefly discussed the concept of demand and how, with supply, it made up what are termed 'market forces.' We also assumed, initially, that these market forces determine a single market price for a good or service. However, subsequently we have recognised that in the real world, one-price markets are not so common. We now need to link market prices with pricing strategies, as a product passes through its life cycle.

When a business introduces a new product it might adopt either one of two pricing strategies. In both cases it will seek to maximise long term profits during the remainder of the product life cycle as a result of the strategy it adopts at the introduction stage.

Skimming the cream

This is appropriate to a new product at the introduction stage of its life cycle. Skimming the cream pricing charges a high price for the product and seeks to secure the maximum revenue whilst the product is new and certain people known as the early adopters, i.e. those who want to lead the market in acquiring new products, are willing to pay a high price for it. This requires the product to be distinctive, with no close substitutes and therefore an inelastic demand, i.e. demand will not be affected by price increases (Chapter 6, Section 6.1). So long as the business can cover its costs and make supernormal profits, in other words profits which are greater than necessary to keep the business in its current activity, it will charge the maximum it can. It will then either cut and run or lower its prices as it moves to the growth stage of the product life cycle. Examples include those willing to pay high prices to have the first mobile phones or the latest first team strip of their favourite football team. In other words these are products which are heavily branded with an emphasis on product quality or differentiation, sold selectively and supported by heavy promotional spend.

Penetration pricing

This pricing strategy is used when the market is much more competitive due to a number of substitute brands. Demand is therefore elastic, i.e. the quantity demanded will change as a consequence of price changes, and the business will charge a low price to secure maximum demand and hence penetrate the market fully to gain maximum market share. It is likely to be used early in the product life cycle if the business seeks maximum market share; however, it might also be used at the maturity stage when competition is really fierce.

Pricing policies

Whereas skimming the cream and penetration pricing are strategies, the following are pricing policies. Hence psychological pricing might be an example of a penetration pricing strategy.

Psychological pricing

An example of this is the high priced Rolls-Royce – apart from reflecting the lack of economies of scale it also reflects that people expect to pay a high price. Another example of a psychological barrier that the vendor does not wish to cross might be a house sold at £79 950 instead of £80 000.

Promotional pricing

This relates to special offers to sell a product, for instance when it is first launched, e.g. 'buy a five litre can of car oil and get a free road map of the UK'. This is to generate extra sales, hopefully to create brand loyalty, but often just to create extra revenue, short term.

Setting the price

This is a much more mechanistic process of determining the actual price, rather than the strategy behind it. Examples include:

- **Cost plus.** This is much less strategic pricing since a business estimates its total costs of producing the good, including production, marketing, distribution, research and development, after sales etc. and adds on to this a margin for profits. Of course, depending on how big or small the margin is, this may in turn be an example of either of the two pricing strategies above. It may also be linked to some pre-determined profit margin – say 10 per cent. Most likely, however, it will be what the market will bear.
- **What the market will bear.** Implicit in the above, and in the business economist's perception of price determination, is this phrase – what the

market will bear. It means that a business should charge the highest price it can, consistent with not affecting the demand for the product. This may be at quite different levels depending on whether a skimming the cream or penetration pricing strategy is employed – but in each case the price is set with a clear eye on its impact on demand. From the business economist's viewpoint it means charging a price as demonstrated by the demand curve, which shows the interaction of price and quantity demanded.

Non-price influences

Non-price factors such as branding, advertising and packaging, and distribution channels first became of real importance in the 1950s and 1960s as a consequence of increased competition among manufacturers. These afforded the means to make products more distinctive. They have been alluded to or discussed to some extent but it is not the role of this book to explore these in any depth. Suffice it to say that the reader should be aware that non-price factors are as important in selling products, and hence helping to maximise profits, as the pricing policy itself. The growth in sales of Japanese cars and electronic goods since the 1970s has owed as much to the reliability, quality and design characteristics of the products as they have to their prices. Again, the reader is referred to specialist marketing texts if he/she wishes to pursue this further.

Adopter categories: who buys what and when

These have already been referred to above. Rogers, in his 1962 book, *Diffusion of Innovation*, argued that consumers who adopt a new product, whether on price or non-price grounds or both, can be categorised under five main headings. These are shown in Table 4.2.

Each of these categories has distinct characteristics and therefore needs a specific marketing strategy aimed at it. The innovators, for example, will be looking for new 'trend-setting' products which no one else has, and which enable them to show that they are ahead of the crowd. This also has

Table 4.2 Adopter categories.

● Innovators	(2.5 per cent of the population)
● Early adopters	(13.5 per cent)
● Early majority	(34 per cent)
● Late majority	(34 per cent)
● Laggards	(16 per cent)

implications for the price they can be charged. However, they are only a very small section of the total consumers.

The early adopters are important because they are a bigger group. They are perhaps influenced in part by the innovators, or maybe, because they have had more time to weigh up the advantages and disadvantages of the product (they are a little more cautious or unwilling to pay a very high price), or take longer to learn about the product, they will buy a little after the innovators. The innovators and early adopters will roughly account for the introduction phase of the product's life cycle.

The importance of these two categories to sales is their impact on the early and late majorities (68 per cent in total) who will account for the growth and maturity phases of the product life cycle. These people need to be reassured that they are doing the right thing in buying the product – its wider adoption is confirmation of this. They may also be slower to learn of the new product or intimidated if it is too technical, e.g. use of Internet banking.

The laggards are the last to adopt and their purchase may well coincide with the decline phase of the product life cycle. They may, for example, need a low price to tempt them to buy because they have lower incomes, or because they do not obtain the same personal satisfaction or utility from owning the product compared with the innovators or early adopters.

These distinct categories of consumers or customers will have implications, therefore, not just for a business's pricing policies but also for its marketing strategy as a whole.

Marketing through the Internet: the growth of e-commerce

Synopsis

This case study explores the growth of e-commerce and the potential it offers for future development. It distinguishes that:

1   e-commerce is the marketing and retailing growth sector in the next decade;
2   many companies have yet to move seriously into this area;
3   future growth is dependent on household takeup of the Internet.

Case Study

Now's the moment. One month's free share dealing for new customers. Deal direct.

At DLJ*direct* we're offering **one month's free UK Internet share dealing for all new customers**. We're confident that once you've tried our service you'll find it second to none. You'll have access to our comprehensive market data and real-time pricing which will help

The above advertisement, for share dealing through the Internet, is typical of many which have appeared in the press in the last year or two. It demonstrates the major growth which has occurred in on-line sales, and the even greater potential for future development. Reflecting the growth of what are called electronic 'quasi-exchanges', these have forced traditional stock markets to re-evaluate how they perform. Most EU stock markets are currently demutualising and selling their own shares to the public; however, attempts to integrate are proving less successful.

In early 2000, just over half of the UK's companies had websites, and 9 per cent were selling via the Internet. In 1999, the value of goods sold via the Internet was approximately £5400 million. To sell means that households must have access to the Internet via PCs, mobile phones or the television and Internet link. Just over 37 per cent of households have a PC, 35 per cent have a mobile phone, and just over 26 per cent have access to the Internet, totalling 12.5 million; of these, 25 per cent shop on-line. Since the Internet permits much more flexible, cost-effective and wider 24 hour access, a major aim of UK businesses is to substantially increase the number of Internet shoppers.

The most popular websites accessed in the UK include: Yahoo.co.uk (Internet portal); Freeserve.co.uk (Internet Service Provider or ISP); MSN.com (Internet portal); Microsoft.com (software provider); America On line (ISP); Amazon.co.uk (Internet booksales); and BBC.co.uk (public sector broadcaster). It is interesting that the top ten most visited sites are mainly ISP or Internet portals. One might speculate that in five years one could see Wal-Mart or Marks and Spencer, or a company which does not yet exist, as a leading site. However, much success will depend on logistics, which means that national postal services and delivery companies will be crucial to the future development of Internet sales, a part of Porter's value chain discussed in Chapter 2, Section 2.2. It will involve changing traditional ordering and distribution chains to e-commerce chains with the aim of cost reductions.

As a result of the huge increase in e-commerce, 1999 and early 2000 saw major stock market demand for Internet, media and communication shares, often where the company had made no profits in spite of being valued at £1 billion or more. Major companies such as the retailer Dixons have reinvented themselves as Internet companies, floating ISPs like Dixon's Freeserve, for huge amounts.

Self testing questions

1   Are there any links between marketing and TQM? Explain your answer.

2   How many of the five 'P's of the marketing mix can you identify in the Marks and Spencer case study in Chapter 4, Section 4.1? What are they?

3   Why might Portland conservatories be classified as a mature product?

4   What pricing strategy should Portland conservatories employ? Explain your answer.

5   Can a business do anything to shift more of its customers into the innovators and early adopters categories when it develops new products?

The reader will appreciate that this chapter has only briefly explored some of the theoretical concepts of marketing, and especially where they overlap with business economics. The reader who is interested in exploring this further is encouraged to consult some of the references cited at the end of this chapter.

4.4 Developing a marketing strategy

Chapter 2, Section 2.2 briefly discussed a business's strategy, outlining its long term objectives. Section 4.1 analysed a marketing strategy as a part of the overall business strategy and the process whereby a business identifies the consumers whom it will target and to whom it will sell its goods, services and/or ideas, and the positioning of its products to gain competitive advantage over its rivals. To ensure that there is a strategic fit between the marketing strategy and its environment, the business needs to map its internal strengths and weaknesses against the external opportunities and threats facing it, i.e. undertake a SWOT analysis, as discussed in Chapter 2, Section 2.3.

Once this has been undertaken, a business then needs to define more precisely its overall objectives and, in the context discussed here, its marketing strategic objectives. It is quite possible to be overwhelmed by the variety of objectives which the company might seek to achieve so a number of theoretical frameworks have been developed to help company directors and senior managers narrow the choice. Two are reviewed here – Ansoff's product/market matrix and the Boston Consulting Group's (BCG) product portfolio matrix.

Ansoff's product/market matrix

Igor Ansoff uses the term 'strategic portfolio strategy' as one way to describe the firm's strategic development. He argues that each business is a combination of distinctive 'strategic business areas' (SBAs); these offer different future growth and profit opportunities and/or will need different competitive approaches. Ansoff's matrix, shown in Figure 4.2, provides a framework for a business to select appropriate strategies for each of these SBAs, based on a number of combinations of market (on the vertical axis) and product (on the horizontal axis). Additionally, each axis is partitioned into current or present products and potential or new products.

Therefore, the top left cell – No. 1 Market Penetration – relates to current products in current markets. If the market is continuing to grow then, assuming that increased sales and hence profits is the objective, this can be achieved so long as the products' sales grow in line with market growth. If, however, the market is static or contracting, then growth can only be achieved by a greater market share at the expense of competitors. The price cutting wars engaged in by supermarkets are an example of the strategy for this latter SBA.

The bottom left cell – No. 2 Market Development – relates to a business diversifying into new markets with existing products, e.g. selling English produced wines in other European Union (EU) countries.

The top right cell – No. 3 Product Development – is the strategy of selling new products in existing markets. An example of this would be the *Innovations* catalogues which come to households by mail or with newspapers, and offer new devices you have never needed.

The bottom right cell – No. 4 Diversification – involves a business developing new products and a presence in new markets. The development of ice creams based on such chocolate bars as Mars, Snickers and Twix would be an example of this. Although one might argue that ice cream, chocolate biscuits and chocolate type bars are all confectionery, clearly they are separate sub-markets appealing to quite different consumer wants.

The reader should be able to relate Ansoff's product/market matrix to the introduction phase of the product life cycle. Any of the cells market

Product / Market	Present	New
Present	1. Market penetration	3. Product development
New	2. Market development	4. Diversification

Figure 4.2 Ansoff's product/market matrix.

development (a business diversifying into new markets with existing products), or product development (selling new products in existing markets), or diversification (a business developing new products and a presence in new markets) is relevant to the development of new products and hence the introduction stage of the product life cycle. An appropriate pricing strategy – whether skimming the cream or penetration pricing – has already been discussed.

The Boston Consulting Group's (BCG) product portfolio matrix

The BCG product portfolio matrix is based on analysing a business's product portfolio and using this as a tool for planning its marketing strategy; it is shown in Figure 4.3. Two key factors are analysed – market growth (the vertical axis of the matrix) and relative market share (the horizontal axis of the matrix). The business has what are termed strategic business

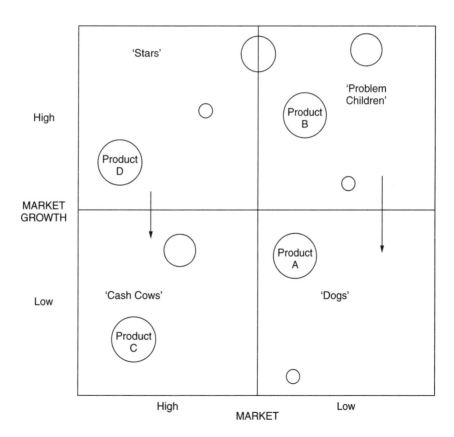

Figure 4.3 The Boston Consulting Group's (BCG) product portfolio matrix.

units (effectively, its products) which are positioned in one of four cells of the matrix. The circles represent sales revenue from products – the bigger the circle the larger the revenue. Their position in the matrix denotes which of the four categories below they belong to.

- **Stars.** The top left hand cell of the matrix shows products in markets which exhibit high market growth and have high market share – what are called the 'stars' of the portfolio of products which the business supplies. These products bring in large amounts of revenue for the business, but to maintain their star status large amounts of money need to be spent on them. Overall, therefore, the net inflow may be relatively small and there could even be a net outflow, i.e. the product consumes more income than it generates.
- **Cash cows.** The bottom left hand cell shows products which have a high market share but low market growth. As their name suggests, they generate large amounts of cash but do not need large expenditure to keep them in this position, which is very good for the business.
- **Problem children.** Situated in the top right hand cell, these are products in high growth markets but with low market share. To get a bigger market share will require the business to spend substantially more money which can soon worsen its cash flow position. As their name suggests, products in this category can cause a business real problems.
- **Dogs.** The bottom right hand cell of the BCG matrix shows products which have the worst of all worlds – they are in a low growth markets and have a low share of them. As such they do not generate a significant cash inflow and are unlikely to have income invested in them over and above what they generate.

Qualifications to the theory

Of course, classifying a product into a particular cell does not mean that it will stay there permanently. For example a problem child may, over time, turn into a dog; or, more hopefully, a star will develop into a cash cow. Additionally, a business is likely to have a range of products in its portfolio which will fit into all the categories, although the fewer dogs it has the better, and the longer they persist in this category, the more likely they are to be removed from the product portfolio. The other thing to remember is that this is not a static or unchanging picture; the situation will change over time and the more the business can favourably influence it the better. It will not want its problem children to turn into dogs but it will want its stars to develop into cash cows and hence help new stars to develop.

Returning to the start of this section, therefore, the business will need to define its marketing strategic objectives and develop a marketing strategy to ensure that it has an optimum product portfolio. In particular this will involve taking decisions about:

- Whether to modify existing products, e.g. marketing research shows that the product needs revision – such as the introduction of diet Pepsi as well as retaining original Pepsi;
- Removing products from the portfolio, e.g. older smokers will remember brands such as Players Weights, a budget cigarette which disappeared many years ago. This occurs when a product is at the end of its life cycle;
- Developing new products. This involves making difficult decisions about whether there is a demand for the proposed new product, whether it fits the existing product portfolio, whether the business has sufficient capacity to produce it with existing resources, the marketing mix which will be required to market it effectively, and what after sales service will have to be provided, among others.

There are also criticisms of the BCG matrix which need to be noted here. There are problems in defining what a strategic business unit actually is. Also implicit in the matrix is that the bigger the market share of a product the higher the business's profits; yet if its costs are high, for example through experiencing diseconomies of scale, this may not be so. Additionally, the BCG matrix is two dimensional, i.e. market growth and market share, whereas marketing strategy is influenced by many variables, for example as PESTLE and SWOT analyses demonstrate.

4.5 The decline of the fine fragrance industry

Case Study

Overview

The main perfume manufacturers of the world are major international companies such as Firmenich, Givaudan, International Flavour and Fragrance, Prestige (the fragrance part of the Unilever empire) and Quest International, a subsidiary of ICI. These businesses produce 'smells' (fragrances) for a wide range of products including cleaning products, air fresheners and deodorants. Perfumes are a small but high profit part of their product portfolio, whilst the biggest growth areas are soap, skincare products and shampoo. Since the manufacturing costs of a perfume account for only 10 per cent of the price of an average bottle of perfume, profit margins are clearly very high so the more they can sell the better; additionally, they can achieve economies of scale. The manufacturers liase with the perfume houses who commission their production capacity and supply the finished product in bulk in drums. It is then put into more familiar bottles on arrival at its destination.

The ideal for these companies is, therefore, a perfume which will be globally popular and which therefore requires volume production, such as

Chanel No. 5 or Miss Dior. However, the fragrance popular in one country will not necessarily be popular elsewhere in the world. Hence pine, which is the preferred aroma for cleaning products in the UK, is not popular in the Far East, where mango is preferred.

Since the late 1980s, strong perfumes (fragrances) have declined substantially in popularity in the UK, with sales of particular brands either static or falling. In 1998, for example, sales of female fragrances fell 19 per cent, whilst male fragrances, traditionally a strong growth market, fell by 5 per cent. In total the fragrance market contracted 14 per cent to £602 million. As a result many retailers have resulted to significant discounting to boost sales. In the US there is a similar picture with sales figures (and hence revenue) contracting in real terms, i.e. after allowing for inflation.

Falling demand

There are a number of main reasons for this declining demand, and hence profitability, one of which is changing tastes. In other words, strong perfumes and aftershave are now seen as socially unacceptable, invading other peoples' privacy by imposing a strong smell on them without their choice. The economic slowdown in 1998–1999 also dented consumer confidence. Changing work habits, such as wearing less formal clothes, especially in the fast growing US high tech industry where people wear khakis and sweaters, and the spreading US idea of a dressing down day on Friday, when people can come to work in casual clothes, have also mitigated against the use of strong perfumes. The most popular US perfumes are Tommy and Tommy Girl which promote casual girl next door images rather than sophistication, sexuality and expense. Another issue is what is termed gender politics; in other words the growth of sexual harassment in the work place. Strong perfumes are perceived as sexually provocative so people are less willing to wear them. Finally, strong perfumes are more closely associated with older rather than younger consumers, yet it is the latter which have more disposable income; perfumes are targeting a contracting market.

In the Far East, perfume sales were also hit by the Asian economic crisis of 1997–1998 which reduced consumer expenditure on what is perceived to be, in times of economic hardship, a luxury good rather than a necessity. All of these forces have combined together to drive down demand and hence exert downward pressure on prices.

Over supply

In the US, fragrance companies' profitability has been hit by their own actions with over 150 new perfume launches a year; yet launching a new product is expensive. Further, perfume manufacturer Givenchy has estimated that, to be successful, sales of £52 million are needed on each new product launched. One executive from a perfume company argued that, although the rate of launches of new perfumes is increasing, many are indistinguishable from each other. This causes brand confusion among customers instead of generating brand loyalty and the consumers switch from product to product, attracted mainly by the novelty of each new launch.

In the US, downward pressures on price have been caused by fierce competitive pressures among retailers. Traditional outlets, such as department stores, are losing customers to newer suppliers such as stores specialising in perfume, clothing stores which also sell perfume and the Internet. In France, over half of perfume sales now occur in hypermarkets rather than local perfumeries as in the past. What is also being seen across many developed countries' markets is retailers giving significant discounts to attract custom. In the UK, for example, the supermarket Asda offered 70 per cent discounts on designer perfumes such as Chloë, Givenchy and Opium. The use of parallel imports is also employed by retailers, i.e. when a brand is imported from another country and sold more cheaply, alongside the same product produced domestically or exported directly from the manufacturer, e.g. a French perfume produced and exported to Italy, is then re-exported to the UK and sold more cheaply than the same brand sent directly from the French manufacturer to the UK. Additionally, many retailers, seeing themselves in a buyer's market, are insisting on significant discounts up front as cash before they will display products.

Summary

The problem facing perfume manufacturers is then a declining, and to some extent ageing, market. Social and economic conditions have caused young consumers, who have the most purchasing power, to move away from traditional heavier perfumes. Although the production costs of new perfumes are not high, the launch costs are. The combination of falling revenues and high costs have caused profits to fall significantly. Further, major discounting by retailers has reduced prices even more.

Self test questions

1 Using SWOT, undertake an analysis of the internal and external environments of perfume suppliers.

2 Using Ansoff's product/market matrix, into which of the four cells (product/market combinations) do the following fit: (a) the sale of Sony Walkman over time; (b) the sale of widescreen televisions; (c) the past development of its product Harp lager by Guinness; (d) the sale of video-recorders; (e) perfumes?

3 Using the BCG product portfolio matrix, under which category would you place perfumes? Explain your answer.

4 Discuss where in their product life cycle you think perfumes are at.

5 Write a one paragraph statement identifying, simply, the marketing strategy objectives which perfume suppliers (fashion houses) should adopt to restore their profit position within five years.

4.6 Summary of chapter

This chapter began with a case study of Marks and Spencer, which has experienced falling profits. It then explored the characteristics of the marketing of products. Marketing strategy was then briefly analysed including a brief overview of the marketing mix. From there, segmentation, targeting and positioning were examined. The undifferentiated market approach and market segmentation were examined in more depth followed by targeting strategies and positioning.

The marketing mix was then discussed in more detail, including the 4 'P's and the 7 'P's as a way to implement a marketing programme. The product life cycle was then examined, followed by pricing theories and non-price influences, including adopter categories.

Developing a marketing strategy was then examined in more detail, examining in particular, Ansoff's product/market matrix and the BCG product portfolio matrix as tools to develop a marketing strategy.

The chapter finished with a final case study examining the decline of the perfume industry and its implications for profit.

4.7 Further questions

1 Where in the product life cycle are the following: (a) cigarettes; (b) pipes (for smoking); (c) alcopops; (d) the Internet?

2 How could a business influence the demand for a product so that it moves from the innovator to the early adopter stage?

3 'It is a waste of time to concentrate any resources on laggards.' Discuss.

4 Will 'cost plus' pricing always be the best policy to ensure that a business makes normal profits? Explain.

5 Why do religious evangelists call at houses rather than place advertisements in the local newspaper?

4.8 Further reading

Ansoff, I. (1988). *Corporate Strategy*. Revised edition. London: Penguin Books.

Brassington, F. and Pettit, S. *Principles of Marketing*, 2nd edition. 2000. London: Prentice Hall.

Dibb, S. and Simkin, L. (1994). *The Marketing Casebook. Cases and Concepts*. London: Routledge.

Fifield, P. (1992). *Marketing Strategy*. Oxford: Butterworth-Heinemann Ltd.

Kotler, P., Armstrong, G., Saunders, J. and Wong, V. (1999). *Principles of Marketing*, 2nd European Edition. London: Prentice Hall.

Lancaster, G. and Massingham, L. (1988). *Essentials of Marketing*. Maidenhead: McGraw-Hill Book Company (UK) Ltd.

Lavigne, M. (1999). *The Economics of Transition. From Socialist Economy to Market Economy*. 2nd edition. Basingstoke: Macmillan Business.

Marketing Pocketbook (2000). Henley-on-Thames: NTC Publications Ltd.

Rogers, E. M. (1962). *Diffusion of Innovation*. New York: The Free Press, p.162.

The Economist

The *Financial Times*

The Times

Amazon booksellers: http://www.Amazon.co.uk

America on Line: http://uk.dir.yahoo.com/Business_and_Economy/ Companies/Internet_Services/Portals/America_Online__AOL_/

The BBC: http://www.bbc.co.uk/

Freeserve: http://Freeserve.co.uk

Microsoft: http://www.Microsoft.com

MSN.com: http://msn.co.uk/homepage.asp

Donaldson, Lufkin and Jennette: on-line share dealing: http:/www.DLJ*direct*.co.uk

Yahoo.co.uk

Chapter 5

Market forces

Learning Outcomes

After completing this chapter the reader will be able to:
- understand the nature and functions of markets;
- explore the problems of non-market economies and their implications for businesses;
- analyse the market forces of demand and supply and the determination of prices.

5.1 How markets function; consumer sovereignty. The collapse of non-market economies in Central and Eastern Europe

What is a market?

Synopsis   This case study explores examples of real world markets and identifies key characteristics which are:

1   they bring together buyers and sellers;
2   they may not have a physical location;
3   they can be formal or informal markets.

Case Study

- **COFFEE MORNING**. 53rd Scouts. Rear Turnbull Avenue, Bosham. **Wednesday May 5 at 10.00 a.m.**
  Jumble and cakes on sale.
  No parking in access road to HQ.

- **The Exclusive Agency** (established 25 years). Personal confidential service for professional and business people. Meet similar people to yourself for friendship/romance. Free home visit. (01703). . . .

- **Unbeatable Pentium III Offer, at Cybertech this weekend.**
  Free 17 inch monitor upgrade worth over £80 inc. VAT.
  Power Online System 450. Intel Pentium III Processor 450 MHz
  Plus: USB colour scanner worth £82.24 inc. VAT.
  Canon Colour printer worth £93.99 inc. VAT.
  Over £150 of software including Microsoft Windows 98, Windows 98 interactive tutorial.
  £899 ex VAT; £1056.33 inc. VAT.
  0% finance – nothing to pay for 12 months, not even a deposit.

- **Manage an MS in Labor Studies and Human Resources and still manage your life.**
  Baruch's Executive MS in Industrial and Labor Relations.
  You want to move up. You want to move on. You want to take a look at the Executive MSILR (Master of Science degree in Industrial and Labor Relations) Program at Baruch. It's a fast track 3-year program with everything you need: job related curriculum, manageable schedule, high caliber professors. We even include your books and your meals. Contact us today for more information: Phone 212 802 5922. Fax: 212 802 5903 or E-mail: spa_admission@baruch.cuny.edu.
  Baruch College. The City University of New York.

- Tesco was the share most heavily traded on the stock market yesterday; over 60 million shares were sold as the price firmed 1½p to 192p, the demand coming from both private and institutional investors. This has reinforced rumours that the food retailing industry will soon undergo further consolidation with many believing a merger is possible between market share leader Tesco and troubled general retailer Marks & Spencer. In spite of the new Competition Commissioner investigating the food retailing sector as a result of allegations of excessive profits compared with Continental European food retailers, many investors clearly believe that there are further profits to be made. There is also a rumour that Kingfisher will buy CRS (Cooperative Retail Society) out of town sites and turn these into Woolworth superstores.

London share prices generally benefited from another record performance by the Wall Street stock market over night, with the Dow Jones Industrial Index rising over 100 points in early trading yesterday; the day's performance was also helped by better than expected figures from IBM minutes before business closed for the day, helping the market to reach new heights. At one time the FTSE 100 index reached 6457.1 before falling back and ending the day 102.6 up at 6413.6. The FTSE 250 index closed the day 28.9 up at 5792.3.

- **THINK SPRING**
  Sandy Point, Long Island. Designed for beauty and easy care, this home was built with the finest materials by an architect for himself. Large rooms, vault ceilings, marble halls, 4 bedrooms, 3 bathrooms. 2 acres with priceless plants. Quiet lane, easy commute, peaceful haven for creative spirit. $725k.

- **Online auctions**
  For the first time ever. Online auctions of important works by blue-chip contemporary and modern artists. Miró. Fontana. Leger. Matisse. Man Ray. Cornell. Warhol. Lichtenstein. Johns. Rauschberg. Nauman, Chamberlain. Picasso.

  Only 5 per cent commission. Buy and sell anytime. Know more before you buy. The news. The trends. The prices.

  artnet.com
  Get the whole picture.

The reader may wonder what the above examples, taken from British newspapers and the *New York Times*, have in common. The answer is that they are all examples of markets; in other words they bring together people and businesses who have goods and/or services to sell and those who wish to buy such goods and/or services.

In some situations, markets may operate through barter, where some goods or services are exchanged for others without money entering the transaction, e.g. the author remembers teaching a student in the 1980s who worked for a UK business making electric blankets. It sold 5000 to communist Poland but the Poles had no hard currencies such as sterling or dollars to pay for them, the Polish zloty not then being freely convertible. To secure payment, the firm accepted jars of Polish plum jam which they then sold to a UK supermarket chain to obtain their money. Normally, however, payment involves money in some form.

The reader will note from the case study that the market may be very localised and in a specific place; people will need to visit a specific location to see what jumble is for sale or what a house looks like. They may, however, never visit a specific place. If Lord Andrew Lloyd Weber sold some of his paintings through artnet.com he would be able to contact them by e-mail, phone or fax and, subject to a suitably negotiated price, sell a Picasso, for example, without ever visiting New York. Again a person living in Melbourne, Australia would buy Tesco shares, for example, through his/her broker without ever visiting the London stock market. So a market does not have to have a physical location where all buyers and sellers meet. The development of electronic commerce clearly demonstrates this.

The other point, which links to Chapter 4, is that there may not be one price. It may be open to negotiation, as in many third world countries where haggling is the norm. When selling a Warhol painting, there would inevitably be negotiation between the vendor and the auction house as to its current price, which would be determined, in part, by the reserve price, the minimum acceptable to the vendor. There would be further bidding by interested parties wanting to own the picture who would each have their own perception of its value; the highest bidder would get it. However, trying to knock down the price of the new computer would probably be much harder since the business would be seeking to skim the cream from the latest top of the range model.

Consumer sovereignty

Chapter 1 discussed how the function of an economy is to allocate scarce resources as efficiently as possible to meet society's demands for goods and services, both now and in the future. The demands for goods and services come from both households and businesses, whilst the latter also supply goods and services. How does the economic system know what to produce? – by whether it makes a profit or not.

To summarise, a rise in consumer demand for a product will cause a price rise. This will increase the profits of the business supplying the product and other businesses, seeing this, will also move into this industry and start supplying the product until all consumer demand is met; then profits fall back to normal levels. This is known as consumer sovereignty, i.e. all economic activities are focused on meeting the needs of the consumer. In some economies however, the situation of producer sovereignty has occurred, where the needs of the producer are foremost and consumers accept what is available. This was most clearly demonstrated in the former Soviet Union and Central and Eastern Europe in the period up to 1990, when communism dominated.

Central planning: the failure of non-market economies in Central and Eastern Europe

In the early 1960s, the then Chairman of the Communist Party of the Soviet Union, Nikita Kruschev, was so confident of the success of communism and central planning that he famously told the American people 'your grand-children will all be communists.' Yet, in 1990, communism collapsed as an economic and political philosophy in Central and Eastern Europe, and in the Soviet Union. These countries had used central planning rather than markets as the basis for answering the key economic questions facing a society: what to produce; how to produce it; and for whom (i.e. to whom is it distributed).

Central planning had a number of key features:

- All resources or inputs were owned or controlled by the state. In Russia, all land was state owned, even that on which houses were built. In the 1980s in Russia, for example, new graduates were directed by the state as to where to work; newly qualified Soviet teachers were obliged to work in Siberia, not the most hospitable of environments, to teach the children of oil workers based there. They had no choice, which is a key feature of market economies. In Poland and Hungary there was a flour-ishing private sector in which businesses operated but it was still small compared with Western European countries.
- Production was to five year plans with production targets set for each industry and factory. Decisions were made by bureaucrats based in Soviet ministries using forecasts of anticipated demand. Once a factory was committed to a five year plan it proved difficult for it to be respon-sive to changing fashions and consumer demand.
- Soviet production was very much focused on heavy industry, e.g. steel manufacture, coal mining, shipbuilding, armaments, partly through fear that it would one day be at war with the West and so needed to be prepared. Consequently consumer goods took second place, something accepted with resignation by most citizens. This meant regular long queues for basic amenities such as foodstuffs and household goods, whilst consumer durables such as cars were even harder to obtain and very expensive, except for high ranking members of the Communist Party.
- The prices of basic amenities such as bread were fixed at very low levels whilst other prices were controlled, such as rent for apartments. Although this benefited those on low incomes such prices did not reflect the economic (opportunity) cost of the resources used. For example, in Estonia, part of the Soviet Union in the 1980s, a flat rate was charged for the use of gas to heat homes. Consumers could therefore leave the gas fired heating on for twenty-four hours per day, seven days per week, yet only pay the flat rate. Supplies were erratic through old equipment

and over consumption, yet the state owned suppliers were not charging consumers enough to cover the costs of supplying the gas, let alone making a surplus to renew equipment. They were eventually helped to undertake new investment by funding from the European Bank for Reconstruction and Development in the early 1990s.

- State industries (which is what businesses were in the Communist bloc) were not required to make a profit in the Western sense of the word, since there were no shareholders, only the state. Hence no market mechanism existed to direct resources, only the bureaucrats. This caused a lack of incentive which is very important for businesses, since without incentives a minimalist philosophy exists. Therefore if a factory met its annual production target by September there was no real incentive to continue working hard for the remainder of the year. This also applied to state owned collectives, i.e. giant farms which regularly failed to meet production targets since equipment was unreliable or lacking and farmers had little incentive to work hard as all foodstuffs were sent to the towns. Serious drunkenness among the workforce also hindered production.

- Economic data were unreliable and the European Union had to send statisticians to these countries in the 1990s to update their data collection services. In many cases factories had over-estimated their production so that their equivalent of Gross Domestic Product figures (the value of goods and services produced in the country during a year) were far higher than reality.

- Foreign trade was carefully controlled and could only take place via government ministries. Therefore a British firm, wishing to sell machine tools to a Ukrainian factory, for example, would need permission from the relevant ministry; a lengthy and bureaucratic process. This was to save scarce foreign currencies (since the rouble was non-convertible). When Elton John performed a series of concerts in the Soviet Union in the 1980s he was paid in roubles. Since these were non-convertible they were left in a Soviet bank account. There was not a great deal to spend the money on in Russia!

- The tight controls on foreign trade meant that the improving standards of other countries were not transmitted to the Soviet bloc countries. As noted in Chapter 2, Section 2.4, in the 1970s the US and European car industries found themselves facing severe competition from better quality Japanese cars. They had to adapt to survive and most did. This did not happen in Eastern Europe. In 1989 East Germany was still producing the Trabant, based on a 1960 Fiat, and there was a waiting list of eight years for these, since foreign cars were largely banned!

Clearly the above is a brief summary of the complex range of problems facing the former Soviet Union and the countries under its economic, political and military control when central planning was used as a substitute for market forces. Some people were better off economically under the Soviet regime, compared with the present regime in Russia. State owned industries lacked operating flexibility and the freedom to formulate strategy which Western businesses had. There have been many problems in recent years which this book does not have time to explore – inflation, the loss of savings through inflation and banking collapses, food shortages, rampant crime and so on. However, these have arisen partly from the ineptitude of Russian governments and Presidents rather than from the inadequacies of market economies (of which there are certainly some, which will be discussed in Chapter 6, Section 6.3). In other countries, such as the Czech Republic, Hungary and Poland, the reform process to market economies has been much more successful, to the extent that these states are hoping to join the EU in approximately 2002.

The best examples of central planning still in force today are Cuba and North Korea.

5.2 Market demand

Definition

The demand for a product may be defined as the amount of it which consumers buy at a given price and at a given moment in time, other things being equal.

When a product is sold there is a price attached – £1056.33 for the computer in the case study above; $725 000 for the house on Long Island. Without a price it is not possible to determine demand. Demand also relates to a moment in time; at a different time demand for a similar product may be quite different. Before Christmas, cards will sell at a certain price, say £2.50 for ten. After 25 December, identical cards will be on sale for much less – say 50p for ten – because the peak demand time has passed. If, however, those cards had been for sale before Christmas for 50p then people would have, in total, demanded more. Therefore, at the same time, different prices will mean different amounts demanded of the same good and, the lower the price, the more that will be purchased. The reader will recall from Chapter 1, Section 1.3 that demand has to be backed by an ability to pay, otherwise it is just a want.

What of the phrase 'other things remaining equal' or 'other things being equal.' This means that we focus just on the relationship between the price of a product and the amount of it demanded at that price; we ignore other factors or variables which can influence demand. These other factors include:

- consumer income, or more accurately household income, since a partner may also work;
- prices of other products;
- tastes and fashions;
- expectations, for example about future prices;

Table 5.1 A demand schedule for audio cassettes of novels.

Price of cassettes £	Quantity demanded
5	20 000
4.5	40 000
4	60 000
3.5	80 000
3	100 000
2.5	120 000
2	140 000
1.5	160 000

• how income is distributed among the population; is it evenly distributed or skewed towards a minority?

We return to these later; at present we concentrate on the price–quantity demanded relationship.

The demand schedule

A demand schedule records the relationship between the price of a product and the quantity of it demanded, other things being equal. A hypothetical schedule is reproduced below for audio cassettes of famous novels read by top actors.

As the reader will observe, there is an inverse relationship between the price of the audio cassettes and the amount of them demanded – the higher the price, the fewer demanded; the lower the price the more demanded.

This table is also produced as a graph in Figure 5.1. It slopes downwards from top left to bottom right, the standard characteristic of a demand curve, although there are exceptions discussed briefly below. The reader will note that the demand curve is a straight line (not very helpfully called a linear curve). In practice the demand curve is actually a concave curve; in other words it curves towards the origin. However, for convenience it will be assumed here that demand curves are straight lines. The reader may recall from Chapter 3 that the demand curve is also a business's average revenue curve.

On the vertical axis is plotted the price of the cassettes, on the horizontal axis is the amount demanded at each price. The demand curve

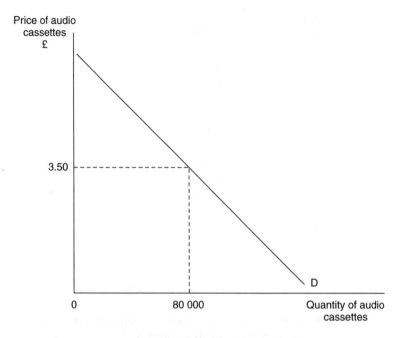

Figure 5.1 A demand curve for audio cassettes of novels.

therefore connects each price to the quantity of it demanded, at a moment in time. For example, if the price of cassettes is £3, then 100 000 will be demanded.

We can therefore say that any change in price will result in a movement along the demand curve. If price rises from £3 to £4, the quantity of cassettes demanded falls from 100 000 to 60 000. This is known as a contraction in demand. If the price changes from £3 to £2.50 we experience an increase in the quantity of cassettes demanded, known as an extension of demand.

Other things remaining equal

So far we have assumed that other factors which can influence consumer demand, such as consumer incomes, tastes etc., do not change. Let us now relax that assumption.

Household income

If household income rises, and families like literature, they may buy more audio cassettes, perhaps to listen to in the car. At any given price, therefore, more will be demanded – this may be shown by, for example, adding say 10 000 to each amount in the quantity column of Table 5.1. It is shown

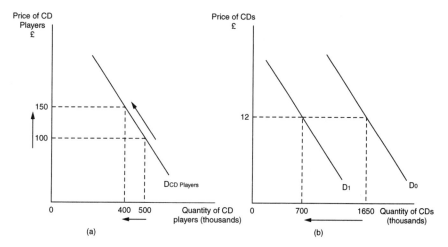

Figure 5.2 Demand curves for complementary goods.

graphically by the demand curve shifting to the right by 10 000 at each price – so we would see a new demand curve, parallel to the first curve; the reader should draw this on Figure 5.1. Conversely, if household incomes fell, say due to a downturn in the business cycle so that people became unemployed, fewer cassettes would be bought and the demand curve would shift parallel to the left, by the amount of the fall in demand at each price; again the reader should draw this on Figure 5.1.

The price of other goods and services

These will affect demand for audio cassettes since they all compete for limited household incomes. For example, if the price of petrol were to rise by 400 per cent, as in 1973, this would reduce the demand for many other products. Essentials such as food and transport would take priority over non-essentials such as audio cassettes, causing demand for the latter to fall. The demand curve for cassettes would, in these circumstances, shift to the left, since households' real income has fallen, after allowing for price increases, and specifically petrol.

Let us now distinguish two sub-categories of goods.

Complementary goods

These are goods where the use of one implies the use of the other, e.g. cars and petrol; CD players and CDs; fish and chips. If the price of CD players rises drastically this causes a fall or contraction in demand for CD players in Figure 5.2(a); in turn there will be a decrease in demand for CDs, shown by the demand curve for CDs shifting to the left in 5.2(b).

Substitutes

These are goods where one may be used in place of the other. Tea and coffee will be substitutes for some people; real milk and powdered milk will also be substitutes for some but not for others. For others, watching soccer on television will be a perfect substitute for watching a live game. In these cases a change in the price of one will also cause a change in demand for the other.

For example, if coffee rises in price as a result of bad harvests in South America and Kenya, this will cause a fall or contraction in demand for coffee. This can be shown exactly in Figure 5.2(a) if the axes labels are changed to reflect coffee rather than CDs. As a result, we will see an increase in the demand for tea as consumers substitute it for coffee. If we use Figure 5.2(b) to show the demand for tea, the demand curve for the substitute good, tea, will shift from D_1 to D_0.

For the other influences, these feature as questions in the section below for you to use your powers of economic reasoning.

In summary we can say that any change in a variable other than price will cause a shift of the demand curve.

The exception to the rule: demand curves which slope upwards to the right

All of the above relate to what economists call normal goods. Very exceptionally a demand curve may slope upwards to the right, looking like the supply curve in Figure 5.3. This suggests that as the price of a good increases people will buy more of it; or conversely they buy less as the price of it falls. This seems illogical since we have assumed people act rationally. However, if the good is wanted because consumers derive satisfaction from its expense, and hence exclusiveness, then a fall in price would make it less attractive and demand could fall. If a Rolls-Royce were as cheap as a Mini then many people might choose another car since the 'Roller' would have lost its exclusiveness.

Another example often quoted is potatoes during the Irish famine of the 1840s. These were the staple diet of many. As the price of potatoes rose people found that their real incomes, after deducting the effects of inflation, which included the rise in the price of potatoes, fell. Although a rise in the price of potatoes would normally make people switch to other cheaper foods (known as the substitution effect) this was more than offset by the fall in their real incomes (known as the income effect). Consequently, people ended up buying more potatoes, not less. Potatoes in these circumstances were known as Giffen goods, named after the Irish economist who discovered this phenomenon. This scenario is very exceptional and potatoes should be viewed as normal goods. The example is included to show the reader that just because economists formulate neat theories it doesn't always mean that everything in real life can be neatly explained.

Self testing questions

1 Use newspapers, your knowledge of your local area where you live or any other information source to give three examples of a market. Explain how each market works.

2 Use the resources of your library to find a case study of life in Russia or other Central and Eastern European countries over the last decade, which demonstrates the problems of making the transition from a centrally planned to a market economy. In no more than 100 words summarise the key problems encountered and explain them in the light of the business economics you have studied so far.

3 Explain in your own words the different causes of: (a) a movement along a demand curve; and (b) a shift of a demand curve. (c) Draw an appropriate diagram to illustrate the change in demand for Tesco shares in the case study in Section 5.1.

4 Draw a demand curve for flared trousers in the 1970s when they were very popular (label the curve D1970). Now, on the same diagram, draw a demand curve for flared trousers in the 1980s, when they were much less popular (label it D1980). Explain your answer.

5 Draw a demand curve for houses. If there is an expectation that house prices will rise by 10 per cent during the next year how will this affect the demand curve now, other things remaining equal?

6 On the same graph draw a demand curve for automobiles if: (a) income is evenly distributed among the population – label it Da; (b) income distribution is skewed so that 10 per cent of the population earn 90 per cent of the nation's income – label it Db. Explain your answer.

5.3 Market supply

If demand for products is one side of market forces then the other side is the supply of products.

Definition

The supply of a product may be defined as the amount of it which producers are willing to put onto the market at alternative prices, other things remaining equal.

As with demand we are concerned with alternative prices at the same moment in time. Since businesses incur higher costs the more they produce, it is safe to assume that at least in the short run higher prices will be needed to tempt businesses to produce more. In the long term this may not hold

Table 5.2 A supply schedule for audio cassettes of novels.

Price of cassettes £	Quantity of cassettes supplied
5	160 000
4.5	140 000
4	120 000
3.5	100 000
3	80 000
2.5	60 000
2	40 000
1.5	20 000

if a business can secure economies of scale from very large scale production.

If for the moment we stick with the audio cassettes of novels, a business producing these is willing to supply onto the market particular amounts at particular prices. A table of such data is provided above.

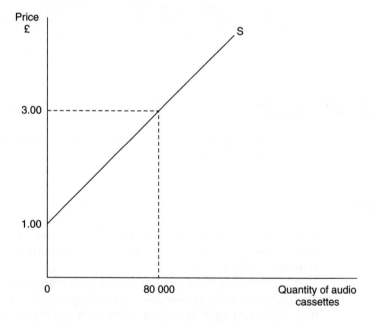

Figure 5.3 A supply curve for audio cassettes of novels.

This shows a positive relationship between price and quantity supplied, i.e. the higher the price of cassettes the more that the manufacturer will supply, other things being equal. We assume here that the situation is, again, at a moment in time.

Table 5.2 may also be represented as a linear supply curve, as in Figure 5.4. Price is shown on the vertical axis and quantity supplied on the horizontal axis. Therefore, for example, if the price of CDs is £3, then 80 000 will be supplied by businesses.

As with the demand curve so also with the supply curve, a change in price will lead to a movement along the curve. If there is an increase in the quantity supplied this is known as an extension of supply; a decrease in the quantity supplied is known as a contraction of supply. The supply curve starts at a price of £1 because if the price were less the business would make a loss; it will therefore supply nothing if the price is £1 or less. We can therefore say that any change in price will result in a movement along the supply curve.

We did assume, above, that this relationship only applies when other things remain equal, i.e. unchanged. These 'other things' on the supply side are:

1   the price of inputs;
2   the price of other products;
3   technology.

If any of the above variables change they will force businesses to re-evaluate their supply schedules.

The price of inputs

Let us assume that a trade union negotiates a wage increase for its members. This raise the business's labour costs and, hence, the cost of producing each cassette. It will therefore have to raise prices to cover the increased costs. Figure 5.4 shows that before the wage increase the business was producing 80 000 audio cassettes at a price of £3. The wage increase has the effect of shifting the supply curve vertically upwards to S1. Now the firm will only supply 80 000 if it can secure a price of £4.25, to enable it to cover the extra labour costs.

To be consistent with shifts in demand curve one could argue that the supply curve has shifted to the left rather than upwards. In that case one could say that if the business keeps the price of the product at £3 it will now only supply 36 000, as determined by supply curve S1. In both cases the end result is the same. Note that, on this diagram, there is no information about demand for these products.

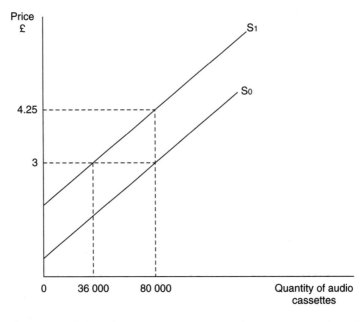

Figure 5.4 Effect of a change in the price of inputs on a business's supply curve.

The price of other goods

If the price of other goods increases then the business producing cassettes may be tempted to switch some resources to this other activity, switching from video cassettes to DVD compact discs. In this case the supply curve will shift upwards and to the left, as in Figure 5.4.

New technology

If new more cost-effective technology is introduced into production then it should lower costs and the supply curve will shift downwards and to the right. If we use Figure 5.4 the curve will shift from S1 to S0.

In reality, however, new technology is expensive to acquire; there are training costs for staff and there may be a long lead-in time before the benefits are felt. Consequently, the supply curve may not move at first. The next case study is a good illustration of this.

Government taxation and subsidies

If the government increases the tax on goods, e.g. excise duties on alcohol, the supply curve will shift upwards and to the left; if a subsidy is granted

Table 5.3 Demand and supply schedules for audio cassettes of novels.

Price of cassette £	Quantity of cassettes demanded	Quantity of cassettes supplied
5	20 000	160 000
4.5	40 000	140 000
4	60 000	120 000
3.5	80 000	100 000
3	100 000	80 000
2.5	120 000	60 000
2	140 000	40 000
1.5	160 000	20 000

this will shift the supply curve downwards and to the right. Figure 8.1 (page 256) illustrates the effects of the latter with further discussion.

In summary we can say that any change in a variable other than price will cause a shift of the supply curve.

5.4 Determining market prices

Having examined demand and supply separately we can now put them together to see how market prices are determined. Let us combine Tables 5.1 and 5.2 and Figures 5.1 and 5.3. These are reproduced as Table 5.3 and Figure 5.5, respectively.

In Table 5.3, at a price of £5, few cassettes are demanded (20 000) but producers are willing to supply a lot (160 000) – as it is very profitable to do so. This is known as a situation of excess supply; supply exceeds demand – by 140 000 CDs. In this situation shops would find cassettes piling up on the shelves since very few would be sold; they would reduce their orders from wholesalers who, finding warehouses filing up with unsold cassettes, in turn would reduce orders from manufacturers. To clear excess stocks, producers will cut prices or, in time, they will become bankrupt as their cash flow reduces. Hence, in situations of excess supply, there is a tendency for prices to fall until demand and supply equalise.

At the other end of the price scale, at £1.50 per cassette, many are demanded (160 000) since they are so cheap; however, only a limited number (20 000) will be supplied by businesses since the price is so low. Here is a situation of excess demand, where demand exceeds supply by 140 000 cassettes. Now shops will order more cassettes from wholesalers who, in

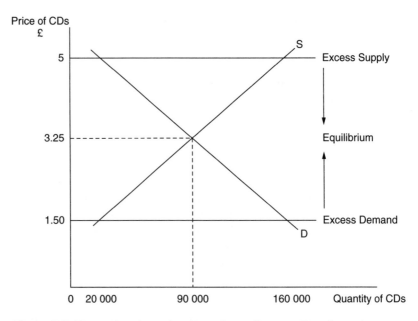

Figure 5.5 Demand and supply curves for audio cassettes of novels.

turn, will pass on increased orders to manufacturers. Because of this excess demand some customers will be willing to pay more to secure the cassettes they want (compare this with the case study at the beginning of Section 5.1, relating to Tesco shares). Prices will rise and this will encourage producers, inspired by higher profits, to produce more. This situation will continue until demand and supply are equal.

If we look, therefore, at the price of £3.25 in Figure 5.5 we shall see that the quantity demanded and the quantity supplied are exactly equal at 90 000 audio-cassettes. At this point the market is in equilibrium, i.e. the situation is stable with no tendency for the market to move in the short term, other things remaining equal. In the longer term, variables such as technology, the price of other goods, household incomes, etc. will change and hence move a market from its equilibrium position. In the real world, therefore, markets are constantly being knocked from their equilibrium positions and seeking to return to this situation.

Some students find demand and supply curves intimidating; the curves merely help to visualise what is actually happening. If you find diagrams difficult to use, try to explain aloud to yourself what is happening when variables change, causing movements along, or shifts of, the demand and supply curves. Some case studies are given below as illustration.

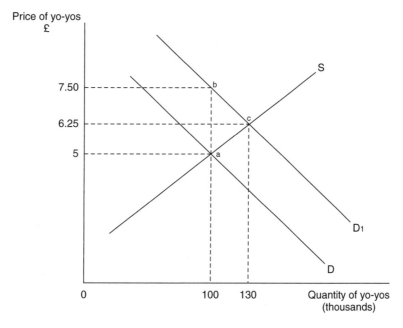

Figure 5.6 The market for yo-yos.

The return of the yo-yo

In 1998, after years of obscurity, the yo-yo returned to popularity as a fun leisure activity, in a new improved form. This caused a big upsurge in demand for them, such that producers were unable, at first, to meet this increased demand. Some shopkeepers, seeking to take advantage of this situation, raised the prices at which they sold yo-yos. As producers expanded their production and yo-yos were imported from elsewhere, the price fell back again. Figure 5.6 illustrates this.

Initially the market is in equilibrium, with the price of yo-yos at £5, and the quantity demanded and supplied are equal to 100 000. Point 'a' marks where the demand and supply curves intersect. Young children who for years had ignored yo-yos, suddenly decide that they must have one. As a result, the demand curve for yo-yos shifts to the right, reflecting this change in consumer tastes. In the very short term, when nothing can be changed, not even overtime for labour, businesses cannot increase output and so the only way to restrict excess demand is to allow prices to rise. Shopkeepers are not just profiteering here; they are also helping the market to function properly. With the quantity on the market still at 100 000 the price of yo-yos rises to £7.50, determined by where the vertical line from 100 000 hits the new demand curve D1 at point 'b'.

Existing suppliers will be encouraged by this high price to supply more onto the market, whilst businesses not producing yo-yos will seek to move into this product. As a result, in the short term, as opposed to the very short term, supply increases (a movement along the supply curve) from 'a' to 'c', since no factors other than price have changed. Labour is now working overtime, more raw materials are bought in etc. Therefore market supply increases from 100 000 to 130 000 to meet the high demand. As supply increases price starts to fall until market equilibrium is restored at 'c', with a price of £6.25, where D1 = S.

If we were to look ahead to the long term, when all factors of production could be varied, e.g. new factories built, new production technology introduced, new entrepreneurs employed etc., we might expect to see the supply curve shift downwards and to the right as the business achieved economies of scale. By then, probably, the yo-yo craze would have ended and something new would have appeared.

Hopefully, the reader can see from this that the graph actually summarises a lot of important detail, which has been unpacked here. Additionally, it enables the business economist to predict exactly what will happen when a change in consumer tastes and preferences occurs.

Case Study

Price ceilings and how the black market bypasses price controls

In the former Soviet Union and Central and Eastern Europe before 1990, prices were often capped at a certain level to ensure that a 'fair' price was charged to all, regardless of income. In Section 5.1 above, examples of this were provided, relating to heating, rent and bread. This is illustrated in Figure 5.7. It is known as a price ceiling and, as its name suggests, it imposes a ceiling or maximum level to which a price may rise. It also applied to goods in the UK during the Second World War. This case study shows how, in spite of attempts to bypass the free market, market forces will always manifest themselves unless the most draconian measures are used.

As can be seen from Figure 5.7, the market equilibrium, if the market were allowed to reach it, is at the price of Pe and quantity Qe. If the government limits the price to the controlled or ceiling price of Pc, then businesses will only supply Qs, whereas consumers will demand Qd – in other words, there is excess demand of Qs–Qd. What is most likely to happen is the emergence of a black market where people are willing to pay more than the control price to secure some of the scarce supply

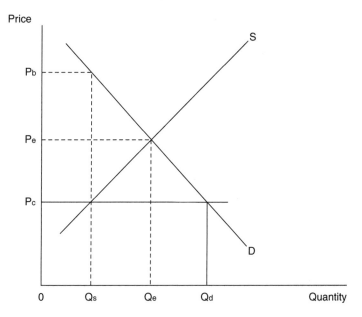

Figure 5.7 Price controls and the black market.

of the good. If the owners of Qs are willing to sell all of it on the black market to the highest bidders then the price will rise to the black market price of Pb, as determined by the demand curve. If only half of the supply were sold on the black market, and the other half were retained for personal consumption, then the black market price would rise even higher. (Mark the midpoint between the origin and Qs on the horizontal axis of Figure 5.7 and draw a line vertically upwards until it hits the demand curve – this will be the new black market price.)

Why will people pay such a high price for a product? Because they obtain satisfaction, or utility, from consuming it. Other examples of black market products include alcohol in prohibition America in the 1920s (one of the major income sources of notorious Chicago gangster Al Capone); many items in Britain during World War II, but especially women's stockings (tights had not been invented then); and narcotics in most modern societies, although black market prices have fallen in recent years as supplies have increased. Therefore, black markets may also arise from a product being banned. Once prohibition ended in the US in the 1930s, alcohol prices fell and speak-easys (illegal drinking dens) disappeared.

How can a government stop a black market developing? The most obvious answer is to remove price controls and allow the market to determine the price – as the reader can see from Figure 5.7, although the market price (Pe) is higher than the controlled price (Pc) it is actually much lower than the black market price (Pb). An alternative option, which ensures that everyone gets a fair share of the good is to introduce rationing via coupons. In the UK during 1939–1945 not only were the prices of goods controlled but additionally households were given coupons – say for one pound of butter per month, four loaves of bread per week etc. Once a household had used its coupons for the month, even if it was only half way through the month, it had to wait until the next month before it could use its next set of coupons. This, of course, encouraged 'horse trading' – I don't like chocolate but I like cheese; you have the reverse tastes – therefore we swap coupons. Of course the swap of coupons might not be on a one to one basis, therefore even here a black market price was starting to emerge – one cheese coupon might be worth two chocolate coupons, for example (like the exchange rate between foreign currencies). Rationing in wartime Britain also put shopkeepers in an extremely strong position since they would be able to give extra to favourite customers – therefore price controls are always open to abuse.

There is a third option to enforce price controls and this is to punish black marketers. In prohibition America, prison sentences were doled out. In the former Soviet Union, dealing in the rouble was illegal since the government operated very strict exchange controls; as well as needing state permission to buy and sell currencies the rate of exchange was fixed by law, at £1 = 1 Rouble in the mid 1980s. Tourists could get a better rate from black marketers, e.g. 5 Roubles to £1, but this was a risky transaction to undertake through fear of the secret police. On a grand scale, speculation, as it was called, was a capital offence; the author remembers, in the mid 1980s, reading of three men executed by a firing squad in Russia for large scale black market currency dealings.

The last point the reader might raise is that surely, in the centrally planned economies, nearly all products were provided by state owned factories? If the government wants to keep the price down to Pc, why not supply Qd of the commodity, an extra Qs–Qd amount compared with if the market were working freely? Demand and supply will then match and there will still be a low price. In Section 5.1 an example was provided of unlimited Estonian gas supplies being provided at a low set price – that is what is happening in this scenario. The trouble is that the market allocates resources as efficiently as it is permitted, as determined by the demands of consumers, and hence the price suppliers want in order to provide the appropriate amounts of the relevant products. If the market were allowed to work freely then suppliers would only provide the quantity Qd at a price determined by where a line going vertically upwards from Qd hits the supply curve (draw this in Figure 5.7). Yet price controls do not allow the price to rise above Pc. Therefore, the bottom line is that supplying the quantity Qd at a price of Pc will result in a misallocation of resources, which could be better used elsewhere.

Conclusions

Chapter 4 drew heavily on marketing theories to show how these were underpinned by, and linked with, the theories of business economics. Among the issues developed was that, in the real world, a market may not produce one price for a good or service; rather there may be several. On the other hand this chapter, drawing on economic theory, has suggested that a market produces only one equilibrium price. There are several answers, which reconcile these seemingly conflicting situations.

Firstly, if prices change over a short period, it may simply be that the market is moving from a non-equilibrium to an equilibrium position. Indeed, different businesses may be adjusting their prices at different rates as they move to one uniform price, so that a range of different prices actually appear. Secondly, different firms will have different levels of costs in producing a product. The lowest cost producers will, therefore, be able to charge lower prices than higher cost producers. Yet consumer loyalty to a brand with higher cost and hence higher price producers, may retain some consumers on the grounds that they have always bought from them; or they may perceive that higher price automatically equates with higher quality. Transport costs also create price differences. For example, goods on the Isle of Wight are often more expensive than say in Portsmouth, on the mainland, because of the cost of transporting them across the Solent. It also depends how big one defines a market to be. One might expect all the televisions in a provincial city to be roughly the same price yet not the same as in London where higher incomes are likely to mean higher prices (what the market will bear). However, in all cities, economies of bulk purchase mean that multiples such as Currys or Comet can buy televisions and stereos in bulk and hence charge lower prices than say a family run store.

There is also the issue that for a market to achieve one price there must be perfect or complete knowledge – that is, each supplier must know what each other charges and each consumer must know what each producer charges. In reality, this does not happen because information is less than perfect. Therefore price differences exist. Bill Gates (1996) argued that people do not have time or the resources to gather all this information. However, he says

> The Internet will extend the electronic marketplace and become the ultimate go-between, the universal middleman. . . . All the goods for sale in the world will be available for you to examine, compare, and, often, customise. When you want to buy something, you'll be able to tell your computer to find it for you at the best price offered by any acceptable source or ask your computer to 'haggle' with the computers of various sellers. . . . We'll find ourselves in a new world of low-friction, low-overhead capitalism, in which market information will be plentiful and transaction costs low. It will be a shoppers' heaven.

Why, therefore, do we bother with economic theory if there are so many exceptions to the theory of markets? The simple answer is because the theory of how markets behave represents the ideal and also explains the reality of their behaviour very effectively. Demand and supply do determine prices and resource allocation; if markets in reality work less than perfectly this does not undermine the truth of market forces and the realities of the free market or capitalist system. There may be a range of prices but they will need to be within a certain band, even if they are not identical, or the highest price businesses will go out of existence.

5.5 The rise of the grey market

Synopsis

This case study explores why EU consumers pay significantly higher prices than their US counterparts. It identifies key characteristics as follows.

1 Companies supply similar goods at different prices in different countries; this is enforced by legislation.
2 Parallel imports or grey markets have developed as market forces seek to unify prices.
3 In time the Internet should help achieve this.

Case Study

A report by the National Economic Research Associates (Nera), commissioned by EU trade ministers and published in 1999, found that EU consumers pay, on average, 40–50 per cent more for all goods than US consumers. In other words, companies regularly supply similar goods at different prices in different countries. In the UK, designer goods such as Levi jeans, Nike sportswear, Chanel No. 5 perfume, Calvin Klein underwear and Rayban sunglasses all command high prices. This, the report argues, is because firms know what they can get away with; in other words, they know what the market will bear. Another factor is the economies of scale achievable from supplying to 280 million American consumers, which is a reason for the creation of the single market in the European Union. Many visitors to the US have found that the cost of a product in pounds in the UK will be the same in dollars in the US (the rate of exchange, at the time of writing, is approximately $1.60 = £1).

The European Trademark Directive 1988

In 1988, the European Trademark Directive was implemented by the European Union. This allows the owners of brands – such as Calvin Klein and Tommy Hilfiger – to control the supply of their products outside the EU. Thus, it prevents EU retailers from importing famous brand goods sold at a low price in another country – known as sourcing from unauthorised suppliers – and selling them at the same low price in the EU, since this would infringe the trademark of the brand owners. Rather, they have to sell the goods at the high price which the suppliers have chosen for the EU. The fact that the supply of such goods in the EU is being limited to authorised supply sources, and that the goods have to be sold in 'appropriate surroundings', e.g. the perfume counters of a major department store, means that prices can be kept high. For example, currently a designer can legally state that its goods cannot be sold in retail outlets where consumers have to walk past fruit and vegetable shelves before reaching the designer product, thus avoiding the goods being sold in supermarkets.

This was reinforced by a 1998 ruling by the European Court of Justice – called the Silhouette Case – which prevented Silhouette sunglasses brought in from Bulgaria being sold cheaply in the EU without the manufacturers' permission. In effect, therefore, the court ruling allowed manufacturers to limit competition and maintain high prices. The manufacturers' defence of this is that they need to protect their brand image and this is what consumers value; Chanel No. 5 has a prestige that other perfumes do not have, for example. Additionally, businesses need to protect their R&D efforts – the cost of developing a new perfume was shown in Chapter 4, Section 4.5, for example.

If the reader looks ahead to Figure 7.5, he/she will see an example of how a monopolist discriminates between different markets, charging different prices in each. One condition is the ability of the supplier to separate different markets, preventing the goods being bought in the cheaper market and sold in the dearer one.

Grey imports

Goods brought into the EU without manufacturers' permission and through non-approved channels of distribution, to sell at lower prices, are known as 'parallel' imports or 'grey' imports. A 1997 New Zealand government study estimated that, for the UK, grey imports were worth over £1.6 billion or 0.2 per cent of Gross National Product (GNP). The retailers that bring them into the EU seek to take advantage of price differences between the domestic market and the country in which they are cheaper. In this sense, the importers – or parallel traders – are effectively embodying market forces since their actions seek to create, as far as possible with geographic separation, one market price and hence one market, from two markets separated by manufacturers exercising their trademark rights. Parallel traders are also able to charge lower prices in the EU when selling grey imports by not charging such a big profit margin on these goods, even if the source from which they bought them is at the same price as the official source.

For example, in 1998 in the UK, grey imports of Honda motorcycles sold by independent motorcycle distributors, as opposed to authorised dealers, brought the price down by 30 per cent on some models and resulted in Honda taking the independents to court to force them to stop selling bikes obtained through unofficial channels, cheaply. The bikes were made under licence by manufacturers other than Honda of Japan and, in practice, it is difficult for brand owners to monitor the production levels of licensees. Therefore, extra production can easily enter the grey market unofficially. This is why manufacturers are increasingly taking court action to enforce their trademark rights and maintain prices.

The other main area where legal action has been taken against UK retailers is with supermarket chains. Tesco ran into trouble with Levi over the sale of its jeans, obtained on the grey market, at a price of £30, compared with a sale price of £50 at most outlets. The other thing to note is that grey or parallel goods are genuine brands not counterfeits. Nonetheless mistakes can be made; in August 1998, Sainsbury's supermarket chain, which had been selling Nike polo shirts obtained from a supplier of grey market designer clothes, cheaply, admitted that the shirts were counterfeit. It was forced to remove 5000 shirts from its Savacentre stores only days after saying that it would go to court to fight Nike over the sale of what it had believed were genuine branded goods.

The UK car industry

Another area where there are restrictions on supply is in the car industry. Throughout the EU, car manufacturers seek to discourage consumers from buying new cars other than from authorised dealers in their own countries and nowhere is this more evident than in the UK. Here, there would be substantial benefits if grey trading were legalised, since UK consumers pay substantially higher prices for cars (on average 35 per cent) than any other EU country. A survey carried out by the European Commission, in 1999, found the following evidence:

- Alfa Romeo 145: £7417 in Spain; £10 776 in the UK (45.3 per cent dearer).
- Fiat Bravo: £7281 in the Netherlands; £10 557 in the UK (45 per cent dearer).
- BMW 214 Hatchback: £7210 in France; £10 953 in the UK (52 per cent dearer) – this car is made in Birmingham!
- Rover 414: £7949 in Portugal; £11 379 in the UK (43 per cent dearer).
- Ford Focus: £7946 in Portugal; £10 157 in the UK (27.8 per cent dearer).

- Range Rover V8i: £25 948 in Portugal; £35 574 in the UK (22.9 per cent dearer).
- VW Polo: £5426 in Sweden; £7163 in the UK (32 per cent dearer).

The Director-General of the Office of Fair Trading (OFT) ordered the Monopolies and Mergers Commission (M&MC), now the Competition Commission, to investigate the relationship between manufacturers and dealers, following the discovery that new cars can cost up to 50 per cent more in the UK than in other EU countries. Director-General John Bridgeman's investigation into the UK car industry found that 'the market isn't working properly and there is an imbalance of power between manufacturers and dealers which is distorting competition.' In other words, the price difference is not just due to the strong pound. He found that car manufacturers refuse to give discounts to dealers for sales volume – this would enable them to pass the benefits onto customers in the form of lower prices. Large price discounts are given on fleet cars to businesses but it is argued that this discriminatory pricing in favour of businesses, and against private motorists, results in the latter subsidising the former. Manufacturers also set a recommended retail price (RRP) from which dealers then offer discounts to customers – yet these conceal the true selling price of cars.

The new legislation is in spite of a similar investigation instigated by the OFT and undertaken by the M&MC in 1990, which led to a 1992 M&MC report. Its recommendations were included in EU legislation which came into force in 1996. The recommendations included:

1   that car makers be obliged to allow their franchised dealers to sell other brands;
2   the promotion of intra-brand competition, i.e. allowing franchised dealers to advertise on each other's territory (normally franchised dealers had a monopoly on their own allocated territory);
3   that dealers could also get involved in related activities such as second-hand car sales (on trade-in models, for example), car hire and servicing.

So why did this legislation fail? The main reason is because car manufacturers still have too much control over their dealers. Moreover, since being a dealer involves a substantial personal investment in premises, stocks etc., dealers are reluctant to upset their manufacturer by seeking grey imports or selling other marques (makes of car) – if they try it is alleged by some that they are 'leant on,' although the Society of Motor Manufacturers and Traders denies this. Additionally, the bonus system employed by manufacturers prevents dealers competing on each other's territory. A further problem is that the car industry has an exclusive distribution system which is currently exempt from the rules of EU competition policy.

These findings regarding the price differences between EU cars and those of the rest of the EU, also resulted in the UK's House of Commons Trade and Industry Select Committee launching an enquiry into whether the European Trademark Directive needs to be repealed. The Department of Transport has also been considering lifting some UK restrictions on parallel imports to help lower UK car prices, which would weaken the power of automobile manufacturers.

Conclusions

If parallel imports are to be permitted much more widely this will certainly improve consumer choice and hence economic welfare, i.e. the well being and satisfaction consumers derive from their expenditure. However, parallel imports will not guarantee price equalisation between the market the goods come from and the market in which they are sold. The differences will be offset partly by transport costs and partly by differences in excise duties and VAT between different countries; hence the argument for the harmonisation of taxes within the EU. However, the advent of the single currency will also introduce transparency which will make price differentials very obvious to consumers. As well as permitting parallel or grey imports there is also a need for a change in European trademark law to remove some of the rights which manufacturers currently have, including the ability to require retailers to charge high prices.

The other area which will help lower prices is the growing sale of goods via the Internet. It is already possible to buy books and CDs from American Internet sites at prices much lower than those in UK stores. In effect, each consumer is able to become his/her own parallel importer, seeking out the cheapest sources for a good – a fulfilment of Bill Gates' assertion quoted earlier in this chapter.

Self testing questions

Self Testing Questions

1 Explain in your own words the different causes of a shift in a supply curve and a movement along a supply curve.

2 Why must a market always return to an equilibrium position (where demand equals supply) if there are no restrictions imposed on the market?

3 Using demand and supply diagrams illustrate the following: (a) the effects of the BSE crisis on the market for British cattle; (b) the effects of a recession on the UK housing market; (c) the effects of New Year's eve on the market for alcoholic drinks.

4 What economic reasons were there, do you think, for executing large-scale black market currency dealers in Russia in the 1980s?

5 Explain in your own words what is meant by: (a) price ceilings; (b) price floors. (c) Give an example of each, not already used in this book, and explain briefly how it operates (you will need to undertake some research for this).

5.6 Summary of chapter

This chapter has explored what is meant by the term market and has given illustration of a wide range of such markets, from a coffee market for scout funds to the London stock market. Consumer sovereignty as a focal point of markets was explored and an analysis was undertaken of centrally planned economies and how these differ from market economies.

The chapter then explored demand, including the use of demand schedules and their importance to businesses. The demand curve was plotted and the causes of movements along the demand curve due to price changes, as opposed to shifts of the demand curve due to other factors, were examined. In the same way the supply curve was examined, including the factors underlying it and what it represented. The distinction between movements along the curve and shifts of the curve was again distinguished. The two forces of demand and supply were then put together and the determination of market prices was examined.

The changes in demand and supply forces and their impact on price were examined and cases were provided as illustration. The impact of the imposition of price floors and price ceilings was then analysed using the market for yo-yos. The development of black markets from price controls was also explored. The chapter concluded with a case study of grey/parallel imports and its impact on domestic prices for goods.

5.7 Further questions

Further Questions

1 (a) Draw up a table with two columns. Head the left column 'The Advantages of the Free Market' and the right column 'The Advantages of Central Planning'. List as many as you can of each, and weight each according to its importance from 1, for most important, to 5, for least important (you can have more than five advantages!). (b) Imagine a parallel universe where communism triumphs over capitalism, as Soviet leader Nikita Khruschev predicted in the 1960s. Write a side of A4 imagining how the economy of the UK might be in 1999, compared with our reality. (See the further reading section below for titles in which authors Deighton, Dick, and Orwell have imagined such a scenario).

2 Draw a demand and supply diagram showing the effects of the Internet on UK retailing. Explain your answer.

3 Although price floors and price ceilings may inhibit the free working of market forces there are strong arguments in their favour, especially regarding helping consumers and producers. Discuss.

4 If unlimited parallel/grey imports are permitted into the UK firms will be discouraged from developing new products and selling existing ones so consumers will lose out in the end. Discuss the validity of this statement.

5 The Common Agricultural Policy is a classic, if overused, example of the use of price floors. Write a report explaining how it works and why it is being reformed (1500 words maximum).

5.8 Further reading

Begg, D., Fischer, S. and Dornbusch, R. (1997). *Economics*, 5th edition. Maidenhead: McGraw Hill.

Deighton, Len (1978). SS-GB. St Albans: Triad/Panther Books.

Dick, P. K. (1976) *The Man in the High Castle*. Harmondsworth: Penguin Science Fiction.

Gates, B. (1996). *The Road Ahead*, 2nd edition. London: Penguin Books.

Orwell, G. (1949). *Nineteen eighty-four*. London: Penguin Books.

Parkin, M. (1999). *Economics*, 5th edition. Wokingham: Addison Wesley.

The Economist

The *Financial Times*

The Times

New York Times: http://www.nytimes.com

Chapter 6

Markets in the real world

Learning Outcomes

After completing this chapter the reader will be able to:
- examine the implications of elasticity of demand and supply for businesses;
- appreciate the implications of market failure;
- explore the implications of market theory for inputs – especially labour.

6.1 Elasticity of demand

The times pricing policy: what impact on demand?

Synopsis   This case study explores the effect of price cutting on demand for *The Times* newspaper. It identifies:

1 complaints that *The Times* engaged in predatory pricing to drive weak competitors out of business;
2 that changing price will affect demand for the paper;
3 how much demand responds to price changes depends on price elasticity of demand which is discussed below.

In late May 1999, the Office of Fair Trading (OFT) rejected complaints from *The Guardian*, *The Independent* and *The Daily Telegraph*, concerning their allegations that *The Times* had been engaged in predatory pricing. This occurs when a business substantially lowers its prices below those of its competitors (which may involve it making losses) with the aim of increasing demand for its product sufficiently to seriously harm its competitors. Subsequently it may then raise prices again. This may occur when a well established business seeks to destroy a new entrant to the market, or when it uses revenue from other sources to enable it to lower prices excessively in one market (known as cross-subsidisation). Predatory policy therefore exceeds normal competitive pricing which is part of the nature of modern business.

The complaints by *The Guardian* etc. concerned the period from June 1996 to January 1998 when *The Times* was sold on Mondays for 10p. Although the predatory pricing allegation was rejected, John Bridgeman, the Director-General of the OFT, did decide, however, that *The Times* had deliberately made a loss during this period which had impacted on competition in the market for daily newspapers.

Since *The Times* reduced its price from 50p in 1993 to 30p in mid 1999 the paper's circulation more than doubled from 354 280 to 744 490.

As Chapter 5 showed, the market price of a product is important to a business since, in part, it determines its profitability. We have also noted that although economic theory suggests that only one price will exist in a perfect market, in reality markets are not perfect. There will be a range within which prices for similar goods will be located and these will be determined partly by market imperfections and partly by deliberate pricing strategies adopted by businesses. The case study above, of *The Times* newspaper, shows that senior management adopted a policy of cutting the price sufficiently low to cause it to make a loss. Although short term this contradicts the argument that businesses are profit maximisers, long term if competitors leave the market, e.g. *The Independent*, which has had an insecure financial history, this will boost the sales and profits of those who remain. Since *The Times* is 40 per cent owned by News Corporation, which also owns BSkyB, some might argue that cross-subsidisation was used here.

In the light of this, businesses will have concerns as to what the impact on their demand and revenues will be if they change the prices of their products – what is known as the elasticity of their demand curve(s). If a big price change leads to a large loss of custom then it may be better to leave prices unchanged; however, if a small price cut leads to a large increase in revenue then the business may well decide to lower prices. Of course, this assumes that other companies do nothing to their prices, allowing the first company to take some of their customers; in practice this is unlikely and will be explored in Chapter 7. The other way to avoid this problem is to assume that all businesses behave in unison and lower their prices together and by the same amount.

It is worth noting that *The Times* boosted its readership very substantially in the 1990s. This was achieved partly by moving down market more or making the paper more readable, depending on one's viewpoint, and partly by cutting price. Other quality newspapers or broadsheets were then obliged to respond in a similar fashion, hitting their profits.

Elasticity of demand

The amount by which demand changes as a business changes its prices is known as the price elasticity of demand. This is defined below:

Definition

Price elasticity of demand is the responsiveness of the demand for a product to a change in its price, other things being equal.

So far we have just drawn a demand curve without any regard to its slope, i.e. whether it is steep or shallow. Price elasticity of demand requires us to look at this more carefully.

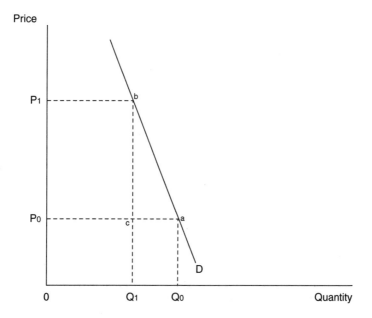

Figure 6.1 An inelastic demand curve.

Initially, the business faces a demand curve of D with a price of P_0 and a quantity of Q_0 demanded at this price. It now decides to raise the price of its product to P_1, and as a result the quantity demanded falls to Q_1. As this is a normal good, i.e. the demand curve slopes down from top left to bottom right, we would expect this.

Has the business gained or lost from its price change? To determine this let us consider the total revenue (TR) which it earns. The reader will recall that this is measured by $P \times Q = TR$, where P is the price of the good and Q is the quantity demanded. At the original price of P_0 the business was earning the area $0, P_0, a, Q_0$. After it has increased the price to P_1 its revenue increases to $0, P_1, b, Q_1$. We can now see that the firm has lost revenue equal to the oblong Q_1, c, a, Q_0. This is revenue formerly earned from customers who have given up the product since the price has risen to P_1. However, the business has gained revenue equal to P_0, P_1, b, c as remaining customers are prepared to pay the price increase of P_0, P_1. Since the area P_0, P_1, b, c is bigger than the area Q_1, c, a, Q_0 the business has clearly gained from increasing the price of its product.

In the same way, therefore, the reader should now work out whether the business should lower its price to P_0 if initially it is selling at P_1.

Business economists also talk about a whole curve being elastic or inelastic as in Figure 6.1. In fact, we are usually concerned with only a small segment of the demand curve, e.g. what happens to demand if the price of *The Times* is cut from 30p a copy to 20p. The demand curve could be plotted from the level of demand if *The Times* were £5 per copy to if it were 1p per copy. However, as neither of those is immediately likely it is more use just to concentrate on the range of the demand curve between say 60p and 10p, assuming these are the limits of any price changes. This is called arc elasticity since it relates to just an arc or segment of the curve. However, economists still generalise and apply the term inelastic or elastic to the whole curve.

Table 6.1 Demand schedule for the use of a local swimming pool.

Price of a swim £	Number of tickets sold per week
4.00	5800
3.00	6300
2.50	6900
2.00	7200
1.50	7500
1.00	7800

Let us now consider some data to examine how precisely elasticity is calculated.

The demand schedule in Table 6.1 related to the demand for tickets to the swimming pool of a local sports centre. Variations such as season tickets, special deals for senior citizens etc. are ignored to simplify matters. The managers are required to maximise revenue from the use of the pool so they need to price the pool admission charges to achieve this. However, if prices are raised too much people will use the new pool in the neighbouring town. Hence knowing the price elasticity of demand for the use of the swimming pool is crucial.

Let us assume the current price charged is £2.50. The pool manager considers lowering the admission charge to £2.00. The formula for calculating price elasticity is given by:

$$Pe = \frac{\% \text{ change in quantity demanded}}{\% \text{ change in price}}$$

$$= \frac{\text{Change in quantity demanded}}{\text{Change in price}} \times \frac{\text{Average price}}{\text{Average quantity}}$$

We substitute the values from the table above into the formula. This gives us:

$$Pe = \frac{300}{-0.50} \times \frac{2.25}{7050} = -0.19148.$$

where Pe denotes price elasticity of demand.

Inelastic demand

We ignore the minus sign, which gives 0.19 to two significant figures. Since this is less than 1, demand is inelastic. In other words demand is not very responsive to changes in pool admission charges. The loss in total revenue from lowering the price will exceed the gain in sales from the lower price. Lowering the price of entry to the pool will therefore lose revenue not increase it. In contrast, as Figure 6.1 showed, raising the price when the demand curve is inelastic will increase revenue.

Some books will suggest that instead of average price (old price + new price/2) and average quantity (old quantity + new quantity/2), we use original price and original quantity, on the right hand side of the formula. The trouble with this is that we get different values of elasticity if the price increases or decreases (try working this out where first the original price and quantity assumes a price increase, then when it assumes a price decrease). Therefore, to avoid this problem, we take the average of the two as above.

Elastic demand

If the value from an elasticity calculation is greater than 1 then demand is said to be elastic, i.e. a change in price will create a greater than proportionate change in quantity demanded. The same formula will be used as above. In this case, lowering the price will increase total revenue whilst increasing the price will reduce it. An elastic demand curve is shown as D3 in Figure 6.2. The reader can draw an elastic demand curve to test the effects of the above assertion.

Other values of price elasticity

Figure 6.2 shows an elastic demand curve and also three other possibilities for price elasticity.

Unitary elasticity of demand

D0 shows a demand curve which is of unitary elasticity – this means that the calculation of the elasticity of the curve will produce a value of unity (1). This implies that any change in price will cause an equal proportionate change in the quantity demanded, and hence total revenue will stay unchanged (revenue gained from the price change = revenue lost). Hence there is no incentive for a business to change the price of its products. The curve is known as a rectangular hyperbola.

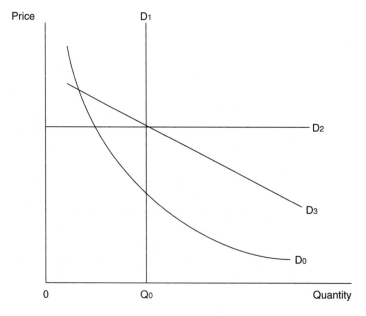

Figure 6.2 Other types of price elasticity.

Perfectly inelastic demand

Curve D1 gives us an extreme type of demand curve. Here, any change in price will have no effect on demand so there is an incentive for businesses facing this demand curve to charge as high a price as possible for their products. However, to avoid consumer exploitation there might be regulators to ensure this does not happen. Water is a product for which there is a relatively fixed demand in the short term so, in theory, a water supply company could charge high prices to exploit this situation. However, OFWAT, the regulatory body for the water industry, monitors firms' prices and profit margins, among other things, to prevent this happening. The value of price elasticity here is 0.

Perfectly elastic demand

D2 is an example of a demand curve which is perfectly elastic (Pe = ∞ (infinity)). This means that there is an infinite demand for the product and consumers will buy any amount which businesses are willing to supply at that price. Again this is an extreme position although we will encounter this again briefly when we touch on perfect competition in Chapter 7, Section 7.4. Perhaps one example of this is the demand for television. At a given price consumers will demand as many channels as producers care to supply. Certainly BSkyB's philosophy of supplying 200 digital channels (when only a few years ago the UK had only four) suggests that they believe the demand curve to be very inelastic, even if not perfectly elastic.

The reader should be aware that the perfectly elastic demand and perfectly inelastic demand are extreme cases only.

The non-linear demand curve

As noted before, demand curves are not, in reality, straight lines. Therefore, the value of the elasticity of demand will vary along a curve's length as price falls, from almost perfectly inelastic at very high prices, through inelastic, to unitary elasticity; then the demand curve becomes elastic before becoming almost perfectly elastic at very low prices. Hence, where exactly the business's product price is on the demand curve it faces will determine the pricing strategy which it adopts. What it will do if in the inelastic segment of the curve is quite different to its actions in the elastic segment.

Factors influencing price elasticity

Early on in this section we defined price elasticity of demand as the responsiveness of the demand for a product to a change in its price, other things being equal. Let us briefly consider what other factors might influence the value of price elasticity of demand.

1   The extent to which there are substitute products. The more substitutes exist the more elastic will demand for each of them be. For example,

butter, margarine and other spreads are substitutes for each other – a rise in the price of butter beyond a certain level will encourage some consumers to switch to the other products, although consumer loyalty will keep some people with butter if the price rise is not too great.

2   The percentage of consumers' disposable income which the price of the product accounts for. Demand for something with a low price, e.g. a postage stamp, will not be directly affected by a price change of 1p since it is not a major part of expenditure. A similar percentage change in average house prices will affect demand for them, other things remaining equal, since they are the largest item of household expenditure.

3   Time – the longer a price change persists the more likely that consumer demand will become more elastic as consumers learn of substitute products, and rival businesses enter the market. The high charges of public transport has, among other things, over time shifted people to private transport, particularly cars.

The impact of advertising on the elasticity of a market demand curve

Synopsis

This case study examines an advertisement for Microsoft Office. Its objectives are:

1   it seeks to promote awareness of the company and its product;
2   it seeks to reinforce the leading position of Microsoft products in the education market;
3   it tells parents that if they wish their children to succeed (the picture shows young people on the beach laughing at the camera, with job titles such as accountant, teacher, lawyer, bus driver, window cleaner above individuals) they need help from Microsoft;
4   it boosts sales;
5   it reinforces consumer loyalty. Once a consumer is tied into Microsoft he/she is unlikely to switch to Lotus or Corel Wordperfect.

Some children get more of a head start than others do. Therefore it's worth remembering that, when you give them Microsoft* Office 2000 Professional, you're not just giving them a piece of software. You're giving them opportunity.

Not only is it the world's best-selling office suite, it's the leading choice for schools and a proven aid in boosting a child's learning ability. With the latest versions of Microsoft* Word, Excel, Publisher, Access and PowerPoint, this essential toolkit offers them the chance to enhance writing skills, the freedom to express their creativity, and so much more. (If you're a parent with children aged 5–18, a full or part time student, teacher or lecturer, Office 2000 is available at the student licensing price of just £129.) Available from these and other leading stockists: PC World, Staples and John Lewis. Or order now from Software Warehouse on 0800 0355 355.

For more information please call 0870 60 70 800 or visit our website. It could make all the difference.

Microsoft
www.microsoft.com/uk/studentlicence

* denotes trademark or registered trademark.

If we examine the effect of this advertisement on the demand curve for Microsoft Office it is seeking to do two things:

1 shift the demand curve to the right, from D0 to D1, to generate more sales;
2 make it more inelastic (consumer loyalty) so that if prices rise consumers will not switch to other software. Note how D1 is much steeper (more inelastic) than D0.

Figure 6.3 shows this.

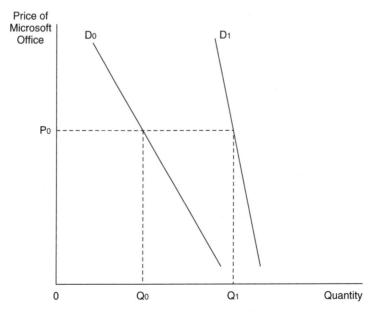

Figure 6.3 The effects of advertising on the demand for Microsoft Office.

In this way consumer loyalty to the product is tied in long term. This is something which the American courts cannot legislate against under the anti-trust laws.

Other types of elasticity of demand

Income elasticity of demand

So far we have examined price elasticity of demand and assumed that other things remain equal. If we hold price constant and vary another influence on demand, namely income, we can consider what influence changes in this have on demand. We call this the income elasticity of demand and it is determined by:

$$Ye = \frac{\text{Change in quantity demanded}}{\text{Change in income}} \times \frac{\text{Average income}}{\text{Average quantity}}$$

We use average income and average quantity for the same reasons as we did with Pe.

Figure 6.4 gives examples of different income demand curves. These are similar to the demand curves we have examined so far except that they plot household income (instead of the price of the good) against quantity demanded. Note also that demand is plotted on the vertical axis in Figure 6.4.

Income demand curve 'a' shows us the curve for necessities, e.g. bread. Since consumers must have bread the value of Ye above will be low, i.e. between 0 and 1; in other words the demand for the goods is income inelastic. People will still buy them even if household income falls. In contrast, income demand curve 'b' shows the income elasticity of demand for luxury goods, e.g. expensive cars or expensive meals out. Demand will be income elastic with a value of Ye greater than 1. Therefore, when household incomes fall people buy second-hand cars or eat cheap takeaways instead.

Cross price elasticity of demand

$$Ce = \frac{\text{Change in quantity demanded of good A}}{\text{Change in price of good B}}$$

$$\times \frac{\text{Average price of good B}}{\text{Average quantity of good A}}$$

Cross (price) elasticity of demand (denoted Ce) measures the impact on one good of a change in the price of another good. This is particularly

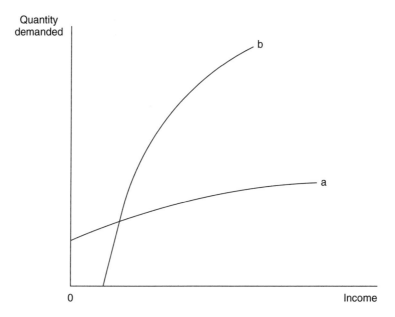

Figure 6.4 Income demand curves illustrating different income elasticities of demand.

useful for businesses to know in terms of whether their products are complements with other goods or substitutes for them.

If goods are complements, e.g. CD player and CDs, or cars and petrol, then the cross elasticity of demand (Ce) will be negative. This means that if the price of cars increases, for example, demand for petrol will fall. Of course, the percentage amount of the price increase is important in terms of its impact on the complementary product – if car prices rise by 0.5 per cent this is not likely to have a big impact on demand for petrol.

If goods are substitutes then the value of Ce will be positive, i.e. greater than zero. Coffee and tea are examples of substitutes, as are margarine and butter. If the price of coffee falls sharply then demand for tea is likely to fall as a result.

Whether goods are substitutes or complements will influence the pricing policy adopted by a business.

Self testing questions

1 If a business faces an inelastic demand for its product should it lower the price?

2 If lowering the price of *The Times* increased demand why have the proprietors subsequently raised the price again?

3 What use is knowledge of income elasticity of demand to a business?

4 Give three examples of goods, other than those mentioned in this chapter, which are complements or substitutes. Explain, in your own words, the value of knowing cross elasticity of demand in each case.

5 If house prices rise we would expect demand to fall more than in proportion since they are a large item of household expenditure (inelastic demand). Why then might demand for houses actually increase?

6.2 Elasticity of supply

We now examine elasticity of supply, which also has important implications for businesses. We may define it as the responsiveness of supply to a change in the price of a good, i.e.

$$E_S = \frac{\text{Change in quantity supplied}}{\text{Change in price}} \times \frac{\text{Average price}}{\text{Average quantity}}$$

where E_S denote elasticity of supply. Figures 6.5 denote examples of elasticity of supply.

In Figure 6.5, S_0 gives an example of an inelastic supply curve ($E_S < 1$); a change in price leads to a less than proportionate change in the quantity businesses will supply. In contrast, S_1 shows an elastic supply curve ($E_S > 1$),

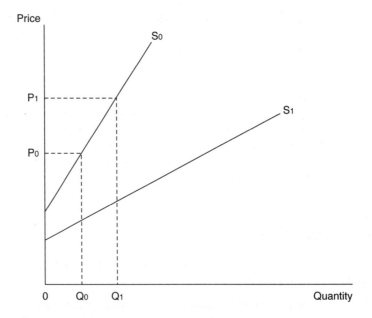

Figure 6.5 Inelastic and elastic supply curves.

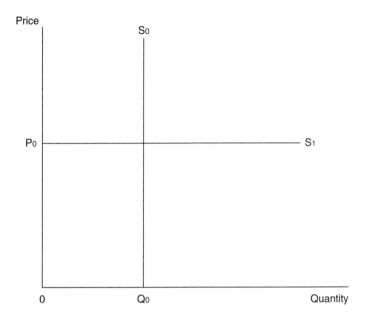

Figure 6.6 Perfectly elastic and inelastic supply curves.

where a change in price will lead to a greater than proportionate change in quantity supplied. These are the two cases most important to business economics. For completeness, however, we should also briefly consider the other cases.

Figure 6.6 shows a supply curve (S_0) which is perfectly inelastic, so $E_S = 0$. Here supply is totally fixed at Q_0 regardless of price, so as demand rises over time (draw in a series of demand curves, one above the other), supply stays constant and only price increases. An example of this would be the supply of original manuscripts of Jane Austen novels since the world will never see more of these written. Figure 6.6 also shows a different supply curve S_1; this is a perfectly elastic supply curve such that businesses will supply whatever amount is demanded at the price of P_0 but none at any price below P_0. Here $E_S = 4$. One example of this, at times, is the supply of crude oil put onto the market by OPEC (the Organisation of Petroleum Exporting Countries). When prices fell to $10 per barrel, oil exporting countries were willing to supply as much as industrial countries would demand to try and keep up their oil revenues as much as possible.

Factors influencing the elasticity of supply

A number of factors influence the elasticity of supply for a product. The main ones are: (i) the time span; (ii) the extent to which costs increase as output increases and (iii) the elasticity of supply of the inputs which make up the product.

The time span

The longer the time span the more elastic will any supply curve become as new supplies or more substitutes are developed. In the very short term supply is totally fixed so the supply curve is perfectly inelastic. In the short term only variable inputs can be increased so the supply curve will be a little more elastic. In the long term, however, fixed factors can be varied and new businesses will enter the industry also increasing supply. Therefore, the supply curve will become more elastic as time progresses.

The extent to which costs increase as output increases

The less costs increase the more elastic the supply curve will be. If, in the long term, economies of scale can be achieved, then the supply curve will be very elastic.

The elasticity of supply of the inputs which make up the product

The more elastic the supply of these, the more elastic will be the supply curve of the finished product.

Boeing's supply curves

Synopsis

This case study explores the supply problems which Boeing encountered through deliberate downsizing to save costs and the merger with McDonnell Douglas. It identifies that:

1 the actions caused Boeing's supply curve to shift to the left rather than the right;
2 its curve became more inelastic, the reverse of what was intended;
3 excess demand could not be removed by rising prices, since contracts fixed prices.

Case Study

The Boeing corporation is the world's largest civil airline manufacturer, so it is interesting to know that even global businesses can get it wrong! In the early 1990s, to increase its production levels and improve its productive efficiency, to enable it to compete more effectively with European rival Airbus, Boeing decided to undertake a major organisational restructuring, involving a major capital expenditure programme and a substantial reduction in its labour force, known as downsizing, to cut production costs by 25 per cent between 1992 and 1998. To achieve this, the labour force was cut by 60 000 between 1989 and 1997, which was one third of its 1989 level. Since each plane could now be produced for only 75 per cent of its previous cost Boeing's supply curve would shift downwards and to the right.

In practice a number of issues caused Boeing substantial problems. Firstly, it sacked too many experienced staff so there were insufficient skilled employees left to produce the planes. This was aggravated by a merger with military and commercial airline manufacturer McDonnell Douglas which meant more staff were shed, since cost savings are a major justification for mergers and labour is the easiest cost to reduce. Consequently, the business subsequently needed to re-hire dismissed staff or poach employees from nearby firms which supplied the components. However, this latter action worsened Boeing's position still more since, with the loss of skilled staff, components firms were unable to supply the components fast enough. As a result, instead of the supply curve shifting to the right, in fact it shifted to the left and became more inelastic, reflecting the production difficulties.

Excess demand, the amount by which demand exceeds supply, can be measured by waiting lists for Boeing planes. By 1997 this was 1629 aircraft. In a free market the price for Boeing aircraft would rise until demand equalled supply, which would choke off excess demand. However, Boeing and its customers enter into contracts which fix the price of new deliveries, so the excess demand remains.

In 1998, as a result of a major reorganisation, Boeing was able to stage a partial recovery producing a record 550 aircraft as against a projected 546, and predicting a 1999 figure of 620 aircraft, showing that the 'production system is starting to get healthy again', argued Alan Mulally, president of the commercial aeroplane division. As a result, the supply curve started to shift back to the right, also becoming more elastic again.

Self testing questions

1 'It is more useful for a business to know the elasticity of the demand curve facing it than it is to know about elasticity of supply.' Discuss.

2 What are the implications for a business of having an inelastic as opposed to an elastic supply curve?

3 Give three examples each of products that would have a perfectly inelastic supply curve and products that would have a perfectly elastic supply curve.

6.3 Market failure

The top ten UK polluters

Synopsis

This case study examines UK businesses which were major polluters. It identifies:

1 the major businesses;
2 the reasons for publishing such a list;
3 the inadequacies of fines in deterring polluters.

Case Study

In March 1999, the Environment Agency listed the 20 businesses which proved to be the most notorious polluters in England and Wales in 1998. The ten worst polluters, with fines, were:

Table 6.2 Top ten UK polluters, 1998.

Company	Fine (£)
ICI	382 500
Tyseley Waste Disposal	95 000
London Waste	38 500
Wessex Water	36 500
Alco Waste Management	30 000
Anglian Water Services	24 250
EOM Construction	21 000
Shell UK	20 000
British Nuclear Fuels Ltd	20 000
Celtic Energy	18 000

Source: Environmental Agency; March 1999 list of worst polluters

The purpose of the list is to shame the offenders, and industry in general, into taking stronger action to prevent the contamination of rivers, lakes and underground water supplies, i.e. external diseconomies of production. There is a need to shame businesses because courts impose relatively low fines on polluters; in 1998 the average fine for a successfully prosecuted company was £2786. As such, the fine for a business, if caught, is far exceeded by the cost savings from committing the polluting acts. For example, EOM Construction saved £180 000 by keeping and disposing of thousands of tonnes of controlled waste in Colne and Burnley.

Yet, when prosecuted, it was fined £21 000 with £1000 costs – a financial saving to the company of £159 000.

The top twenty worst polluters include five water companies (Wessex Water, Anglian Water, North West, Welsh, and Severn Trent) and a number of waste disposal companies (including the three above and Alco Waste Management, and Caird Environmental; the latter are meant to clean up the environment!) Other examples of pollution include:

- Wessex Water – prosecuted five times in 1998 and fined £36 500 mainly for sewage pollution.
- ICI – fined £300 000 for polluting ground water with 150 tonnes of chloroform in Runcorn, Cheshire; £80 000 for accidentally releasing 56 tonnes of trichloroethylene (a cleaning fluid), also at Runcorn; and £2500 for contaminating marshlands and killing wildlife and plants when 200 tonnes of naptha escaped from underground tanks in Brinefields, Cleveland.
- Tyseley Waste disposal – fined £90 00 for losing two 'radioactive sources' whilst demolishing an incinerator.

It should also be remembered that the firms listed here are the ones which have been detected.

So far, the market has been discussed as a resources allocator. Markets will emerge and an equilibrium stable price and quantity will be determined, assuming buyers and sellers behave rationally. Additionally, allocative or social efficiency will be achieved. However, if buyers and sellers do not behave rationally, equilibrium price and quantity do not emerge and markets do not allocate resources with maximum efficiency. There is then said to be market failure. This may be defined as a situation which occurs when an unregulated market cannot allocate resources with maximum efficiency, i.e. achieve allocative efficiency, in all circumstances.

Market failure

There are a number of reasons why market failure might occur.

Inefficiencies

Although businesses may wish to maximise profits, in reality some may be inefficient and so not use resources optimally. As a result, they will not produce at the lowest point on their average cost curves. Similarly, although consumers may wish to maximise the satisfaction or utility they derive from their purchases, they may at times, erroneously, buy the wrong products. If sufficient people make such mistakes resources will be misallocated from their optimum position.

Imperfect information

Imperfect information may be the cause of wrong decisions and inefficiencies, causing consequent sub-optimal resource allocation. This is because, in the real world, not all buyers and sellers have access to all sources of information – in other words there is imperfect information. Not all businesses know each others' costs, or pricing policies, or profit levels or business plans. Hence businesses which otherwise might be tempted to diversify into new products or markets do not do so at all, or not until it is too late, because they are unaware of potential opportunities.

Similarly, consumers do not know the price of every good in every retail outlet within travelling distance. Nor do they often have detailed technical knowledge about, for example, consumer durables which they buy, e.g. second-hand cars with mechanical problems or video-recorders impossible to programme. Often problems are only discovered after purchase, which is why the Consumer Association's *Which* magazine is so popular, as it seeks to provide as much of this type of information as possible. Alternatively, consumers are persuaded by advertising to ignore information on the known harmful long term effects of smoking which, if they behaved rationally, they would use to modify their behaviour, i.e. give up smoking. Therefore, in reality, incomplete information means that allocative (or social) efficiency is often not achieved.

As noted in Chapter 5, Section 5.4, Bill Gates addressed the issue of imperfect information in 'The Road Ahead.' His argument is that information technology will overcome this and enable buyers and sellers to get much closer to the optimal resource allocation of the efficient market. Whilst it is certainly true that electronic commerce and electronic business are growing very rapidly, as is discussed in Chapter 12, nonetheless, there is still a long way to go until we reach Gates' ideal world.

Imperfect competition

Secondly, market failure may occur because of the existence of imperfectly competitive market structures, such as monopoly or oligopoly, which cause output to be restricted. This means that the business will produce at a point other than the lowest point on its AC curve and resources will not be used optimally. Prices charged to consumers will be higher than in a perfectly competitive market, whilst entry barriers will prevent other businesses from entering the market. This is discussed more fully in Chapters 7 and 8.

External economies and diseconomies of production

A third reason for market failure is the existence of external economies of production and external diseconomies of production, which occur when a business supplies goods or services or ideas. Collectively these are known as externalities. An externality may be defined as an effect of production or consumption which is not allowed for by the producer or consumer and which affects the welfare of other producers or consumers who were not parties to the original decision.

For example, a business provides first aid training to its staff, in case they need to use these skills at work. However, they can then use these away from work if needed; this is an example of an external economy of production since it beneficially affects the welfare of citizens who were not involved in the company's decision to offer its employees first aid training. Similarly, the pleasant smell enjoyed by residents living near an Indian takeaway restaurant is an external economy to those who enjoy Indian food but an external diseconomy to those who dislike it. Another external diseconomy is pollution of the environment by a business, as demonstrated in the case study above.

If there is no means to recompense those who suffer the external diseconomies of production from the activities of a business, or to pay those businesses which provide external economies to society, then these will not be recognised in market transactions. In other words, only private costs and revenues, as discussed in Chapter 3, will be recognised.

In Chapter 3, Section 3.4, we saw that a business will produce to the point where its marginal costs equals it marginal revenue, i.e. MC = MR. To recognise that these are, in fact, private costs and benefits, i.e. as shown in the company's accounts, let us now call these marginal private costs (MPC) and marginal private benefits (MPB), where benefits are the same as revenue. We examine a situation where a business's activities also generate external economies of production, which we measure in money terms and call social benefits. A business may also generate external diseconomies of production, which we measure in money terms and call social costs, but these are not shown in the diagram below. The social cost of consuming a last or marginal unit is known as the marginal social cost (MSC) and the social benefit derived from the marginal unit is the marginal social benefit (MSB).

Valuing external economies and diseconomies

The reader may ask, how do we measure these in money terms? In most cases there is no market to determine a price for an external economy or diseconomy of production. One option is to use the consumer's willingness to pay (WTP) for an external economy. This will be reflected, although not completely, in the price he/she actually pays for the good whose production has generated the external economy. Where there is an external diseconomy the consumer can be asked what he/she is willing to pay to prevent the nuisance. He/she doesn't actually pay the money in either case; it is merely a means to obtain a surrogate or shadow price so as to value the external economy or diseconomy. The alternative, more acceptable approach is to ask the consumer what he/she is willing to accept (WTA) to live with the external diseconomy. Again, no payment is actually made. It is probable that the consumer will value the WTA at a higher value than the WTP.

Marginal social costs and benefits

In Figure 6.7 we show a situation where production by a business generates social benefits as well as incurring its own private benefits and costs. The social benefits are represented as the Marginal Social Benefit (MSB) curve, sloping downwards to the right. This shows that, as more of the product is produced, so the benefit derived from each extra unit diminishes, as we might expect. It lies to the right of the Marginal Private Benefit (MPB) curve, which is the business's marginal revenue curve, showing that, as the business's private benefits increase, so do the benefits to society. The marginal (private) cost curve slopes upwards and to the right as we saw in Chapter 3, Section 3.1.

If we consider just the private costs and benefits (revenues) of the business, as we did in Chapter 3, the optimum production point is at a point a where MPB = MPC, giving a market price of P_0 and an output of Q_0. This is the business's competitive equilibrium.

If there are social benefits generated by the business's production process, but no social costs, then the socially efficient point of production is at point

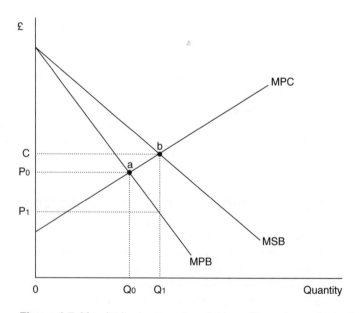

Figure 6.7 Marginal private and social benefits and marginal private costs.

'b' where MSB = MPC, i.e. where there is allocative efficiency. This gives an output of Q_1. However, because there is market failure, i.e. MSB are not recognized in market transactions, the market will only produce Q_0. If the business were to produce Q_1 it would be at a cost of C.

If the government intervenes in the market, to correct the allocative inefficiency, it can subsidise the business by the amount CP_1. This will encourage the business to produce to Q_1.

For example, the more a business produces, the more employees it hires and the more training it therefore gives them. When these employees move on to new jobs, the training which they have received benefits society as a whole. The government subsidy in the example above is remuneration for the training costs which the business has incurred.

External economies and diseconomies of consumption

In the same way as with a business, so a household or an individual consumer may, by the act of consuming goods or services, generate external economies of consumption or external diseconomies of consumption. An example would be a woman wearing an attractive perfume which people smell and enjoy; if valued as above by WTP this is a measure of the social benefit. Conversely, an example of an external diseconomy of consumption is a person who plays loud music in his/her home with all the windows open, forcing others who may not like his/her tastes to listen to it. The social cost is the monetary valuation of this external diseconomy.

In both the examples above not everyone will like the perfume and not everyone will dislike the music. So, in reality, we would need to consider the average effects of each.

Pure private and pure public goods

There are circumstances where the market is even less suited to the production and consumption of products due to the nature of the goods or services concerned. This involves making a distinction between private and public goods.

Pure private goods are those where most of the benefits from consuming the good are derived by the purchaser to the exclusion of other people, even though there might be external effects. A person drinking a beer would be an example of consumption of a private good, although consumption of many beers may well have unpleasant external effects (diseconomies of consumption) on others. A private good has the two characteristics of rivalry and excludability. Rivalry means that if one person consumes something – the beer in our example – no one else can. Excludability means that the owner of the beer in our example can exclude other people from its consumption. A person may share her beer with a friend if she wishes but rivalry still exists in that the part of the bottle of beer drunk by its owner cannot also be drunk by the friend.

Conversely, pure public goods are those which can benefit a large number of people and where consumption by one person does not prevent others consuming them. In other words, non-rivalry and non-excludability exist. National defence is often cited as such an example. It benefits everyone who lives in the UK and the fact that I am protected against foreign attack by the UK's armed forces does not exclude others from the same sense of well-being. Pure public goods may be, but do not have to be, provided by the public sector of the economy.

If I walk along a local beach on a bright winter's morning, that doesn't stop other people from also doing so (non-rivalry); nor can I prevent them from doing so (non-excludability). However, if many people do the same as me, the beach will eventually get so crowded that there will not be room to walk, or the quality of the experience will diminish very substantially – in other words congestion creates rivalry. Where this occurs such goods are known as quasi-public goods.

How does the government address market failure?

The government, or a local authority, acting on behalf of society, can and often will intervene in a market to redress its failure.

As we saw in Figure 6.7, where external economies of production exist, one main option for government is to subsidise businesses to produce the socially optimal level of output, i.e. where MSB = MPC, rather than the business's optimal level where MPB = MPC.

Where there are only external diseconomies, one way to deter these is for the government to pass laws to prevent them. However, legal action has to be sufficiently powerful to actually deter; as we saw in the case study above it was sometimes more cost effective from the business's viewpoint to pollute and pay a small fine than to dispose of the waste legally.

External economies of consumption also exist. If a good confers external benefits on society it is known as a merit good. This means that a government may, therefore, encourage citizens to consume more of it, up to what is termed the socially optimal level. Examples of merit goods would be education and exercise. It may be that people who consume less, those in socio-economic groups C2, D and E in Chapter 4, do so through lack of income.

One way the government can promote greater consumption is, again, through law. An example of this is compulsory 'free' secondary education until the age of 16. Another way is to reduce the cost of consumption, again through a subsidy, thus reducing each individual's cost of consuming the marginal unit of the good or service. Local authority public libraries are an example of this. Of course, this assumes that the authorities know each individual's marginal benefit curve. A third way is to encourage consumption through some form of public information service, e.g. to stress the benefits of regular exercise and an effective diet to combat the risks of having a stroke or a heart attack; or to promote the use of the Internet.

For external diseconomies of consumption, again legal action may be employed, e.g. to combat someone who persistently has large bonfires; or a public information campaign to combat the effects on children in the womb of expectant mothers who smoke. The consumption of goods which are detrimental to society are known as merit bads. Taxation may also be employed by a government to deter consumption of merit bads. For example a differential vehicle licence tax is currently used by the government which depends on the size of a car's engine to combat the effects of car pollution; green or unleaded petrol is cheaper than lead replacement petrol; and tobacco products are heavily taxed to deter the effects of smoking, both on the individual and on other people affected by his/her smoking.

What of public and quasi-public goods? These provide benefits to many people and as such are often provided by the government or local authority, financed from taxation or council tax revenues. This is to avoid one difficulty with public goods, which is known as the free rider problem. If it is possible to consume the service without paying for it there will be a temptation to do so, i.e. some people will choose to be free-riders. For example, an unadopted road with large potholes is made up by its residents. Some residents refuse to contribute to the cost yet still benefit from the new surface; nor can they be excluded from access to their own properties. Of course, if only two or three people were willing to contribute to the new road surface then the resurfacing might not take place at all, with the attendant social disadvantages that might have, e.g. easy access by ambulances to residents who are taken ill.

Conclusions

So, what can we conclude from this brief analysis? This chapter is looking at markets in the real world and we have learned that they do not always function as predicted. Rather market failure occurs, resulting in resources not being allocated optimally, because of the existence of external costs and external benefits in the production process. Imperfect information may be one cause of market failure. Market structures, such as a monopoly or cartel, which inhibit free or perfect competition so that businesses do not produce their goods or services at minimum possible cost, also cause market failure. Additionally, the existence of economies and diseconomies of production and consumption, and public goods and quasi-public goods cause market failure.

The implication of market failure is the need for the government to intervene. It does this, for example, by using taxation and subsidies to try and restore social equity. Other options are legal measures and persuasion.

Self testing questions

1 Explain, in your own words, why market failure occurs.

2 What do you understand by externalities? List as many examples as you can.

3 What is a public good? Explain its two main characteristics and give three examples of public goods.

4 (a) What are merit goods? Give two examples. (b) What do you think merit bads are? Can you think of any examples of merit bads?

5 What will be the optimum level of output in a market: (a) when externalities are ignored? (b) when externalities are allowed for. Why do your answers differ?

6.4 Input markets

Here we can examine the market for inputs or factors of production, which are also real world markets concentrating, for illustration, on the labour market. The reader wishing to explore all the factor markets is referred to other texts at the end of this chapter.

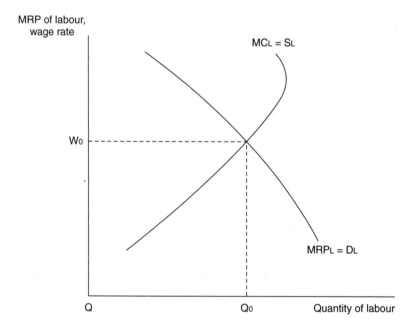

Figure 6.8 The marginal revenue product and marginal cost of labour curves.

Whereas products are demanded in their own right, the demand by businesses for an input is a derived demand, i.e. it is not wanted for its own sake but for the products it helps produce. Programmers, for example, are wanted for the software they write, not because they are nice or attractive people.

As a business employs more labour, other things being equal, i.e. the quantities of fixed inputs being unchanged in the short term, so the product or output of each extra person employed (called the marginal physical product of labour or MPP) declines, because of the law of diminishing returns (see Chapter 3, Section 3.1). The change in total revenue earned by the business from the output of the marginal person employed is called the Marginal Revenue Product (MRP) of labour. It is measured by MPP multiplied by the price of the product. Like the MPP, this will decline the more people are employed. This is shown in Figure 6.8 for the labour market as a whole, i.e. the summation of all businesses employing labour; as can be seen the MRP curve slopes downwards and to the right, and is also the demand curve for labour.

A business will hire or demand labour so long as the value of the output of the last person is greater than or equal to the wage rate he/she earns. Therefore, a quantity of labour Q_0 will be employed at a wage rate of W_0, which also equals the MRP.

MC_L is the market supply curve of labour and has, largely, the same shape as the supply curves we met in the markets for goods and services, i.e. output. This says that the supply of labour will be determined by the wage rate offered – the higher the wage rate the more people will be willing to work. However, the reader will note that it bends back to the left. As wages get very high people can have a good living standard and work fewer hours; in other words they substitute leisure for income, working fewer hours.

Where the two curves intersect determines the equilibrium wage rate in the labour market – W_0 in Figure 6.8, with quantity Q_0 employed. If there are any changes in the factors determining the demand for and/or supply of labour then the curves will shift to left or right in the same way that curves shift in the output markets.

The elasticity of demand for labour will be determined by a number of factors including:

1   The elasticity of the demand for the output produced by labour; the more elastic the demand for the product the more elastic the demand for labour will be.
2   The extent to which other factors, particularly capital, including communication and information technology, can be substituted for labour, i.e. the more elastic their supply curves (the easier it is to substitute them for labour), the more elastic the demand for labour will be.
3   The more wages account for total costs of production, the more elastic will be the demand for labour, since businesses will want to substitute other cheaper factors.

4 The longer the time period under consideration; since a longer period allows more time for new substitutes for labour to be developed.

The elasticity of supply of labour will be determined by:

1 The ease of changing jobs; the easier and cheaper it is to do so, the more elastic the supply curve will be. As one gets older it can become more difficult to change jobs because of family and social ties keeping one in a particular location, known as geographical immobility of labour, or because training is required which takes time and loss of income from the job one has given up, known as occupational immobility of labour.
2 The time period; the longer the time period under consideration is the more elastic will the supply curve for labour be.

How useful is this theory in explaining business economics?

In reality, labour markets do not function as precisely as this theory, known as neo-classical theory, suggests, which has drawn criticism of it. There are a number of reasons why neo-classical theory does not fully represent the real world of business economics.

Inadequacies of neo-classical theory

The theory assumes that the market will produce one price for labour in a particular activity, e.g. shop assistants, or draftsmen, but this is not so. Labour is not homogenous; different people have different levels of skills, aptitudes and self-promotion, and will therefore have very different MRP curves, and hence earn different wages.

Even where workers have the same skills, they may earn different wages for similar work because the labour market is imperfect. Education is one factor determining earnings levels, graduates earning more during their working lives than those with only 'A' levels, for example, due to their higher marginal revenue product. Additionally, age brings experience; up to the age of approximately forty, one might expect an older person to earn more than a younger person doing the same work. However, age makes workers more vulnerable in the labour market since it is equated with higher costs which can be cut if younger workers are employed instead (ageism is not illegal, whereas racism and sexism are).

The other way to increase labour productivity, and hence MRP, is through higher levels of business investment. The more capital equipment a worker has, the greater should be his/her productivity; the UK, with low per capita investment levels compared with Germany and Japan, finds its workforce has lower productivity levels.

Additionally, the labour market is imperfect in that not every worker has total knowledge of job opportunities, or of what others earn; this is particularly so in many businesses where performance related pay is used so that the workforce are encouraged to be secretive about what they earn. This militates against the existence of one wage for a particular job or level of skills.

The role of unions

Trade unions have a significant impact on the labour market. Through collective bargaining on behalf of their members, and the threat of strikes, they are able to secure higher wage levels, better working conditions and hence better living standards than if workers bargained individually. Hence, members of unions normally earn higher wages than non-union workers, such as office cleaners etc. Of course, if a union demands wages higher than the market equilibrium in a competitive market then the supply of labour will exceed the demand and there will be unemployment. This is discussed more fully in Chapter 10, Section 10.1. The reader should note that union power has diminished very substantially in the last twenty years, partly through Conservative governments' anti-union legislation, partly through the changing nature of work from manufacturing to services where union power is much less, partly because more British now perceive themselves as middle class whereas trade unionism was associated with working class struggles, and partly through the disappearance of nationalised industries which were major centres of trade unionism. High unemployment in the early 1980s and 1990s also hit union membership very hard so that most unions have now shed their previous confrontational attitudes and see themselves as co-operating with management to some extent to help promote better opportunities for the business as much as their members alone.

In 1996, 31 per cent of all employees belonged to a trade union; 35 per cent of all full time workers belonged and 20 per cent of all part time workers. Membership figures for the five leading unions are shown in Table 6.3.

Inequalities between the sexes

The other area where there are clear differences in earnings for similar work is between men and women. In spite of legislation in the mid 1970s, such as the Equal Pay Act 1970, and the Sex Discrimination Act 1975, women in the UK still earn, on average, only 80 per cent of what men earn. A recent study by the European Commission suggested that these disparate wage rates are unlikely to equalise before 2025. So why do women earn less?

Table 6.3 Top five trade unions by membership, 1995.

Ranking	Union	Membership nos
1	Unison – Public Services Union	1 355 000
2	Transport and General Workers Union	897 000
3	GMB	740 000
4	Amalgamated Engineering & Electrical Union	726 000
5	Manufacturing Science & Finance Union	446 000

Source: Labour Force Survey. The Office for National Statistics, © Crown Copyright 2000.

One answer is that many management posts are occupied by men who therefore make the rules to favour men, although this is changing. Because women have time off work to bear children, some businesses prefer men. Again, many women work part time, fitting in work around school hours; so they fill supermarket shelves, work on the tills etc. Part time rates of pay in these jobs are low. Other types of work such as cleaning, catering and hotel work, home working making toys etc. also earn low rates of pay, partly because they are low skilled and partly because these jobs are non-unionised. However, this is changing. More women are now securing management posts and, for example, more women are now qualifying as solicitors than men. Additionally, women are perceived by employers as cheaper, more adaptable and with better inter-personal skills, making them increasingly more attractive to employ than men. The minimum wage has also improved many workers' lots.

In conclusion, marginal productivity theory does explain the outcome of business decisions in the labour market even if businesses do not consciously equate MC of labour and MRP of labour as textbooks suggest. They are still trying to achieve the point of maximum profitability, assuming that is their objective, even if they do not precisely know the MRP of each extra worker employed. Indeed it is extremely unlikely, in a big organisation, that managers would look at an individual worker's output if an extra 300 staff are taken on to build a new a fighter plane or a new model of car. However, in a sense the whole 300 new staff are the 'marginal unit of labour' and managers will look at their output in terms of its contribution to the construction of the new plane or car.

6.5 The minimum wage

Background

A minimum wage (or more accurately two minimum wages) was introduced by the Labour government on 1 April 1999 at a rate of £3.60 per
hour for workers over 21 years of age, and £3 per hour for 18–21 year olds;
this was raised by 10p per hour in 2000. At the time, the Low Pay Unit
estimated that 2 million people (8.3 per cent of the work force) would gain
from this, the main beneficiaries being women, especially in social care (e.g.
child care) and cleaning jobs. Other areas where there is traditionally low
pay, and which would benefit, were young people (200 000); hospitality
(295 000); and retail (300 000).

Arguments for introducing a minimum wage

Many arguments were advanced for a minimum wage in the UK. These
included:

1   Social justice – market forces may drive the equilibrium wage to levels
    too low for the work force to subsist. There is, therefore, a need for
    government intervention on equity grounds to protect weak members
    of the work force such as the poorly qualified, immigrants and women
    part time workers.
2   It is argued that if you pay people more they can increase their consump-
    tion of products, thus increasing total or aggregate demand in the
    economy. To meet this, businesses will produce more, leading to
    increased economic growth. Germany has grown, since the Second
    World War, on the basis of being a high earning and high spending
    economy.
3   A minimum wage is common throughout Western Europe and rein-
    forces the Social Chapter of the Treaty of Maastricht, which sought to
    identify the benefits accruing to consumers from the Single Market,
    rather than merely to businesses. In the past, the UK has been viewed
    as a low pay 'McJobs economy', where the majority of people will under-
    take low skilled, low pay jobs such as working for McDonalds. Low
    wages also force workers into the black economy, e.g. working in the
    building trade for cash in hand, or encourage workers to resort to
    unlawful employment practices.
4   Income inequalities between rich and poor have increased since 1979
    in the UK, although not as markedly as in the US. During Ronald
    Reagan's presidency the 'trickle down' theory of wealth creation was
    advanced, which argued that if the rich become even richer it would
    cause the wealth created to 'trickle downwards', making poorer people

better off. In reality this has not worked; there is therefore the need for a minimum wage to redress this.

5   Since the abolition of minimum wage councils in 1993, evidence showed that wages in some industries had declined, often to below what might reasonably be defined as subsistence level wages.

Arguments against introducing a minimum wage

1   Markets which are deregulated, i.e. without government restrictions, function nearer to the theoretical models of markets discussed earlier in this book, as typified by the UK and the US, as opposed to the more regulated model of continental European economies. Resources, which include labour, will be allocated more efficiently. If wages fall sufficiently, as opposed to the fall being restricted by a minimum wage, labour will be sufficiently cheap for employers to want to hire it, hence reducing unemployment. (However, it should be noted that many American states have minimum wages.)

2   Unemployment and low earnings, two sides of the same problem, are due to the skills gaps between the working well qualified, and hence well paid, on the one hand and the low skilled on the other, who may work for low wages or not work at all. Rather, improved education and training is what is needed. The OECD (the Organisation for Economic Cooperation and Development) identified the UK's poor position regarding this when it looked at otherwise increasing UK competitiveness.

3   Introducing a minimum wage above the market or equilibrium rate harms British competitiveness as firms pass on higher labour costs as higher prices. This leads to inflationary price increases and the government will have to pursue other economic policies to offset this, such as lowering the value of Sterling against other currencies, and/or raising interest rates. Additionally, competitiveness also depends on such issues as the level of investment in the economy and the level of R&D expenditure.

4   There is the problem of deciding what is the correct minimum wage. The higher the minimum wage the more impact it might be assumed to have on unemployment and declining competitiveness. Before the introduction of the minimum wage, debate in the UK ranged between £3.50 and £4.15 per hour. Business economists do not have a clear answer to this issue of what is the appropriate minimum wage.

5   A minimum wage will not help the poorest 7–10% of the working population, since they do not work anyway.

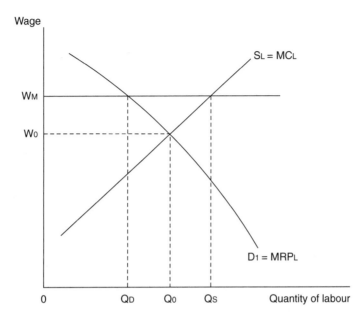

Figure 6.9 The introduction of a minimum wage.

Economic analysis

Firstly, we assume that each worker has broadly similar skills. Figure 6.9 shows a perfectly competitive labour market where the market clears, i.e. there is equilibrium giving the wage of W_0 and quantity of labour Q_0.

The government now introduces a minimum wage. If this were below the equilibrium level the former would have no effect since the market will automatically go to equilibrium, which is higher than the minimum wage. This would be an example of a maximum price or price ceiling and is normally used, for example, when a government wishes to keep essential commodities such as bread and the rent for housing at levels which poor people can afford.

So, let us set the minimum wage at W_M, i.e. above the equilibrium rate. This is known as a price floor since the minimum wage cannot fall below this. For those who previously were receiving the lower equilibrium wage there is a clear gain; individually they are better off. However, looking at the whole economy, we can see that employers only wish to employ Q_D of labour whereas the labour force offers Q_S. Therefore, there is forced, or involuntary unemployment of Q_D–Q_S.

In the short term, therefore, the labour market may not be in equilibrium due to inflexibility introduced by the minimum wage, nor can the wage rate fall to clear it. In the long term, we may see the demand curve for labour shift to the left. The increased cost of producing each extra unit of output will lead to less of the product which is produced, being sold.

In turn this will lead to greater involuntary unemployment. Additionally, to minimise costs, capital will be substituted for labour where feasible, causing still greater involuntary unemployment.

Of course there are qualifications to the above analysis. Firstly, the amount of involuntary unemployment depends how high above the equilibrium wage the minimum wage is set. It also assumes that markets are perfect which they are not, e.g. as noted before people are not homogeneous; workers and employers do not have perfect knowledge of all wage rates, job vacancies etc. in the market; and there are transaction costs in moving from one job to another.

It should also be noted that the earnings gap between skilled and unskilled workers is likely to increase in future due to fundamental changes in technology and global competition.

Following the introduction of the minimum wage in the UK

At the time a variety of arguments were advanced for and against the introduction of the minimum wage. George Bain, an economist and Vice Chancellor of Queens University, Belfast, and the chairperson of the independent advisory Low Pay Commission argued that it could take up to three years before the minimum wage was 'settled down into the UK labour market'. He argued that the regulations drawn up by the DTI were over-complicated and that success would depend on 'self-enforcement' by employers.

Bain saw the commission as operating like the public sector pay review bodies, with regular reporting, but said it could not deal with specific queries made by individuals or companies. There is no separate enforcement body for the minimum wage; rather the Inland Revenue and the combined Contributions Agency ensure that rates are upheld. Employees who think they are not being paid enough can go to an employment tribunal or civil court to seek to remedy this.

One main problem for employers was that the regulations underpinning the minimum wage were very complex, creating a significant burden on business and its competitiveness. This was further exacerbated by the employment relations reforms, including the EU directive on the maximum length of the working week (the working time directive).

Bain argued that the minimum wage would have little impact on unemployment and that pressures from other workers seeking to restore pay differentials would be minimal. The commission also argued there would only be a limited effect on inflation, with the Bank of England arguing for a 0.4 per cent increase over two years. It said the national wage bill would rise by only 0.6 per cent and there would be a 'broadly neutral' effect on public finances. By early 2000, evidence collected by the Commission suggested that the £3.60 minimum wage had had little effect on employment or inflation.

This is interesting as Business Strategies, a group of economic consultants, had argued in 1999 that 80 000 jobs would be lost over two to three years, with businesses having to reduce profits or raise prices to pay for the extra labour costs. These included 25 000 job losses in the hospitality sector and 9000 in the retail sector. In contrast, the Engineering Employers Federation argued that what was needed was not a minimum wage but rather a workforce with improved skills to be able to fill some of the job vacancies for skilled workers.

Empirical evidence

Economists test their theories to determine their validity – yet in a dynamic world this is often difficult to undertake. Therefore, previous evidence was somewhat inconclusive as to the impact of a minimum wage.

In 1992, Paul Gregg, an economist at the National Institute for Economic and Social Research, forecast that Labour's proposal for a minimum wage would cost 170 000 jobs. However, subsequently in 1994, he argued that more recent research had invalidated this; a minimum wage of half male median earnings (£4 per hour in 1994, not applying to those under 21) would have no significant impact on jobs.

David Card and Paul Kreuger of Princeton University analysed the 1992 effect of New Jersey increasing the minimum wage from $4.25 to $5.05 per hour, whilst neighbouring Pennsylvania kept to $4.25. Regarding the fast food industry, they found that, with the introduction of the minimum wage, employment grew by 13 per cent more in New Jersey (NJ) than in Pennsylvania. However, these findings were subsequently attacked by David Neumark of Michigan State University and William Wascher of the Federal Reserve. They were critical of Card and Kreuger's methodology; they found that the 19 per cent increase in the minimum wage in NJ reduced employment in fast food industry by 4.6 per cent, rather than it growing by over 13 per cent as the former had argued.

Subsequent, research by Stephen Machin and Alan Manning of the London School of Economics related to nursing homes on the South Coast of England. They found that wage rates could rise by 15% (which would, therefore, include the introduction of a minimum wage) without jobs being lost.

Therefore, overall the evidence is not conclusive. What can be said from the research is that, at particular times and in particular jobs, a minimum wage might not destroy jobs.

Conclusions

1   Low wages and worse, unemployment, have an economic cost to society though their social effects. These include: tax evasion through the black economy; benefit fraud; increased mental and physical health problems,

and their cost to the National Health Service, associated with low pay; increased crime; less incentive to work hard and produce better quality output. If a minimum wage can raise the living standards of the lowest paid then it must help the quality of the work force, but needs reinforcing with other aspects, discussed above.

2 Adopting a minimum wage does not have to mean that the benefits of labour market deregulation are lost. It depends on the rate at which the minimum wage is set and who is excluded from it. The higher the minimum wage the more impact on the macro economy it will have, with implications for UK competitiveness. However, the Labour government also had to consider social priorities.

Self testing questions

Self Testing Questions

1 What is the difference between the Marginal Physical Product (MPP) and the Marginal Revenue Product (MRP) of labour?

2 Draw a diagram showing the determination of wages in an industry. How useful is this theory in reality?

3 Why do different people earn different wages for doing the same work?

4 Will the introduction of a minimum wage in an industry cause demand for the industry's product to fall?

5 In your own words write a briefing paper (one side of A4) presenting the case for or against the implementation of a minimum wage.

6.6 Summary of chapter

Having considered the theory of markets earlier in this book, Chapter 6 has looked at the operation of markets in the real world. The importance and the significance of elasticity of demand and supply were considered, including why businesses need to know price elasticity of demand for their products. This, we saw, had major implications for their pricing policies. We also considered income and cross-price elasticities of demand and elasticity of supply.

We then looked at the issue of why markets do not always work as theory predicts, i.e. why there is market failure. The significance of external costs and benefits (externalities) was explored including their impact on deciding the optimum level of output which should occur in a market. The use of taxes and subsidies was also discussed.

The labour market was discussed as another example of real world markets including how wages are determined and why theory and reality diverge. The introduction of a minimum wage was introduced as a case study to show government intervention, on the grounds of equity, to correct perceived inequalities.

6.7 Further questions

Further Questions

1   Do you think demand for the following would be price elastic or inelastic? Explain your answers. (a) BMW cars; (b) white sliced bread; (c) bottles of table wine; (d) newspapers.

2   What would be your attitude to a price increase for your product if the price elasticity of demand for your product was: (a) elastic; (b) inelastic?

3   Would supply of the following be elastic or inelastic? Explain your answers. (a) Home grown potatoes; (b) potatoes in general; (c) nuclear power stations; (d) newspapers; (e) houses.

4   If pollution is so harmful to the world why do governments allow it to continue? What measures could a government use to reduce it?

5   If a minimum wage is an example of a price floor give an example of a price ceiling. Draw a demand and supply diagram to illustrate this.

6.8 Further reading

Atkinson, B., Livesey, F. and Milward, B. (eds) (1998). *Applied Economics*. Basingstoke: Macmillan.

Begg, D., Fischer, S. and Dornbusch, R. (1997). *Economics*, 5th edition. London: McGraw Hill.

Cooke, A. (1994). *The Economics of Leisure and Sport*. London: Routledge.

Harris, N. (1999). *European Business*, 2nd edition. Basingstoke: Macmillan Business.

Labour Force Survey, Office of National Statistics (published annually).

Le Grand, J., Propper, J. and Robinson, R. (1992). *The Economics of Social Problems*, 3rd edition. Basingstoke: Macmillan.

Lewis, R. (1992). *Recent Controversies in Political Economy*, Chapter 8. London: Routledge.

Parkin, M. (1999). *Economics*, 5th edition. Wokingham: Addison Wesley.

Sloman, J. (1999). *Economics*, 4th edition. Hemel Hempstead: Prentice Hall Europe.

The Environment Agency: http://www.environment-agency.gov.uk/

The Low Pay Commission: http;//www.lowpay.gov.uk/

Microsoft: http://www.Microsoft.com

Office of Fair Trading: http://www.oft.gov.uk/

Chapter 7

Competition and competitive strategy

Learning Outcomes

After completing this chapter the reader will be able to:
● use theoretical models as a framework to explore market structures and concentration;
● evaluate the economic implications of different market structures;
● analyse business strategies in relation to market structures.

7.1 Business strategies: the structure–conduct–performance paradigm. Porter's five forces model

'Eggstra' interest guarantees more customers

Synopsis   This case study explores Prudential's move into Internet banking with Egg. The key characteristics of the case study are:
1 banking and insurance markets increasingly overlap;
2 the existence of the Internet has lowered entry barriers to banking;
3 Internet banking is much more cost effective.

Case Study

In recent years the overlap between the three formerly discreet areas of the financial services sector – banking, insurance and building societies – have become increasingly blurred as each has moved into the others' activities. For years the high street banks – Barclays, HSBC, NatWest etc. – have sold insurance and, to some extent, affected insurance companies' profits, although they have never secured more than 10 per cent of the market. Where they did succeed was in taking 70 per cent of the money released by maturing insurance policies.

By the mid 1990s, insurers had retaliated, offering direct savings accounts to offset the impact of bancassurers, as banks who sell insurance are known, on their profits. This was extended by the subsequent insurance company moves into Internet banking, especially the Prudential with Egg in 1998. This attracted over £6 billion of deposits in its first year through offering depositors high interest rates, and also loaned out £1.5 billion. Initially, customers could access their account by telephone or via the Internet but, to keep operating costs low, new customers may only use the Internet.

When Egg was created, it was estimated to cost £200 million to establish and that it would break even in 2001. Its advantage over traditional banks is the lack of a high cost branch network to establish or maintain, with the associated costs of insurance, maintenance, business rates and staffing. For comparison, the average cost of a transaction at a branch bank is £1.20; the same transaction through the Internet at Egg costs 10p. Consequently, the entry barriers to banking, previously very high, are now realised to be relatively low.

Egg's low operational costs underpin its strategy of maximising its customer base and hence market share. Egg initially offered very high deposit rates compared with its competitors, attracting many customers; as these are lowered to boost Egg profits, the bank will find it harder to retain these. However, British bank customers are more likely to divorce than change their banks, so inertia will help Egg retain many customers. Additionally, if in future Egg can sell higher profit margin products to its customers then it can provide a wide range of financial services and become very profitable.

Business strategy

Chapter 2, Section 2.2 discussed business strategy, i.e. a plan to achieve the defined medium to long term business objectives. Prudential's strategy is to successfully establish a telephone/Internet banking arm, Egg. In turn, objectives are what the business intends to have achieved by the end of the specified period. One objective for Egg is to break-even by 2001; others, which are commercially confidential, will include target figures for the number of Egg customers, market share etc. These objectives provide direction for the business, whereas its strategy is the plan for achieving them.

The development of Egg, and the use of Internet banking, has certainly helped to update the Prudential's stuffy and old-fashioned image, as typified for many years by the image of 'the man from the Pru' collecting weekly insurance payments from households. It presents the business as being at the cutting edge of modern technology, with all the implications this has for effective competition.

Market power and the impact on competitors and consumers

In all market structures, much business strategy is concerned with gaining competitive advantage over rivals. Where a market is dominated by a few large firms, such as supermarkets, or in a market where one firm is dominant, such as computer software, excluding potential competitors to maintain or extend market share is fundamental. This may involve collaboration between rivals or the erection of entry barriers making it costly or difficult for new businesses to enter existing markets, e.g. the development costs of new products in the pharmaceuticals industry. Where businesses do not collude they will compete on both price and non-price grounds. Therefore, competition is fundamental to lower prices for consumers and normal profits for businesses. The more competition is inhibited the more the firms in a market can exercise their power to the detriment of rivals and consumers.

Market power also affects consumers. A market dominated by a few large sellers, or one business, can charge excessive prices, as evidenced by the 1999 Competition Commission investigation into supermarket pricing. Although the main supermarket chains do not overtly collude, but rather compete, they still achieve profit margins of 4–6 per cent, far higher than US or Continental European supermarkets. This has resulted in food prices being higher than in other countries. In the extreme case, a sole seller of a good can, in theory, charge any price it wishes because of its total market control. Consequently, governments have passed laws and introduced regulatory bodies to limit such producer power and protect the interests of consumers. Chapter 8 discusses this in more detail.

In conclusion a business's strategy is likely, to seek to increase its market power to increase its influence on both its competitors, actual and potential, and on its consumers. Of course, the converse may also happen; a customer may be so powerful as to exercise influence over suppliers. An example of this would be the government placing defence contracts with armaments manufacturers.

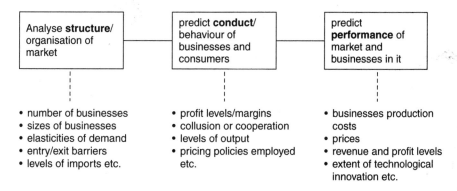

Figure 7.1 The structure–conduct–performance model.

The structure–conduct–performance (S–C–P) model of analysing market structures

Since market power is important for a business to influence competitors and consumers, the business economist needs a theoretical framework to analyse businesses and the markets in which they sell their products. From this he/she can predict the likely behaviour or conduct of the buyers and sellers. The business economist can then forecast how the market may perform over time. Together, these three stages are known as the structure–conduct–performance (S–C–P) model or methodology; this will be used to explore different types of market structure in the UK today.

Structure

Analysing the structure or organisation of a market requires the business economist to examine a number of different factors such as:

● the number of businesses operating in the market;
● their relative sizes;
● elasticities of demand for the goods they sell;
● their levels and types of production costs;
● the extent of entry barriers preventing new firms from joining the market to supply products or exit barriers preventing existing businesses leaving the market. Entry barriers include: product differentiation which wins consumer loyalty and makes it hard for new firms to win customers; absolute cost advantages such as a cheap source of inputs; and economies of scale leading to lower production costs.

Economists also distinguish between entry barriers deliberately erected by firms and innocent entry barriers. Absolute cost advantages may be innocent, e.g. firms already in an industry will have cost advantages over new entrants who have to establish sources of supply, retail outlets etc. Economies of scale are also innocent. If businesses have to be of a certain size to be profitable, i.e. have a large minimum efficient scale of plant (the lowest point on a firm's long term average cost curve), such as the car industry, then a new firm entering the market will increase market supply substantially. This will drive down prices to the extent that the newcomer may not be able to survive economically. Product differentiation is obviously deliberate:

- the extent of overlap with other markets;
- levels of imports, since foreign imports are substitutes for domestically produced goods;
- the speed of technological change, since this changes the market's structure, as can be seen above with the advent of telephone/Internet banking and so on.

Conduct

Next, the business economist must consider the conduct or behaviour of both businesses and customers as they meet together to buy and sell in that market. The smaller the number of firms the more likely they are to be able to exercise control over market prices and entry barriers, make monopoly profits etc.

A number of factors or variables need to be considered at this stage. These include: profit margins; the extent to which businesses in the market cooperate (collude) with each other or whether they vigorously compete; what sort of pricing policies they employ (see Chapter 4, Section 4.3); what levels of output are produced, i.e. the extent to which economies of scale/scope can be achieved; how marketing is employed, including the extent of branding and advertising; the extent of R&D programmes and so on.

This is very wide-ranging and some data will be much harder to obtain than other partly because of its commercial confidentiality. In this case substitute or proxy data have to be employed which are second best but will still enable informed opinions to be reached.

Performance

Once the structure and conduct of a market have been determined the business economist can make predictions about how the market, and the businesses in it, will perform. These predictions will again encompass a range of variables including the business's costs of production, prices, revenue and profit levels, the extent of technological innovation etc. In this way, a picture can be built up as to how the market will behave in the foreseeable future, i.e. the short to medium term.

Porter's five forces model

The discussion of market power and the structure–conduct–performance methodology leads us further along the path which says that if a market is to perform its functions effectively, i.e. achieve allocative efficiency, then it needs to be competitive. The issue of competition was discussed by Michael Porter in his five forces model, which is discussed here.

Porter argued that competition in an industry is determined by five main forces:

1 The threat of new entrants. This is determined by the height of entry barriers. The higher these are the greater the competitive advantage existing firms in the industry have.
2 The intensity of rivalry between direct competitors. This relates to the degree of concentration in an industry. As noted, an oligopolistic market with a high degree of concentration (few suppliers) will mean less competition if there is collusion between its members, such as a cartel. This will enable the businesses to influence prices charged and the quality of their products. If the market is non-collusive the firms will compete by product/service differentiation to maintain price levels and competitive advantage.
3 The pressure of substitute products. The greater the range of substitute products the more their impact on a firm's ability to maximise profits, with the effects on elasticity of demand of the products.
4 The bargaining power of buyers. The greater the power of buyers in influencing price, quality of product, or service, the greater the impact this will have on corporate profitability.
5 The bargaining power of suppliers. This relates to the number of suppliers of inputs to the businesses producing outputs. The more input providers that exist the stronger the position of the output producer in terms of its ability to demand price reductions, improved quality etc. (Porter, 1980).

In part, this links back to the structure section of the previous structure–conduct–performance methodology. Additionally, as was seen in Chapter 2, Section 2.2, when Porter's value chain was considered, it was argued that a business can secure two types of competitive advantage over its business rivals – producing its products more cheaply than others (cost advantage) and/or differentiating them from other businesses' activities.

Porter also discusses competitive scope in the context of the value chain. Competitive scope relates to the range of a firm's activities including:

1 which segments of the industry it covers, i.e. the varieties of products produced and the range of buyers served;
2 integration – how far activities are performed in-house rather than buying in from independent firms;
3 the geographic markets it supplies – the range of regions or countries the business supplies to;
4 how it co-ordinates competition in related markets.

A firm may seek to broaden its competitive scope or range of activities by pursuing these internally or by entering into a coalition, such as a joint venture, with independent firms. The optimal value chain for competing in different arenas, and how the chains are related, will define the boundaries of the business unit, which is Porter's term for the particular sector of an industry in which a business operates, e.g. budget airlines within the airline industry. These issues will be explored more fully in Chapter 8.

In conclusion, we have a framework for analysing business performance. Business strategy seeks to gain competitive advantage over its rivals, and this may be achieved on cost or product differentiation grounds. The structure–conduct–performance methodology enables us to analyse markets to predict their behaviour and future performance; Porter's five forces model, which links to structure and conduct, enables us to analyse market structures in terms of what determines competition in them.

Self testing questions

1 What are the main differences between a business's strategy and its operations? Give examples from any business of which you have knowledge.

2 Undertake a brief PESTLE analysis for the development of Internet banking.

3 Write a brief summary of what is meant by the structure–conduct–performance model and explain its main strengths and weaknesses for analysing market performance.

4 Pick any industry of which you have knowledge and test the extent to which Porter's five forces apply to it. How competitive is this industry?

5 Analyse the same business in terms of its competitive scope.

7.2 Oligopolies; competition and collusion strategies. Porter's generic strategies for gaining competitive advantage

Types of market structures

The reader is referred back to Figure 1.3 for a reminder of the different types of market structure. Business economics distinguishes these by the number of businesses supplying each market.

Oligopolies

To remind the reader, an oligopoly market structure is one in which a few large businesses dominate. Some small businesses may also exist in the market but will have such little economic power as to be negligible in terms of their market influence and market share. For example, the high street banks dominate the building societies sector of the financial services market. They include both traditional banks such as Barclays and also the new banks, which were formerly building societies but which have demutualised and converted, e.g. Abbey National, Prudential and Halifax. Nonetheless, small building societies remain and will compete but to a very limited extent. Filling stations are another example of an oligopoly.

The importance of an oligopoly is that whatever any one large business does will impact on the others, encouraging them to respond similarly. When one bank introduces a telephone banking system the others copy; when one opens on Sundays so do the others. Such businesses may compete with each other vigorously but usually through the branding and marketing of their services rather than prices, since price cuts are likely to be copied by the other businesses, whilst price rises are not, lest custom be lost. The other key characteristic of oligopoly is the existence of entry barriers to the industry.

There is the risk that businesses will decide competition is futile and that it would be better to share the market, agree common prices etc. This will enable them to exclude potential entrants by various barriers to maintain high profit levels. This is known as collusion and is illegal since it inhibits competition and harms consumer interests. In its extreme form, businesses may establish a formal agreement, known as a cartel, to monitor their collusion. Both the UK and the European Union (EU) have passed legislation to control the behaviour of businesses in oligopolistic markets. Chapter 8, Sections 8.3 and 8.4 discuss this in depth. The most likely circumstances for favouring collusion are when there are a limited number of firms, one of which is dominant; they have similar production methods and cost levels and these are generally known among the firms in the industry; another example is when products are fairly similar, permitting common prices to be established.

Internet book sales

Synopsis

This case study explores price-cutting wars among Internet booksellers. It identifies as key issues:

1 the need to make profits to survive long term;
2 how the actions of one firm will cause competitors to react similarly;
3 how non-Internet book sellers have had to respond to the threat to their traditional markets.

Case Study

In mid 1999, it was reported that Internet book price wars were intensifying as both Amazon.co.uk and then its rival uk.bol.com offered discounts of up to 50 per cent on a range of best selling books. Following the strategy of its US parent Amazon.com, Amazon.co.uk introduced discounts of 50 per cent on its top 40 books, as determined by BookWatch, the independent book information business. The discounts covered all of paperbacks and hardbacks, fiction and non-fiction. The only extra cost which the UK arm of Amazon.com charges is £1.95 to cover postage and packing for one book and 50p for each additional book. This is in spite of Amazon.co.uk not yet making a profit in the UK, nor being willing to say when it will, and in the US only gaining a 3 per cent market share of book sales.

These 50 per cent discounts replace discounts of 40 per cent already being offered by Amazon and are in response to an aggressive pricing strategy adopted by WH Smith's Internet book sales service, the aptly named WH Smith Online, which has halved the price of 20 best-sellers.

Traditional high street bookshops mostly have their own online operations, although at the time of writing it was not clear how precisely they would respond. Many operated a 'three for the price of two' scheme during the summer of 1999, whilst another scheme was £2 off the price of selected paperbacks. What is clearly happening, however, is that the gap between the online booksellers and the high street bookshops is narrowing.

The case study above, illustrates the very competitive nature of oligopoly. Although there are entry barriers to online book selling, these are not particularly high, as illustrated by the number of traditional or high street sellers establishing an Internet presence. Consequently, the division between exclusively online sellers and traditional sellers has blurred as the latter have adopted Internet selling as a strategy. As one business adopts new strategies to boost sales so others copy or try new strategies to gain competitive advantage – hence Amazon.co.uk's response to WH Smith Online halving the price of its 20 best sellers. What is interesting is that Amazon undertook such actions without regard to its lack of profitability but rather, it seems, merely for tactical reasons to better its competitors.

You wait at the bus stop for 20 minutes then four buses all come along together – and they all charge the same price!

Synopsis

This case study explores alleged collusion in an oligopolistic market. It identifies:

1 fixing prices and allocating market share as weapons to limit competition;
2 the impact on local citizens in terms of higher costs.

In late 1998 the Office of Fair Trading (OFT) accused Stagecoach of being involved in an agreement to fix prices and allocate market shares in the home-to-school bus services in the city of Kingston upon Hull. Stagecoach is the FTSE 100 (Financial Times Stock Exchange top 100 companies) transport group, which owns South West Trains, a rolling stock company and many bus companies. The agreement between Cleveland Transit, a Stagecoach subsidiary, and 12 other local bus operators was referred to the Restrictive Practice Court by OFT Director-General John Bridgeman, who is seeking to prevent the bus operators from putting the cartel into operation.

The OFT was advised of the proposed cartel by (Kingston upon) Hull City Council which said that the operators had met to discuss its putting the school bus services out to tender. There was evidence that the 13 local bus operators had secretly met in a local hotel and had agreed what prices they would bid for running the service and the bus routes for which each would tender. The OFT's legal director argued that cartels destroyed competition and that, if the tenders had been accepted, the alleged agreement would have caused higher costs to (Kingston upon) Hull City Council and possibly higher charges for council tax payers. She also said that under the new Competition Act, anti-competitive agreements such as these could lead to fines for the companies up to 10 per cent of their turnover.

Stagecoach, which in the past has been the subject of two Competition Act investigations and one reference to the Monopolies and Mergers Commission, responded that it was co-operating with the OFT investigation and also running its own internal investigation. A spokesman said 'we are not aware that we are involved in any price-fixing. We do not support cartels. The Stagecoach philosophy is one of competition.'

The second case study presents a different picture. Here it is alleged that a cartel was in the process of being established by transport operators to agree common transport prices and allocate market share, rather than compete and risk driving down prices to levels below those which are profitable. Collusion rather than competition was alleged to be the order of the day. If true, prices could be fixed by:

1 the dominant company in the thirteen since it is the most powerful; this is known as dominant firm price leadership;
2 the highest cost business, to ensure that all the companies make a profit, with the most efficient making the biggest;
3 the smallest company, since this appears the least threatening to the others;
4 The firm best able to analyse changes in costs and market demand over time, in the same way that a barometer monitors atmospheric pressure; hence it is known as barometric price leadership. This firm then alters its market price and the other firms in the industry will follow. Over the time the business assuming the function of the barometer may change.

The other key characteristic of oligopoly, entry barriers, is also demonstrated in the above case study. There would be no point in a new company seeking to gain a share of the Hull school bus market if the companies were operating market sharing. Additionally, the cost of establishing a bus fleet, although not creating very high entry barriers, will still deter some potential entrants.

In an extreme form, a cartel might involve revenue sharing between members according to some pre-agreed formula; or businesses which violate the cartel agreement might be fined, with the money then distributed to the other members.

So far this section has looked at practical examples of oligopolistic markets. We have used the structure–conduct–performance (S–C–P) methodology to examine:

1 The structure of such markets – a small number of large businesses; the existence of entry barriers; differentiated products through advertising, branding, price discounting etc.;

2 The conduct of such markets – either competition, with price discounting, or collusion, with price fixing. In the case of the Internet based booksellers the concern is to secure market share by low pricing; in the alleged case of the Hull bus companies the aim is to secure market share through collusion.

3 Performance – this is harder to analyse since the case studies have no commercially confidential data. Theory suggests, however, that businesses will make abnormal or monopoly profits in the long term through entry barriers and in the latter case study through alleged collusion. In the case of the Internet book selling, although monopoly profits will not be made initially, if the main businesses can drive the others out of the market through developing customer loyalty or through economies of scale permitting lower prices, then it may be possible to achieve high profit levels. However, the low entry barriers in the case of the Internet booksellers suggests that, currently, minimal profits, if any, are being made. Porter's five forces model suggests that Internet book selling is very competitive for an oligopolistic market. This is because there is always the threat of new entrants, there is intense rivalry between direct competitors, and there are close substitutes in the form of books sold through bookshops, as well as audio books, videos etc.

Criticisms of the structure–conduct–performance methodology

The reader should note that in recent years the S–C–P methodology has come in for criticism from business economists. In particular, the chronological separation of structure and conduct has been argued to be unrealistic; rather they occur simultaneously. This is because how firms already in a market behave strategically (conduct) can affect entry by new businesses and, therefore, the market structure.

Secondly, although a market may, at first glance, have a particular structure, in practice it may behave differently from the way that basic economic theory predicts. For example, an oligopoly where there are very low or zero entry and exit barriers means that new firms could enter the market, set up businesses, siphon off the abnormal or monopoly profits, and then leave. The risk of this occurring may well deter the existing oligopolistic firms from exploiting their market power. In other words, they may be happy to accept only normal profits to discourage potential new entrants. These are known as contestable markets.

A third criticism of the S–C–P methodology is that it suggests that the way in which businesses behave is a direct function of the structure of the market in which they operate. However, in reality, this is not so. Businesses who experience similar competition levels may behave quite differently and achieve different levels of performance.

Nonetheless the S–C–P model still has some value in that it helps to distinguish the characteristics of each market even if its value is not as great as previously perceived.

We now need to look at the theory which has been developed by economists to try and predict exactly how oligopolists actually behave. Firstly, we consider game theory to explore the behaviour of oligopolists who do not collude.

Game theory

Every action by one oligopolist in a market will have an impact upon its competitors; in turn their reactions will have an effect on the first business. Therefore, the strategy which a business adopts, to gain market preeminence and power, recognises this inter-dependence or interaction. The strategy will describe every action a business can make in every possible situation. In a sense it is like a game of poker or chess, which is why the theory which explains business behaviour is known as game theory, each business being a player in the game. Businesses have to 'second-guess' how their rivals will react to their initial actions, to choose the best initial action. The best initial action will be the one which gives it the highest profits, or 'pay-off.'

As we have seen previously, businesses seek to be in equilibrium where profits are maximised, and markets seek to move to equilibrium, where demand equals supply. In game theory this equilibrium occurs when each business has chosen its best strategy, given the strategies chosen by all the other businesses (and which each business has accounted for in deciding its strategy). This situation is known as a Nash equilibrium. A table – known as a pay-off matrix – can be drawn up to show the pay-off for each business in a market as a result of every possible action by every other business or player in the market.

Dominant strategy

It may be the case that a business will adopt a strategy regardless of the actions of its rivals – this is known as a dominant strategy. Table 7.1 illustrates, for a simplified two business oligopolistic market, where each business (Arrow Computers and Betta Computers) adopts a dominant strategy. We assume that each firm: has similar production costs; assembles similar (homogeneous) products – personal computers – which are sold with colour printer, scanner, software and free Internet access; and faces a similar demand curve. They also seek to maximise profits. The only choice they have to make is which of two prices, £499.99 or £479.99, to charge for the PC plus add-ons.

Table 7.1 A dominant strategy pay-off matrix.

Betta Computers / Arrow Computers Price		£499.99	£479.99
	£499.99	Profits Arrow £50 million Betta £50 million	Profits Arrow £65 million Betta £30 million
	£479.99	Profits Arrow £30 million Betta £65 million	Profits Arrow £40 million Betta £40 million

If each firm charges £499.99 then they will each make a profit of £50 million, or £100 million in total – shown in the top left cell of the table. Now we assume that, independently, each firm is considering reducing the price of its PC to £479.99. If we examine Arrow Computers first, they need to contemplate how Betta Computers might react:

1   If Arrow Computers do not lower their price, and Betta Computers do, this will be the worst case scenario for Arrow, since Betta will take some of Arrow's potential customers. Let us assume that, in this scenario, Arrow's profits would fall to £30 million, whilst Betta's would rise to £65 million – as shown in the bottom left cell of Table 7.1.

2   If Arrow do lower the price of their PC, again the worst case scenario is if Betta also lowers its price. In this situation both companies' profits fall to £40 million each, as shown in the bottom right cell of the table. However, for Arrow, £40 million profit is more than the £30 million profit if it does not lower its price. Therefore, if its senior managers are cautious, i.e. risk averters, Arrow will lower the price of its computers to £479.99.

If we examine Betta Computers, its managers will argue in the same way, and therefore will also cut their computer prices to £479.99. Each business is following a maximin pricing strategy, i.e. it is adopting a strategy which will maximise its minimum possible profit.

If however, each business had senior managers who were optimists, i.e. risk takers rather than risk averters, they would assume that the other business would react in the most favourable way (to them) as a result of their actions. Therefore, Arrow Computers will adopt a strategy to achieve the highest possible (maximum) profit. This will occur if, when it lowers its price, Betta Computers do nothing. This can be seen in the top right cell, where Arrow Computers earn £65 million, and Betta Computers only £30 million. This strategy is known as a maximax strategy since Arrow seeks the maximum profits possible.

Again, of course, Betta may think in the same way. It would hope that Arrow does not respond to its price cut. In this case the relevant cell would be the bottom left one, where Betta makes £65 million profit and Arrow £30 million.

In the two cases we have examined here, both the maximin pricing strategy and the maximax pricing strategy have involved price cutting, rather than doing nothing. This is therefore called a dominant strategy game.

The final outcome, of course, is that both Arrow and Betta will be tempted to lower their computer prices to £479.99. They will therefore end up in the bottom right cell, making £40 million profit each. Both the maximin and the maximax strategies lead to price cutting; hence the name dominant strategy.

Had the two businesses colluded, and kept prices at £499.99, they could have stayed in the top left cell, each making £50 million profit. However, as each business would benefit individually by cutting its price, it will be tempted to do so. Cartels have sought to address this problem in the past by forming agreements, written or sometimes verbal, to work to the same mutually agreed rules, restricting future actions. This is known as a precommitment. However, since collusion is illegal, such an agreement could not be enforced in the courts, nor would the businesses wish others to know of its existence, as the case study on the alleged collusion between bus companies in Hull demonstrates. Nonetheless, colluding firms may agree to penalties or punishment so that if one firm lowers its prices or increases its output, the other will respond in a similar fashion.

The kinked demand curve

Another model to explain oligopoly where businesses do not collude is by the use of the kinked demand curve. This seeks to explain why there is price stability in oligopolistic markets even when there is no collusion. Figure 7.2 illustrates.

The diagram shows standard demand/average revenue and marginal revenue curves. However, the marginal revenue curve has a vertical discontinuity AB. Equilibrium is determined, as normal, by where MC = MR, which in turn determines the firm's output (Q_0) and price (P_0). As the business's production costs rise – denoted by the shift of the MC curve from MC_0 to MC_1 – price and output stay the same. In other words, the firm is absorbing the increased costs through reduced profit margins, rather than raise its price.

Only if costs continue to rise, so that the MC curve intersects MR above point A, will the firm be obliged to raise its price and reduce output. If other firms do not copy, the demand for this firm's product will fall signifi-

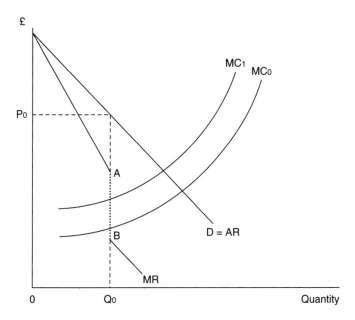

Figure 7.2 The kinked demand curve.

cantly, and rivals will gain. Therefore, there is no incentive to raise prices unless absolutely necessary. If the firm were to lower its price other firms would copy and there would be no gain. Therefore, the price of P_0 will be maintained if at all possible.

Although the kinked demand curve has the virtue of explaining price stability it also has a number of weaknesses. It does not explain how the firm reached the price level P_0 in the first place, only what happens if production costs change. Price changes are also costly: catalogues need to be changed; advertising is affected; revenue forecasting has to be undertaken again. Therefore, price stability may occur for this reason, rather than as a result of fear of retaliation from competitors.

Collusion

The issue of collusion has been discussed before. Here we present a theoretical model to explain such collusion. For illustration the reader is referred to Figure 3.4.

When businesses collude they effectively act as one firm – a monopolist. They therefore calculate the marginal cost and marginal revenue curves of the industry as a whole (the sum of the individual firms), which are shown as MC and MR in Figure 3.4. Where these intersect determines the optimum output (23 250 in Figure 3.4), and, in relation to the industry demand curve, the market price 'b', which the firms in the cartel will charge.

This will maximise the total output. The shares of the output and the resultant profits will then be negotiated between the members. Competition between the colluding businesses is still possible on a non-price basis, through advertising, branding, promotional campaigns etc.

If the colluding firms were all to increase their output, the market price would fall. But if only one firm in the cartel were to cheat on the agreement, and lower its price, it could sell more of the good, and hence increase its profits. In Figure 3.4, as long as other firms in the cartel do not cheat, the firm which does will perceive the demand curve it faces to be horizontal, i.e. perfectly elastic at the price it charges, which will be below market price 'b'. In other words, there is infinite demand by customers for its good at this price, so long as other cartel members do not lower their prices. If other cartel members do copy the cheating firm the market price will fall and the cartel will break up.

The cartel will, by collusion, have created entry barriers which newcomers will have to overcome. We distinguished earlier the concept of innocent entry barriers; clearly these are not that! Barriers include:

- product proliferation, e.g. two companies, Proctor & Gamble and Unilever dominate the UK soap powder market by 'flooding' it with a variety of different brands, thus making it very difficult for new firms to enter and gain market share;
- high research & development budgets;
- advertising and branding;
- price cutting wars, known as predatory pricing, where prices are lowered as newcomers enter the market to drive them out of business, then raised again subsequently;
- spare capacity, so that output can be quickly expanded to flood the market and hit potential new entrants. This is another example of pre-commitments of the type identified before, whereby a business commits resources demonstrating to potential entrants the threat they face if they try to enter.

Entry barriers need to be effective to prevent contestable markets, a situation in which outside (the market) firms can enter the market, cream off monopoly/abnormal profits, then leave again.

Porter's five forces, which determine competition in an industry, and which we considered earlier in this chapter, can be seen, therefore, to present an accurate picture of the strength of competition in an industry and how collusion, entry barriers etc. reduce this.

7.3 Monopolistic competition; how firms compete

Monopolistic competition in the real world

Case Study

The Soft Furnishings Centre

Sale
15% off all fabric (on production of this advert. Valid until 25/9/00).
Free measuring and estimates
Expert Fitting Service
Quality Curtains and Blinds Made to Measure

Just Ahead

25% off Everything with this voucher
Includes cuts, colours and perms

Posh Windows

The difference is, you'll see what we've done, not where we've been!

At **Posh Windows** the standards we maintain in caring for your home are as high as the quality of our products and service.

The last things that go into a Posh van and the first to come out are the dust sheets. Call us fussy, but sometimes, we even use them outside to cover your garden.

Attention to detail and the quality of our windows and conservatories make us different from most other window companies – we'd like to show you how different we are.

The largest window and conservatory showrooms in the UK.

Almost at the other end of the scale from oligopoly is a market structure with many small businesses. They offer broadly the same services or products but compete by differentiating these through advertising and branding to create slightly different consumer perceptions. As such, they may be local monopolies dominating a local area or market so there is not the interaction or interdependence between them seen in oligopoly. Hence, there are no opportunities to achieve scale economies. Newsagents are one example, the boundaries of a newsagent's market largely defined by how far the paperboys/girls can be expected to cycle in the morning or evening to deliver. Chinese takeaways are another example. The case study above

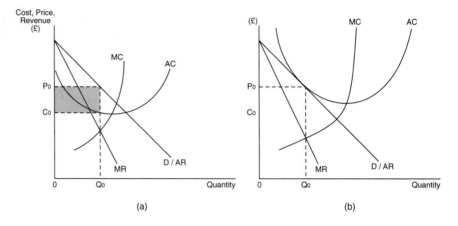

Figure 7.3 (a) Monopolistically competitive firm making supernormal profits in the short term. (b) Monopolistically competitive firm making normal profits in the long term.

gives further examples: a soft furnishings company, a hairdresser, and a double glazing company, all drawn from a local newspaper. They are good examples of many small businesses competing against each other in similar or overlapping activities.

This market structure is monopolistic competition. It is relatively low cost to enter whilst the expertise needed is not great, i.e. entry barriers are low. Products are differentiated as the advertising in the case study above shows, but essentially are very similar. Monopolistic competition is sometimes grouped with oligopoly under the collective heading of imperfect competition. Each firm faces the normal downward sloping demand curve and if supernormal (i.e. temporary) profits are being made by existing firms in the industry, then newcomers will enter until the supernormal profits fall to normal. These markets may at times be contestable if the newcomers then leave again. Figure 7.3 illustrates this.

Figure 7.3(a and b) show the situation for a monopolistically competitive firm. In Figure 7.3(a), in the short term the typical business is producing an output of Q_0, where MC = MR. The market price is determined by the demand/average revenue curve (D/AR) at this output and is shown as P_0. The cost of producing this output is shown by the business's average cost curve and the cost is C_0. Since this is lower than the price (and hence the AR curve), i.e. AR > AC, the firm is making supernormal profits which are shown by the shaded area.

Because there are low entry barriers, new businesses will enter this market to secure some of these, e.g. the development of the video rental business in the mid 1980s. As the new firms move in, existing businesses will find that their market share contracts – the demand curve facing the firm will shift to the left until eventually all firms, old and new, make only normal profits. This can be seen in Figure 7.3(b) where each firm is producing Q_0, where MC = MR, and making normal profits as shown by the fact that AC = AR, i.e. the AC curve is just touching the AR curve at the output of Q_0. It should be noted that this business is not operating at optimum efficiency since it is not at the lowest point on its AC curve.

Hence, the monopolistically competitive firm cannot maintain super-normal profits in the long term whereas oligopolistic firms may be able to (hence we call the latters' profits abnormal or monopoly profits, implying that they are long term.)

Small and medium sized enterprises (SMEs)

Business economists talk of SMEs as an important sub-group of UK businesses. These have between 1 and 500 employees, and many of them are at the low end of the scale. There are 18 million SMEs across Europe and these account for 66 per cent of EU jobs. This growth is particularly important in terms of high tech businesses such as software companies, Internet based businesses etc.

Self testing questions

1   What are the essential differences between oligopoly and monopolistic competition? Give examples of both types of market.

2   Why do oligopolistic firms collude as opposed to compete? Is collusion something which can be maintained by oligopolists long term? Explain your answer.

3   What does the kinked demand curve tell us about price stability in oligopolistic markets?

4   How exactly does game theory help us explore the behaviour of oligopolists?

5   Why do monopolistically competitive firms not collude or set up entry barriers to block new entrants?

7.4 Other market structures: monopolies; perfect competition as the template

Monopoly; competition commission threat to British Gas

Synopsis   This case study explores a possible monopoly situation. It identifies:
1 why this might be a monopoly;
2 what action could be taken against it.

It has been reported that British Gas, owned by Centrica, could be referred to the Competition Commission (which has replaced the Monopolies and Mergers Commission) because of its national network of customers and spending capacity. The Commission would then ask the Office of Fair Trading and the energy regulator, Callum McCarthy, to investigate whether British Gas has excessive market power. Both the gas and electricity markets are completely deregulated. Competition in the gas market began in 1995, yet currently British Gas still supplies 80 per cent of households, compared with almost 100 per cent before deregulation. In the electricity market, deregulation was completed in 1999; currently British Gas supplies 1.5 million of the 26 million households with electricity as well.

There is, therefore, concern that its dominance of the household power market will inhibit competition from businesses wishing to supply gas or electricity. If this is found to be so, then in the extreme case the Competition Commission could cause the company to be broken up. There is concern that British Gas has been using pricing tactics, dual-fuel offers (offering electricity and gas at a cheaper rate if purchased from British Gas, raising fears of cross-subsidisation), cross-selling and multi-million pound advertising campaigns (which rivals cannot afford to match) and its strong brand name, to hinder competition. The sale of complementary products, e.g. gas and gas fires is also being investigated.

Power companies have argued that, unless British Gas is cut down in size, there will be little competition in the energy market. All the electricity trading companies were reduced to regional operations when they were privatised; however, British Gas was allowed to stay intact. As a result small companies trying to join the market, and those trying to trade in regions other than their own, are unable to compete. Additionally, now that British Gas is also allowed to offer electricity supplies in the deregulated energy market, the problem is perceived to have got worse. Only the Scottish Power and the Eastern Group are net gainers of customers among the power suppliers; all the other regional electricity suppliers are losing customers to British Gas.

British Gas has argued that, although it has a dominant position, it has not abused its status.

There is real concern over a company with a dominant market share because of its ability to misuse its market power if it were to choose to do so; hence the possible need for the investigation demonstrated in the case study above. Therefore, a business can be perceived as having monopoly power even if it does not control 100 per cent of the market supply. However, from a theoretical viewpoint a monopoly is a market structure where one business supplies the entire market and where there are no close substitutes for its products.

Typically, UK monopolies have been state owned through the fear that they would abuse their power, e.g. by charging high prices and blocking new entrants to make long term greater than normal, i.e. monopoly, profits. The former British Rail and the former state owned public utilities such as water and nuclear power were other examples and were known as natural monopolies, i.e. the size of the market is such that only one firm can exist in it and fully exploit economies of scale. If there is more than one firm, the long term average costs of each would be higher than the natural monopoly. For example, it would waste resources to have seven railway tracks all running from Birmingham to Manchester and competing with each other.

In the last twenty years, in the UK and other countries, many state owned industries have been privatised. However, this has not introduced competition but merely transferred monopolies from the public to the private sector. To ensure that these do not abuse their power, the UK government has therefore created regulators such as OFWAT, to regulate the water companies, OFTEL, to regulate telecommunications companies, particularly BT, and OFGEN, to regulate gas and electricity companies. Chapter 8, Sections 8.3 and 8.4 explore this in more detail.

A monopoly has many similar characteristics to an oligopoly in that there are very high entry barriers, which may be legally enforced in the case of state owned companies. Whereas monopolistically competitive firms are price takers, oligopolies and monopolies are price makers, i.e. the monopolist can set the price at which its products will be sold. However, it cannot also set the quantity since this will be determined by the market demand curve; or it can set the amount it wants to sell but will then have to accept the price determined by the demand curve.

Figure 7.3(a), which showed the monopolistically competitive business in the short term is also the relevant diagram for the monopolist. The monopolist here is making abnormal monopoly profits since they persist in the long term, because they are protected by high entry barriers. In contrast, under monopolistic competition, the entry barriers were very low and so the profits were supernormal, i.e. would not persist long term. In Figure

7.3(a) the shaded area shows monopoly profits. Hence the equilibrium conditions are:

1   MC = MR determines the equilibrium output;
2   AR > AC determines the existence of monopoly profits.

Discriminating monopoly

The other interesting monopoly situation is the discriminating monopolist who charges different prices for the same services to different consumers at different times. This can also apply to oligopolistic firms. For example, telephone companies charge different rates at different times of the day; a doctor charges different rates to private and NHS patients; and football clubs charge different prices for season tickets for different parts of the ground etc. Therefore, discrimination is common practice in business. To be effective, three conditions must be met:

1   The elasticity of demand for the product must differ between the different products.
2   There must be a way to separate consumers – by age, geography, time etc.
3   Those being charged higher prices cannot buy in the cheaper market – otherwise the prices will equalise.

There must also only be one supplier with total control over that supply. Consumers will often be unaware that there is price discrimination since markets do not give perfect knowledge to all. Additionally, geography means that people will not travel ten miles to save 10p on the cost of a jar of coffee, so resale becomes unrealistic.

By discriminating, the monopolist is able to maximise profits, and this is proved by the business producing at the point where $\Sigma MC = \Sigma MR$ (Σ (sigma) means the total of). This is the simple rationale for such action.

Figure 7.4 demonstrates how price discrimination works. We assume a monopolist supplying the same good from the same factory to two separate markets. Because the goods are produced in the same factory, the discriminating monopolist will have one MC and one AC curve – the MC curve is shown in diagram (c) of Figure 7.4 as ΣMC.

However, market A (diagram (a)) and market B (diagram (b)) have demand curves with different elasticities, A's being more inelastic than B's. They also have separate MR curves. If the two MR curves are added together we get the firm's MR curve, shown in diagram (c). Where ΣMR intersects MC in diagram (c) determines the optimum output for the monopolist, at Q_T.

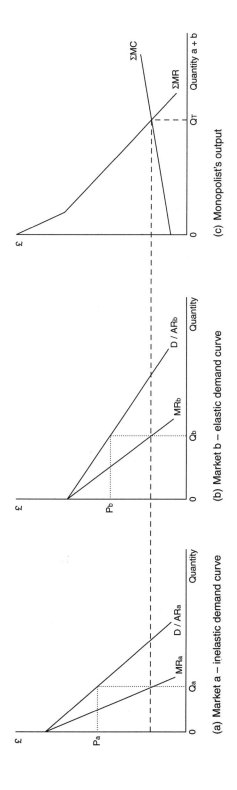

(a) Market a – inelastic demand curve

(b) Market b – elastic demand curve

(c) Monopolist's output

Figure 7.4 Discriminating monopoly.

The monopolist will set the optimum output in each market, A and B, where ΣMC (shown by the horizontal dotted line going left from where $\Sigma MC = \Sigma MR$ in (c)) is equal to the individual market MR.

In market A, $\Sigma MC = MR_a$, to give an output of Q_a and a price of P_a. In market B, $\Sigma MC = MR_b$, giving a lower output of Q_b, and a lower price of P_b.

Perfect competition

This last type of market structure is largely theoretical and is known, by economists, as perfect competition. The reader will note that a main difference from the second market structure we examined, monopolistic competition, is that the goods and services the very many businesses sell are not differentiated in any way, i.e. they are homogeneous. Therefore, for example, consumers will have no preference between one brand of baked beans and another. There are very many buyers in the market, so neither any business selling the products, nor any consumer buying them, is economically powerful enough to be a price maker; so they are price takers. Price is determined solely by market forces. It is also assumed that everyone has a perfect knowledge of who is selling what, where and at what price, so there will be only one price in the market. There are also assumed to be zero transport costs and no entry or exit barriers.

The reader may say at this point 'why bother with such an unrealistic situation? It doesn't relate to the real world, which business economics should be all about.' The answer to this is that a market structure which is perfectly competitive gives an ideal of how markets should work. It is the template against which the other market structures are measured and which economists and legislators use to judge the efficiencies of these other markets – since they all interfere with the free working of the market in some ways, e.g. through advertising and branding; through entry barriers; through being price makers etc., thereby preventing the economy's scarce resources being used most efficiently.

It is not realistic, or even desirable, of course, to try and make all markets perfectly competitive. For example, since there are so many businesses in a perfectly competitive market, they would not be big enough to compete globally against multinational American and Japanese businesses operating in several different continents (known therefore as multinational enterprises or MNEs).

Figure 7.5(a) and (b) show the equilibrium conditions for the industry and the individual firm under perfect competition.

Figure 7.5(a) shows the industry equilibrium, where demand = supply, as we saw in Chapter 5, Section 5.4. This demand–supply intersection determines the market price which the individual firm, in Figure 7.5(b) accepts, since it is, by definition, a price taker. We will assume that this firm is representative of all firms in the industry.

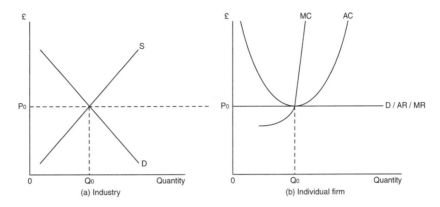

Figure 7.5 Equilibrium conditions for the industry and firm under perfect competition.

Although the market demand curve is downward sloping, the individual firm faces a horizontal demand curve. In other words, at the prevailing price P_0, consumers will demand whatever amount the firm cares to supply, since it is such a small contributor to total industry supply. In other market structures the demand curve is also the AR curve; however, in perfect competition the horizontal or perfectly elastic demand curve will the firm's AR curve, and also the MR curve. This is because the revenue earned from each extra unit of output sold is equivalent to the price.

As usual the firm's MC curve cuts its AC curve at the latter's lowest point. The firm will produce where its MC = MR, which gives an output of Q_0. Since this is also the point where AC = AR, the business is making normal profits.

If demand for the product were to fall, the industry demand curve will shift downwards and to the left in Figure 7.5(a). The point where it intersects with the supply curve will determine the new market price. In Figure 7.5(b), the horizontal demand curve will also shift down to cut the MC curve at a lower point on it. This will determine the firm's new output. However, AR will now be less than AC and the firm will be making a loss. If this persists in the long term the firm will have to leave the industry.

Comparing perfect competition and monopoly

It has been argued that the monopolist is less efficient than the perfectly competitive business because its output is lower and the price it charges is higher.

Additionally it uses its resources less efficiently since it is not producing at the minimum point on its AC curve, whereas the perfectly competitive firm is. In Figure 7.3(a), which represents the monopolist in the long term, as well as the monopolistically competitive business in the short term, the monopolist produces where MC = MR. However, for a competitive industry it would produce where MC, which is the firm's supply curve, intersects the firm's AR curve, which is its demand curve. This would give a higher level of output at a lower price. The monopolist also uses entry barriers to make monopoly profits.

There are some qualifications we need to make to this simple analysis. Firstly, a business which is the sole producer in an industry is unlikely to have the same cost curves as a very small firm which is part of a perfectly competitive industry, so the initial comparison is suspect. Secondly, a monopolist, through its size, can achieve economies of scale, which a perfectly competitive firm could never do. This will mean lower production costs which could be passed onto the consumer as lower prices, whether through the desire to sell more of the product or through being forced to do so by an industry regulator (see Chapter 8).

With large scale production a business can become an effective competitor in global markets, taking on multinational firms – what has been termed a 'Euro-champion' – since only very large firms can compete effectively in new global markets. A Euro-champion is also placed to take advantage of the opportunities, particularly scale economies, offered by the Single European Market. In contrast a firm as small as those operating in a perfectly competitive market would take many years to grow to a significant size, if at all. Hence, economically, they are insignificant.

Additionally, a monopolist can afford a large R&D budget whereas a perfectly competitive firm cannot. We have seen that a large R&D budget can be used as an entry barrier to deter potential newcomers; however, it may be merely essential for new product development and diversification into other markets. Therefore, there is a delicate balance at times between a monopolist being economically harmful or beneficial to a national economy. This issue is pursued again in Chapter 8.

Many of the above arguments also apply to oligopolists compared with perfectly competitive firms.

7.5 Competition for British retailing

The UK supermarket sector

The supermarket sector in the UK is a good example of an oligopolistic market structure since it is dominated by a small number of large businesses. UK supermarkets have high profit margins – typically 4 per cent to 6 per cent – compared with Continental European and US supermarkets which have much lower margins – around 2 per cent. This has resulted in a Competition Commission investigation into the prices charged by UK supermarkets.

Although this makes the UK businesses more vulnerable to foreign take-over, especially since the virtual completion of the Single European Market, there are also high entry barriers facing would-be entrants. Existing UK supermarkets have established customer loyalty and hence market share, although there is movement between different supermarkets of course. In 1994, for example, Tesco's market share was 17.8 per cent, whilst Asda's was 11.2 per cent, compared with 1999 figures of 24.1 per cent and 14.8 per cent, respectively. UK supermarkets also have an established network of retail outlets, including a growing number of out-of-town hypermarkets, which a newcomer would have to match, at very high cost. Although European firms such as French hypermarket firm Carrefour and German chain Aldi have had some stores in the UK, these were relatively few in numbers compared with established British firms; indeed Carrefour soon lost interest in the UK, selling out to Dee Corporation (now Somerfield) in the early 1980s.

Supermarkets now sell as many non-food items as they do food, including CDs and books, clothing, household goods etc., some of which offer much higher profit margins than food. Hypermarkets offer even more facilities to shoppers, such as crèches, very large car parks, snack bars etc., as well as a much wider range of goods, including computers, furniture and even mopeds.

In June 1999 the UK supermarket calm was shattered by the news that Wal-Mart, the US discount retail giant had bought Asda, the UK's third largest supermarket business, for £6.72 billion. In so doing it defeated rival bidder Kingfisher which had wanted to merge with Asda.

Wal-Mart

Wal-Mart was founded in 1962 by Sam Walton when the first store was opened in Rogers, Arkansas. Since then it has grown at a prodigious rate to become the most profitable retailer in the world, based on a philosophy of competitiveness through selling at low prices. Wal-Mart's motto is 'we sell for less, always.' Its expertise lies in its ability to secure cheap and reliable sources of goods, other than food, and sell them in volume from very large stores at discount prices on low profit margins, goods such as gardening equipment, electrical consumer goods, health and beauty products. Currently, its sales from its 3000 US retail outlets are around $137.6 billion (£86 billion), making it the third largest business in the US. Wal-Mart also runs a very customer focused business which incorporates the attention to consumer needs, so often missing from UK stores. This is achieved by good staff motivation and thorough training and includes someone greeting each customer as they enter a Wal-Mart store – the so-called 'people greeters.'

It has never been certain that Wal-Mart would establish itself in the UK. Planning permission to construct hypermarkets is hard to secure, while land is expensive and traffic congestion also imposes high costs.

As well as hitting the supermarket chains, Wal-Mart's arrival in the UK will impact on businesses such as electrical retailer Comet, part of the Kingfisher group which also includes Woolworth, Superdrug and B&Q. Kingfisher, the defeated rival for Asda, offered a share for share deal valued at £5.6 billion, whereas Wal-Mart offered a 220p cash bid per Asda share. In failing to secure Asda, Kingfisher was unable to obtain the food and clothing businesses it had long wanted to complete its business empire.

Wal-Mart's arrival also has implications for stores such as troubled Marks & Spencer, the food and clothing retailer, and MFI the furniture retailer, since the goods which Wal-Mart sells will cut right across their product ranges. Wal-Mart has also talked of moving into financial services, copying such supermarket chains as Tesco and Sainsbury which have established their own banks. This will also impact on the high street banks, already under pressure from the supermarket banks, and other financial services providers such as the Virgin group.

Its strategy, according to its senior vice-chairman Don Soderquist, is to retain the Asda brand name but, if the opportunity arises, also open Wal-Mart stores. These are very much larger than UK hypermarkets and cash and carry discount warehouses such as Makro; in the US the average size of a Wal-Mart store is 160 000 square feet compared with an average 60 000 to 80 000 square feet for Asda, Tesco and Sainsbury hypermarkets. However, retailers complain that it is very difficult to get planning permission in the UK for new stores, compared with Germany, France and Italy.

At the time of the announcement of the acquisition, Soderquist argued that no staff would be sent from Wal-Mart to offer advice on how run Asda since it already had strong customer support. The chief executive of Asda, Allan Leighton, argued that Asda would, however, draw on Wal-Mart's expertise in its computer systems and supply chain management. By combining its purchasing with that of Wal-Mart it would also be able to secure substantial economies of bulk purchase, enabling it to lower prices still further. However, he argued that both Wal-Mart and Asda had similar corporate cultures, which enhanced the potential benefits from Wal-Mart's acquisition.

7.6 Summary of chapter

Chapter 7 has examined market structures and given case studies from the real world as evidence that such distinctions or classifications are important. The structure–conduct–performance methodology or model was explored as a means to analyse market structures, and was applied to oligopoly. Its weaknesses were also noted. Porter's five forces model was also examined which analyses what determines competition in an industry.

Oligopoly was examined through the use of game theory to examine strategy, and also through the kinked demand curve to explain price stability. Collusion as a means to maximise profits was also examined and its inherent instability was discussed. Monopolistic competition, the other strand of imperfect competition, was also examined. The inability to establish entry barriers was contrasted with that of oligopoly, as was the inability of monopolistically competitive firms to maintain supernormal profits in the long term.

The two market extremes of monopoly and perfect competition were then discussed. Monopoly was examined in terms of its ability to be a price maker and maintain very high entry barriers; discriminating monopoly was also examined. It was then compared with the theoretical benchmark of perfect competition and there was a debate about how harmful and inefficient monopoly actually is.

The chapter concluded with a case study of Wal-Mart's take-over of Asda.

7.7 Further questions

1   Is a monopolist always less efficient than a perfectly competitive firm?

2   What are the advantages and disadvantages afforded by a discriminating monopolist?

3   Is the study of perfect competition of any use to business economists? Explain your answer.

4   What underlies Wal-Mart's strategy of acquiring Asda. Write a side of A4 justifying the decision to Wal-Mart stock (share) holders.

5   What is the effect of Wal-Mart's action likely to be on other supermarket chains?

7.8 Further reading

Ansoff, I. (1988). *Corporate Strategy*, Revised edition. Harmondsworth: Penguin Books Ltd.

Crainer, S. (1997). *The Ultimate Business Library. Fifty Books that Made Management.* Oxford: Capstone Publishing Ltd.

Porter, M. E. (1980). *Competitive Strategy. Techniques for Analysing Industries and Competitors.* New York: The Free Press.

Smith, J. G. (1990). *Business Strategy*, 2nd edition. Oxford: Basil Blackwell Ltd.

The Economist

The *Financial Times*
The Times
The Office of Fair Trading website: http://www.oft.gov.uk/
WH Smith Online: http://www.whsmithgroup.com/
WalMart website: http://www.walmart.com

Chapter 8

Regulating market power

Learning Outcomes

After completing this chapter the reader will be able to:
- understand how and why firms grow and, in particular, the nature of mergers and acquisitions and their effectiveness;
- understand the need for regulatory legislation;
- analyse UK and EU regulation of monopolies and mergers.

8.1 How and why firms grow. Mergers and acquisitions. Diversification as a competitive strategy

The struggle for market power in the European defence industry

Synopsis   This case study explores rationalisation in the European defence industry. It identifies as key characteristics:

1 global competition, especially American, driving rationalisation;
2 national and state intervention problems hindering rationalisation;
3 the potential economies of rationalisation.

Case Study

Airbus Industrie, the European consortium which manufactures commercial airlines, is a limited partnership of four main companies, although attempts are being made to convert it into a company in its own right. The partners in the consortium are France's partially privatised Aérospatiale (now Aérospatiale Matra), Germany's Deutsche Aerospace (Dasa), Spain's Construcciones Aeronauticas (Casa) and Britain's British Aerospace (BAe). There is also another consortium to produce the long awaited Eurofighter, consisting of Dasa, BAe, Casa and Alenia, the aerospace part of the state controlled Finmeccanica of Italy.

In May 1999, Dasa, the German defence group which is the aerospace arm of the German–American car manufacturer, DaimlerChrysler, signed a strategic alliance to secure control of Casa. In so doing it beat British Aerospace, Aérospatiale Matra of France and Alenia, all of whom had also bid for control of Casa.

Dasa's control of Casa will inevitably make it more difficult for Airbus Industrie to be converted into a company. It also further strains relations between Dasa and British Aerospace, which had regarded ownership of Casa as 'desirable but not essential.' Originally there had been discussions between the German and British groups concerning a possible merger but these collapsed when, to Dasa's annoyance, BAe acquired GEC Marconi Electronics, the defence electronics arm of GEC, for £7.7 billion.

Dasa subsequently announced that, after the merger with Casa, the new company might well be floated on the stock market, creating a company valued at £6.6 billion. The Chief Executive of Dasa, Manfred Bischoff, also argued that other partners would be welcome in the new merged company and cited as one possibility Alenia, one of the unsuccessful bidders for Casa. In turn, Alenia, which the Italian government is looking to privatise, has been eyed up as a potential partner both by BAe and by Thomson–CSF, another French defence group. Bischoff also suggested the possibility of a partnership with Aérospatiale Matra, but the continued part ownership of it by the French government will hinder this. Subsequently, Thomson–CSF bought British defence electronics firm Racal.

This spate of mergers has occurred for a number of reasons. Most importantly, there is a need to rationalise the European defence industry because of over-capacity through too many less than optimal sized companies for global competition, preventing the achievement of economies of scale. Some of these are partly or totally controlled by national governments which makes rationalisation more difficult. For example, the French government has put Thomson–CSF at the centre of its defence strategy and blocked non-French companies from merging with it. The end of the Cold War in 1990, and the collapse of the former Soviet Union, meant high levels of armaments expenditure could be reduced; however, this also substantially reduced the value of defence contracts placed by govern-ments. UK, French and German governments have recognised the need for rationalisation and urged European defence businesses to rationalise through mergers and strategic alliances.

The US had already gone through a rationalisation process in the 1990s, reducing its defence contractors from fifteen to three in the period 1993–1997. This put further pressure on the European defence busi-nesses, seeking to compete with the US for Eastern European and third world defence contracts.

Dasa's securing of Casa, and its proposals for a link up with Alenia and/or Aérospatiale Matra, were partly a response to British Aerospace's acquisition of GEC Marconi Electronics, which made the size of the new British company much more threatening to the German group.

The above case study demonstrates why mergers and acquisitions occur, highlighting over-capacity in an industry, the need to effect cost savings and achieve scale economies, and the importance of competing globally. Underlying this is an oligopolistic market with high entry barriers in setting-up costs and R&D, and the fact that the actions of one firm will impact on the others – as shown by the effect of BAe's acquisition of GEC Marconi Electronics on Dasa.

The case study also highlights the strategic dimension of business deci-sions with the medium to long term development of the European defence industry affecting the defence firms and national governments. Finally, it tells us something of how companies grow – which we now explore.

How and why firms grow

Organic growth

As a business makes profits its directors plough them back to finance further growth, for example by renting bigger premises, hiring more staff, updating computers etc. Most small businesses fail within the first two years of being established and one reason for this is that the costs of future growth are underestimated. It is most likely that a business will need to borrow money from its bank at some time, yet banks are notorious for calling in loans as soon as there is a downturn in the business's activities, when finance is most needed. Many small businesses fail because the directors try to take too much money out of them too soon, as their reward for being entre-preneurs, and hence the business encounters cash flow problems; in other words insufficient money coming in to meet outgoings.

Other reasons for business failure include underestimating the strength of the competition in the market when the business is first set up (inadequate marketing research), falling consumer demand because of a downturn in the economy, reducing consumer confidence, and customers – particularly larger businesses – not paying their bills until several months after the credit period afforded to them has expired, again causing the new business cash flow problems.

External funding

Businesses cannot normally grow by internal funding alone; external funding must be secured, most commonly bank finance as loans or overdrafts. Trade credit is another source of external funding, when a business is allowed, say, 30 days credit before it has to pay its bills. If, long term, it does really well a business may raise money by issue shares.

The nature of mergers and acquisitions: rationale

The other growth option is mergers and acquisitions, and is associated with businesses of a certain size rather than new companies. However, some software houses, which have only existed for a year or two, have been bought by larger software companies in recent years to secure their products before competitors do.

Mergers

A merger occurs when two companies willingly come together, normally as equal partners, to form a new business, e.g. in mid 1999 British Steel merged with Koninklijke Hoogovens of the Netherlands to form a new £3 billion steel producing company, known as Corus. The rationale for this was to enable them to compete more effectively in both a European and a global market, where there are regular cycles of boom and slump in steel producing activity, seriously affecting long term profitability. This is aggravated by cheap steel imports from Far East countries such as Korea, Japan and India.

Acquisitions

Also known as take-overs, these occur when one business, the predator, seeks to gain control of another, the victim. This may be undertaken willingly, as with the blocked BSkyB take-over of Manchester United, discussed in Chapter 1, a take-over where the victim company being taken over does not wish to be acquired by the predator. An example of the latter would be Vodafone's acquisition of Mannesman of Germany.

After the take-over, the victim company may continue as a named organisation, e.g. Scottish Widows following its acquisition by Lloyds–TSB, or it may be subsumed by its new owner and the name disappears, as with many British cars, such as Hillman. Of course some names have come back from the dead, e.g. MG cars. Whether the name continues or not, the organisation and operations will change as the acquired business is made to fit its new owner's structure. This often involves large-scale redundancies since rationalisation is a major merger motive.

There will often be a battle to acquire a business, with rival bidders each making offers; Kingfisher and Wal-Mart's rival bids for Asda is such an example. The higher bidder should normally win, whilst the bidder offering cash as opposed to shares in the predator company, or a mixture of cash and shares, normally has the odds in its favour. In spite of the recommendations of the victim company's directors, it is the shareholders who decide, since they own the company; although many shares are owned by directors or institutional investors, which reinforces the directors' recommendations.

Another example where two rivals fought for the same business was the bitter battle between Punch Taverns and Whitbread for the control of Allied Domecq's chain of 3600 public houses, valued at £2.925 billion, which took place in mid 1999. Whitbread's bid was blocked, much to its surprise, when the Trade and Industry Secretary referred it to the Competition Commission, on the grounds that it ran 'contrary to the spirit of the beer orders', i.e. the last Conservative government's attempts to separate the beer brewing and retail (public house) industries, to reduce the number of tied houses (pubs which are forced to sell a certain make of beer because the brewery owns the pub chain). The Trade and Industry Secretary's action automatically caused the bid to lapse.

In some cases a take-over bid by a predator company will cause the victim to ask another company, known as the white knight, to intervene with a rival bid, since the victim company believes that it could work better with the white knight than with the predator. Again the shareholders will choose. Since many institutional investors such as pension funds and insurance companies are major shareholders, their decision is often the crucial factor since they hold more shares than small private investors do. They must consider the best interests of their policyholders and pension fund contributors first, and whether the predator or the white knight will be best for the long-term success of the victim company.

Horizontal and vertical integration

Mergers and acquisitions may be either horizontal or vertical in nature, or conglomerate diversification.

1   Horizontal integration occurs when a business merges with or acquires another business, e.g. BMW's ill-fated acquisition of Rover. In contrast, vertical integration occurs in one of two ways.

Table 8.1 Purchase of UK businesses by foreign investors, 1995–1997.

Year	Value of transactions $ billion
1995	36.34
1996	39.21
1997	53.04

2 Forward horizontal integration occurs when a business acquires another business, which brings it closer to the customer. For example, Whitbread's attempt to acquire Allied Domecq's chain of public houses was forward vertical integration because it would have brought the brewer into the retail sector.

3 Backward vertical integration: in contrast if Whitbread had sought to move closer to its sources of supply, e.g. by buying a farm which grows hops, this would be backward vertical integration, since the business is now moving further away from the customer.

4 Conglomerate diversification occurs when a business moves into a totally different area. For example, the Virgin Group is a classic example with initial activities based on a 'pop' music magazine and then recording studios and record shops. Subsequently, however, Branson has diversified into such unrelated activities as airlines, cola drinks, condoms, trains, cinemas and the Internet.

The rationale for mergers and acquisitions

There are a number of reasons identified by the European Commission to explain why businesses merge or seek to acquire other businesses:

1 Mergers and acquisitions are seen as ways to reduce costs. This may be by closing branch offices where there are two in the same high street, as when the Lloyds Bank took over the TSB. Computer systems may also be combined so that one system can handle information management for both parties; this will also save costs when the system is next upgraded. Labour is usually the easiest cost to reduce, e.g. the merger of British Steel and Koninklijke Hoogovens was anticipated to shed at least 2000 jobs in both organisations, mainly in administration and management. The big fear of the British unions was that most of the wastage would be in British Steel since employer-friendly labour laws make it easier to sack staff in the UK than in the Netherlands.

2 Another reason for mergers and acquisitions is the desire to grow bigger and more profitable, to compete more effectively in existing and potential markets. The acquisition of Casa by Dasa in the earlier case study shows this. The larger business size should enable it to compete more effectively and achieve economies of scale, effecting cost savings on future production. If the assets of a company are not fully reflected in its share price, i.e. the price is too low, this may also tempt a predator to seize the opportunity and bid for the victim. It may then incorporate it into its existing business or it may asset strip, keeping some parts and selling off others with the hope of at least covering the purchase price. When Marks and Spencer's shares fell to 230p these no longer covered the asset value of the company, making it vulnerable to acquisition.

3 Synergy occurs when it is beneficial to combine two or more activities rather than undertaking them in isolation. It is often described as $2 + 2 = 5$. This will overlap with growth since, if synergies can be gained, then it will reduce production costs and permit scale economies. For example, modern car assembly often has component suppliers based under the same factory roof as the car manufacturers, and in many cases component suppliers transfer their products directly to the assembly line. Synergy gains should also help the new company to grow, become more efficient and secure greater market power. It can then raise entry barriers by virtue of its larger size and greater cost effectiveness.

4 Research and Development expenditure synergies are important; developing new information systems in one area of defence work, for example in the case of Dasa and Casa, can lead to spin-offs into other areas of development. In pharmaceuticals, defence, software and many other industries, high R&D budgets are essential; however, just spending a lot of money does not guarantee success. Merging or acquiring a competitor pools research effort and shares costs.

5 A merger or acquisition may be seen as the means to restructure a business to make it more competitive and efficient. BAe's acquisition of GEC Marconi Electronics can be cited as an example of this. Of course, in many cases, the above categories will overlap substantially.

6 A merger or acquisition may seek to promote co-operation. In 1999 Vivendi, the French Media and Utilities group acquired an extra £825 million of shares in BSkyB, to lift its holding to almost 25 per cent, giving it a blocking minority in any vote. Vivendi was previously known as Générale des Eaux, and initially started as a water supply company. At the same time as it bought extra BSkyB shares it also bought more shares in Canal Plus, the French pay television company, giving it a stake of just under 50 per cent. It was assumed that its strategy was to try and restart stalled merger talks between BSkyB and Canal Plus, which collapsed early in 1999, although Vivendi said that this was not its immediate intention.

7 Diversification occurs when a business moves into new areas of activity by acquisition or merger, e.g. BSkyB's acquisition of shares in a number of Premiership football clubs (see Chapter 1).

Some of these motives for mergers and acquisitions clearly relate to cost savings and hence profit maximisation, our assumed main motive for business behaviour. However, some are more strategic, relating to the ability of a business to position itself in the market place to gain greater power; points 2 to 5 above may all be assumed to fit into that category.

Economists have also argued (see Chapter 2, Section 2.1) that there are other motives for business behaviour inspired by the wish of managers to maximise their utility. Research suggests that these managerial motives may be significant. The ability of a business to survive and influence its environment seems as important as cost minimisation or achieving scale economies. Market power seems to be at the centre of merger and acquisition activity and this fits in with our analysis of business strategy and oligopolistic theory.

How effective are mergers and acquisitions?

The other important test of merger activity is how effective is it. The bulk of merger theories suggest that profits should be increased as a consequence of the merger or acquisition. Yet analysis of US mergers finds that, for the majority, there is a small but significant decline in profitability post merger. Perhaps this is not so surprising when one considers redundancy payments made to staff no longer needed, the costs of introducing new systems, staff setting up new organisational structures and learning to work with each other etc. What does occur however is that share prices rise, benefiting shareholders. Therefore, most mergers appear to be financial in nature, with a rise in the stock market value of the company but no gain in profitability which, at least ostensibly, the merger was about.

This is supported by other research in the UK, which found that most mergers achieve only minimal cost reductions. This is either because they fail to exploit economies of scale or because the merger actually causes diseconomies of scale. Other research has found that three quarters of UK mergers and acquisitions do not reach their financial targets whilst half never recover the premium which the predator had to pay the victim to secure its shares. Therefore, although merger activity may allege cost savings in practice it appears to be much more about market power.

Competitiveness and competition

The reader should now be able to distinguish between competitiveness and competition. The former is about the ability of a business to compete effectively with its rivals on the grounds of price, quality of product, marketing, delivery times, after sales service etc. It therefore encompasses having lower average costs, making bigger profits, being able to undertake larger capital expenditure programmes, running a bigger R&D programme, securing a greater market share etc.

In contrast, competition relates to the nature of the market in which businesses operate. They can bid for customers without restrictions by governments or other businesses and also for the resources necessary to produce these goods. The more businesses in a market the less their ability to be price makers; the lower the entry barriers the easier it is for new firms to enter. If there is competition, prices will be lower, the quality of goods should be better and so on. Additionally, the greater the competition in a market the more the incentive for firms to be competitive.

Joint ventures

The other form of business arrangement which enables firms to work together without losing their independence is a joint venture. This may be a separate business set up by say two companies, each of the founders owning part of it. This may enable them to move into a new market, share R&D costs, and cut distribution costs by sharing networks. In other words, risks and costs are spread. An example of this would be Airbus which was created to manufacture commercial aircraft in competition with Boeing. Technically it is a consortium, but the net effect is the same.

8.2 The need for legislation – monopolies, oligopolies and market failure

Car prices – protecting the UK car buyer

Case Study

For several years there has been concern within the UK regarding the high price of new UK cars, and hence, linked to this, the price of second-hand cars, compared with those in other parts of the EU. A European Commission survey found that the UK is the most expensive market for 57 out of the 76 best selling car models, with prices up to 50 per cent higher than similar marques (brands) and models in other EU countries. The Society of Motor Manufacturers and Traders blamed the differences on exchange rate movements and tax differences between the different countries.

Between July and December 1999 the Competition Commission's inquiry panel met to investigate whether UK car prices were being rigged by manufacturers and dealers. Initial meetings of the panel were boycotted by car manufacturers which expressed concern about the confidentiality of the proceedings. In contrast, the Consumer's Association argued that manufacturers were operating 'a price discriminating oligopoly' and dictating to retailers what models were available and at what prices.

Car dealers at the inquiry blamed manufacturers for squeezing their profit margins and erecting barriers to them obtaining cars from abroad, where they are cheaper, and reselling them in the UK. Alan Pulham of the Retail Motor Industry Federation argued 'suppliers have the power of life and death over a dealer. It would be frowned on' (if dealers sourced from abroad).

The start of the inquiry followed a previous admission by Volvo that it supported a price-fixing cartel among dealers in new Volvo cars by punishing dealers who did not keep discounts to customers within agreed limits. Volvo dealers restricted discounts by up to 2.5 per cent for private buyers and up to 5 per cent for commercial (fleet) buyers. If dealers exceeded these limits they were threatened with losing their bonuses. An investigation by the Office of Fair Trading (OFT) determined that the price fixing cartel operated between March 1995 to early 1996. In its defence Volvo argued that the price fixing was not company policy. Rather 'a limited number of field force staff had acted against company policy by indicating support for dealer pricing agreements.' The staff involved were not sacked or disciplined in any way.

Volvo Cars UK, now a subsidiary of Ford, has pledged not to support price fixing cartels in the future. Had the offence been committed in the year 2000, the company could have been fined by the OFT up to 10 per cent of its turnover, a total of £70 million in the case of Volvo.

In late March 2000, it was reported that the Competition Commission had concluded that car buyers were being exploited by manufacturers and that the government was intending to force them to cut prices; this could be by to 35 per cent.

Mergers and acquisitions may well lead to increased concentration in a market, unless it is possible for other businesses to enter because entry barriers are low, or because the newcomer is powerful in another market and so brings economic muscle into the new market. Increased concentration means, simply, that fewer firms now supply a product to a market. As Chapter 7, Section 7.2 showed, firms may subsequently collude rather than compete and end up fixing prices, or output levels or market sharing, as the case study above shows. Alternatively, if one firm continues to grow by organic growth and/or mergers and acquisitions, it may even become a monopoly with all the market power which that implies.

As we saw in Chapter 6, Section 6.3, monopolies can also lead to market failure. In a monopolistic or oligopolistic market structure, the firm(s) will produce where MC = MR. At this quantity, AR > AC, meaning the firm makes monopoly/abnormal profits. Therefore, the final outcome, as we saw in Chapter 7, Section 7.4, is that a monopolist produces less output at a higher price than does an industry which is perfectly competitive. Since the monopolist does not produce at the lowest point on its average cost curve it is also not producing at its most efficient point, i.e. the monopolist inhibits allocative efficiency.

There are problems with measuring just how big the social costs of allocative inefficiency are, but they are undoubtedly big enough for concern and hence for governments to adopt policies to promote competition. These are discussed in the next section.

Self testing questions

1 What is the difference between a merger and an acquisition?

2 Why do mergers occur? Give three examples of mergers not in this book and explain their rationale.

3 What might be the dangers of conglomerate diversification as opposed to a merger or acquisition?

4 Volvo supported a price fixing cartel among its dealers in new Volvo cars. What was the reason for this when allowing dealers to give bigger discounts would surely ensure greater car sales?

5 What is meant by the social costs of monopoly?

8.3 UK policy – the Office of Fair Trading and the Competition Commission. Regulating privatised industries

Ofwat imposes price cuts on water companies

Ian Byatt, the water supply industry regulator and head of Ofwat, the water industry regulatory body, ordered the water companies to cut household water bills by an average of 14 per cent for the years 2000 and 2001. The water companies will then be allowed small increases in 2002 and 2003 to fund investment programmes.

Byatt's action is a result of growing concerns over the last decade that the privatised water companies, which are private sector monopolists, have been more concerned with the interests of their shareholders, and in some cases the financial rewards to the water company directors themselves, rather than with household and business customers, who have no choice as to their suppliers. The price cuts will, for once, benefit consumers rather than shareholders; they also recognise that, with falling interest rates, water companies' borrowing costs are lower, offering them further cost savings. In estimating appropriate price cuts Byatt made assumptions about the costs of the maintenance and investment programmes that the water companies must undertake, the extent of future productivity gains (required to exceed 2.5 per cent per annum), and the cost of borrowing which the companies will have to pay. Byatt assumed 5.25 per cent whereas Thames Water argued that the more accurate cost was 6–8 per cent.

Byatt also demanded more emphasis on environmental improvements; indeed the case study in Chapter 5, Section 5.3 showed that one of the top ten polluters was one of the water companies, Wessex Water. The government also argued that its £8.5 billion environmental programme over the five years of this price review is part of the re-examination of the water industry. Companies will have to find this as part of a £15 billion spending programme, and it must be largely funded by borrowing rather than raising prices charged to consumers.

Subsequently, Thames Water, announcing a 6 per cent rise in interim pre-tax profits to £214.2 million, argued that the price cuts imposed by the water regulator risked alienating customers. It said that, after 2005, prices would have to rise steeply to pay for future investment programmes.

The UK has two main regulatory bodies covering the economy – the Competition Commission (formerly the Monopolies & Mergers Commission – the MMC) and the Office of Fair Trading (OFT). Additionally there are regulators for the individual industries which formerly were state owned nationalised industries, but which have now been privatised, such as Ofwat in the case study above.

The UK has operated on the basis that mergers and acquisitions need to be investigated independently since there may sometimes be benefits when a merger gives market power to a business. Current UK legislation concerning monopolies and mergers was determined by the 1973 Fair Trading Act and the 1980 Competition Act, but has since been modified by the 2000 Competition Act. Under the 1973 and 1980 legislation, if any firm, or group of firms acting as one, has a market share exceeding 25 per cent (formerly 33 per cent) of the market, there was a risk that they could influence competition, and hence should be investigated. This applies whether the firm is a sole seller (monopolist) or a sole buyer (monopsonist), and also to local markets as well as national (as with Kingston-upon-Hull school bus services, Chapter 7, Section 7.2). In the case of more than one firm, two interrelated businesses may be investigated, e.g. a parent company and a subsidiary; firms colluding informally, for example by price leadership, may also be investigated.

The legislation also relates to mergers if the outcome of the merger is that the newly merged business has a market share exceeding 25 per cent, or with gross assets exceeding £30 million.

The Office of Fair Trading

The 1973 legislation created the Office of Fair Trading (OFT), presided over by its Director-General (the DGFT). This person has the power to refer cases of suspected monopoly to the Monopolies and Mergers Commission, now the Competition Commission, which is discussed below. The DGFT also chairs a panel to gather information on proposed mergers falling under the legal limits defined above. He/she then advises the Trade and Industry Secretary whether the panel believes that the businesses about which it has gathered information should be referred to the Monopolies and Mergers Commission; however, the DGFT does not have the authority to enforce the decisions, which may or may not be accepted by the Trade and Industry Secretary. Having said that, most are accepted; between 1987 and 1997, the DGFT advised the Trade and Industry Secretary on 2112 proposed mergers, as to whether or not to refer them. In only 13 of these cases did the Minister disagree with this advice. Since 1965, only 3 per cent of all UK mergers have been referred to the MMC; however, most of these have been subsequently abandoned or ruled against by the Trade and Industry Secretary. The basis for the Director-General reaching his/her decision is whether the mergers would have harmful effects on competition and hence be against the public interest (see the discussion below on the Competition Commission). Many firms have been persuaded by the OFT, over the years, to modify their behaviour to avoid being referred to the MMC.

The Monopolies and Mergers Commission

Until its replacement, this decided whether or not mergers were against the public interest. Once the MMC completed its report the Director-General then advised the Trade and Industry Secretary as to what actions should be taken. Of the 2112 cases between 1987 and 1997, in only ten of these cases was there disagreement between the Trade and Industry Secretary, the MMC and the OFT at the end of the investigation. Of course, the boards of the companies being investigated may defend themselves and about 30 per cent do so; of these approximately four out of every ten defences are successful. In the past, in some cases, merely being referred to the MMC caused the merger to be abandoned because of the uncertainty it imposed. In most cases, however, the MMC accepted the evidence which firms put forward, so a potential investigation by the MMC did not cause too much worry.

A similar situation existed with EU mergers in the 1990s, in terms of the time taken to investigate, with long time lags by the European Commission in dealing with a growing number of mergers. Under previous competition commissioner Karel van Miert, there was an increasingly aggressive policy towards them, discouraging some firms from completing them. For example, a 1998 £17 billion proposed merger between Reed Elsevier, the Anglo-Dutch information and publishing group, and Wolters Kluwer of the Netherlands was cancelled through fears that the Commission might require large scale sales of some of their activities to secure approval for the merger. Section 8.4 discusses EU legislation.

The 1973 Fair Trading Act strengthened the MMC, enabling it to define more freely what was meant by the term 'in the public interest.' This permitted it to act more more effectively to ensure that competition was maintained. The 1980 Competition Act reinforced the powers of the MMC enabling it to investigate mergers where there was a possible resultant loss of competition, as well as on the grounds of exceeding the 25 per cent market share. Anti-competitive practices identified by the 1980 Act included: price discrimination; predatory pricing (lowering prices to drive newcomers out of the market); selective distribution (where only certain retailers are supplied with the good, as with car dealerships in the past); and tie-in sales (where a company selling one product requires a second one also to be bought, e.g. a computer printer and ink cartridges).

UK governments' policy has, therefore, been that the MMC has to demonstrate whether a monopoly, or a prospective merger, is against the public interest – either on the grounds of market share (25 per cent) or gross assets exceeding £30 million, as discussed above.

The Competition Commission

The Competition Act, passed by the Labour Government which came into force in March 2000, imposes much tougher controls over cartels. It has strengthened the OFT substantially, giving it considerable powers of investigation and punishment, particularly where there is price fixing. Seeking to end the exploitation of consumers by business, or what he called ending 'rip-off Britain', Stephen Byers, the Trade and Industry Secretary, argued that firms exploiting their market powers could be fined up to 30 per cent of their UK sales, whilst businesses which continue to break the law could be closed down. This would be policed by the OFT. Additionally, Byers hoped this would lead to more litigation by the public against anti-competitors, as in the US, which could result in huge civil damages against these businesses. Additionally 'whistle-blowers' (people who report the actions of businesses from inside the company) will also be encouraged to reveal illegal practices. He also argued that it would protect smaller businesses in a market against the anti-competitive behaviour of big firms.

From March 2000 the OFT has also been empowered to enter premises, seize documents, take interim action against companies suspected of anti-competitive actions, and ultimately, levy large fines. This is supported by an OFT based anti-cartel task force. It is now a criminal action for a business to supply the OFT with false or misleading information when it undertakes its investigations. The final arbiter of actions will be the Competition Commission.

On the merger side, the Trade and Industry Secretary has decided to give the final decision on most mergers and take-overs to a more powerful independent Competition Commission, rather than leave it with ministers, where the power has long resided. A 1999 white paper argued for the depoliticisation of merger and acquisition policy by giving much greater independence to the Competition Commission. Previous Trade and Industry Secretaries had very substantial powers to delay or block mergers or impose conditions on mergers they did allow. Often this decision was delayed for months after a MMC or OFT inquiry, causing considerable frustration and economic disadvantage to the parties wishing to join together. There were also past accusations that decisions were made in the light of the political interests of the party in power, rather than purely on public policy grounds, although published OFT records indicate that ministers rarely went against independent advice given under the previous mergers regulation system.

Under previous laws a minister had two separate powers. He/she could decide whether to refer mergers to the MMC and he/she could decide whether to accept an MMC decision to block a merger or attach conditions to one which had been approved. Once the MMC approved a merger a minister could not overturn it. Nonetheless, removing the Trade and Industry Secretary from the decision making process solves this situation and eliminates what many see as secretive and arbitrary decisions in particular cases.

Transparent decision making by an independent Competition Commission reinforces early Labour government reforms which have sought to give a much clearer legal foundation to UK competition policy, prohibiting specific actions rather than relying on vague tests of what is in the public interest. Byers argued that merger decisions would be taken by the independent authorities on the basis of a test based on the need to protect competition. However, he also argued that there were some areas where ministerial intervention was still necessary; these relate to over-whelming public interest, for example proposed mergers and acquisitions of newspapers, or defence (for security reasons).

What Byers failed to spell out, however, was what the test based on the need to protect competition would be actually be, and what the test would be in the minority of areas where ministerial intervention was still necessary. The first investigation by the Competition Commission was an investigation into car prices, a case study illustrated in Section 8.2.

Conclusions

The fact that only three per cent of mergers in the UK have been referred to the MMC in the last 35 years suggests that, in spite of the existence of the two main bodies the OFT and the MMC, successive UK governments have had a fairly supportive attitude to mergers, a policy very different to that of the US where mergers and concentration are considered inherently bad. Indeed in the US, monopolies can be broken up and the former constituent parts required to compete with each other as with the Bell telephone company which, because of its market power, was broken up into seven smaller companies – the so-called 'baby Bells.' In the UK, once investigations have proved satisfactory no further action is taken, prompting accusations that the current regime is nowhere near as effective as it might be. Clearly the Competition Act of 2000, with its newly empowered OFT, and the Competition Commission, are means of putting real teeth into competition legislation.

Regarding monopolies, the underlying UK assumptions are that large firms can be more cost effective through the achievement of economies of scale, and that businesses need to be large to compete in global markets. Additionally, the near completion of the Single European Market in 1993, and increased global competition, mean that in many cases UK firms now face competition from overseas which moderates any temptation to exploit their market powers. However, this does not apply to all, as case studies elsewhere in this book concerning car sales and supermarket profit margins clearly demonstrate.

The other reason why only three per cent of mergers have been investigated by the MMC is the lack of sufficient resources. Nonetheless, where they have been investigated, they have either been ruled against or they have modified their behaviour. However, as was discussed earlier in this chapter, the majority of mergers have not achieved their stated objectives, but rather have increased market concentration.

The privatised industry regulators

Although covered by the MMC and the OFT, when a number of the nationalised industries were privatised, specific industry regulators were established to ensure that these newly created private monopolies did not exploit their new positions. A case study of the water industry has been provided above; other regulators were for electricity (Offer – the Office of Electricity Regulation); gas (Ofgas – the Office of Gas Supply); trains (ORR

– the Office of the Rail Regulator); and telecommunications (Oftel – the Office of Telecommunications).

Where there are activities in these industries with little chance of competition the regulators have imposed price controls to stop the businesses exploiting their market power – known as Retail Price Index (RPI) minus X per cent. For example, for switched national and international calls and line rentals, British Telecommunications had the price increases that it could levy, limited to RPI minus 3 per cent. Therefore, if inflation was 5 per cent BT could only raise its charges by 2 per cent. If there is a disagreement between the regulator and the businesses as to the relevant price increases then the MMC will act as arbiter. The purpose of this is to require the privatised business to pass any cost reductions, arising from increased efficiency, on to the consumer.

The regulator is also empowered to force other conditions on the privatised industries. For example, BT has to allow other companies entering the market, such as Cable and Wireless, to use its lines to households. In the same way, Centrica, formerly British Gas, is now able to supply electricity to households using the cabling formerly controlled exclusively by regional electricity companies. Yet, in turn, it has had to allow other companies to use its pipelines to supply gas to domestic households. Normally, negotiation between the regulator and the companies has been the approach that has worked since the appeals to the MMC are unpredictable in terms of outcomes. However, regulators have, in the late 1990s, tended to take tougher stances against privatised companies as the case study concerning the water industry, illustrates. High salary increases paid to the directors of these businesses, especially gas and water, and a seeming emphasis on paying high dividends to shareholders rather than providing the best service to customers, have prompted this.

8.4 The role of the EU – policies; state aid and subsidies; public procurement

£33 million fine levied on British sugar businesses

Synopsis   This case study examines the work of the European Commission in combating anti-competitive behaviour. It identifies as key characteristics:

1 secret price fixing by supposed competitors through a cartel;
2 the rationale for this being the need to end a price cutting war;
3 heavy fines levied on the companies.

In late 1998, the European Commission levied fines of £33 million on a number of British retail firms in the sugar market for engaging in secret price fixing deals between 1986 and 1990. British Sugar, which was accused of being the instigator and ring leader of the deals, was fined ECU (European Currency Units – now replaced by the euro) 39.6 million. Tate & Lyle had fines of ECU 7 million levied on it, whilst Napier Brown and James Budgett, who are sugar merchants and act as intermediaries between the growers and the retailers, were each fined ECU 1.8 million. Tate and Lyle's fine was considerably lower than British Sugar's because it co-operated with the investigation. It provided letters which were not only self-incriminatory but also confirmed the cartel's existence.

According to the Commission, the price fixing arose from a price cutting war in the early 1980s, which had been led by British Sugar. At a 1986 meeting, the Commission argued, British Sugar tried to end this. Eighteen subsequent meetings followed at which issues such as target prices which both would charge, and discounts to retail customers were discussed by the companies. British Sugar, which appealed against the fine, consistently argued that there had been no effect on prices as a result of the meetings.

Section 8.3 discussed UK legislation to ensure that markets remain competitive. This section explores European Union (EU) policies and legislation. It begins with a case study showing European Commission action against a number of sugar refiners for price fixing, which as we have seen is an example of collusion found in oligopolistic markets.

The EU places considerable importance on competitive markets since these underpin the single market. The Single European Act 1987, building on the Treaty of Rome 1958, sought to remove national restrictions, both quantitative (tariffs and import duties) and qualitative (also called non tariff barriers – such as bureaucratic administration), to achieve the lowest possible prices and the widest choice of goods for consumers. Additionally, businesses could hope to secure economies of scale through unfettered access to the then twelve (now fifteen) national markets of the European Union.

However, if there were restrictions on single market competition through the existence of cartels and monopolies, particularly state owned ones, predatory pricing, discriminatory pricing and public procurement policies (where governments offer public work for tender but only to national businesses rather than all EU businesses), then the benefits of the single market would be substantially reduced. The EU has therefore sought to create a business environment where firms can operate without restrictions, other than those required by law, to maximise profits and where consumers can receive maximum benefits from the completion of the single market. Legislation is implemented by the European Commission and enforced by the European Court of Justice.

Competition legislation was first introduced by the Treaty of Rome, articles 85 to 94. It has subsequently been updated by the Treaty of Amsterdam 1999; the latter's numbering system is showed here.

Article 81: Restrictive practices

This purpose of this article is, as its name suggests, to control practices by firms which restrict competition. These include: fixing the price of products so that all businesses in a market charge similar prices; businesses sharing out the market so that each has a certain amount, inhibiting competition between existing firms and making it much more difficult for newcomers to secure market share (the EU is only concerned where a firm's market share exceeds 5 per cent); and businesses determining output quotas so that each can only produce a certain amount, thus keeping up market prices.

The European Commission will examine all restrictive practices of which it is aware if the turnover of the business involved exceeds 200 million euros. Restrictive practices will be investigated whether they are horizontal, i.e. between businesses producing similar products, or vertical, i.e. between a firm and its raw material/components supplier(s), or between it and its retailers.

Case Study

European Commission levies record fines on shipping cartel

A cartel of container shipping companies, including P&O Nedlloyd, has been accused by the European Commission of fixing prices on North Atlantic container routes. A container enables cargo to be carried in standard shaped boxes to cut handling and other operating costs. It is easily transferred from ship to rail or truck by means of special cranes. The shipping companies are members of a 15 company conference or cartel, the Trans-Atlantic Conference Agreement (TACA). This co-ordinates common rates or prices to avoid competition between the companies driving prices down to a level so low as to incur losses for them in times of economic depression, when the volume of goods traded internationally falls. In the 1990s, the container industry was also trying to recover from an excess supply of container ships driving down rates, following a ship construction boom in the early 1990s.

The fines levied by the Commission amounted to $35 million (£22 million) for each member of the conference. TACA appealed on the grounds that it had notified the European Commission under the proper procedures and was exempt from EU competition policy under Regulation 4056, which was granted by the Council of Ministers. However, the EU's Competition Directorate, which supported the then competition commissioner Karel Van Miert, argued that shippers (exporters who send cargo) and carriers (the shipping companies) should be able to cope with the competition.

Article 82: Dominant positions

A business with a dominant position is one with significant market power, such as a monopolist or a group of firms acting as one, i.e. a cartel. The EU combats the actions of businesses in this situation if they seek to abuse this dominant position, rather than acting against them merely because they are dominant. Indeed, as noted previously, this is the real dilemma which the EU faces. On the one hand it seeks to prevent abuse of market power by dominant firms, who are usually dominant because of their size; on the other hand it needs dominant firms of substantial size in markets to be able to compete globally with US and Japanese firms as Euro-champions.

The key tests which the European Commission applies in determining whether a business has a dominant position include:

- whether its market share is greater than 40 per cent;
- whether this dominance is in a significant area affecting consumers or other businesses;
- whether the business is abusing its dominant position through charging excessively high prices;
- whether it is discriminating by charging different prices to different customers for the same products (see Chapter 7, Section 7.4);
- whether it is using loyalty rebates, whereby loyal customers are given a discount on their purchases to tie them to their existing supplier(s), making it harder for new entrants to the market to secure their custom;
- whether the business refuses to sell its goods/services to a customer without legitimate reason.

This article of legislation relates, therefore, to the problem of monopolists or oligopolists in a cartel exploiting their market power to secure monopoly profits, as discussed in Chapter 7.

Articles 87–89: State aid

Governments can also restrict competition by:

- giving grants, subsidies, low or zero interest loans, tax relief etc. to failing industries, enabling them to compete against other businesses which do not receive help but, rather, have to survive, or not, depending on their ability to generate profits;
- state acquisition of shares in businesses to enable funds to be channelled to them (a common practice in France);
- regional aid to depressed regions. This can also be viewed as another form of state aid, although in practice it is usually treated separately. If it persists it can confer unfair financial advantages on businesses located in the region, compared with those situated outside.

The EU does allow exceptions to this, however. State aid to help areas with high unemployment or where living standards are exceptionally low is permitted. Aid to promote projects which will benefit the EU as a whole are also permitted, such as: state aid to support Airbus Industrie; aid to disaster areas; aid to help the former East Germany because its economy and infrastructure was so run down by the Communist regime; aid to help regions in decline, e.g. where coal mining or steel manufacture was the major employer; and aid to promote improvements of a social character to assist individual consumers.

If a government wants to introduce a new aid scheme the European Commission must be given advanced warning. It will then review procedures as they are implemented to ensure that no discriminatory or anti-competitive policies are employed. In the same way it monitors existing state aid. Additionally, the European Commission operates a policy of 'one time, last time;' this means that a government giving aid for the restructuring of an industry, or rescue aid, should normally only be able to do this once. The rationale for this is that in the past, European governments gave large amounts of state aid to industries to enable them to secure competitive advantage over their rivals; this was, and to some extent still is, true with state airlines and steel producers, both of which suffer from severe overcapacity. The French government has used state aid and state partial or total ownership of many other businesses as means to protect and promote French industry and retain French ownership of it.

Figure 8.1 illustrates the effects of a subsidy on the price of and demand for a product, compared with a good not receiving a subsidy. Initially the goods in the market are sold at the equilibrium price of P_1 with Q_1 sold. When one government introduces a subsidy on the production of the good in its country, its country's businesses are able to sell the good at a new lower price of P_2; at this price Q_2 is demanded if all firms copy the subsidised firm and lower their prices as well. The supply curve has meanwhile shifted to the right and the amount of the subsidy is the vertical distance between

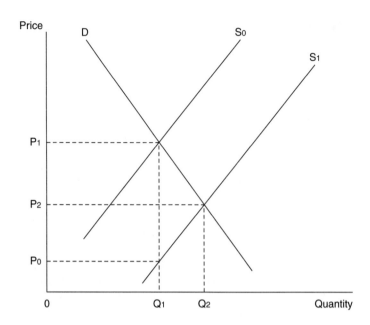

Figure 8.1 The effects of a subsidy on the demand for a good.

the old and new supply curves, i.e. P_1, P_0. The consumer receives P_1, P_2 of the subsidy, the amount by which the market price has fallen; the producer receives the market price made up of the remainder of the subsidy, i.e. P_2, P_0 plus $0P_0$, which is the cost of production of $0Q_1$ units.

The other area of state interference affecting competition in the single market is the issue of public procurement. When national and regional governments need work undertaken, e.g. constructing a new highway, or a university, they offer it for tender; this is public procurement. Businesses then submit their prices for undertaking the work and, normally the lowest price wins the contract, assuming they offer comparable quality work, similar timescales for completion etc. The value of these contracts can be substantial and, in the past, national and regional governments offered them only to businesses located within their own country because they wished to retain the income, jobs etc. generated by this work.

However, this defeats the whole purpose of the single market whereby businesses from Finland, for example, should be able to bid for contracts in Germany or Spain with an equal chance as German or Spanish businesses of securing the work. It also inhibits the benefits which the 1989 Ceccini Report said should arise from the single market, namely: cost savings from buying at the cheapest source; lower prices due to rival firms tendering for public sector contracts; the ability to achieve economies of scale as a result of the completion of the single market; that the single market, and hence greater competition, will encourage firms to be more innovative and invest more; and that private sector buyers will benefit from cheaper prices by firms supplying to the public sector.

In the last two years the European Commission has sought to amend legislation to make public procurement more open and transparent, by making the information about new public contracts to be tendered for more widely known across the EU, and by easing contact between buyers and sellers.

Regulation 4064/89

This regulation, which supplemented the competition legislation as defined by the Treaty of Rome, seeks to prevent the development of dominant positions by European businesses, whether by mergers or joint ventures. It sets limits on aggregate world-wide turnover (5 billion euros) which, if exceeded, requires prior clearance from the European Commission.

Additionally, large companies outside the EU, which have a turnover of at least 250 million euros in the EU must secure European Commission approval if the merger will impact upon competition within the EU. This was clearly illustrated by the previously cited example of the 1996 agreement to merge by US plane manufacturers Boeing and McDonnell Douglas. The European Commission objected on the grounds that the new company would have a 70 per cent global market share of commercial plane sales, and that McDonnell Douglas, also being a defence contractor, received large subsidies from the US Department of Defence. It argued that it had authority to police the terms of a US business deal with implications for EU competition. After much brinkmanship in negotiations and bitter dispute between President Clinton and the Commission, the latter finally agreed to the merger provided that Boeing–McDonnell Douglas met certain mutually agreed conditions, preventing cross-subsidisation between the military branch of McDonnell Douglas and the civil aircraft manufacturing of Boeing. It also required Boeing to drop exclusivity of (Boeing aircraft) purchase which it had with a number of US airlines to enable Airbus to compete for new contracts as airlines sought to buy new planes.

Self testing questions

1 Why has Ian Byatt, the head of Ofwat, recently taken a much tougher stance against the privatised water companies?

2 Briefly explain the work and responsibilities of (a) OFWAT; (b) the Competition Commission.

3 How did competition regulation change under legislation which came into effect in 2000?

4 What is the main focus of EU competition policy?

5 Summarise briefly, in your own words, the main articles of legislation governing EU competition policy.

8.5 Scottish Widows carried off by Lloyds–TSB

Case Study

Introduction

In the late 1990s a number of building societies and insurance companies demutualised, turning themselves into public limited companies (Plcs). A mutual building society or insurer is one which is owned by its savers or borrowers, or both, rather than by shareholders, as with a company. Mutual societies date back to the early to mid 1800s. However, many now perceive them to be dated organisations which need to be modernised by becoming Plcs. Others, members of a building society or insurance company often for just a short while, are tempted by the windfall profits when a building society or insurance company demutualises, and gives shares to its depositors, mortgage holders and insurance policy holders, so are also in favour of their demise (these people are known as carpet-baggers). In contrast, others, particularly directors of mutual societies, argue that the mutual status is worth preserving because they can provide a better quality service at lower cost, e.g. cheaper insurance premiums or lower cost mortgages by not having to worry about shareholders' dividend and share growth expectations.

One main reason for demutualisation is the desire of the mutuals to diversify into areas of financial services other than the narrow segment of the market in which they are currently concentrated, to offer more competitive products and secure external funds. In other words, by becoming a Plc, a mutual can borrow more easily from banks, and raise funds by issuing new shares, or even become a bank as with Halifax and Abbey National. Otherwise it would have to use its reserves which would place its members' monies at risk. As a Plc, however, an insurance company has first responsibility to its shareholders, rather than to its members, and many of the shareholders are likely to be institutional investors such as pension funds, banks and other insurance companies.

Another reason for demutualisation is that the UK financial services sector has faced substantial overcapacity. Relatively small sized building societies and insurance companies, and even banks, are seen by many to be calling out for rationalisation through mergers and acquisitions. Demutualisation followed by acquisition or merger is a clear way of achieving this.

Scottish Widows

In mid 1999, the 184-year-old insurance company Scottish Widows, the UK's fifth biggest, announced that it was planning to demutualise, with the market value of the company being worth an estimated £6 billion. It had been set up in 1815 to help the widows of Scottish soldiers killed in the Napoleonic wars. Earlier in the year Scottish Widows had announced that it was considering shedding its mutual status by floating the company on the stock market or by a merger with another financial institution.

At the same time as the demutualisation announcement, Scottish Widows stated that it was involved in talks with Lloyds–TSB about being acquired by the bank. These talks were subsequently to prove successful and created a bank assurance group with a market value of £56 billion, making it the fourth largest company in the UK. It also made Scottish Widows the fourth Scottish life assurance company to demutualise in recent years, following Scottish Amicable bought by the Prudential in 1998, Scottish Mutual bought by Abbey National, itself the first building society to become a bank, and Scottish Equitable, bought by the Dutch Group Aegon.

Scottish Widows was under no pressure from carpetbaggers to demutualise, unlike some building societies. However, after April 1999, when it hired Morgan Stanley, the US Investment Bank as external consultants to investigate whether it should float as a Plc or merge with another organisation, it was deluged with applications for insurance policies from carpetbaggers. It manages funds totalling £33 billion, although as noted above, joining with another company would give it access to more capital to grow further. A Scottish Widows director, Orie Dudley, who was brought in to make Scottish Widows more up to date, was thought to want to increase the company's assets under management, from £33 billion to £100 billion. It was believed that a merger, or being acquired by another business, was the best way of achieving this.

Lloyds–TSB

Lloyds–TSB had been looking to acquire another financial services provider for some time and stated in its annual results earlier in 1999 that it felt share prices of financial institutions had fallen sufficiently in value for an acquisition to be feasible. Lloyds–TSB already had its own life insurance company – called Lloyds Abbey Life – but this could only sell tied products, i.e. those originating from the Lloyds–TSB group. What it also wanted, to give a wider and more balanced business, was access for the distribution of its products in the independent financial adviser market, i.e. one that can sell the products of all companies rather than just tied products. Scottish Widows, in contrast, distributes nearly all its products through independent financial advisers (IFAs). Lloyds–TSB insurance products had also not been very successful, with only 4 per cent of its customers buying life assurance policies from it.

The merger

The acquisition of Scottish Widows by Lloyds–TSB created an organisation with funds under management of £80 billion, and 17 million customers, and made Lloyds–TSB the second largest life insurance company in the UK after the Prudential which has £150 billion under management. It also became the UK's largest bancassurer, i.e. banks with interests in insurance as opposed to a straight insurance company, like Prudential.

Instead of floating as a Plc, therefore, Scottish Widows was acquired by Lloyds–TSB. Under the terms of the acquisition deal, Scottish Widows became the part of Lloyds–TSB, representing the life insurance and investment brand, just as the acquisition of the Cheltenham & Gloucester Building Society by Lloyds–TSB became the mortgage brand for the financial services group. In this way the goodwill from existing customers, valued as £1 billion within the take-over price, was kept by the retention of the existing names, rather than branding it all under the name Lloyds–TSB. The group itself, in the meantime, secured a wider spread of activities to give it a strong presence in all areas of financial services, as well as additional market muscle – a wise series of acquisitions over a period of time. The Lloyds–TSB existing life assurance and investment businesses, Lloyds–TSB Life and Hill Samuel Asset Management, were then tied in with Scottish Widows, the new structure generating new premium income of about £800 million per annum.

The benefits to Scottish Widows from the acquisition have already been discussed. Their 900 000 policyholders with Scottish Widows, who had with-profits policies, each received a cash windfall of about £5900 plus £1.3 billion extra profits on their policies paid out over time; other policy holders each received a £500 cash handout.

For Lloyds–TSB, the main attraction of acquiring Scottish Widows was securing ownership of a valuable brand name. As noted above, the Lloyds–TSB brand name had not exactly been a runaway success in selling insurance policies to its customers; acquisition of Scottish Widows gave Lloyds–TSB one of the best brand names in the life assurance market, helped by a long term multi-million pound series of press and television adverts using an attractive young woman dressed in black.

There will be cost savings (£60 million) from the combining of the bancassurance business under the Scottish Widows umbrella, through voluntary redundancies and natural wastage.

In spite of the seeming benefits of the acquisition, Lloyds–TSB share prices fell after the initial announcement as dealers felt the bank had paid 'a very full price' for the insurance company. In contrast, Sir Brian Pitman, chairman of Lloyds–TSB, argued that the deal would deliver higher returns for shareholders and would boost dividends. Sir Brian also argued 'this is not the end of the story. We remain a very ambitious group, hungry for further expansion both in the UK and overseas.'

8.6 Summary of chapter

This chapter has examined how market power might be regulated. It began by examining how and why firms grow, distinguishing between mergers and acquisitions; it also distinguished between horizontal and vertical integration and conglomerate diversification. Research evidence on mergers and acquisitions suggests, however, that the expectations of mergers are not normally realised. Profits actually decline in US mergers investigated, rather than increase; cost savings are minimal, often because the merger causes diseconomies of scale.

The social costs of monopolies were then explored and this led into UK and EU legislation concerning monopolies and mergers. For the UK, the work of the Office of Fair Trading and the Competition Commission (formerly the Monopolies and Mergers Commission) were examined, including the increased powers given to them from the year 2000. The role of the privatised industries regulators was also examined. EU legislation to promote competition was also examined, including articles of the Treaty of Amsterdam dealing with restrictive practices, dominant positions, and state aid. Public procurement was also discussed.

The chapter finished with the examination of a case study on the acquisition of Scottish Widows by Lloyds–TSB.

8.7 Further questions

Further Questions

1 Monopolies can bring major benefits to their consumers and their shareholders through achieving economies of scale, which lead to lower production costs. Therefore, they should be encouraged. Discuss.

2 If privatised industries have to be regulated, might it have been better to keep these industries under state ownership?

3 'Collusion is inevitable in oligopolistic industries since firms will always seek to minimise competition. Therefore, the government should actively discourage mergers.' Discuss.

4 Should subsidies to industry always be banned on the grounds that they stifle competition?

5 Why did Lloyds–TSB acquire Scottish Widows? What does empirical evidence concerning previous mergers and acquisitions tell us about its potential for success?

8.8 Further reading

Curwen, P. (1997). *Understanding the UK Economy*, 4th edition. Basingstoke: Macmillan.

Griffiths, A. and Wall, S. (1999). *Applied Economics: An Introductory Text,* 7th edition. Harlow: Longman.

Harris, N. (ed.) (1997). The economics of organisational change. In *Change and the Modern Business*. Basingstoke: Macmillan.

The Economist

The *Financial Times*

The Times

The Adam Smith Institute: http://www.cyberpoint.co.uk/asi/

The Competition Commission: http://www.competition-commission.gov.uk

The European Commission: http://www.cec.org.uk

The Institute for Public Policy Research: http://www.Ippr.org.uk/

Lloyds–TSB website:http://wwwlloydstsb.co.uk/

The Office of Fair Trading website: http://www.oft.gov.uk/

OFTEL: http://www.oftel.gov.uk/

OFWAT: http://www.open.gov.uk/ofwat/index.htm

Chapter 9

The macroeconomy and its impact on business: I

Learning Outcomes

After completing this chapter the reader will be able to:
- understand different measures of national income and the problems of calculating these;
- appreciate the circular flow of income and Aggregate Demand–Aggregate Supply models of the economy and their use as tools of macroeconomic analysis;
- understand the effects of inflation in a modern market economy, how government policies seek to address this and its impact on businesses.

9.1 Defining national income

The return of the feel-good factor

Synopsis

This case study explores the return of 'the feel-good factor' in the UK and its impact on total, or aggregate, consumer demand. It discusses:

1 what constitutes the 'feel-good factor';
2 why consumer confidence in the UK improved so significantly in 1999;
3 the potential implications of this.

Case Study

The return to the UK of the 'feel-good factor' was reported by British broadsheet newspapers, at the time of writing this case study. The proof advanced was the development of a summer credit and housing boom, the latter evidenced by average house prices having risen by 10 per cent over the previous twelve months. This, in turn, was fuelled by increased household borrowing from banks and building societies, with bank lending peaking at a monthly figure of £6.3 billion, 18 per cent above the previous month's total of £5.3 billion. The average new mortgage was £72 000, compared with £63 000 twelve months previously.

The British Bankers' Association said that this was a reflection of the growing confidence of house buyers that interest rates were likely to stay low and stable, and also reflected sellers' confidence in securing the property prices they were seeking. However, the 14 per cent increase in the size of the average mortgage in the previous year raised fears that house prices would escalate out of control, as they did in the late 1980s.

Other forms of bank lending to customers also rose significantly, by 17 per cent over the previous year, reflecting growing consumer confidence and growing total or aggregate demand in the UK economy. The use of credit cards also picked up as consumers overcame their fear of incurring credit card debts in case they were made redundant. Lending on credit cards totalled £16.6 billion at the time of writing, whilst credit card spending, which is never the same as lending since some people pay back their outstanding balance each month, gained 4.3 per cent to £6 billion.

Newspaper commentators noted that buoyant consumer demand was likely to rule out further short term reductions in interest rates in the UK.

In Chapter 5 we examined demand and supply and saw how these determined the price of a product. Here, we shall examine demand and supply in the economy as a whole, as part of the study of macroeconomics. In other words, we shall consider all the markets in the economy added together rather than just an individual one, and we shall look at total or aggregate demand and aggregate supply and price determination in the economy, rather than just in one market.

The case study above illustrates aggregate demand and the factors influencing it, particularly growing consumer confidence, or the 'feel-good' factor as journalists call it. It also focuses on the major area of consumer spending, housing, and shows the impact of rising consumer confidence and hence expenditure, financed by borrowing, on house prices. Therefore, businesses, in this case study house builders, need to know the current state of the economy and how consumers will react. They also need to know how the economy will develop in the short to medium term future, government macroeconomic policies, and their impact on the economy. Most importantly for businesses, growing consumer confidence should translate into higher expenditure on products which will cause businesses to produce more.

The focus of this chapter, and subsequent ones is, therefore, on the relationship between businesses and the macroeconomy. One of the problems of macroeconomics, compared with microeconomics, is that there are a number of competing schools of thought as to how the macroeconomy works and the policies to be adopted to manage it effectively. These schools of thought are classified as the Keynesians, the Monetarists, the new Classical economists and the New Keynesians. The reader who wants to explore these in depth is referred to standard economic texts identified in the further reading section. This book does not have the scope or the space to do so. Rather, it seeks to discuss generally accepted theories of macroeconomics, their implications for businesses and how the latter react to economic change, both within the UK economy and externally.

Definitions

We begin our exploration of macroeconomics by defining national product.

National product

When examining microeconomics we saw that, if demand equalled supply, this determined the equilibrium price and quantity. Similarly, we can examine the economy and calculate the quantity of output of goods and services supplied by all businesses, however defined. This is called national product. However, in the economy as a whole, there is no guarantee that aggregate demand will automatically equal aggregate supply; we return to this later. In the meantime, there are several definitions of national product to consider.

Gross domestic product (GDP) at factor cost
This measures the total value of output produced in a country during a period of time, usually one year. It doesn't matter if the businesses are British or foreign owned, so long as the goods and services are produced in the UK.

Gross domestic product (GDP) at market prices
When goods are produced and sold they are taxed, by value added tax (VAT) or by excise duties for alcohol, petrol and tobacco. These are indirect taxes since they are levied on the consumer indirectly, as opposed to direct taxes, like income tax and capital gains tax. Businesses also receive

subsidies to encourage them to produce particular products; British Aerospace, for example, to encourage them to contribute to the Airbus consortium, or Ford and Rover cars to help maintain jobs. As we saw in Chapter 8, these determine the market prices at which the products are sold. We must allow for these indirect taxes and subsidies when calculating the GDP of a country, or we will get false values. Therefore:

GDP at market prices – taxes on expenditure (e.g. VAT and excise duties)
+ subsidies
= GDP at factor cost

Gross national product (GNP)

GNP is the value of output produced by a country regardless of where in the world the services from its factors of production are supplied. Therefore, money invested overseas in the shares of foreign companies will generate income for the UK as dividends. Other overseas income include royalties from the sales of compact discs and videos by British pop stars, UK developed computer games and profits from overseas investments such as constructing an oil refinery in Nigeria. All revenues generated in these and many other ways, which may be in the form of interest on loans or rents, need to be taken into account, since this money, called property income, will return to the UK. Conversely, property income will leave the UK as payment to foreign investors who provide similar services to the UK, e.g. Nissan's profits repatriated to Japan. The difference between the in-flows of income and the out-flows is net property income from abroad. GNP can also be measured at market prices or factor cost.

GNP = GDP + net property income from abroad

National income (NI)

Also denoted by the letter Y, since I is reserved for investment, national income is linked to the other three definitions of national product. Assets depreciate over time, i.e. lose economic value through wear and tear, or technological obsolescence. Hence, some of a country's GNP is the production of capital goods to replace other capital goods which have depreciated. As such it cannot be used by consumers, businesses or the government. We therefore deduct depreciation from GNP to determine the net additions to wealth of the country.

GNP at factor cost – depreciation = national income

National income is also known as net national product (NNP).

Let us now go back to our first definition, GDP, to consider, in more detail, how it might be measured.

9.2 Ways to measure real gross domestic product

We can measure real GDP, i.e. after removing the effects of inflation, in any one of three ways: output, income and expenditure. All these totals should, broadly speaking, equal each other, allowing for the complexities of calculating these amounts, which total billions of pounds sterling, across the whole economy.

National product (NP)

This measure of the value of real GDP is known as the product method. We calculate the value of goods and services produced in the economy by the country's businesses and other organisations, e.g. government agencies, over a period of time, usually one year.

National income (NI)

This measure of the value of real GDP is the income method. NI is calculated by the total of all incomes earned by the owners of the four factors of production. This will be by households as wages and salaries, from both employed and self-employed sources, and by businesses as profits. Rent from land and interest on capital are also included. Since the value of all the national product must be distributed to the owners of the inputs which have produced it, then national income must equal national product.

National expenditure (NE)

The third way to measure real GDP is the expenditure method. It is estimated by the total expenditure on goods and services during the same period of time. We include expenditure by foreigners on domestically produced goods, i.e. UK exports, but deduct expenditure by our citizens on foreign produced goods, i.e. UK imports. Since the income earned by households and businesses is spent on producer and consumer goods and services either currently, or in the future as household savings or retained earnings by businesses, then national expenditure must equal national product.

So, we find that NP is equal to NI is equal to NE.

Problems with valuing GDP

First, there is the problem of how to classify output. We have already given an example of this with a computer; it may be regarded as a consumer durable if used for domestic/family purposes, or a producer good if used by the same person for work purposes. Therefore, we must look at its end use to decide what it is.

The product method

The main problem here relates to what is called double counting. When we value the output of an economy we can do so by estimating the value of the final product or good. For example, we take the total value of a car. However, it contains an engine and five wheels (counting the spare). If we count the value of the engine and wheels when produced, and also in the final value of the car we are counting them twice, and hence overestimating the output produced by the economy. This is double counting. To get round this problem we have two options.

1 Added value at each stage. Here we value the engine and the wheels as they are produced. When we calculate the value of the car we include only the value added by the assembly of all the components, rather than the value of the components themselves. So, if the components are valued individually at £5000, and the car is valued at £8000, then the added value from assembling the car is £3000. (Value Added Tax, or VAT, is, of course, based on precisely this principle. As the name suggests, the Inland Revenue taxes the value added at each stage of the production process.) Therefore, GDP from this activity is £5000 + £3000 = £8000.
2 The other alternative is to take the final value of the car as £8000, but exclude the value of all the components; so we do not count the value of the engine, wheels etc. when first produced. Therefore, GDP from this activity is £8000.

There are, of course, problems with this. Services can be hard to value if provided by the public sector since there is no market for these, e.g. breast cancer screening, police and education. The usual way to get round this is to value these services at the cost of provision. Inflation poses another problem requiring business economists to distinguish between the real and money value of stocks of goods at the beginning and the end of the year for which GDP is calculated. Inflation will increase the money or nominal value of stocks of manufactured goods and goods in progress held by businesses, whereas, in real terms, there may have been no increase in output during that year. Therefore, the effects of inflation must be deducted – hence the use of real GDP above. Additionally, it is important to include only the value of goods and services during the year being measured, not goods carried over from previous years.

There is also the problem that many goods and services which are produced do not enter GDP statistics because they are not market trans-actions. For example, the tomatoes given to me by neighbours, grown in their own greenhouse, do not show up in GDP figures because no market transaction has taken place. In contrast, had those tomatoes been bought in a local supermarket they would have been shown as part of GDP. Work done which is paid for by cash, to avoid income tax and VAT, particularly in the building trade, similarly does not show up in records and hence understates GDP. Indeed this is a major problem with national income statistics, no matter which measure is used; the statistics can have signifi-cant errors through the sheer scope of the collection process, data discrepancies etc. As a result, a statistical discrepancy element has to be included in each method of calculation.

The income method

The problem of double counting also arises with the income method, specif-ically with transfer payments. These are incomes such as unemployment and maternity benefits, pensions etc. transferred, via the government, from some citizens to others. The recipients of these monies have not generated output; it is merely transferred by a government agency from someone else who has worked to earn it. To count the transfer payments would be to count them twice; once when earned by taxpayers, from whom it is then taken as taxes, and once as a transfer payment, when it is given to the benefit recipient. The latter are therefore excluded from the calculations.

The issue of indirect taxes and subsidies has already been discussed. Subsidies are included in national income calculations, since these are given by government to businesses and so become part of their income. In contrast, indirect taxes are deducted. This distinguishes between GDP at factor cost and market prices.

National expenditure

We discussed above the importance of avoiding double counting to avoid expenditure by businesses on inputs from other businesses. In the same way expenditure by government on transfer payments must be excluded for the reasons discussed in the income method. We must also make allowance for taxes and subsidies by subtracting the former and adding the latter to give us GDP at factor cost instead of GDP at market prices – factor cost giving the true value of output in a country. Another problem is that goods – such as cars and televisions – which last a number of years, are measured by their value at the year of purchase, even though the flow of services from the product spreads over a number of years. The exception is owner-occupied houses, where the value that the owner-occupier could have achieved had he/she rented it out, is used as the imputed or estimated rent.

Factors influencing national income

Many factors influence a country's national income and, through space constraints, only a few are briefly discussed here. The resources of a country clearly matter; this includes the size of the population, amount of natural resources, land mass, length of coastline etc. The amount of capital investment is important since this provides the tools and equipment for the workforce. Education is crucial to the development of human capital, as is the culture of a country. In the UK, for example, it has been alleged that business people are afraid of failing through loss of face, whilst those who do succeed are sometimes resented. In contrast, in the US, risk taking, and hence failure, is much more a part of the culture.

There must also be mechanisms such as access to venture capital, i.e. money loaned for higher risk new business ventures to enable potential entrepreneurs to secure the funding they need to develop their ideas. The political stability of a country is important; for example, the economic prospects of developing nations such as Afghanistan have been harmed by decades of conflict.

There is also the issue of whether resources are used productively or for non-wealth creating activities such as defence, which is part of national income. Economic policies and how they are implemented will also impact upon the size and growth rates of a country's GDP.

The uses of GDP statistics

GDP statistics are important in measuring how a country is performing economically over time. By making comparisons over time the extent to which a country's wealth is increasing can be measured. As well as comparisons over time, comparisons between countries can also be made and, indeed, this is one measure of countries' competitiveness.

Table 9.1 Comparison of leading countries' GDP, $ billion, 1998.

Country	GDP $ billion
EU members	
Austria	212.5
Belgium	250.5
Denmark	174.9
Finland	124.8
France	1433.9
Germany	2135.7
Greece	120.5
Ireland	83.2
Italy	1172.3
Luxembourg	16.7
Netherlands	377.5
Portugal	105.9
Spain	553.3
Sweden	226.9
UK	1357.2
Other	
Japan	3777.2
US	8230

Source: OECD, Economic Outlook, December 1999, NO. 66 © OECD 1999

The reader should note that the figures above are at prices and exchange rates current at the time of writing.

There are a number of problems, with using basic GDP statistics. If comparisons are made over time then this does not allow for increasing population, as with China and India. GDP per head of the population (GDP per capita) is therefore a better way to analyse GDP growth. The other problem is inflation. If nominal GDP grows at 5 per cent per annum, for example, and inflation is 6 per cent, then real GDP has actually reduced by 1 per cent per annum. The data above, being at current (nominal) prices does not remove the effects of inflation. Therefore, real GDP per capita is a better measure and comparator over time and between countries than nominal GDP.

Additionally, comparing GDP of different countries involves converting to a common currency, e.g. dollars in Table 9.1. However, the exchange rate may not show the purchasing power of a currency very well, e.g. £1 = $1.60 but, as a rule of thumb, in the US one can buy for $1 what it costs

£1 to buy in the UK. Economists therefore use a purchasing power parity rate. This enables GDP to be measured in a common currency such that a given amount of money can buy the same amount and type of goods in both countries. If the reader wishes to explore this further he/she is referred to more comprehensive books; for the purposes of this book we do not address this further.

9.3 The components of real GDP

In terms of expenditure, let us now remember that we distinguished between gross domestic product (GDP); gross national product (GNP), which was GDP minus net property income from abroad; and net national product (NNP) which was GNP minus depreciation at factor cost. NNP, we said, was also equal to national income.

Let us now consider the components of real GDP. We denote this as Y; this letter is also used to denote national income.

For simplicity, we assume an economy with no government to intervene, and no foreign trade, i.e. we have a closed economy.

Consumption (C)

One major element of gross domestic product is the production of consumer goods, both those used up in consumption, such as a pint of lager, or which can be used over time, such as a television set or a table and chairs, i.e. consumer durables.

Table 9.2 gives final consumption expenditure for 1995–1999. As can be seen, households account for the largest amount. NPISH are non-profit making organisations, serving households.

Table 9.2 Final consumption expenditure, £ billion, 1995 prices.

Year	Households £ billion	NPISH £ billion	General government £ billion
1995	438.5	15.7	140.4
1996	454.7	15.9	142.8
1997	472.7	16.2	140.8
1998	488.5	16.9	142.2

Source: National Statistics – the official UK statistics website, The Office of National Statistics. © Crown Copyright 2000

Table 9.3 UK investment: percentage of GDP, 1995–1998.

Year	% of GDP, 1995 prices			
	Business	General government	Private sector dwellings	Manufacturing
1995	10.7	2.2	0.6	2.5
1996	11.4	1.8	2.7	2.4
1997	12.3	1.5	2.8	2.6
1998	13.7	1.5	2.9	2.7

Source: HM Treasury

Investment (I)

This is the production of investment or producer goods such as assembly lines to make cars, ocean liners, a car when used by a company rep. as a necessary tool of his/her trade, a motorway etc.

Add these together we have

$$Y = C + I \tag{1}$$

In other words, GDP consists of consumption plus investment.

Table 9.3 shows UK investment components as a percentage of GDP at constant 1995 market prices. Business, general government, private sector dwellings and manufacturing exclude purchases, with the exception of sales of land and existing buildings. Business consists of private sector and public sector corporations (excluding NHS Trust hospitals), non-residential fixed investment.

Savings (S)

If we consider households, rather than the economy as a whole, they have two options: to spend their income on consumer goods and services (C), or to save it (S). If we aggregate this for the whole economy then whatever is not consumed must be saved.

$$Y = C + S \tag{2}$$

These savings will be borrowed, via banks etc, by businesses, to invest. In other words:

$$Y = C + I \quad \text{for the economy}$$
$$Y = C + S \quad \text{for households}$$

Table 9.4 UK household savings ratio, 1990–1998.

Year	Household savings ratio % of household income
1990	7.4
1991	9.4
1992	11.5
1993	10.9
1994	9.4
1995	10.3
1996	9.5
1997	9.3
1998	6.4

Source: HM Treasury

Therefore:

$$S = I \qquad\qquad 3$$

In other words, when the (closed) economy is in equilibrium then, by definition, savings will be equal to investment. The problem comes when the amount people want to save differs from the amount businesses wish to invest; but actual savings must always equal actual investment.

Savings can be thought of as deferred consumption. People go without now, i.e. save, to have more later, i.e. future consumption. People may save because interest rates are high, so they get a good return on their money, or they may save because this is part of a country's culture, as in Japan. Savings are also likely to be linked to income levels, with poor people unable to save because they don't have any surplus income, in spite of government attempts to persuade them to do so.

Since savings are, in our simple example, what is left over after consumption expenditure, we can think of savings as a withdrawal of money from the economy, especially if under the mattress, for example. If money is saved it is not being spent. Conversely, if businesses invest – building a new factory, for example – then they are putting income into the economy. We call this an injection of income, as opposed to savings, which is a withdrawal.

Savings are influenced by many factors, including interest rates, level of household income, the state of the economy (people save more when the economy is in recession in case they are made redundant), expectations about the future etc. The reader might like to compare this with Southeast Asian countries where the percentage of household income saved exceeds 25 per cent of household income.

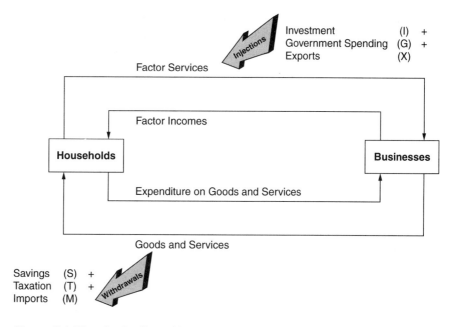

Figure 9.1 The circular flow of income.

It might be helpful, at this stage, to consider Figure 9.1, which shows the economy, and particularly the relationship between businesses and households, in a simple diagrammatic format.

The circular flow of income

Figure 9.1 is a circular flow of income diagram. It shows the two main types of economic unit in the economy: households, which represent consumers; and businesses. The top loop shows that households supply factor services or inputs to businesses: their labour; capital (either directly by investing in a business or indirectly via depositing money with banks who then aggregate it and lend it to businesses); land; and enterprise (entrepreneurs live in houses!). In return they receive: wages for labour; interest on capital; rent for land supplied; and profits for entrepreneurial skills. These factor incomes are shown on the return top loop.

The incomes which consumers receive are spent on goods and services which businesses sell, shown by the higher of the bottom two loops. In return they receive the goods and services, as shown by the bottom loop.

The role of government and international trade

Let us now introduce government and international trade into Figure 9.1

Government

A government interacts with businesses in two main ways already considered; it levies taxes and makes payments. It also manages the economy but we discuss this later. Taxes, denoted T, are levied on households by government and local authorities as income tax, capital gains tax, value added tax, council tax etc. and on businesses in the form of corporation tax, VAT, business rates etc. Since a government takes income away from households and businesses, taxes may be viewed as withdrawals from the circular flow of income. We denote public sector taxes by the letter T.

Conversely, governments make payments to households as supplementary income benefits, unemployment benefits, disability benefits etc. and to businesses in the form of subsidies, and grants. These may be viewed as injections into the circular flow of income, and are denoted by the letter G. Depending on whether taxes are bigger or smaller than government expenditure, the net effect will be a withdrawal from the circular flow of income (if T > G) or an injection (if G > T). Governments can also finance their expenditure by borrowing, so there is no reason why G and T must necessarily be equal.

If we add government activities into equation 1, we have:

$$Y = C + I + G \qquad\qquad 4$$

International trade

Finally, we allow for international trade. When British firms sell products overseas (exports), or receive dividend or interest payments from overseas investments, money is entering the UK's circular flow of income, and boosting the UK's wealth, i.e. it is an injection into the circular flow of income. We denote this by the letter X for exports. Conversely, when UK businesses and households buy imports, or payments are made overseas, as Ford repatriates its profits to the US, for example, then income leaves the UK. We denote this by the letter M for imports; these are a withdrawal from the circular flow of income. Depending on whether X > M, or vice versa, this will determine whether the net figure is an injection or a withdrawal to the circular flow of income, and a trade surplus or deficit.

Adding (X – M) to the income equilibrium equation, number 4, gives:

$$Y = C + I + G + (X - M) \qquad\qquad 5$$

For 1998 we may consider this in relation to Table 9.5.

Summarising, in an open economy, with international trade and government activity, we have

1 Injections into the circular flow of income: (I + G + X);
2 Withdrawals from the circular flow of income: (S + T + M).

Table 9.5 Components of UK aggregate demand, 1998.

Final consumption expenditure	£ billion, 1995 prices
Households (C)	488.5 +
*NPISH (C)	16.9 +
General Government (G)	142.2 +
Gross capital formation	
Gross Fixed Capital Formation (I)	144.4 +
Change in Inventories (I)	3.6 +
Foreign trade	
Export (X)	241.1 −
Imports (M)	265.3 =
Gross domestic product at market prices = £771.4 billion	

Source: HM Treasury

*NPISH, non-profit making institutions serving households.
See below for a discussion of aggregate demand.
Exports and imports are values of goods and services.

Injections will boost real GDP; withdrawals will cause real GDP to contract. These are shown as arrows entering and leaving the circular flow of income in Figure 9.1. Just as with the closed economy we said that, in equilibrium, S = I, so in our open economy, in equilibrium:

$$(I + G + X) = (S + T + M) \qquad\qquad 6$$

Governments strive to get the economy to an equilibrium position consistent with low inflation and low unemployment, steady economic growth, a stable exchange rate and a trade surplus with the rest of the world. Nonetheless, the reader should note that, in reality, the world is dynamic and at a moment in time the economy is more likely to be moving to or away from equilibrium rather than actually being there. So, if we were to take a snapshot of the economy, then at that moment (I + G + X) might well not equal (S + T + M).

Aggregate demand and aggregate supply

Finally, we link the above ideas with our earlier use of demand and supply curves to show how we may develop a demand and supply analysis for the whole economy.

We have already said that total expenditure in the economy will be on a range of goods and services, both domestically produced and, although

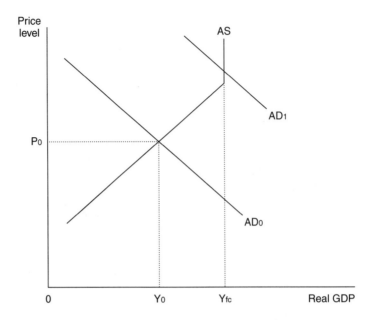

Figure 9.2 Aggregate demand and aggregate supply curves.

we deducted these from our estimations of GDP, foreign produced. Since demand has to be backed by an ability to pay we can measure aggregate demand in the economy as the total of the expenditure components defined above, i.e.

$$AD = C + I + G + (X - M)$$

We show this as AD_0 in Figure 9.2.

As the reader will note, the aggregate demand curve AD_0, in Figure 9.2, has exactly the same shape and characteristics as a demand curve for a single product, so the lower the prices in the economy, the more goods and services will be demanded. The main differences are the axes; the vertical axis shows an index of retail prices across all goods and services in the economy, at a moment in time.

By index we mean that the total cost of buying the typical shopping basket of goods and services is equated to 100 at some period of time – say January 2002. Monthly changes in prices of the basket of goods and services are then shown as changes from 100. For example, if prices rise 1 per cent between January and February 2002 because of inflation then the index will increase from 100 to 101. The horizontal axis shows the quantity of all goods and services produced, and is real gross domestic product, denoted by the letter Y. The reader should note that whereas government statisticians estimate the value of GDP over a period of time, Figure 9.2, like other demand and supply diagrams shows both prices and real GDP at a moment in time.

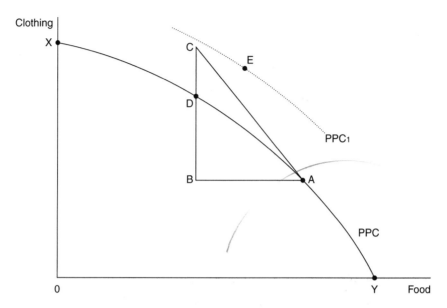

Figure 9.3 A production possibility curve.

In the same way we draw the aggregate supply curve, AS. This is the supply of all goods and services produced in the economy at a moment in time at each price level, other things remaining equal. Again it has the same characteristics as a conventional supply curve, so the higher the prices in the economy the more goods and services businesses will supply. Where the aggregate demand and supply curves intersect gives equilibrium in the economy at a level of GDP, Y_0, and a level of prices P_0.

However, when the economy reaches full physical capacity, i.e. all inputs in the economy are fully employed, the supply curve becomes vertical. This is shown on the horizontal axis at the point Y_{fc}, denoting the level of income of GDP consistent with full capacity or employment. This applies to all factors of production, not just labour. No more can be produced beyond Y_{fc} and if demand continues to rise, as shown by AD_1, then prices will rise rather than real GDP.

Figure 9.2 also shows that when the economy is in equilibrium at Y_0, it is not working at full capacity, i.e. resources are under-utilised, and the economy is not producing as much as it is potentially capable of. Economists use the production possibility curve to illustrate this, as is shown in Figure 9.3.

Figure 9.2 is more useful for economic analysis, i.e. explaining why events happen and their implications; in contrast Figure 9.3 is illustrative, although some analysis can be undertaken. For simplicity, we assume that the UK can only produce two goods, clothing and food. The production possibility curve (PPC) or frontier shows the limit of the UK's production, in the short term, given the fixed amount of its resources. It could produce all clothing (point X on the diagram), or all food (point Y) or some combination of the two, such as A or D, depending on whether it prefers more food or more clothing. Point B maps with the equilibrium P_0Y_0 in Figure 9.2. In both diagrams, the UK is under producing compared with its potential output. In Figure 9.3 it needs to move to its PPC to maximise its output; the opportunity cost of being at B, rather than A or D, is the output the UK could have had but which is now lost for ever because of its under performance.

Given an economy with no trade, the UK cannot be at point E in the short term since this is beyond its PPC; it does not have the resources to produce this combination of food and clothing. However, in the long term, with economic growth it could move to E, perhaps by investing in new capital equipment. As this happens the PPC moves outwards from the origin until it reaches E, where it is shown by the dotted line PPC_1.

We return to explain the triangle ABC a little later in Chapter 11.

9.4 Inflation – causes and costs of; money supply and monetary policy

Falling inflation and rising interest rates

Synopsis

This case study explores newspaper reports that inflation fell in the UK to its lowest level for 36 years. The case study discusses:

1 the low levels of inflation in relation to the previous week's increase in interest rates by the Monetary Policy Committee (MPC);
2 short and long term inflationary pressures;
3 the implications of the low inflation rates for other economic indicators such as the value of sterling.

UK inflation fell to its lowest level since 1963, in September 1999. The headline rate of inflation, which is the rate of change of the Retail Prices Index (RPI), and includes mortgage interest rates, fell 0.2 per cent (known as two percentage points) to 1.1 per cent in the previous month, the lowest since July 1963.

The underlying rate of inflation, which excludes mortgage interest payments (denoted RPIX), fell by one percentage point to 2.1 per cent, its lowest level since October 1994. This rate, which is targeted by the Bank of England, has remained below its 2.5 per cent target for five consecutive months.

The unexpected reduction in inflation was mainly due to falling seasonal food prices, especially potatoes; however, since seasonal food prices tend to be erratic, their effect could soon cease. If the inflation figures are broken down into their constituent parts they show that inflation persists in the services sector of the economy, whilst petrol prices are also rising sharply, mainly due to the increasing price of crude oil on the world markets as the Organisation of Petroleum Exporting Countries (OPEC) restricts supplies.

The previous week, the Monetary Policy Committee (MPC) of the Bank of England had raised the base rate by 0.25 per cent; the low levels of headline and underlying inflation were, therefore, used as evidence by affected parties to support their argument that the base rates should not have been raised. The Confederation of British Industry (CBI) argued that interest rates should not be raised further whilst the British Chamber of Commerce claimed that the previous week's rate increase had been 'misguided and inappropriate.' However, City analysts argued that the MPC is targeting inflation two years ahead. By raising interest rates the week before, the MPC was recognising that, although there would be a dip in inflation in the short term, in the long term pressures were building up. These included rising wage increases due to shortages of workers with the requisite skills as the economy moves to full employment, and rising oil prices and house prices, which could push up inflation. Indeed, one City bank had forecast that UK house prices would rise by over 30 per cent in the next fifteen months unless the MPC increased interest rates sharply. So, the MPC's raising of interest rates was an attempt to pre-empt such long term inflationary pressures.

The data caused sterling to fall in value against other currencies, especially the US dollar, whilst the stock market share price index rose in value.

Defining inflation

In Chapter 1, inflation was defined as a sustained rise in average prices over time. Normally, for newspapers, inflation is associated with retail prices, i.e. those paid by consumers for goods and services in retail outlets, as in the case study above. As the reader can see from this, the actual measures, headline and underlying, differ by whether mortgage interest payments are included or not. Changes in the headline rate of inflation measure of retail prices are calculated by changes in the observed prices of the contents of a typical shopping basket of goods and services bought by households, each component weighted according to its importance in household expenditure. The contents of this basket will change over time as new products are bought by consumers and old ones discarded. For example, changes in the prices of video-recorders, personal computers and mobile phones are included in the current basket of goods and services, whereas thirty years ago they would not have been. However, at that time black and white televisions and mild beer were included.

Businesses are also concerned with the inflation rate for raw materials since these will feed through to retail prices; the government therefore monitors these as well. For each measure of inflation, the data are published as an index series by the Office for National Statistics.

Why inflation poses problems

The fact that the Bank of England monitors the rate of inflation, and that it is a key economic indicator of how well an economy is performing, suggests that stable price levels are preferred to rising price levels, i.e. inflation. If inflation is anticipated then adjustments can be made, such as trade unions seeking wage increases at least equal to the rate of inflation. However, if inflation is unanticipated, which includes varying rates of inflation over time, this poses problems for consumers and businesses. We can therefore identify a number of reasons why inflation is perceived to be undesirable:

Erosion of living standards

With inflation, pensioners and others on fixed incomes are particularly vulnerable to changes in their real as opposed to their nominal incomes. In the same way, inflation erodes the value of savings if the interest rate paid by banks and building societies is less than the rate of inflation. This may actually boost savings since people worry about the inflationary effects and spend less to increase the real value of their savings. Others, seeing their savings fall in real terms may actually spend more.

Conversely, if people do borrow money, and the rate of interest is below the rate of inflation, i.e. the real interest rate is negative, then inflation redistributes wealth from the lenders to the borrowers since, in real terms, the borrowers pay back less than they have borrowed. In the late 1970s, for example, UK inflation was 28 per cent per annum, yet banks were only charging interest rates of 18 per cent for borrowing; it therefore paid to borrow as much as one possibly could, yet many people chose not to. This is because it takes time for people (and banks) to change their expectations of inflation levels and their attitudes towards it and borrowing and lending.

Uncertainty

Unanticipated inflation creates uncertainty for consumers and businesses. As indicated above, it means that households are uncertain as to their future real incomes; people may, therefore, spend less and save more to offset the falling real value of their savings. In times of high inflation, high interest rates may also deter people from long term debts and hence borrowing, e.g. mortgage loans, because of the high nominal cost of borrowing; although conversely, if consumers anticipate rising house prices for the foreseeable future, they will be anxious to buy a first house or move to a more expensive house before prices rise still further.

For businesses, inflation may deter new investment programmes for the same reasons. Additionally, there is the uncertainty arising from potential profits; although inflation means rising prices and hence rising revenues for businesses, it also means rising costs of raw materials, labour etc. If costs rise faster than revenues then profits will fall, unless businesses can reduce costs, for example, by downsizing. Yet this action will have further costs in terms of redundancy payments and restructuring the organisation to enable it to function at least as effectively with fewer staff. Uncertainty is an essential characteristic of business activity but inflation can exacerbate that uncertainty.

The implications of rising costs for businesses

As well as rising labour costs businesses will, in inflationary times, have to continually change the prices they charge for their products. For businesses which produce catalogues, such as mail order firms, this can be very costly and the faster prices rise the more frequently new editions must be produced. Rising prices also make British goods less competitive in both domestic and foreign markets. In domestic markets, British firms will face increased competition from foreign goods produced in countries where the inflation rate may be lower and, therefore, the price of the foreign goods is lower. The latter are likely to increase their market share at the expense of British goods. In foreign markets British goods will, through inflation, also be less competitive and therefore likely to sell less well against foreign produced goods. This in turn has adverse effects for the UK's balance of payments. The UK economy has a long history of inflation and one government policy to combat these adverse inflationary effects has been to allow sterling to fall in value against other currencies, i.e. a falling exchange rate. This makes British exports cheaper and foreign imports dearer. This is explored more fully in Chapter 11, Section 11.3.

The causes of inflation

In discussing the causes of inflation, the reader should again note that economists do not agree on the exact causes, although there are elements of commonality among them. As discussed at the beginning of this chapter, this book seeks to give a broad overview; again, for a more detailed analysis, the reader is referred to the texts at the end of this chapter.

Demand pull inflation

Non-monetary demand pull

In Figure 9.2 we saw how, if the aggregate demand curve shifts to the right, then both output and prices will increase. If demand increases to AD_1, the fact that the economy is already working to full capacity, or full employment, means that prices will rise even more sharply since, in the short term, no more can be produced. Economists say that this excess demand over the amount of goods and services supplied is pulling up prices to higher levels. This is called demand pull inflation. As we have seen, the increases in aggregate demand may result from: increased demand by businesses through increased investment programmes (I); increased consumer demand (C) either through tax cuts or growing consumer confidence; the government through an increased expenditure programme on education, the National Health Service etc. (G); and from overseas customers demanding British exports (X). In reality, goods can be imported from abroad and this will happen reducing, to some extent, the effects of demand pull inflation. However the UK's balance of trade, the difference between its exports and its imports, will then worsen. The economists who supported this theory of inflation, which is most typically associated with full employment, were called Keynesians, and took their ideas from the work of John Maynard Keynes. They were particularly influential in the UK, the US and other market economies from the late 1930s to the end of the 1960s.

Monetary demand pull

Most economists believe that growth in a country's money supply also causes demand pull inflation. The government uses a number of different measures of money supply, but in broad terms we will take it to mean notes and coins in circulation in the country, plus bank accounts, either in the form of deposits, as when workers' salaries are paid in monthly, or in the form of bank loans and overdrafts. Bank accounts, and especially loans and overdrafts, are by far the biggest element of money supply, as can be seen in Table 9.6, with the first three components of M4.

Table 9.6 Main measures of UK money supply.

M0	**known as narrow money**
=	notes and coins in circulation
+	bankers balances (banks' non-statutory deposits with the Bank of England).
M4	**known as broad money**
=	notes and coins held by the private sector
+	private sector £ non-interest bearing sight bank deposits
+	private sector £ interest bearing sight and time bank deposits
+	private sector holdings of £ certificates of deposit
+	private sector holdings of building society shares and deposits and £ certificates of deposit
+	building society holdings of bank deposits and bank certificates of deposit and notes and coins

Bankers are the clearing or high street banks. Sight deposits are, effectively, current accounts; time deposits are deposit accounts. Certificates of deposit are receipts issued by banks to acknowledge that a sum of money has been deposited with them at a fixed rate of interest for a fixed period of time. It may be in sterling or another currency.

If, through its economic or monetary policies, the government allows the supply of money in the economy, particularly loans and overdrafts, to increase by more than the expected growth rate of real output, i.e. GDP after removing the effects of inflation, then people will use these loans and overdrafts to buy more goods and services. This will cause their prices to rise, whether the economy is at full employment or less than full employment. In the short term it will also cause output to increase as businesses, seeing prices rise, are encouraged to produce more. Further, an increase in money supply relative to the demand for money will cause interest rates, which are the price of money, to fall. However, in the long term, all the increase in the money supply will be absorbed by an equal proportionate increase in prices; there will be no effect on GDP. Therefore, increases in money supply are always inflationary. This theory was developed in the early 19th Century and was known as the Quantity Theory of Money. In the late 1960s it was refined and re-presented to the world by a group of Chicago University economists known as Monetarists, the most important of whom was Milton Friedman; they were particularly influential in government circles from the late 1960s to the mid 1980s.

Table 9.7 shows increases in the two main measures of money supply in the 1999s. The data show, for each measure, year on year percentage increases.

Table 9.7 Money supply increases, 1990–1999.

Year	M0 %	M4 %
1990	5.3	15.9
1991	2.4	7.9
1992	2.4	5.1
1993	4.9	3.5
1994	6.4	5.1
1995	5.9	7.3
1996	6.7	10.0
1997	6.2	11.2
1998	6.1	11.2
1999	7.2	N/A

Source: HM Treasury

Cost push inflation

Another theory of inflation argues that it is caused by rises in costs, particularly labour costs (wages) and raw material costs, e.g. crude oil. Where raw materials and components are imported from abroad, costs may rise through a variety of reasons such as prices being forced up by suppliers, as with the OPEC cartel and crude oil prices in 1973 and 1979; these are known as exogenous shocks because they originate from outside the economic system and have a major impact on the economy. Other examples include bad harvests as with South American or Kenyan coffee crops being damaged by frosts, or even by adverse movements in exchange rates. For example, if sterling falls in value against other currencies, then more sterling has to be given to buy each other currency; so prices of the UK imports will rise, pushing up UK prices – what is known as import cost push inflation. This situation is exacerbated when the imports are components or raw materials to be used in the manufacture of goods in the UK, since these then have to rise to cover their higher input costs.

Wage cost push inflation

Let us take rising wages as a good example of cost push inflation; what we call wage cost push inflation. If the UK's work force sees inflation increasing then trade unions will demand higher wages to compensate for the decline in the real living standards of their members. Other wages will also rise on comparability grounds, even though other workers will not be trade union members. To cover rising production costs businesses will raise the prices of their goods and services sold to consumers. This, in turn, will trigger further wage demands at the next round of negotiations which in turn will push prices still higher, causing what is known as wage price spiral.

The problem will be exacerbated still further if, when unions negotiate higher wages, their expectations as to next year's price increases fall short of what subsequently transpires, since their members' living standards will then fall. For example, they anticipate 2 per cent inflation but it is actually 4 per cent. At the subsequent year's round of negotiations, they will seek to obtain wage increases equal to what they expect inflation to be the next year (say 4 per cent again), plus the 2 per cent that their expectations fell short of the previous year. This will create still greater inflationary pressures. Therefore, influencing the inflationary expectations of consumers and businesses is perceived to be important by the government. If it can convince the population that inflation will be low in the next year then the labour force will moderate its wage claims and businesses will be less inclined to build large price increases in to their forecasts.

In this case, the effects of cost push would be shown in Figure 9.2 by the aggregate supply curve shifting upwards and to the left. Prices rise and output falls as firms reduce demand for inputs, especially labour, to try and control production costs; this is in contrast to demand pull inflation where both prices and output increase.

Demand pull and cost push inflation working together

It is possible for an economy to experience both types of inflation together, and they will interact with each other. For example, a government may embark on an expansionary spending programme, financed by borrowing, to stimulate economic growth. This was the type of policy typically adopted by governments in the 1950s and 1960s when influenced by Keynesian economic theory. This causes aggregate demand to increase and the AD curve in Figure 9.2 shifts to the right, with rising prices, i.e. demand pull inflation. In the pre-Thatcher governments prior to 1979, when the trade union movement was overly powerful, this would trigger wage demands to compensate for rising prices, shifting the AS curve to the left. In turn this would cause further price increases, i.e. wage cost push inflation. In turn, higher inflation causes the value of the money supply or currency to fall, both in its own right and against other currencies, i.e. the exchange rate falls. This will cause import prices to rise and may trigger import cost push inflation to further contribute to the trend of rising prices. The AS curve in Figure 9.2 will shift upwards and to the left pushing prices up further.

Policies to combat inflation

Demand management policies

These could also be called demand side policies but the above is more common, so is used here. Two main demand management policies may be distinguished, monetary policy and fiscal policy. Both of these will impact on businesses.

Monetary policy

Monetary policy in the UK has, as its main objective, the control of inflation to achieve price stability and to provide a framework for non-inflationary economic growth. To achieve this it seeks to keep aggregate demand in the economy approximately in line with the economy's productive capacity, or aggregate supply, by varying the base rate as appropriate.

Monetary policy works by varying the short term interest rate, which is the price of money. The key short term interest rate is the base rate of the Bank of England. This is the central bank of the UK and is often known just as the Bank, with a capital B to distinguish it from high street and merchant banks. The base rate is the rate on which all other UK short term interest rates are based. The base rate therefore determines the cost of borrowing money, such as overdraft rates and mortgage rates; it also determines rates paid on savings. Changes in interest rates feed through the economy in a variety of ways. They affect:

1　the demand for assets such as houses, and thus house prices, via mortgage rates, and also government stocks and shares; in turn, the value of these affects consumer confidence;
2　consumer demand for goods and services via bank loan and credit card rates, and the rates earned on savings;
3　business demand to undertake new investment via loan rates and mortgages on existing assets such as factories and office blocks;
4　the rate of exchange of sterling against other currencies. For example, a rise in interest rates makes sterling more attractive to foreign investors who will deposit money in UK banks, buy UK stocks and shares etc. To invest in the UK these investors must use the domestic currency; so the demand for sterling will rise in the foreign currency markets causing its price (the exchange rate) to rise. As sterling is now dearer, exports will cost more in foreign markets whilst imports coming into the UK will be cheaper;
5　ultimately, GDP and employment.

If interest rates are set too high, known as tight monetary policy, this will discourage aggregate demand, reduce business activity, economic growth and employment and cause the economy to work inside its production possibility curve. If, conversely, interest rates are too low, then aggregate demand will exceed aggregate supply and inflationary pressure will build up in the economy, causing rising prices, since businesses will not, in the short, term, easily be able to meet the increasing demand.

The short term interest rate has been set, since 1997, by the Monetary Policy Committee (MPC) of the Bank of England, as opposed to by the Chancellor of the Exchequer, on behalf of the government. When it was under the Chancellor's control, there was always the worry, often justified, that a government would operate a loose monetary, i.e. low interest rate, policy before an election to boost aggregate demand and growth to help it win the election, even if subsequently there were adverse economic effects. In contrast, the Bank of England is politically neutral. The objective of the Bank's monetary policy is to achieve a target of 2.5 per cent per annum for the underlying rate of inflation, which excludes mortgage interest payments (RPIX). The MPC meets monthly to review current economic data and forecasts of UK and international economic and monetary variables for two years hence, and to decide the base rate for the next month. If it fails to keep inflation within plus or minus one per cent of its 2.5 per cent target, the Governor of the Bank of England must write an open letter to the Chancellor of the Exchequer explaining why the target has not been met.

Therefore, to combat inflationary pressures in the economy, the MPC will raise the base rate; if pressures are abating and economic growth is slowing, the MPC will lower interest rates. Its main weakness is that, at times, using monetary policy to achieve one goal may not be suitable for other goals. If inflationary pressures are increasing, the MPC will raise the base rate, and other rates will follow. Yet, if sterling is also overvalued, as in the late 1990s/early 2000, raising the base rate makes sterling even more attractive as a currency in which to invest and so drives the exchange rate up still more – which is not desirable as it makes exports more expensive/less competitive in foreign markets.

In conclusion, monetary policy is currently perceived by the government to be a flexible policy weapon which has a direct impact upon both non-monetary and monetary demand pull inflation.

Table 9.5 shows changes in UK base rates since the beginning of 1997, which is just before the MPC acquired responsibility for setting the base rate.

It is worth noting that a report in October 1999 by the National Institute for Economic and Social Research (NIESR), found that economic growth would have been little affected, although output would have been slightly more volatile, and inflation would still have stayed under control, albeit marginally higher, if the MPC had left the cost of borrowing at its May 1997 level of 6 per cent, during the two and a half years up to October 1999. The report's author, Garry Young, concluded 'much less activism (in varying interest rates) would probably have been better over the last two years.'

Table 9.8 Changes in UK base rate, 1997–2000.

Year	Date	Base rate %
1997	6 May	6.25
	6 June	6.5
	10 July	6.75
	7 August	7.0
	6 November	7.25
1998	4 June	7.50
	8 October	7.25
	5 November	6.75
	10 December	6.25
1999	7 January	6.00
	4 February	5.50
	8 April	5.25
	10 June	5.00
	8 September	5.25
	4 November	5.50
2000	13 January	5.75

Source: HM Treasury

Fiscal policy

This is concerned with varying the balance between public sector expenditure (G) and public sector revenue (T). Basically, the public sector consists of central government, local authorities and remaining state owned businesses such as the London Underground and Air Traffic Control.

If public sector expenditure exceeds revenue, this is a budget deficit, and has to be financed by the government borrowing to make up the shortfall. This revenue shortfall was formerly known as the Public Sector Borrowing Requirement (PSBR), but is now known as the Public Sector Net Cash Requirement (PSNCR). Conversely, a budget surplus occurs when public sector revenue exceeds public sector expenditure; the government may use this surplus to pay off part of its previous accumulated debts which, in total, are known as the National Debt. This budget surplus is known as the Public Sector Debt Repayment (PSDR).

By varying public sector expenditure and revenue, and hence the amount of the PSNCR and PSDR, a government can influence the level of activity in an economy, and hence its impact on businesses. If the reader refers back to the circular flow of income in Figure 9.1, he/she will recall injections and withdrawals and their constituent parts. If the government increases taxation (T), a bigger withdrawal from the circular flow of income, and contracts its spending (G), a reduced injection into the circular flow of income, then this will reduce the level of activity in the economy. If for example, in Figure 9.2, the economy were at full employment of its resources, with the AD curve intersecting the vertical part of the AS curve, then increasing T and reducing G would shift the AD curve to the left and reduce inflationary pressures. This is a contractionary economic policy since the level of activity in the economy contracts as a result of the government's fiscal stance.

Alternatively, a government may operate a PSNCR, spending more than it raises by taxation, with the excess expenditure funded from government borrowing, for example by selling government stocks or bonds (normally fixed interest, fixed term debt) to households, businesses especially banks and pension funds, and others willing to buy it. In this case the increase in G, perhaps supplemented by reduced T, will have an expansionary effect on the economy, increasing GDP and prices. If AD intersects AS on the latter's vertical segment, then any increase in G or reduction in T will be purely inflationary, whereas where AD_0 intersects AS, any increase in G will cause increases in both prices and GDP. When the government seeks to influence the level of injections and withdrawals, as in the two examples above, this is known as discretionary fiscal policy, since such policies are at the choice or discretion of the government. In contrast, automatic fiscal stabilisers such as progressive taxes, which rise as consumers become better off (e.g. income tax), or benefits which reduce as GDP increases, dampen down the effects of any growth in GDP and so reduce fluctuations in the economy. In other words they dampen movements of the business or economic cycle, which was introduced in Chapter 1.

The impact on the economy of the government's particular fiscal stance will depend on whether the other components of the injections and withdrawals increase or decrease. If, for instance, business investment rises because of growing business confidence then, if the government is also running a PSNCR, the two elements of aggregate demand will work together and push the demand curve further to the right than if G alone were increasing.

Government expenditure and revenue policies for the next year are set out in the annual Budget, which is published in broad terms in November of each year and delivered in March of the following year. In the past, when Keynesian economic theories held sway, fiscal policy was perceived to be the main way of influencing the economy. Adjustments to tax rates and expenditure were seen to be ways to 'fine tune' the economy to ensure that steady upward economic growth was achieved. Nowadays monetary policy, particularly the use of interest rates, is seen to fill that role. Interest rate changes can be made quickly, whereas expenditure changes and, to a lesser extent tax changes, are normally only made once a year at Budget time (see Section 9.5); and, when they are introduced, there will usually be a time lag before they become fully effective. Moreover, their effectiveness depends on how good government forecasts are of future changes in the economy; in practice economic forecasting is less than perfect, which mitigates against the effectiveness of fiscal policy.

Fiscal policy is therefore much less influential and, to a great extent, fiscal prudence is now the dominant rationale of fiscal policy, i.e. the desire to minimise the PSNCR, even better to balance the budget and, ideally, to run a surplus to pay back part of the national debt. Running a large long term PSNCR is therefore not acceptable; indeed this has been reinforced by the rules which EU countries have had to meet to qualify for membership of the single European currency – known as the Maastricht Convergence Criteria. This is because a PSNCR has to be funded by borrowing from the public, businesses etc. through the sale of government stocks and bonds. Since the pool of funds available to borrow is finite (there is only so much households and businesses can save for example), the government competes against the private sector of the economy when it borrows. Its greater borrowing power can force up interest rates and prevent businesses from borrowing to finance investment projects, since they cannot afford such high rates; this is known as crowding out.

Having said all that, a combination of fiscal and monetary policy is currently seen as the best mix to manage the economy, seeking a longer term balanced or even surplus budget as demonstration of a prudent fiscal policy and monetary policy for short term adjustments as economic circumstances change. Inflation is targeted, currently not to exceed 2.5 per cent, and this is intended to provide a stable economic environment within which businesses can flourish and become increasingly competitive. To quote the Chancellor of the Exchequer Gordon Brown, a 'pro-active monetary policy' (is necessary, since) 'far from choking off recovery, pre-emptive action is essential in order both to sustain growth and to meet our inflation target.'

Supply side policies

Whereas demand management policies are concerned with influencing the aggregate demand curve, and hence prices in the economy, so supply side policies seek to influence the aggregate supply curve. The underlying philosophy of these is to make input and output markets more competitive and hence boost productivity, particularly of labour. In the case of the input markets, it has meant seeking to make labour more flexible by: removing the power of trade unions to operate closed shops, where all workers in a business have to be union members; preventing secondary picketing, where union members demonstrate outside businesses other than the ones where they are employed to prevent other workers and inputs entering the factory gates; and making wildcat strikes illegal, where strikes are called spontaneously on the strength of a show of hands of union members at a meeting, rather than by a formal ballot. All of these were outlawed by the Thatcher governments of the 1980s. On the input side, supply side policies also involve providing better training and retraining for employees to enable them to acquire new skills and move to new jobs that they were not previously qualified to attempt; in other words, to become more employable. It also involves cutting the marginal rate of income tax to leave people with more of their income to take home after all deductions; it has been argued that this will encourage them to work harder, longer and more willingly.

Cutting corporation tax paid by businesses has the same logic under-pinning it and also the expectation that this will encourage businesses to invest more. Supply side policies therefore also involve output markets. It has been realised that, for many goods, UK consumers pay far higher prices than either US or EU consumers. This ranges from cars to CDs and from food in supermarkets to financial services. For example, planning restrictions have: stifled competition in retailing; in financial services, unit trust providers have levied high initial charges and management fees, as they operate cartel-like arrangements; whilst the car industry has subsidised company cars at the expense of retail sales, and has prevented cheaper right hand drive cars from being imported into the UK from Continental Europe, in direct contravention of single market regulations. Much of this is due to the lack of competition in these markets and these issues were discussed in Chapter 8. Supply side policies seek to remove these anti-competitive forces and free up markets. The privatisation programmes adopted in the UK, and in many other countries of the world, over the last two decades, are further examples of this. Not only does this free up markets previously dominated by state owned businesses; it also reduces government spending and hence the PSBR which is used to finance it, and thus avoids the problem of crowding out discussed earlier.

Some economists argue for more interventionist supply side strategies, such as government schemes to encourage businesses to locate in areas of high employment; the financial support for Nissan to locate its car plant in Sunderland in the 1980s and in late 1999 were examples of this. Of course, when factories such as this start producing, the intervention also impacts on the aggregate demand curve through increased demand for inputs from the business and for consumer goods from those who work at the factory.

In Figure 9.2, therefore, the purpose of supply side policies is to shift the aggregate supply (AS) curve downwards and to the right, leading over time, to increased employment, increased real GDP and lower prices, i.e. reduced inflation.

Exchange rate management policies

One other policy, not so far discussed here, is manipulation of the exchange rate to influence inflation. The exchange rate is the price of one currency against another and is discussed more fully in Chapter 11, Section 11.3. The government may influence the price of sterling against, say the deutschmark, either through interest rate policy or by buying and selling sterling.

If the government raises interest rates this means that those who invest in the UK will earn a higher return on their money. Investors might include pension funds, banks and insurers, and multinational companies who have cash flow in a number of currencies. The investment may be longer term, e.g. by buying government bonds, or it may be short term, e.g. by just placing money on deposit in the London money markets. As interest rates rise investors will buy sterling since this is what they must use to place money on deposit or invest in businesses. Increased demand for sterling will cause its price (the exchange rate) to rise. As a consequence, UK exports become dearer, since foreigners must give up more of their currency to buy one pound, but UK imports will be cheaper, since now one pound buys more foreign currency and hence more goods, services and raw materials. This will help keep the inflation lower than would be the case if the exchange rate were lower, i.e. sterling were cheaper. The only adverse side effect is that the UK's balance of trade, i.e. the record of the value of its exports and imports, is likely to worsen and go into an even bigger deficit than it normally is.

Even here there is a final constraint. Another of the Maastricht Convergence criteria requires potential single currency members to have been in the exchange rate mechanism (ERM), an arrangement which links currency values to each other and to the euro for two years, with each currency having a variation not exceeding plus or minus 2.25 per cent of its agreed exchange rate. Although the UK left the ERM in 1992, the government must be mindful of this condition which it will have to meet if a national referendum decides that the UK will join the single European currency. Hence even the ability to use this weapon to reduce inflation is circumscribed.

Self testing questions

Self Testing Questions

1 It has been argued that a low rate of inflation is desirable for a country in that business profits will be rising, the labour force will earn more and there will be increased confidence. How valid is this argument? Explain your answer.

2 What are the essential differences between demand pull and cost push inflation?

3 How might: (a) Monetary policy, (b) Fiscal policy, be used to combat inflation?

4 How do demand side and supply side policies differ? Should a government consider using both at the same time? Explain your answers.

5 Why did the Labour Government give control over monetary policy to the Monetary Policy Committee, rather than keeping it under its own control?

9.5 The 1999 Budget

Synopsis

This case study explores the 1999 Budget as a means of managing the macroeconomy and achieving political aims. It identifies a number of key characteristics which are:

1   the Budget philosophy;
2   the measures;
3   analysis of the measures.

Case Study

It is said that yesterday's news is history – so last year's Budget is even more so. Nonetheless, it can be very informative in terms of applying the theoretical knowledge developed in this chapter and so that is why it is explored here. Further, the Budget is as much political as economic – a way to hit the opposition parties. The Budget delivered on 9 March 1999 was also drafted with one eye on the (then) forthcoming 1999 Scottish parliament and Welsh assembly elections, and on elections to the Northern Ireland assembly, as a means to secure votes for the Labour Party.

The Budget philosophy

The Budget speech usually has four main sections: the big themes of the Budget speech; where the economy is now at; policy changes affecting industry; and taxes on consumption. It deals with both revenue and expenditure by the government.

Before delivering it, Chancellor of the Exchequer, Gordon Brown, had argued that it was a Budget for 'enterprise, the family and work.' It was also anticipated to be largely neutral (i.e. not causing the economy to grow or decline), but that there would be some redistributive effects (taking money from middle income earners and giving to low income earners) – which in fact proved to be the case. Although these were going to be its themes, much had been 'leaked' to the newspapers through unattributable briefings or by already declared policies such as the November pre-Budget statement. For example, it had already been announced in 1998 that £40 billion would be spent on education and health; that the duty on petrol would rise by at least 6 per cent above the rate of inflation; that child benefit would increase in the Budget; and that the income tax personal allowance would rise. Nonetheless, Chancellors also like to have surprises up their sleeve to gain 'political points.'

The UK economy

Gordon Brown was helped by the fact that the economy was in a relatively strong position. Public finances were good with a projected £10 billion surplus, helped by rising tax revenues from previous Budgets and fiscal drag (when earners automatically move into the higher tax bracket as their earnings increase). This was in spite of an unexpected tax revenue loss of £2 billion from cross-channel tobacco smuggling. Unemployment was 4.6 per cent of the workforce, the lowest since June 1980; headline inflation (which includes the cost of mortgages) was 2.4 per cent; and wage rates were moderating to 4.5 per cent. Sterling was still strong, which was bad for exporters but also meant cheap imports, which helps keep down production costs, and hence inflation. Additionally, under the control of the Monetary Policy Committee of the Bank of England, interest rates were only 5.5 per cent and forecast to fall to 4.5 per cent by the end of 1999. This is why Brown did not introduce a growth Budget.

The measures

The main Budget measures, grouped by main areas, were:

1   Measures to help those on lower incomes (by income redistribution from higher earners), or by helping people back to work.
    ● The introduction of a 10p income tax rate on the first £1500 of taxable income earned after the (tax free) personal allowance of £4500.
    ● 1p off the basic income tax rate (from 23 to 22 per cent) from April 2000.
    ● The abolition of the married couples allowance (tax relief paid to married couples and worth £285 per annum in 1998/99), and its replacement by a new children's tax credit.
    ● The abolition of MIRAS, the scheme which gives tax relief on the interest paid on the first £30 000 of a mortgage.
    ● Child benefit up to £15 per week for first child, £10 for others from April 2000.
    ● 900 000 people taken out of national insurance by raising thresholds.
    ● Rise in national insurance for those earning more than £26 000.
    ● An increase in stamp duty of 0.5 per cent on properties over £250 000.
    ● Pensioners' winter fuel allowances increased from £20 to £100.

2   Help for business
    ● A new 10p corporation tax rate for small businesses.
    ● A share ownership scheme for workers to take a stake in the firms for which they work.
    ● New research and development tax credit for small businesses.
    ● £60 per week credit for over 50 year olds moving off welfare into work.

3 Help for the environment
- A £55 cut in excise duty (road tax) on small cars, whilst road tax on other cars rises in line with inflation.
- A new energy tax on business from April 2001.
- Company car tax reform.

4 Taxes on consumption
- 17.5p on a packet of 20 cigarettes.
- 4.25p on a litre of leaded petrol; 3.79p on a litre of unleaded petrol.
- However, duty on wines, spirits and beers were frozen.

5 Extra public expenditure
- An extra £1.1 billion for schools, hospitals and crime prevention.

Analysis

The reader should note that this list is not exhaustive since space does not permit everything to be included. However if he/she wants to see the full details then back copies of the quality newspapers or CD-ROMs of back copies are available from libraries. Additionally, the websites of the broadsheets or quality newspapers have archives with back copies. The above headings may contain measures which may fit into more than one category.

The main beneficiaries of the 1999 Budget were families and older people. This can be seen, for families, with such measures as the abolition of the married couples' allowance, partly because more unmarried couples now live together, partly because couples are now assessed separately. Therefore, the allowance was an anachronism. The new children's tax credit which will give a flat rate £416 tax credit for children, and the raising of child benefit, also help lower income families with children. Additionally, the cut in the basic rate of income tax in 2000 and the introduction of the 10p band again helps the poorer paid. The raising of the national insurance contributions threshold excludes low income earners from having to pay, whilst those earning over £26 000 pay more – all clear income redistribution effects. Finally, increased stamp duty on the sale of houses costing more than £250 000 again penalises the better off with expensive houses. Pensioners benefited from the 500 per cent increase in their winter fuel allowance and an increase in pensions in line with inflation.

For businesses, the main aims were to help small and medium sized enterprises (employing fewer than 500 workers) to be established and to grow – especially those in the high technology area of the economy. The creation of a single small business service was proposed to provide loan guarantees (banks are reluctant to lend to small new higher risk businesses), support innovation and help the growth of electronic commerce (this latter reinforced by a £0.5 billion computers for all initiative). To achieve this, corporation tax was cut by 1 per cent for large companies (down to 30 per cent) and by 3 per cent for small companies (to 20 per cent), whilst for new companies starting up it was cut to 10 per cent. Again, the new tax credit to promote research and development was aimed at small businesses – it is firms such as these which have been so successful in areas like America's Silicon Valley in the last fifteen years. Indeed, one criticism was that this should have been introduced years ago.

Other areas might be seen as benefiting businesses but might also be seen as helping the poorer paid or unemployed. The £60 a week credit for over 50 year olds to get them back into work will bring to businesses expertise and experience lost when such people have been unable to secure work on age grounds. The risk is that, since older people are perceived to be more expensive to employ, the £60 credit may merely encourage employers to hire older workers for a year at lower wages, and then get rid of them. The introduction of individual learning accounts to promote life long learning reinforced this.

Again, share ownership is perceived by Brown to be an incentive to encourage people to work harder. However, there is no research evidence to prove this whilst private companies are reluctant to allow their employees to become shareholders since this dilutes control.

There are also many smaller measures in the Budget which are too detailed to examine here.

Green, or environmental policies seek to reduce carbon pollution by 3 million tonnes and include a new energy tax on carbon fuels from 2001 which will, of course, impose extra costs on the businesses which the previous section of the Budget was trying to promote. Energy efficient sectors of the economy will get tax reductions. Again, the other two measures listed seek to shift people to smaller cars, which consume less fuel, and to make the use of company cars more expensive, since these have been partly responsible, in the past, for the growth in car numbers on UK roads.

The increased excise duties on fuel and cigarettes are classic examples of the ability to raise prices on goods which have inelastic demand, without losing revenue. One might also argue that in raising fuel prices there are environmental benefits if it discourages car usage, although research suggests that fuel prices would have to rise very much higher to deter private car usage. Again, the proven health risks of cigarette smoking could be used as health grounds for the high price increases here.

Other issues of direct relevance to business economics include a new competition policy where products are provided by a sole supplier, e.g. water.

9.6 Summary of chapter

This chapter is the first of two exploring the operations of the macroeconomic environment and its impact on businesses. It began by considering national income and the various measures of this. These included gross domestic product and gross national product, measured at market prices and factor cost. The three ways of estimating GDP were discussed, as were the factors influencing GDP and the use of GDP statistics. From there the chapter examined the components of GDP and the circular flow of income. This was then linked to the aggregate demand/aggregate supply diagram.

The chapter then went on to examine inflation. This included how to define it, why it poses problems and what causes it. As part of this, the narrow and broad measures of money were defined. The section finished by analysing demand management (monetary and fiscal) and supply side policies to combat inflation, and the use of the exchange rate.

The chapter finished with an integrating case study tying together all the concepts and theories developed in this chapter through the 1999 Budget.

9.7 Further questions

Further Questions

1 Write a report covering two sides of A4 to the chairman of your company discussing the implications of current low inflation rates for your hotel business compared with the 1980s when inflation was high.

2 Explain three measures of national product and the problems associated with measuring them.

3 Why is inflation undesirable? Are there any circumstances when it might be desirable? Explain your answer.

4 Why is fiscal policy alone not the best way to manage the economy?

5 Look up the details of the most recent Budget. Summarise what it was seeking to achieve and by what means.

9.8 Further reading

Cohen, L. and Manion, L. (1997). *Research Methods in Education*, 4th edition. London: Croom Helm Ltd.

Curwen, P. (1997). *Understanding the UK Economy*, 4th edition. Basingstoke: Macmillan Business.

Johnson, C. (1991). *The Economy under Mrs Thatcher 1979–1990*. Harmondsworth: Penguin Books.

Morris, D. (ed) (1990). *The Economic System in the UK*, 3rd edition. Oxford University Press: Oxford.

OECD (1999). *Economic Outlook*, December 1999, No. 66. Paris: OECD.

Parkin, M. (1999). *Economics*, 5th edition. Wokingham: Addison Wesley.

Vickers, J. *Price Stability in the UK*. Given as the Glasgow Trades House Lecture, 26 May 1999.

Bank of England: Bank Briefings

Bank of England: Fact Sheets

The Bank of England: http://www.bankofengland.co.uk

The European Commission: http://www.cec.org.uk

The Office of National Statistics: http://www.ons.gov.uk

The Treasury: http://www.hm-treasury.gov.uk

UK Chambers of Commerce: http://www.britishchambers.org.uk

Chapter 10

The macroeconomy and its impact on business: II

Learning Outcomes

After completing this chapter the reader will be able to:
- understand the theories of unemployment, its relationship with inflation and the means to remedy unemployment;
- appreciate the importance of the business cycle and economic growth in a modern market economy;
- discuss how government policies seek to address these and analyse the impact of such policies on businesses.

10.1 Unemployment – types, causes and remedies

Unemployment at lowest level since 1980 as UK jobs market risks overheating

Synopsis

This case study discusses the fall in UK employment to its lowest level since 1980. It explores:

1 the causes for this drop in unemployment (or rise in employment);
2 the relationship between high employment and the attendant risks of inflationary pressures;

3 the differences in the levels of employment in different sectors within the labour market.

Case Study

Unemployment fell to its lowest level since April 1980, figures from the Office for National Statistics (ONS) revealed, with the number of people claiming benefit dropping 22 300 to 1.21 million. Using the broader International Labour Office (ILO) measure, the unemployment rate fell to 5.9 per cent. Between May and June 1999 employment rose 54 000 to a record total of 27.41 million. The main reason for this was rising employment among the over 35-years-olds by 110 000 to over 16 million, boosted by increasing job opportunities in the services sector. However, the number of people in work in the 16 to 24 age group fell by 24 000, which caused the Government concerns as it was anxious to help more people in this age group into work. The figures also showed a polarisation between the manufacturing and services sectors of the economy; whilst the number of jobs in the former sector fell by 26 000 in the second quarter of the year, the number of jobs in services rose by 129 000.

When the figures were released they caused concerns that, with such low unemployment, wage deals could be increasing. In July 1999, the headline growth in average earnings (which averaged out earnings changes for May, June and July) rose by 0.2 percentage points to 4.6 per cent, according to ONS statistics; this was just above the 4.5 per cent level which the Bank of England felt was compatible with its inflation target of 2.5 per cent. Some business economists argued that this further showed how tight the labour market was and that the recent action by the Monetary Policy Committee, in raising interest rates by 0.25 per cent, had been a sensible move to pre-empt further inflationary pressures.

Others argued, however, that inflationary pressures were moderating and that there was no need for concern. The monthly figures for July had shown that there was a slowing down in recent high bonus payments, which contribute to total earnings, after the passing of the half year bonus period, and the monthly earnings growth rate eased from 5.2 per cent to 4.4 per cent. Services sector growth, which had been more buoyant because of the high growth in employment, eased from 6 per cent in June to 4.9 per cent in July. It was argued that this would help contribute to a fall in headline inflation over the next few months.

The above case study is useful in tying together a number of issues as well as discussing unemployment. First, it is about unemployment and its mirror image, employment; as unemployment falls, or employment increases, the demand for labour, particularly that with certain skills, begins to exceed the supply. This has major implications for businesses in that in order to secure employees from other competing businesses, or to persuade people to retrain which may be much longer term, they have to offer higher pay. As the case study shows, this may be in terms of a wage or salary and perhaps a bonus linked to sales or business profitability. In turn, as wages rise, cost push inflationary pressures start to rise and this may trigger a wage price spiral when demand push inflation also kicks in. Therefore, monetary policy, i.e. interest rates, becomes crucial in taking the pressure out of the labour market. There were also variations between different sectors and whilst the number of jobs in manufacturing fell, the number in the services sector increased.

Defining unemployment

The case study refers to the broader International Labour Office (ILO) measure of unemployment. This is defined as people of working age (16–65 years) who do not have a job but who are available to work and are actively seeking a job, or waiting to start one. The data are collected from a survey which asks unemployed people whether they have actively been seeking work through job applications over the last month. The alternative way of measuring unemployment is the claimant count. This takes the figure of those registered for unemployment benefit or, as it is now known, job seeker's allowance. The ILO figure tends to give a higher value than the claimant count. Unemployment is expressed both as an absolute number – 1.21 million in the above case study – or as a percentage of the total labour force at a moment in time – 5.9 per cent for July in the above.

The UK has used many different measures of unemployment in the last 20 years, as a result of many changes in definitions. This occurred especially when unemployment was high, provoking claims that the changes were politically motivated to exclude many people from the statistics and hence to make unemployment look better than it was in reality. Currently, the UK uses claimant unemployment as its main measure. This records all those who are receiving unemployment benefits as a consequence of being out of work. Since there are a number of categories excluded from receiving benefits, this underestimates the true situation. Exclusions include: school leavers and men between 60 and 65 years who are looking for work; people returning to work after time out, e.g. bringing up children; people looking for part time work, and those in part time work who are looking for full time jobs; those temporarily out of work; and the very long term unemployed who have given up hope of ever getting a job. As the reader can see, compared with the ILO definition, the UK government's claimant count definition will give a lower figure.

Table 1.5 presented UK figures for unemployment in recent years and, as was seen, unemployment changes substantially over time, rising and falling. The reader should refer back to this table.

Why is unemployment undesirable for society and for businesses?

Unemployment is undesirable both to society and businesses for many reasons. For society, the opportunity cost of unemployment is the output foregone forever. Society finds itself within its Production Possibility Curve in Figure 9.3 instead of being on it. In turn this affects the rate of growth of the economy, both in absolute terms and relative to other countries, and also its balance of trade. Some goods will need to be imported because they will not be produced sufficiently in the UK, whilst exports will fall as less is produced.

Unemployment imposes costs on central government finances since those who do not work have to be paid social security benefits; either this will be financed from tax revenues or by borrowing, which will increase the government's PSNCR. Further, potential tax revenues, both income and VAT, which would have been paid to the government had the unemployed been working, will be lost. Unemployment has social costs in that those who do not work, especially when unemployed long term, are more likely to suffer from depression, which in turn creates extra pressures on the National Health Service. Furthermore, the quality of life, both for the unemployed and their families, is likely to be lower than that of a person in work. There has also been concern in the past about increasing crime and social unrest being linked to rising unemployment.

For businesses, unemployment means a loss of potential customers and hence revenue. With a lower growth rate for the economy, resulting from higher unemployment, businesses are less likely to invest in capital equipment since there will be lower potential demand for their products. Therefore, in times of high unemployment, businesses fail because of lack of demand for their goods or services. Often cash flow is the major problem, where businesses face bills yet their customers delay making payments to them; consequently more cash is leaving the business than is coming in. If banks refuse to extend overdraft and loan facilities then a business will cease trading. Of course, businesses do make employees redundant. This may be because of falling demand for their products and/or because they wish to reduce their operating costs. As we saw earlier in this book making part of the work force redundant, and in the longer term replacing them with machinery, is the most obvious solution. Therefore, businesses, by such actions, themselves contribute to unemployment.

The types and causes of changes in unemployment

There are many reasons why unemployment changes over time; some will only have a short term impact while others will have long term effects.

Classical

This type of unemployment, also known as disequilibrium unemployment and much more common in the 1960s and 1970s, involved trade unions driving up real wages to levels which exceeded the equilibrium real wage rate. If the reader reconsiders Figure 6.9 he/she will see that if unions are able to force average real wage rates up to W_m, only Q_d of labour will be demanded by businesses whereas Q_s will be supplied by the workforce.

As noted in Chapter 6, a minimum wages policy imposed by a government could also have this effect if the minimum were set above the equilibrium level.

Seasonal

In the short term, unemployment will, in some activities or areas of the country, vary from season to season. For example, in Cornwall there is much more work in the summer than in the winter due to the influx of summer holiday makers and the demands of agriculture. Therefore, in winter, more people will be unemployed; this is known as seasonal unemployment. Alternatively, people may be underemployed when they only have enough work to fill part of the week; yet they cannot claim benefits so are not classified as unemployed. Additionally, a small family farm, for instance, may support five people when, in reality, there is only sufficient work for three during the whole year; this is known as disguised unemployment. In all three cases unemployment is seasonal and hence varies across the year.

Frictional

Short term unemployment may also occur when people are between jobs, for instance having been made redundant from one job they are in the process of looking for another. This is known as frictional unemployment and can occur when the economy is at full employment.

In this case it is given the name the natural rate of unemployment, which is discussed more fully below.

Cyclical

Unemployment will also vary from year to year according to the movements of the business cycle, which lasts approximately five years (see Chapter 1, Section 1.4 and Chapter 10, Section 10.3). In times of recession, when the economic or business cycle is at its floor and the level of economic activity is lower (AD shifts to the left in Figure 9.2), unemployment will rise. Many economists argue that this is specifically due to insufficient aggregate demand in the economy; hence this type of unemployment is also known as demand deficient unemployment. As the cycle moves to the upswing phase, economic activity picks up, aggregate demand rises and businesses seek to hire more labour. When the cycle peaks, the shift of the Aggregate Demand curve to the right encounters the vertical section of the Aggregate Supply curve in Figure 9.3; the demand for labour is very high and, conversely, unemployment is low. The cycle then moves into its downswing. This is known as cyclical unemployment because of its direct link to the business cycle.

Structural

In the long term, industries decline and the people who worked in them are made redundant. Steel, shipbuilding and coal all used to be important but have now declined substantially or almost ceased operating. Where large numbers of people lose their jobs, as with coal mining in South Wales, this has a major impact on the local economy, with significant job losses. Miners who worked in the pits all their lives cannot, nor would they want to, retrain as computer programmers or foreign exchange dealers. Hence long term unemployment, known as structural unemployment, is inevitable. It is so named because of the changes in the structure of the economy over time, particularly the shift from manufacturing to services provision. It only reduces in the long term when new businesses enter the region, often persuaded by the government through subsidies, such as Japanese electronics firms in South Wales. In contrast, the South East of England, where services rather than manufacturing are the dominant source of employment, has not suffered as much in this way.

Full employment

Although not a type or cause of unemployment, the concept of full employment is directly relevant here. In 1944, the government published a white paper, authored by Lord Beveridge, which argued that in the post World War II society, UK governments should aspire to achieving full employment; this was defined as not more than 4 per cent of the labour force being without a job. For many years this was government policy and Keynesian based policies to boost aggregate demand in the economy were motivated by this goal of achieving full employment. However, full employment as a policy objective was effectively, although not explicitly, abandoned in the 1970s when unemployment rose and governments were unable to achieve this. In the late 1990s, the UK clearly had full employment by the old definition and, in some parts of the economy, over-full employment, i.e. the situation where there is excess demand for labour, or greater demand for labour with certain skills, than there is a supply of it. The case study in Section 10.5 pursues this further.

The natural rate of unemployment

There is some controversy over the definition of the natural rate of unemployment, discussed under frictional unemployment. Some economists define it as under frictional unemployment; others distinguish between voluntary and involuntary unemployment. They argue that when the labour market is in equilibrium there can still be unemployment; this is voluntary, i.e. those who do not work at the prevailing wage when the demand for labour equals its supply. Voluntary unemployment includes frictional unemployment and structural unemployment (since the unemployed steelworker could work as a cleaner for a lower wage).

If the wage rate were to be forced up by unions above the equilibrium rate, as W_m in Figure 6.9, then classical unemployment would also be counted as part of voluntary unemployment since union members would have acquiesced in the policies of their union in forcing up wages. Hence the only involuntary unemployment, these economists would argue, is demand deficient or cyclical unemployment. Together, voluntary unemployment plus involuntary unemployment equals total unemployment.

For reasons to be explained, the natural rate of unemployment is also consistent with a constant rate of inflation.

Policies to combat unemployment

The reader now needs to revisit Chapter 9, Section 9.2 to be reminded of the main weapons which can be used to combat inflation, since these also apply to unemployment. In other words, governments have monetary and fiscal policies to influence aggregate demand and supply side policies to influence aggregate supply in the economy.

Monetary policy

Monetary policy can be used to boost aggregate demand in the economy by lowering interest rates, thus encouraging consumers and businesses to borrow more from banks as loans and overdrafts; in turn this generates extra expenditure and, as demand for goods and services increases, businesses hire extra labour to increase output. However, since the government passed responsibility for interest rates to the Monetary Policy Committee, monetary policy is used, essentially, to control inflation and so, for the UK since 1998, it cannot easily be used to boost employment. This almost sounds as if there is a tradeoff between inflation and unemployment; to control inflation, interest rates are raised, yet higher interest rates discourage aggregate demand, businesses do not demand extra labour and unemployment rises. We return to this in Section 10.2.

Fiscal policy

Fiscal policy will clearly have an impact on aggregate demand and hence unemployment. In times of recession, when the business cycle is in its trough, the government can spend more and/or lower taxes. This can be financed by increasing its PSNCR and spending the money on new roads, schools, hospitals etc. This will boost aggregate demand and, therefore, employment.

However, as discussed earlier, the emphasis in recent years on fiscal prudence, and the possible need for the UK to meet the Maastricht Convergence Criteria to qualify for the single European currency, whereby the budget deficit should not exceed 3 per cent of GDP, means that governments do not wish to run large budget deficits unless forced to do so in times of recession, through extra social security payments or to compensate for lost tax revenues. Therefore, fiscal policy becomes less of an option than it was in the 1960s, for example.

Supply side policies

These have already been discussed in depth. Essentially, we saw that the aim of these policies was to shift the economy's aggregate supply curve to the right as a consequence of making input and output markets more flexible. If this occurs in the ways described previously then output and hence employment will rise. The current government puts much emphasis on this, with monetary policy, as a means to combat unemployment.

Exchange rate management policies

Again, these have been discussed. If the exchange rate of sterling against other currencies is high then export prices will be high, less will be sold abroad – the exact amount depending on the price elasticity of demand for UK exports – and there will be less demand by businesses in the UK for labour to produce these goods. Even worse, as cheaper imports gain market share over domestically produced goods, again sales by UK businesses will reduce, the precise amount depending on the price elasticity of demand for imports. Therefore, the demand for labour, and thus employment falls.

Conclusions

In reality governments seek to employ a mix of demand management and supply side policies to stimulate employment. However, the idea that the UK government has freedom to implement whatever policies it wishes can be seen to be untrue. The politically independent MPC controls monetary policy whilst the EU and the single currency requirements constrain untrammelled use of fiscal and exchange rate management policies. Only supply side policies offer total freedom, but implementing them is a long term process which may not always succeed. Whichever policies the government adopts, however, will have significant impacts on businesses and the business environment within which they operate.

Self test questions

1 What has been the trend in UK unemployment in the last six months? Explain why this has been so?

2 If unemployment is so undesirable why do you think that the governments of the UK have periodically allowed it to rise above 3 million?

3 Discuss the essential differences between cyclical and structural unemployment, including their time spans.

4 How do unemployment and the natural rate of unemployment differ?

5 Which policy measure seems, to you, to be most effective in controlling unemployment? Explain your answer.

10.2 The inflation–unemployment relationship and its effect on business

Analysing the policies used to combat inflation and unemployment suggested a tradeoff between the two. If the government wants to control inflation then interest rates are raised, and it reduces expenditure (G) and raises taxes (T). However, higher interest rates and tighter fiscal policy reduce aggregate demand in the economy and hence employment. Therefore, if the government wants to avoid the iniquities of inflation it has to accept the iniquity of unemployment being higher than it would otherwise wish. Conversely, if government's main objective is to reduce unemployment, it will cut interest rates and adopt a looser fiscal policy of increased G and/or reduced T, but it then has to accept higher inflation. In both cases supply side policies and exchange rate management may also be used.

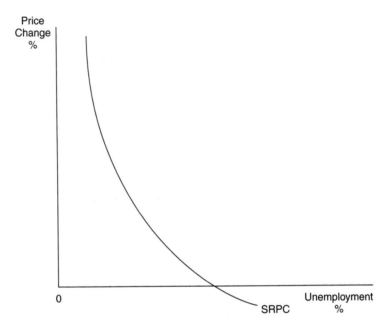

Figure 10.1 The short term Phillips curve.

The Phillips curve

In the late 1950s an English economist A.W. Phillips postulated an inverse relationship between the rate of wage changes (wage inflation) and the rate of unemployment, based on one hundred years of data observation. This was subsequently modified to the relationship between changes in the retail prices and the rate of unemployment, and is shown in Figure 10.1. On the vertical axis of the short term Phillips curve, is the rate of change of prices, i.e. inflation, whilst on the horizontal axis is the rate of unemployment. As can be seen, this suggests that there is an inverse relationship of the type postulated earlier. This theory held dominance until the late 1960s.

However, from the observations relating to the late 1960s onwards, there appeared to be a breakdown in this formerly stable relationship, such that the UK was experiencing both higher inflation and higher unemployment. In other words the Phillips curve appeared to be moving upwards and away from the origin in the 1970s and 1980s. In effect there were a number of Phillips curves at different levels, each showing the inverse inflation–unemployment relationship.

This necessitated a revisiting of the original Phillips curve theory and its modification by the monetarists, as the expectations–augmented Phillips curve.

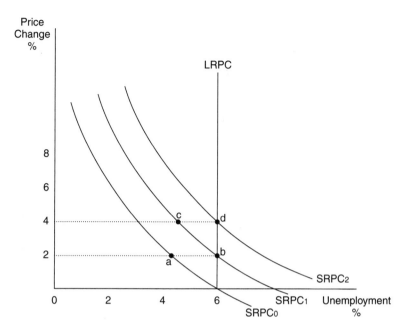

Figure 10.2 The expectations–augmented Phillips curve.

The expectations–augmented Phillips curve

The importance of expectations was briefly discussed earlier under the heading of cost push inflation. One school of economic thought, the new classical economists, place at the centre of their assertions, the concept of rational expectations, i.e. that people base their expectations on the current information which they have, even if this is imperfect. Exploring this in any depth is beyond the scope of a business economics book of this size, and the reader is advised to consult the further reading section at the end of this chapter if he/she wishes to pursue this further. Rather, for the current analysis, we concentrate on what are known as adaptive expectations, i.e. the argument that people base their expectations, in this case of inflation, on past information about it; in other words on its past rates. Therefore, in its simplest form, this year's expectations of the rate of inflation might be based on last year's actual rate. This necessitates a distinction between short term and long term Phillips curves. Figure 10.2 illustrates this.

In Year 1, $SRPC_0$ is the initial (short term) Phillips curve which is the same as the Phillips curve in Figure 10.2. We assume there is zero price inflation and unemployment of 6 per cent. The government seeks to reduce unemployment through appropriate demand management policies such as reducing interest rates and running a budget deficit. This causes unemployment to fall to 4 per cent. However, demand pull inflation develops and increases to 2 per cent; so the economy moves upwards to the left along $SRPC_0$ to the new co-ordinates at point 'a'.

In Year 2, consumers and businesses adapt their expectations to assume inflation at 2 per cent, based on the previous year's experience, which causes $SRPC_0$ to shift upwards by 2 per cent and become $SRPC_1$. This increase in inflation wipes out any short term increase in real wages so workers are no better off; businesses have to pay higher wages to their labour force to offset inflation and also, based on their knowledge of the past, expect inflation to continue at 2 per cent; so they will substitute capital for labour and reduce their labour force. Unemployment will return to 6 per cent but will now be associated with 2 per cent inflation, at point 'b'. Therefore, monetary and fiscal policies are of no use, according to the Monetarist economists, in reducing unemployment below the natural rate in the long term; any effects will only be inflationary. Other economists, of the new Keynesian school of thought, argue that the growth of monopoly power by businesses in the UK, and globally, is a major cause for the upward shifts in SRPC. They also argue that increases in aggregate demand in the economy will increase output and employment, even in the long term.

The government now pursues more of the same policies to reduce unemployment again and this causes a further movement, along $SRPC_1$, to point 'c'. However, this has caused inflation to rise to 4 per cent. This increase in inflation will affect consumers' and businesses' adaptive expectations and the short term Phillips curve will shift upwards to $SRPC_2$. Subsequently, for similar reasons to above, unemployment will increase back to 6 per cent at point 'd' on $SRPC_2$.

The more the government seeks to reduce unemployment by monetary and fiscal policies, the more it increases inflation and hence society's expectations about future inflation. Any reductions in unemployment will only be temporary and will inevitably move back to the 6 per cent figure. The different combinations of rates of inflation and the 6 per cent unemployment rate give us what is called the Long Term Phillips curve (LRPC) in Figure 10.2. Economists who subscribe to the monetarist school of economics argue that this figure, of 6 per cent in our example, is the natural rate of unemployment which was examined above, i.e. the long term unemployment rate when the labour market is in equilibrium.

This scenario which has been outlined explains why it is possible to have situations of rising inflation and rising unemployment at the same time, a situation not capable of being explained by the short term Phillips curve alone. The solution, for the Monetarist economists, is to remove inflationary expectations from the economy, for example by businesses resisting high wage demands, or by deflating the economy through contractionary monetary policy; the more severely the economy is deflated the quicker inflation will be eliminated from it. Unemployment can only be reduced by supply side policies; in contrast new Keynesian economists argue that increases in aggregate demand in the economy will increase output and employment, even in the long term. The latter believe that, to control cost push inflation, the dominant type, there is a need to control union power through legislation.

So how does this tie up with business economics specifically? Most importantly, it shows that depending on the economic and political beliefs of a government, different policies are likely to be adopted with different implications and outcomes for businesses. If a government believes that fiscal policy can reduce unemployment then it will run a large budget deficit which will involve large public sector contracts benefiting the construction sector, for example, through building new hospitals and schools.

In contrast, if a government believes fiscal policy to be ineffective in the long term reduction in unemployment, and causing crowding out, then monetary policy will be the main weapon. Yet if the government tries to squeeze inflation from the economic system by raising interest rates, this will affect businesses' abilities to invest, and the exchange rate, raising the price of British exports and reducing business competitiveness.

If the belief is that monopoly power is a main explanation of shifts of the short term Phillips curve, then competition policy will be widely used to moderate such influences. This may have implications for businesses wishing to merge or acquire others. If, on the other hand, expectations are perceived as the main cause of shifts of the short term Phillips curve, then it has to be determined whether these are adaptive or rational expectations. Then the question has to be asked how these might be reduced; for monetarists the answer is deflationary monetary policy, i.e. high interest rates. This is clearly a very different policy from the ones the new Keynesians would pursue.

10.3 The business cycle – causes and trends

Recap

In Chapter 1 we noted that the economic activity of a modern economy will vary over a time span of approximately five years, in the form of what is known as a business or economic cycle (and in the past was known as the trade cycle). The actual length of each phase may vary from cycle to cycle and the magnitude of the phase, i.e. the height of the boom and the depth of the recession, may also vary so that business cycles are to some extent, unpredictable. Nonetheless, the broad pattern of each cycle has largely been the same. Let us now examine the theory more fully. We identify four distinct phases to the business or economic cycle. These are:

1 the boom, which is the peak of the cycle
2 the downturn or downswing, when economic growth slows down and the economy moves towards recession;

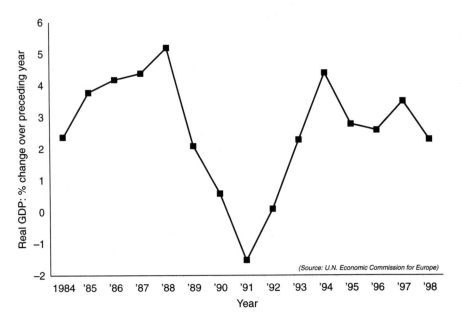

Figure 10.3 The UK business cycle, 1990–1998.

3 the slump or trough of the cycle when the economy is in recession and economic growth is negative;

4 the upturn or upswing when the economy recovers.

The economic theory underpinning the business cycle

There are a number of competing theories explaining the business cycle, depending on whether one believes that it is aggregate demand or aggregate supply which is the crucial variable. We will focus primarily on the former. To do so we need to return to Keynesian economic analysis and introduce two further economic concepts, the multiplier and the accelerator, and consider how they interact.

The multiplier

This may be defined as the number of times by which national income increases in response to an initial increase in an injection of income, which might be any of consumption, investment, government expenditure and exports, as shown in Figure 9.1. C + I + G + X is national expenditure, or aggregate demand.

We begin with a simple example. Assume that for each £100 of gross income which households earn £85 (85%) is spent on UK consumer goods and services; by gross income we mean that it does not include taxes paid to the government, benefits received from the government or expenditure of foreign goods, i.e. imports. The figure of 85 per cent, or 0.85, is known as the Marginal Propensity to Consume (MPC) and may be defined as the proportion of a small increase in income which will be allocated to increased consumption. We also assume that the remainder, i.e. 0.15 of income is saved. This is the marginal propensity to save (MPS) and is defined as the proportion of a small increase in income which will be allocated to increased savings. Therefore:

$$\text{MPC} + \text{MPS} = 1 \qquad\qquad\qquad\qquad\qquad 1$$

$$\text{I} - \text{MPC} = \text{MPS} \ (\text{or } 1 - \text{MPS} = \text{MPC}) \qquad\qquad 2$$

For consumption, the £85 spent in shops on goods and services becomes income to shopkeepers who also spend 85% (£72.25) and save 15% (£12.75). Their expenditure becomes income to manufacturers who make the goods who, assuming the same ratios, spend 85% of the £72.5 they receive (£61.41) and save the rest (£0.59). The reader can follow the diminishing series. He/she should note that at each stage of the expenditure the money which is saved leaks out of the system (i.e. it is a withdrawal in Figure 9.1).

For the economy, the total amount of money spent will, therefore, be £100 + £85 + £72.25 + £61.41 + £52.12 + £44.37 + £37.71 + . . . = £666.66.

The total amount of income generated in the economy, as a result of the initial injection of £100 of consumer expenditure will be given by the multiplier (often denoted k) which is:

$$k = \frac{1}{1 - \text{MPC}} \quad \text{or} \quad \frac{1}{\text{MPS}} \qquad\qquad\qquad 3$$

In our example, total national income created in the economy will be:

$$= £100 \times \frac{1}{1 - \text{MPC}}$$

$$= £100 \times \frac{1}{0.15}$$

$$= £100 \times 6.67$$

$$= £667 \ \text{(rounding to two significant figures)}.$$

The reader should note that, the larger the MPS (the smaller the MPC) the bigger are the leakages from each new round of expenditure, and the smaller will be the total increase in national income.

By the same logic, for savings the amount saved or leaking from the economy will be £15 + £12.75 + £10.59 + £9.21 + . . . = £100.

The multiplier comes to an end when total leakages equal initial injections.

Further withdrawals

In reality, as we saw in Figure 9.1, there are other leakages from the system which further reduce the value of the multiplier from the one based solely on the MPS. These are taxation paid by households to central and local government (and the households also receive back benefits from government) and payments overseas for imports. In the same way as we identified the MPS so we can also distinguish:

1 the marginal propensity to import (MPI), which is defined as the proportion of a small increase in income which will be allocated to increased imports;
2 the marginal propensity to tax (MPT) which is defined as the proportion of a small increase in income which will paid as taxation.

If we add these to MPS we obtain as our multiplier:

$$k = \frac{1}{MPS + MPT + MPI} \qquad 4$$

Let us assume a marginal tax rate of 0.37 and an MPI of 0.30. This gives a multiplier of:

$$= \frac{1}{0.15 + 0.37 + 0.30}$$

$$= 1.22$$

As the reader can see, when we take account of these extra leakages, the value of the multiplier falls from 6.67 to 1.22; so any injection into the circular flow of income in an open economy, i.e. one which trades internationally and where there is government activity (which means every economy in the world), will have much less effect than in the simple model where we just had the MPS. The higher any withdrawal, the less effective the multiplier will be. A further issue is that income does not respond immediately to changes in consumption; in reality there will be time lags before injections and withdrawals impact on real GDP, employment and income.

The other qualification is that, although the government withdraws money as taxes, it also puts money back into the system as benefits to the unemployed, as family allowances etc., which is income to households. It also undertakes major expenditure such as building new hospitals etc.; this creates work and hence incomes for those undertaking these civil engineering projects. In return they spend their money and the multiplier kicks off again. Indeed, if the government is running a budget deficit it will put more back into the economic system than it is withdrawing, which will result in a boost to economic activity. In other words it will push the aggregate demand (AD_0) curve in Figure 9.2 to the right. Conversely, if the government spends less than it raises in taxes, i.e. running a budget surplus (PSDR), then the net effect will be an overall withdrawal from the circular flow of income, and the economy will contract by a multiple amount of the net withdrawal (AD_0 curve shifts to the left in Figure 9.2). Therefore, the multiplier can work in both directions, to increase expenditure by a multiple amount and, conversely, to reduce it by a multiple amount depending on the net size of the injections and withdrawals.

What the reader should now be able to conclude is that when a government uses fiscal policy, varying expenditure and taxation, it will have an impact on the economy greater than the amount of the expenditure or taxation.

The accelerator

The other main theory which needs briefly to be considered is the accelerator principle. This relates particularly to manufacturing industry and the need for businesses to acquire capital equipment to undertake production. The level of investment in an economy is unstable and contributes to fluctuations in the business cycle. The accelerator principle argues that the level of investment depends on the rate of change of real GDP; a small change in real GDP will lead to a much bigger change in investment. This investment will accelerate economic growth or, conversely, economic decline if the business cycle is in its downturn. A simple example illustrates this.

Lunnis & Sons own a factory with 50 machines which produces sportswear for a major retailer. Each machine makes £5 million worth of clothing per year. Because of wear and tear (depreciation) and technological obsolescence, the machines need to be replaced after ten years. Consequently, assuming that the rate of change of real GDP, and hence the demand for its clothing, is constant, the business needs to replace five machines per year to ensure an even flow of capital expenditure. In Table 10.1 we begin at year 11, when the first machines have worn out.

Now assume that in year 12, because of an increase in real GDP, there is an increase in consumer demand for Lunnis's clothing from £50 million to £75 million per annum. This means that it must buy 10 machines; the five replacement ones plus five additional ones, i.e. there has been a 100 per cent increase in demand for machines in total.

In year 13, demand continues to grow by an accelerating rate and 15 machines are now needed, 5 replacement and 10 additional. However, the rate of change of total investment is now only 50 per cent. In year 14, demand rises by another £50 million and the number of machines increases by another 15; however, the percentage change in the number of machines is now 0. In year 15, demand stays constant and so only replacement investment now occurs; the annual change in the number of machines is now minus 66% (the brackets around a number mean it is negative). In year 16, consumer demand falls by £25 million and total investment falls to zero.

Table 10.1 The accelerator principle.

Year	Consumer demand £ million	% Annual change, consumer demand	Replacement demand	Additional machines	Total machines	% Annual change, total no. machines
11	50	0	5	0	5	0
12	75	50	5	5	10	100
13	125	66	5	10	15	50
14	175	40	5	10	15	0
15	175	0	5	0	5	(66)
16	150	(14.3)	0	0	0	(100)

The third column, percentage annual change in consumer demand, and the last column, percentage annual change, total number of machines, illustrate the accelerator principle most effectively. For example, in year 12, an annual increase in consumer demand of 50 per cent leads to a 100 per cent increase in gross investment (the total of the replacement + new machines). Conversely, in year 15, constant consumer demand results in a fall in gross investment of 66 per cent. Therefore, to repeat our assertion above, the accelerator principle argues that the level of investment depends on the rate of change of real GDP, of which consumer demand is the measure; and a small change in real GDP will lead to a much bigger change in investment.

Criticisms of the accelerator theory

There are a number of criticisms of the accelerator theory. In reality there is not likely to be the precise relationship between increasing consumer demand and new investment by businesses that Table 10.1 suggests (neither is machinery suddenly obsolete after ten years, as in our example). If demand is only short lived businesses will probably seek to work their existing equipment more intensively, even if there is the risk of diminishing returns. Even if they believe that increased demand will be sustained there may still be a delay before businesses respond with new investment; in other words new investment will lag consumer demand rather than responding immediately (the same issue of lags also applies with the multiplier). This may be because those businesses which make the machinery may not be able to respond instantly with new producer goods.

It is also the case that the accelerator will only apply if the economy is at full capacity, i.e. on its production possibility frontier. If a business has surplus capacity it will use the machines it already has, and only order new machinery when full capacity is reached. There is also the case, as we saw in Chapter 2, Section 2.2, that businesses undertake forecasting which will shape their expectations of the future; so they will not just respond to current demand but also to expected demand. If a business has committed itself to major capital expenditure it will not be able to easily curtail investment to which it has committed itself.

Linking the multiplier and the accelerator

One theory to explain the cyclical nature of the business cycle has been derived by the interaction of the multiplier and the accelerator; we will use it now. Let us begin with the upturn phase of the cycle.

Upturn

We assume that the economy has just left the slump due to the government undertaking a major expenditure programme coupled with tax reductions and reduced interest rates. The latter may also trigger a fall in the exchange rate, encouraging increased export sales. These will also be helped by lower prices since the economy is working at less than full capacity; additionally, lower prices will encourage consumers to buy domestic goods rather than imports, helping consumer confidence to recover.

Increased government expenditure and consumer expenditure, due to tax reductions, boost the economy and, through the multiplier, cause a multiple growth in national income. As consumer demand increases, and spare capacity in the economy is taken up, the accelerator triggers increased capital expenditure by businesses which, as another injection into the circular flow of income, increases national income still further via the multiplier. Unemployment also falls.

Inflationary pressures may pick up but this will lead to increasing business profits and wages in nominal terms. Until businesses and consumers adjust their inflationary expectations this will help confidence in the economy to continue to improve. Exports should start to improve but, due to improving household incomes, so will imports. This continues until the boom is reached.

Boom

In the boom period, real GDP continues to rise but more slowly, partly due to the economy reaching the limits of its productive capacity, i.e. at its production possibility frontier, and partly due to rising prices reducing the real value of consumer incomes as aggregate supply struggles to match aggregate demand. In Figure 9.3, demand will intersect supply at the rising segment of the AS curve. Exports are also likely to be diverted from overseas to the domestic market to meet the extra demand with the resultant loss of overseas market shares, whilst imports increase to meet unfilled demand, causing the balance of trade to worsen.

There is full employment, so businesses will find that labour with the requisite skills they need is short in supply. This may force them to bid up wages to secure suitable people from their competitors or, if they cannot obtain who they want, output may have to be limited relative to the targets they have set themselves, with consequent reduced profits. Shortages of raw materials or components will also limit manufacturing businesses. Additionally, businesses will run down their stocks of existing goods to meet high consumer demand. Higher costs may well have to be passed on as higher prices; although consumers will have more money to pay higher prices, demand for specific goods and services may fall, depending on the price and income elasticities of demand for goods and services sold by businesses.

For the economy as a whole, economic growth will slow. This slower growth of real GDP will, via the accelerator, slow net investment by businesses; in turn this reduced investment will cause a greater slowdown in income via the multiplier which, in turn, will slow private sector investment still further, via the accelerator. In time, businesses will start to disinvest, i.e. sell off excess capacity and, via the multiplier, real GDP will begin to contract. The economy is now entering the downturn phase.

The boom is, therefore, a time of potential inflationary pressures, with the economy's resources being fully utilised, at its natural rate of unemployment. The government will need to think carefully about its use of monetary, fiscal and exchange rate policies to moderate potential inflationary pressures. However, high tax revenues and lower expenditure on unemployment benefits should reduce the government's budget deficit.

Downturn

Once the economy slips from its peak, economic growth slows, the declining 'feel good factor' shows diminishing consumer confidence. Demand begins to contract (the aggregate demand curve shifts to the left in Figure 9.3) and inflationary pressures in the economy should begin to reduce. As aggregate demand falls, national income contracts by a multiple amount. Businesses cut back on production as stocks of goods accumulate due to lower sales, labour is laid off causing unemployment to rise, and consumer borrowing and expenditure therefore reduces. Businesses may also reduce their investment plans for new buildings, via the accelerator by an accelerated amount, until the economy recovers. They may also slow diversification into new products and markets, although conversely they may seek to diversify more into foreign markets to offset the domestic decline especially if, as with Continental Europe, their business cycles do not coincide with the UK's.

However the reduced domestic demand and consequent reduced production may cause the volume of exports to contract. Demand for imports, both finished goods and raw materials and components, is also likely to reduce. Depending on the price and income elasticities of demand for exports and imports, the trade balance, the difference between the value of UK exports and UK imports, may improve (if imports reduce more than exports).

The government's fiscal balances will be affected as VAT, and income tax revenues reduce, with fewer people and businesses working and spending, whilst expenditure on unemployment benefits has to increase. This is likely to increase the size of the PSNCR and may cause upward pressure on interest rates. However, as a general rule, the government will need to ease monetary policy as the economy enters the downswing to avoid a hard landing, i.e. high unemployment and a major contraction in the growth rate. If left alone, the decline will worsen.

Slump

Technically, a recession is two consecutive quarters of negative economic growth; so, when the economy is in the slump phase or trough of the business cycle, the economy may be recessed. Businesses now reduce demand for labour still further as order books and sales contract and stocks of unsold goods accumulate; this in turn will affect component suppliers. Unemployment will therefore rise still more but inflationary pressures should be at their lowest, including in the housing market. The balance of trade may improve as imports reduce due to lack of domestic demand but this may be counteracted by reducing exports due to a lack of domestic production. The economy is now operating well within its production possibility curve.

In the slump phase of the business cycle it might seem that nothing short of government intervention, or a favourable exogenous shock, can ever help the economy recover. However, businesses, which have been disinvesting, i.e. selling off machinery and not replacing old machinery as it wears out, eventually will reach a point when some new investment is necessary merely to continue in business, lest they have no fixed capital left. Once investment begins to pick up then, no matter how small, this will have a multiplier effect on real GDP. Consumer demand will begin to pick up and, as it does so, it will begin to trigger an accelerated increase in private sector investment. In turn this injection into the circular flow of income will trigger a further multiple increase in income and the economy continues its recovery, moving further along the upswing. Exports should also recover and act as a further injection into the circular flow.

The government will also use demand management policies, i.e. loose fiscal and monetary policies, to reinforce this upturn and start businesses and the economy moving again, at the price of an increasing budget deficit.

Conclusions

The above analysis shows two key issues:

1 Left to itself the economy will go through the four stages of the business cycle due to the multiplier–accelerator interaction.
2 The government can use monetary and fiscal policy to minimise business cycle fluctuations.

Criticisms of business cycle theory

The business cycle theory has come in for a number of criticisms in addition to those discussed above, which relate specifically to the accelerator. They assert that modern economies have now changed and might be termed post-industrial, with a major emphasis on services rather than manufacturing; they are discussed in the next case study.

Can the Chancellor of the Exchequer banish the business cycle?

Synopsis

This case study paraphrases a newspaper article examining the causes of the economic or business cycle, which was touched on in Chapter 1. It discusses:

1 the potential causes of the business cycle;
2 how current circumstances and structural changes in the national and international economies might mean that the worst fluctuations of the business cycle no longer hold;
3 which new variables might cause business cycle fluctuations.

Case Study

In late 1999 one broadsheet newspaper advanced the following argument. Not only had the Labour Government achieved, by building on previous Conservative governments' economic policies, low inflation, low unemployment and a budget surplus (PSDR), but also the Government was implying that Gordon Brown, the Chancellor of the Exchequer, had put an end to 'boom and bust', i.e. the business or economic cycle.

The author of the article argued that the economy had merely slowed down over the previous year, rather than moving into recession, in spite of the adverse forces of strong sterling and the SE Asian economic crisis. Indeed, the UK economy now seemed more stable than at almost any time since the end of World War II. However, it was a very long step from this to arguing the end of the economic cycle.

The causes of the economic or business cycle have generated much debate among economists for a long time. A lot of their work, the author of the article argued, has concentrated on 'describing and analysing [cyclical] fluctuations [in aggregate demand] which are part of a self-sustaining system'. Each peak creates the forces that move the economy to the next trough and again to a recovery, according to a regular pattern. This is the economic or business cycle, pure and simple. To some extent, it has been a feature of all industrial economies. This model is discussed more fully above.

However, the article's author argues that the fluctuations in aggregate demand which create the business cycle may now be far less influential than they used to be for a variety of reasons. Firstly, the UK economy is now primarily services based rather than manufacturing based. When manufacturing dominated the UK economy, businesses had to hold large stocks of goods to meet possible upsurges in customer demand; the so-called just-in-case system of stock control rather than modern JIT (see Chapter 2, Section 2.3). With the latter, stock holdings are, by definition, low whilst, in a services based economy, there is virtually no need for businesses to hold stocks – as with an Internet provider or a firm of accountants or a university, for example. Further, in a manufacturing based economy, as the UK was pre-World War II, businesses need to build new factories and acquire heavy machinery etc., e.g. such industries as ship-building, or steel manufacturing, or coal mining. These fixed investments last a long time but then have to be replaced at similar times, creating major upsurges in business demand for the new fixed capital, which in turn causes the economy to turn upwards. Subsequently, as businesses meet their new investment targets, their demand for further heavy invest-ment goods falls back and the economy turns down (as discussed previously).

A second reason for the fluctuations in the UK economy, over time, has been poor macroeconomic management by successive governments. The article argues that governments have exaggerated the capability of the economy to grow; consequently, as aggregate demand has increased it has not been matched by a comparable increase in aggregate supply. Inflation has therefore accelerated and governments have then had to tighten monetary and fiscal policy substantially to regain control; this has pushed the economy from boom to recession. In the 1970s, this erratic lurching from boom to slump and back again was known as 'stop–go.' The article argues that this has usually been associated in some way with the exchange rate, either by the government trying to ignore it completely or by tying the economy to it too rigidly, as during the UK's membership of the ERM, 1990–1992. We shall explore this more fully in Chapter 11.

Past fluctuations of the economic cycle have also been aggravated by the policies of governments loosening economic controls before an elec-tion, to boost the economy and win votes, and then having to retighten economic policy subsequently to dampen down the excess demand and inflationary pressures which they had generated.

The other major factor which can cause substantial fluctuations in the economy is what are known as exogenous shocks, either to aggregate demand or to aggregate supply. These occur outside the UK economy and can knock it off course, for example, pushing a recovering economy back into recession or prolonging an existing one. An example of exoge-nous shocks in the 1970s was the oil price increases of 400 per cent in 1973 and 100 per cent in 1979, which generated major recession with high unemployment, low growth and high inflation. Another major exogenous shock, in 1990, was the reunification of Germany, which had a substantial impact on Continental European economies, delaying their recovery from recession until the early to mid 1990s; a third one was the SE Asian economic crisis of 1997–1998.

So, why are things different now? The author of the article suggests a number of reasons. Firstly, inflation is now low and it is generally recognised that it needs to be kept low. This is reinforced by the requirement for the Bank of England to work to a 2.5 per cent inflation target and by the Maastricht Convergence Criteria which require any potential member of the single currency to meet the target that its inflation be no higher than 1.5 per cent above the average for the three EU members, with the lowest rates during the previous year. In the past, UK governments were willing to live with higher inflation than other countries and allow the value of Sterling to fall against other currencies, making exports cheaper and offsetting their rising prices through higher inflation.

The article argues, finally, that exogenous shocks, as discussed above, will possibly pose the greatest shocks to the business cycle in future as the global economy becomes more and more intertwined. The network economy, which is increasingly becoming the dominant model, the author argues, means that it is only as strong as its weakest link. If a war, or a stock market crash or a natural disaster occurs it can cause a major shock across the world and push economies into recession, i.e. the slump section of the business cycle. Additionally, as trade barriers fall as a consequence of the work of the World Trade Organisation and capital mobility is greater due to the ending of exchange controls by many countries, the risks of a shock impacting across all economies becomes still greater.

Self test questions

1 Why is the business cycle important to businesses?

2 What is meant by the multiplier and why does it not increase real GDP by the amount of any injections?

3 How does the accelerator differ from the multiplier?

4 Explain: (a) why the economy cannot grow for ever; (b) why a slump will, in time, end; (c) how exogenous shocks influence the business cycle.

5 In the light of the previous case study, is the business cycle an outdated concept?

10.4 Economic growth – theories, causes and costs

US economic growth in the twenty first century

Synopsis
This case study reports a lecture by Alan Greenspan, the Chairman of the Washington based Federal Reserve, the central bank of the United States. In it he articulates what he perceives as the main causes of sustained American economic growth in the last decade of the 20th century. The case study discusses:

1 what Greenspan believes are the benefits of a free market system;
2 The importance of an efficient economic system being based on the rule of law and ethical behaviour;
3 the factors likely to contribute to future US economic growth.

Case Study

This lecture on the millennium, sponsored by the Gerald Ford Foundation in Michigan, was delivered by Alan Greenspan in late 1999. Essentially a laudatory discourse to modern capitalism, it argued that modern US economic success was built on a culture of freedom and trust, specifically respect for the rule of law and individual fair dealing; material success was not incompatible with honesty and integrity. Speaking triumphantly about the collapse of communism ten years previously, Greenspan argued that the collapse of the Berlin Wall had revealed both the political success of civilised democracy and its economic achievement. He claimed 'it is safe to say that we are witnessing this decade [the 1990s], in the United States, history's most compelling demonstration of the productive capacity of free peoples operating in free markets [and achieving economic growth].'

Greenspan claimed that recent fundamental changes in communication and information technologies had improved US growth prospects fundamentally. Companies were now far less dependent on holding large piles of inventories [stocks of goods] just in case consumer demand for them increased. Rather, technology had helped to eliminate expensive distribution networks and had raised productivity. However, he also admitted that there were faults in the system, identifying inequalities of income and wealth, and arguing that racial and other forms of discrimination needed to be eliminated if continued success were to be achieved.

The above case study is interesting for a number of reasons. It is clearly self-congratulatory and looks back to the fall of communism ten years previously to say 'we won at the time but now it is widely recognised that we won.' Secondly, it identifies the links between economic growth and a market economy without barriers to inhibit the former. Linked to this is the importance of trust and the rule of law, issues not common in many countries of the world where successful business depends on who one knows or bribes. Finally, Greenspan's lecture recognises that economic growth alone is not the only criterion of success in a society. If wealth ownership and income earning potential are inhibited by racial, sexual or religious discrimination, then this can inhibit future economic growth. What the lecture does not acknowledge, of course, is the US's major role as a polluter, or that economic growth which does not recognise environmental and resource sustainability cannot be maintained long term.

What is economic growth?

We distinguish, firstly, between actual growth and potential growth. Actual growth may be defined as the actual annual increase in national product or real GDP per annum, normally expressed as a percentage. This may also be expressed on a per capita basis. In contrast, potential growth is the annual increase in a country's productive capability. Actual growth may fall short of potential growth if the economy is working at less than full capacity, i.e. if it works within its production possibility frontier.

Economic growth is perceived to be desirable since the higher growth is, the better off the population of the country is. However, as noted earlier, if high shorter term economic growth uses up non-renewable resources then the cost of this is slow long term growth.

What causes economic growth?

In the case study, Alan Greenspan advances a number of reasons which he believes underlie US economic growth. Economic growth might be due to growth in one or more productive resources such as labour over time, or improvements in its skills base, or the discovery of new resources such as oil fields in Alaska in the 1960s, or the development of new communication and information technologies. In Figure 9.3 potential economic growth would be shown by a shift of the production possibility curve outwards from the origin.

One analysis of short term economic growth, which we have already considered to explain fluctuations in the business cycle, is the multiplier–accelerator interaction. This demonstrated how business cycle upturns, i.e. economic growth, occur as firms begin to undertake basic replacement investment just to stay in business. This interacts with the multiplier to create an interaction which will cause national product to grow, i.e. actual growth to move nearer to potential growth. However, we also noted criticisms of this theory.

The above is essentially short term, examining the movement of actual output around potential output. However, theories of economic growth are concerned with the long term, examining the effects of increases in aggregate supply in an economy.

Aggregate demand

If we think back to our diagram of the aggregate demand and aggregate supply curves in Figure 9.2, this will help us to distinguish potential causes of economic growth. On the aggregate demand side we saw that increases in any of the variables consumption (C), private sector investment (I), government expenditure (G) or exports (X) are injections into the circular flow of income and hence, via the multiplier, will increase national product, i.e. cause economic growth, which corresponds to an upturn in the business cycle. Therefore this is essentially short term economic growth since, by now, we know that the cycle will, in time, turn down.

Of course, we know that an economic system also experiences leakages, in this case in the form of imports which detract from expenditure on, and hence output of, domestic product, and so economic growth.

Investment

Investment, which is the accumulation of capital by an economy, is the major factor influencing economic growth; in turn it is financed by savings, either from businesses as undistributed profits, or from households. The latter then save with banks and other financial intermediaries who loan it to businesses, among others. It is interesting, therefore, that recent research by the Department of Trade and Industry (DTI) has found that investment by UK companies lags behind that of its major competitors. As Lord Sainsbury of Turville, the Minister for Science and Innovation, argued 'overall, UK investment levels are below those shown by the top international companies, in some cases markedly so. This is prima facie evidence that many UK firms are missing out on the cost, speed and quality benefits that new investment in plant and machinery can bring. . . .This contributes to the lower levels of labour productivity that are seen in the UK.' One author of the report, Norman Pike argued 'capital expenditure is material wrapped around knowledge; without it and other knowledge investment, companies will struggle to innovate and remain competitive in the global market ... competitiveness requires appropriate capital ... a worker can be 100 per cent efficient with a shovel, but it won't count if his international counterpart is equipped with a JCB.'

Across all the 33 industrial sectors covered by the report, British companies in 1998 spent £10 000 for each employee compared with £15 200 for international businesses.

Other influences

There are a number of reasons why UK investment levels are low but one explanation often levied is that UK companies are short-termist, i.e. they focus too much on short term profit maximisation and give too much of their profits away to keep shareholders happy. In contrast, in Continental Europe and Japan, where businesses finance their activities from banks rather than equity, profits are retained to finance capital expenditure, among other things. Other factors influencing investment include: expectations about the future – the so-called 'feel-good factor'; interest rates (UK rates are significantly higher than those of Continental Europe); corporation and other business taxes; and economic growth which, paradoxically, is influenced in turn by the level of investment.

Aggregate supply

On the aggregate supply side of the economy, economic growth will depend on the supply of inputs and their productivity. The level of investment alone is not the only factor of importance regarding investment. The productivity of capital invested – known as the marginal efficiency of capital (MEC) – is also significant. This shows the relationship between the amount of capital invested and the productivity of each extra unit invested; the more capital that is invested the lower the productivity of each extra unit, i.e. diminishing returns are experienced, other things being equal. In other words, if we plot the quantity of capital on the horizontal axis and the marginal rate of return on capital on the vertical axis, the MEC curve will slope downwards and to the right, looking like a demand curve. However, as new technologies, especially information technology, are introduced so the productivity of capital increases rather than diminishes and costs are driven down rather than increasing. This can be seen where technology has substantially replaced labour in many industries from automobile manufacture to banking to retailing. Of course the productivity of capital has also been increased by improved managerial techniques, e.g. to achieve economies of scope. The net result of this is that the MEC curve shifts to the right over time.

If we examine labour, the size of the UK's workforce will actually decrease in the next 20 years, as a larger percentage of the population retires. However, supply side policies, discussed in Chapter 9, which increase the relevant skills base of the labour force through retraining, are a means to overcome the declining workforce since those remaining in work will be more productive. Government attempts to raise to 40 per cent the number of school leavers who undertake further or higher education, and to encourage all higher education courses to have a vocational element, are attempts to improve the quality of education and skills of the UK workforce.

In the same way, land cannot normally be increased; indeed it may actually contract as global warming raises sea levels and reclaims parts of

Southern England. However, intensive farming, whatever the harmful effects it has had on wildlife, has increased the productivity of land very substantially. For enterprise, education is perceived as a main means to increase the amount and quality of entrepreneurial skills. However, a business environment where entrepreneurs can flourish without bureaucratic restrictions, is also important; this is the basis of supply side policies.

Of course for economic growth to be sustained over time all factors of production must be increased or diminishing returns will set in. Additionally, exogenous shocks can have a major impact on economic growth and these may be demand side or supply side led. The oil price hikes of the 1970s had a major adverse impact on inflation, unemployment and economic growth; similarly the impact of German reunification in 1990 slowed down economic growth in other Continental European countries as they raised interest rates in response to Germany's increases to combat inflation, in order to keep their currency values stable against the deutschmark.

A final aggregate supply issue we should note is the product life cycle which was examined in Chapter 4, Section 4.3. We saw how the life of a product goes through a number of phases from introduction to decline. The very process of products growing and then new products being developed to replace them, generates new consumer demands, new levels of investment by new businesses anxious that their output be successful, and hence economic growth. This is also reinforced by products lasting much less time than they did say two generations ago; in other words, built-in obsolescence exists. As we saw earlier, increases in consumer demand are an injection into the circular flow of income, which creates growth of actual output.

Is unlimited economic growth desirable?

At first glance, sustained economic growth may seem highly desirable. People become better off as their living standards rise. There are sufficient jobs for everyone and the range, quantity and quality of goods and services also increases. We are much better off than our parents and our children will be better off than us. That appears to be the self-fulfilling expectation.

However, economic growth also has harmful effects. If it depletes non-renewable resources, then the generation behind us will be disadvantaged since we have destroyed resources which they would have wished to use. Uncontrolled economic growth, without recognising the side effects or external costs of production, can also cause serious environmental harm, as global warming appears to demonstrate. The countryside disappears under more roads and housing; additionally, in the UK, economic growth is particularly strong in the South East of England which consequently suffers from road congestion, high house prices and increased pollution.

Indeed some business economists and pressure groups argue that a state of stasis is preferable, i.e. we maintain living standards as they are to reduce the continuing adverse effects of production on the environment. We might then allow less developed countries to catch up with us. Others argue that uncontrolled growth makes for a greedy, selfish materialist society which neglects the spiritual side of its nature; more is not necessarily better, and the more people have the still more they will want. Additionally, not everyone benefits from economic growth, as was demonstrated by the polarisation of wealth in Russia in the 1990s.

Self testing questions

1 Write bullet point answers to how a government might combat each of the types of unemployment discussed in this chapter.

2 'When the US economy sneezes the UK economy catches cold'. Obtain data from your library for the UK and US economies of GDP, inflation and unemployment to see to what extent the UK economy follows the US one.

3 Explain in your own words the multiplier–accelerator interaction as a theory to explain movements in the business cycle.

4 How valid is the multiplier–accelerator interaction as an explanation of the business cycle in the early 21st century. Explain your answer.

5 Should a country always seek maximum economic growth?

10.5 The role of economic briefings for business

Presenting an overview of the UK economy: current state and future prospects

Synopsis

This case study explores, at the time of writing, the current state of inflation in the UK economy, its relation to other key economic variables which constitute aggregate demand, and unemployment and exchange rates. Such reports are regularly published by economic consultants as well as by official bodies such as the Bank of England, the OECD, and the IMF. They are important in that they provide valuable information to businesses regarding the current state of the economy and its future developments. Businesses need to understand exactly how the economy is performing and what implications there are for their current activities and their plans for the future. Additionally, by now, the reader should be able to read this report and make sense of it. The case study:

1 reinforces concepts developed earlier in this chapter;
2 shows the inter-connections between key variables;
3 explores the use of monetary policy to control the macroeconomy.

Case Study

Whilst inflation remains subdued, UK economic growth has begun to increase significantly with forecasts of a 3.5 per cent rate for 2000, helped by a substantial increase in household consumption and business investment, both major components of final domestic (aggregate) demand. GDP has grown by almost 1 per cent in the third quarter of the year which is much higher than anticipated. Government statisticians have also revised upwards their UK economic growth figures for the first six months of the year 2000, giving a new annual growth rate of 1.8 per cent. The services sector has shown the strongest growth but manufacturing has also improved recently. However, increasing cost pressures are being identified which will cause some concerns in the coming months.

Final domestic (aggregate) demand was 4.5 per cent higher at the end of the second quarter compared with twelve months ago. In contrast, net trade (exports minus imports) and stockbuilding (mainly of manufactured goods by businesses for future sale) have been very subdued in the past, although net trade has boosted economic growth in the second quarter of this year, helped particularly by recovering demand for British exports as world trade has grown. In part, businesses have met this demand by running down their stock levels. Now, stockbuilding is also beginning to recover, contributing further to greater hope for future growth. However, assuming that net trade and stockbuilding stabilise in the foreseeable future, the growth rate of final domestic (aggregate) demand will need to moderate in the next year to ensure that it stays in line with the capacity of the economy (aggregate supply).

The labour market has got tighter in recent months as demand for labour, particularly with relevant skills, has exceeded its supply; unemployment has fallen again, to 5.9 per cent, when the Labour Force Survey measure is used and to 4.2 per cent when the Claimant Count Measure is used. This is causing the growth in nominal pay (i.e. before deducting the effects of inflation), which, as measured by the Average Earnings Index, has increased to 4.9 per cent for the last three months, mainly in service industries in the private sector of the economy. On average, however, wage claims have remained broadly flat, i.e. neither increasing or decreasing. Pay growth, in real as opposed to nominal terms, has been rising for some months; this is partly because inflation has been lower than expected, and partly because of the tightness of the labour market.

The growth of narrow money (M_0) continues to remain firm but the growth of broad money (M_4) has weakened further, and is now at its lowest level on record. This weakness is mainly because non-bank financial institutions, such as finance houses, have undertaken a major reversal of their previous policy of expanding their deposits. Household borrowing to finance houses and consumer durables and services is buoyant; additionally, house price increases appear to be broadly based across the UK rather than just in the South East, as with previous housing market booms. To pre-empt inflationary pressures, the Bank has twice raised its base rate by 0.25 per cent in the last two months.

The world economy has substantially recovered from the 1998 SE Asian economic crisis. Downward pressures on international prices have eased whilst the prices paid by producers for inputs have begun to rise. Sterling has again become stronger, causing higher British export prices and cheaper import prices. Forecasts of exchange rate prospects by the Bank of England start with an effective exchange rate index (ERI) of 105.6 and predict that, in the central value among a range of forecasts depending on different assumptions made, Sterling's ERI will decline to 101.8 in two years.

In spite of these growing inflationary pressures, however, at the time of writing, the RPIX measure of inflation had been below its target 2.5 per cent for the six previous months. The Bank of England predicts that inflation is most likely to fall to just below 2 per cent over the next year or so, before rising to the 2.5 per cent target two years hence. Compared to its previous forecast the Bank argued that upward inflationary pressures generated by domestic demand pull and earnings growth (cost push) are being offset by the declining value of sterling and declining price–cost margins (i.e. businesses are reducing the gap between their costs and the prices they charge).

The Bank also argued that the medium term outlook for inflationary pressures is less good; hence the Monetary Policy Committee must set interest rates with a view to forecast inflation rates, even though the assumptions on which the forecasts are made are uncertain. Hence the last two interest rate increases have been pre-emptive to head off possible price rises a year down the line.

The recovery of the international economy demonstrates strong growth matched by low inflation, particularly in the US; however, worries of a Wall Street downturn still remain, with the knock-on effects this will have for other countries' stock markets. Forecasts also suggest stronger economic growth in the euro area and indications of an upturn in the Japanese economy. Additionally, economic indicators of the emerging market economies suggest that, for Central and Eastern Europe, things are looking brighter. These positive signs, coupled with restrictions on supply, explain why the price of crude oil prices has risen from $10 to $25 per barrel in the last year; this price increase has also been mirrored by other commodities. As a consequence, monetary policy has been tightened both in the US and in the Eurozone, the area where the euro will be introduced into circulation in 2002.

10.6 Summary of chapter

This chapter began by exploring unemployment; various definitions of it were examined and the reasons why it is undesirable for businesses and society were discussed. Types and causes of changes in unemployment were examined and the use of economic policies to combat unemployment were also discussed.

The chapter then went on to examine links between inflation and unemployment, beginning with the Phillips curve and subsequently discussing the causes for the development of the expectations–augmented Phillips curve. This also involved discussion of different schools of economic thought concerning the Phillips curve and the appropriate policies to employ to combat inflation and unemployment.

The business cycle was the next area considered in this chapter. The various stages of the business cycle were explored, including the implications of each stage for the economy as a whole. The multiplier–accelerator interaction was put forward as one theory seeking to explain why fluctuations occur; the validity of this model in the post-industrial society of the 21st century was also explored. Policy measures to offset cycles were examined.

The chapter concluded with a case study which sought to draw together the main elements of Chapters 9 and 10.

10.7 Further questions

Further Questions

1　Discuss how the claimant count measure of unemployment differs from the ILO measure.

2　Analyse the differences in approach between (a) demand side; and (b) supply side measures to lower unemployment in an economy.

3　Is unemployment ever a good thing for an economy?

4　Why is the international economy so important to the UK. What impact does it have on inflation and employment?

5　If you managed a business resident in the UK what note would you take of forecasts such as the one in Section 10.5 and why?

10.8 Further reading

Atkinson, B., Livesey, F. and Milward, B. (eds) (1988). *Applied Economics*. Basingstoke: Macmillan.

Begg, D., Fischer, S. and Dornbusch, R. (1997). *Economics*, 5th edition. Maidenhead: McGraw Hill.

Bootle, R. (1999). Brown cannot banish boom and bust. *The Times,* 11 October, p. 25.

Johnson, C. (1991). *The Economy under Mrs. Thatcher. 1979–1990.* Harmondsworth: Penguin Books.

Lipsey, R. G. and Chrystal, K. (1999). *Alec Principles of Economics,* 9th edition. Oxford: OUP.

The Economist

The *Financial Times*

The Times

The Bank of England: http://www.bankofengland.co.uk

OECD: http://www.oecd.org/

The Office of National Statistics: http://www.ons.gov.uk

Chapter 11

International trade and finance

After completing this chapter the reader will be able to:
- understand the reasons for international trade;
- appreciate the importance of the balance of payments for a national economy and its implications for business;
- analyse the implications of exchange rate instability and the impact of the single currency on business operations and strategy.

11.1 International trade: theories, gains and implications. The terms of trade

Record US trade gap causes big share fall

Synopsis   This case study, modified from newspaper reports, explores the importance of international trade to world economies. It discusses:

1 the impact of trade figures on share performance;
2 the implications for the value of the currency;
3 the potential for monetary policy responses.

Case Study

London stock market shares fell to their lowest level for seven months after the US announced a larger than expected record trade deficit of $25.18 billion (£15.45 billion) in July. The US Commerce Department released figures showing that a massive increase in imports was the cause of the adverse July trade figures. American imported consumer goods rose to $104.22 billion, causing record monthly trade deficits with the EU, Japan and PR China.

These trade figures prompted growing concerns over the weakness of the dollar, and these were further aggravated by the growing strength of the Japanese Yen and the Bank of Japan's refusal to do anything to restrain this. As a result Wall Street fell more than 200 points whilst the UK's FTSE 100 leading shares index fell by 99.2 points, closing at 5957.3.

As a consequence of the weaker dollar, analysts surmised that there could be a further increase in interest rates at the next meeting of the US Federal Reserve, the US central bank, which sets American interest rates.

What is international trade?

International trade occurs when the sale of goods and services crosses national borders, for example, the UK selling television programmes to the US, or buying wines from Australia, or a French business, intent on acquiring a German company, hiring the services of a firm of US management consultants to advise it. It includes the sale of primary products such as fish, grain and crude oil, and manufactured goods such as clothing, cars and microprocessors for computers. It will also include processed primary products such as petroleum, chemicals and plastics made from crude oil and semi-manufactured goods which, elsewhere, will be converted into manufactured goods, such as steel plate and bars which will, for example, be made into cutlery. Further, trade will occur in services, which are of major and growing importance. These include tourism, financial services such as banking and insurance (both of major importance to the City of London), shipping, and many more.

As the case study demonstrates, the impact of trade is not just confined to government statistical records. It also impacts on international stock markets and the value of currencies.

Why trade internationally?

International trade occurs between countries in order to increase their prosperity, including securing goods and services to which, otherwise, they would not have access.

Figure 9.3 examined a country's production possibility curve (PPC) or frontier and showed, for the UK, the limit of its production in the short term given the fixed amount of its resources. For simplicity we assumed that only two goods were produced; food and clothing. We also saw that in the long term the production possibility curve could shift outwards as a result of economic growth achieved, for example, by higher levels of investment by businesses. In the short term a country may be able to achieve a point beyond its production possibility curve through international trade. This is shown in Figure 9.3.

Without international trade the UK is at point A. It then trades AB of food with the rest of the world, securing in return BC of clothing. As a result it ends up, in the short term, at point C. This is beyond what it is otherwise, in the short term, capable of achieving. Of course, the ability to be at point C depends upon the fact that it can trade BC of clothing for AB of food. If it were the case that it could only secure BD of clothing for its AB of food it would be no better off, having merely moved along its existing curve. Having said that, if society as a whole prefers clothing to food then the UK will still have gained, albeit to a lesser extent, since it now has more of the clothing.

The reader might also like to think back to Chapter 9 where the circular flow of income was analysed. We saw there that there were three main sources of income or injections into the circular flow of income which could boost it: business investment, government spending and exports. Of course there were also three withdrawals or leakages from the circular flow which, other things being equal, would cause it to contract: savings, government taxes and imports. Therefore, if exports exceed imports, other things remaining equal, international trade will boost employment, national income and promote economic growth. In reality all other things do not remain equal but the general principle still holds. International trade permits countries to maintain much higher living standards than they would otherwise be able to sustain and the UK, which relies very heavily on international trade, is living proof of this.

International trade also enables consumers to have access to goods and services not otherwise available to them and often of better quality and at lower cost. Tropical fruits such as bananas, oranges and mangoes are examples of items which UK consumers would not have without international trade. Japanese cars have been cited elsewhere in this book as products which revolutionised the world car industry in the 1970s in terms of their quality; the Internet and access to it would not have been possible without the US defence industry initially. Global trade permits bigger production

Table 11.1 Main UK trading partners, 1996.

Country/region	Imports to the UK £ million	Exports from the UK £ million
European Union of which	99 988	95 915
Germany	27 202	20 752
France	17 719	17 119
Italy	8783	8048
Netherlands	12 418	13 481
Belgium & Luxembourg	8625	8548
Ireland	7222	8669
US	22 812	19 831
Japan	8994	4265
Australia	1296	2467

Source: National Statistics – the official UK statistics website, the Office of National Statistics. © Crown Copyright 2000

runs and lower unit costs of production, i.e. the achievement of economies of scale through specialisation and division of labour.

Indeed, one key characteristic of international trade is that countries specialise in those goods and services which they have the greatest aptitude for producing due to natural resource endowments (South Africa and diamonds; California's climate suitable for growing vines; Saudi Arabia and oil), or because of the acquired skills of their workforce, such as the US and computer software or the City of London and financial expertise. India has plentiful labour but limited capital, so produces labour-intensive products such as furniture and clothing. These factors of production are largely immobile between countries so trade takes place in the goods which they produce.

Theories of international trade

Table 11.1 is descriptive. By now the reader will know that economics and the work of business economists is based on theories which seek to explain how and why economies behave as they do and what the implications are of different policies. Therefore, there are theories of international trade in the same way as there are theories of how markets behave and of the causes and remedies of inflation. Here we look specifically at theories which explain why countries specialise in producing and trading internationally in certain goods and services rather than others.

As before, for simplicity of analysis, we make limiting assumptions. In this case, we assume two countries (the UK and Canada), each producing two products, food and armaments. The reader may argue that this is simplifying to the point of losing all realism. There is some validity in this criticism but with 160 plus countries in the world and literally hundreds of thousands of different goods and services being traded, a full world analysis would lose any explanatory or predictive ability as well as being immensely complex. There are, additionally, more complex models than the one outlined here and this is intended only to be an introduction to business economics for students undertaking broad based degree courses.

The law of absolute advantage

The UK is well endowed with capital and skilled labour (including entrepreneurship) compared with Canada, so can produce armaments more efficiently (i.e. with less resources) than Canada. In this case we would say that the UK has an absolute advantage in armaments. Conversely, Canada has sweeping prairies, highly mechanised labour and cheap phosphates and other fertilisers, so can produce food more cheaply than the UK through achieving economies of scale, i.e. it has an absolute advantage in food. In this case each country can gain by specialising in the product in which it has an absolute advantage and trading some of it for the product of the other country. This will seem fairly obvious to the reader; but what of the situation where Canada, for example, is more efficient than the UK at producing both goods. Can trade then occur?

The law of comparative advantage

Let us assume that, before international trade, the UK and Canada produce food and armaments as in Table 11.2, with the labour force in each country sufficiently flexible to be capable of moving easily from one activity to the other. Canada can produce 150 000 tonnes of food, or 125 000 tanks or some combination of the two. The UK can produce 30 000 tonnes of food or 100 000 tanks or some combination of the two. Total world production is provided as the bottom line of the table.

Table 11.2 Pre-specialisation production.

Country/products	Food tonnes	Armaments hundred tanks
Canada	150 000	1250
UK	30 000	1000
Total World Production	180 000	2250

Table 11.3 Post-specialisation production.

Country/products	Food tonnes	Armaments hundred tanks
Canada	300 000	
UK		2000
Total World Production	300 000	2000

This may seem to suggest that Canada is more efficient than the UK at producing both types of good and therefore international trade is not likely to occur. Let us now compare the comparative advantages of each country.

With food Canada is more efficient than the UK by a ratio of 150 000: 30 000, or 5:1. However, with armaments Canada's efficiency is only 125 000: 100 000 or 1.25:1. This tells us that there is actually scope for each country to specialise. Canada has a greater comparative advantage in food (5:1) than armaments (1.25:1) and therefore will, in our simple model, shift all its resources into food production and leave weapons production to the UK.

The reader will note that world production of grain has increased by 120 000 tonnes but tank production has fallen by 250. In the post cold war era since the 1990s this might well be very acceptable to governments in the real world – what was known as the peace dividend.

Let us now assume that trade takes place between the UK and Canada. The exact gains to each country will depend on the rate at which food is traded for armaments. This is known as the terms of trade. If trade occurs at the rate of 100 000 tonnes of food for 1000 tanks, Canada exports 100 000 tonnes of grain to the UK and the UK exports 1000 tanks to Canada. We end up with the figures in Table 11.4.

If we compare Tables 11.3 and 11.5, we see that, post trade, Canada has gained 50 000 tonnes of food but has 250 fewer tanks; the UK has gained 70 000 tonnes of food and still has the same amount of armaments as before, so it can be highly pleased with the results of international trade. Will Canada be pleased however? This is a little more complicated to calculate, but not a lot!

Table 11.4 Post-trade situation.

Country/products	Food tonnes	Armaments hundred tanks
Canada	200 000	1000
UK	100 000	1000

Before specialisation Canada had 150 000 tonnes of food, now it has 200 000 tonnes. It has gained 0.33 extra food (50 000/150 000), or 33 per cent, which is equivalent to being given an extra 33 per cent of work force employed in agriculture before specialisation. Conversely, with armaments, before specialisation it had 1250 tanks; after trade it has 1000. Therefore, it has lost 250 tanks which is 0.2 (20 per cent) of its pre-specialisation supply (250/1250). In other words it has lost the equivalent of 0.2 (20 per cent) of its workforce. If we balance the effects, post trade, of the two products, we find a net gain to Canada of 0.33 − 0.2 = 0.13 (13 per cent). In other words, after trade, it has extra output which could only have been produced pre-specialisation if its labour supply had suddenly increased by 0.13 or 13 per cent. Even with massive immigration that would not occur. Therefore, Canada has also gained from international trade, albeit not to the same extent as the UK.

The other assumption of the above theoretical model is that there are no transport costs. If these are significant then the gains from international trade will be reduced.

The terms of trade

We referred above to the terms of trade. These may be defined as:

$$\frac{\text{the average price of goods exported by a country}}{\text{the average price of goods imported by that country}} \times 100.$$

So in year 1 (the base year) the terms of trade will be:

$$\frac{100}{100} \times 100 = 100.$$

Suppose now that in year 2 the price of exports rises by 5 per cent. This will give as the terms of trade:

$$\frac{105}{100} \times 100 = 105.$$

Since the index has risen in value it is said that the terms of trade have improved. This is because the country now has to sell less exports to secure the same volume of imports. Why should the price of exports rise? One reason is that there has been an increase in demand or a reduction in supply by the country from which they originated, which causes the price to rise. The other possibility is that the exporting country's currency has risen in value (appreciated), causing the exports to rise in price. Of course the danger of this is that, depending on the price elasticity of demand for the exporting country's goods, a rise in price of exports might reduce the demand for them; so the more inelastic the demand for a country's exports the more beneficial this is for a country's terms of trade.

The terms of trade of a country might change as the result of a change in the composition of its exports or imports, or a change in the price of its exports or imports. For the former, businesses selling higher priced products such as software as opposed to low level manufactures would be one cause of an improvement in the terms of trade; the latter was discussed earlier.

Free trade vs protectionism

Why protectionism?

As can be seen from the previous analysis, the benefits of international trade to an economy, and to the businesses involved in it, depend on there being specialisation and complete freedom to trade internationally, i.e. an absence of protectionist policies adopted by other governments. In practice many governments, especially of developing nations, use protectionist policies. This may be to avoid a heavy imbalance between their exports and their imports which would cause a large balance of payments deficit which would be hard for them to finance. Indeed, if a government is receiving loans from the International Monetary Fund (IMF) or World Bank, a condition of receiving the funds will probably be that any balance of payments deficit is reduced.

Linked to this is the fact that such countries will normally operate very tight exchange controls. This means that possession of foreign currencies is controlled by the central bank and no foreign currencies may be acquired or held without their permission. This is a very effective means of protectionism and also holds the value of the currency at an artificial level (normally higher) which is not related to its true value if the currency could be freely bought and sold in the Forex market. When leaving India, for example, one is frequently warned that attempting to export Rupees is a criminal offence, so all domestic currency, no matter how small, must be converted.

Another reason for protectionist policies is to boost domestic production and hence employment which, otherwise, could be adversely affected by an influx of cheaper or more attractive foreign produced goods. This is particularly important for countries with very large populations, such as India and PR China, where high unemployment can cause severe social and political unrest. Small businesses are major creators of wealth yet can be wiped out by more efficient and larger foreign businesses which export to that country. However, the downside is that exports to the countries facing the protectionist policies may be restricted in retaliation, losing export sales, revenue and potential jobs in the home country. Therefore, across the whole economy, protectionism may actually reduce job opportunities.

Protecting new or infant businesses until they have grown strong enough to stand up against external competition is an argument often advanced by governments which support protectionist policies. However, if the subsidies and other protection continue for too long there is a real danger that the business will stay reliant on state protection and be unable to ever compete effectively.

Restrictions on imports and exports may also be undertaken for political or strategic reasons. In the 1970s UK firms were discouraged from trading with South Africa because of its policy of apartheid or racial segregation. Exports to the former Soviet Union (and now Russia) and PR China, of the most modern computer technology, has normally been blocked by the US Government on strategic grounds, which is why industrial and other espionage activities are undertaken by these countries against the US. Conversely, a country which is politically 'at odds' with other countries may seek to achieve greater self-sufficiency by deliberately restricting foreign trade and trying to supply all its own needs, viz. Nazi Germany in the 1930s as it prepared for war.

Types of protectionism

Governments use a number of different protectionist policies including:

1   Import tariffs – imports into a country have to pay a tariff or tax or import duty (all much the same thing), usually a percentage of the price of the good or service. This makes the imports dearer and hence less competitive compared with domestic goods, encouraging citizens to buy the latter. Since the foreign supplier receives the price charged, less the tariff, this also raises revenue for the central government; the more inelastic the demand curve for the foreign imports the more money the government raises. Conversely, the more elastic the demand curve the more effective the tariff will be in reducing demand for the imports.
2   Quotas – these limit the amount of goods which may be imported into a country and are imposed by governments to promote domestic production at the expense of foreign produced goods, and to reduce domestic expenditure on imports. In some cases quotas may be voluntary. A government may operate a licensing scheme as a way to enforce quotas. For example, in the 1990s Nissan operated a voluntary quota system for its car exports to the UK because of UK government concerns that Japanese cars were swamping the UK market at the expense of other producers.
3   Exchange controls limit the amount of foreign exchange which can be purchased with domestic currency. This will limit the amount of imports which can be purchased and the amount of money which travellers can spend abroad.

4 Export subsidies are also a form of protectionism. Here the purpose of giving financial help to domestic producers is to enable them to charge lower prices in foreign markets, thus making their goods more competitive. To the government providing the subsidies the cost of these is, from their viewpoint, more than offset by the foreign currency they earn. This can then be used to buy urgently needed goods such as computers or, sadly for many developing nations, new armaments. In the 1970s and 1980s the communist countries of Central and Eastern Europe relied heavily on subsidies, often selling goods in western European markets at below production costs in order to secure hard (i.e. convertible) foreign currencies such as sterling, dollars and deutschmarks; this is known as dumping. Subsidies may be in the form of development funds or export credit guarantees whereby if foreign customers default on their debt, government backed insurance will compensate them.

5 Restraints on exports which have strategic value or to countries which are politically unacceptable: this was discussed earlier.

6 Administrative barriers and the attendant paperwork may be so complex as to inhibit international trade. This was the case with the European Union's single market in the early to mid 1980s and prompted the Single European Act 1987, which sought to remove these barriers by the end of 1992.

The economic effects of protectionism

Clearly protectionism reduces international trade and the gains it brings. Choice is reduced for consumers whilst for businesses new markets are denied and there is reduced opportunity to achieve economies of scale. This will also impact on the ability of businesses to achieve economies of scale. For illustration, Figure 11.1 shows the effects of import tariffs on an economy.

The demand curve and the supply curve show domestic demand for and domestic supply of a good. In isolation, i.e. without international trade, its market price would be P*. However, international trade exists, and the world price is P_w. Since this country does not have the power to influence the world price, i.e. it is a price taker, it has to accept the prevailing world price. The world supply curve is shown by the line S_w which, the reader will note, is perfectly elastic, since the world can supply any amount. At this price, domestic demand is Q_2 but domestic suppliers will only put Q_1 onto the market. The difference Q_1Q_2 will be supplied by foreign businesses as imports.

To restrict imports the government now imposes a tariff equal to T, which raises the price prevailing in the domestic market to $P_w + T$; the world supply then curve shifts up to $S_w + T$. The new price is still below that which would have prevailed domestically in isolation. Domestic demand

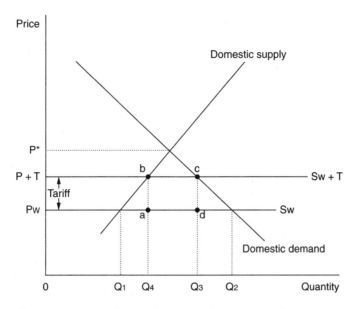

Figure 11.1 The effects of protectionist import tariffs.

now reduces to Q_3, whilst domestic supply increases to Q_4; the difference Q_4Q_3 will be supplied by imports.

The net effect of the protectionist policy is that the price to consumers rises from P to P + T. Of course domestic producers could still charge just P and undercut the price of the imported goods; however, in reality, the chance of making bigger profits will probably tempt them to raise prices. Therefore, consumers end up paying more as a result of the tariff imposition, whilst buying less (Q_3 instead of Q_2); importers sell less (Q_4Q_3 instead of Q_1Q_2); domestic firms supply more goods (Q_4 instead of Q_1); and the government earns tax revenue from the import tariff equal to $Q_4Q_3 \times T =$ abcd.

11.2 The balance of payments accounts. Problems and remedies. The impact of capital flows

Record level of exports

Synopsis   This case study illustrates UK trade statistics and their use to monitor imbalances between exports and imports. It identifies as key characteristics:

1 the record growth in UK exports and where these increases were most significant;
2 concerns that the gap between exports and imports remains high and not in the UK's favour;
3 the implications of rising exports for the UK economy and monetary policy.

Case Study

Data from the Office for National Statistics (ONS) revealed that exports reached record levels totalling £19.9 billion in August. As a result, the monthly trade deficit in goods and services fell to £825 million and raised hopes that there would be a continuing improvement in the UK's trade gap. Traded goods showed the greatest improvement, with the deficit falling from £2.2 billion in July to £1.9 billion in August, helped by economic recovery in SE Asia. Revenue from (North Sea) oil exports remained steady at £700 million, whilst exports of services also increased a little.

The volume of goods exported rose by 7 per cent in August which was the largest monthly increase for over two years; cars and chemicals were products where increases were greatest. Economists suggested that the improvement in export figures showed that UK exporters were coping better with the high value of sterling, although several suggested that increased exports would increase inflationary pressures and hence the risk of an increase in interest rates.

However, preliminary data for September suggested that exports outside the EU were slipping back. Imports of goods and services also reached record levels.

Defining the balance of payments

The balance of payments of a country is a statistical record of its transactions with the rest of the world over a period of time, usually one year. As such it consists of a number of sections which are shown in Table 11.5. These are the current account, transactions in external assets and liabilities, and the balancing item.

The current account

This balance of payments account consists of visible transactions and invisible transactions. Visible transactions or items relate to trade in physical items such as coal, grain, oil, televisions, computers, aircraft and so on.

When the UK exports visibles, payments return to the UK in sterling or another currency, usually of the country purchasing the exports. Conversely, when the UK buys goods from overseas it has to make payment in the currency of the exporting country or sterling or a third country's currency. The difference between the inflows and outflows of payments is known as the balance of trade. Therefore, if payments into the UK (credit or plus items) exceed payments out of the UK (debit or minus items) the UK is said to have a surplus on its visible trade or on its balance of trade.

Invisible items consist of services such as tourism, finance, watching foreign films, transport etc. Therefore, if you holiday abroad the payment you make to the hotel, and spending money, will be debit items on the UK's current account since your money leaves the UK. Conversely, the expenditure of foreign businessmen visiting the UK and who use British Airways to get here will be a credit item since their money is coming into the UK. Invisible items also consist of interest on loans, share dividends and profits from foreign direct investment entering and leaving the UK. If I hold shares in foreign companies, the dividends paid to me each year will be a credit item on the invisible items of the UK's balance of payments on current account, since money enters the UK.

If we add visibles and invisibles together we get the balance of trade in goods and services; it is to this that the case study at the start of Chapter 11, Section 11.2 relates.

Transfers of funds are also included in the current account, for example financial aid given to the Bangladeshi government after severe floods, or transfers of money between the UK government and the EU Commission. If we add these to visibles and invisibles we have the balance of payments on current account, i.e.

visible trade + invisible trade + transfers of funds = balance of payments on current account

Table 11.5 gives the main components of the balance of payments on current account for the years 1996 to 1998. All figures are in £ million, and not seasonally adjusted. The number in brackets after the year denoted which quarter; so 1996(1) denotes January to March 1996. The reader will note the variations in the current account balance and also that the visible balance is always in deficit, as are transfer incomes, e.g. pensions paid to retired people living abroad. However, this is offset by a surplus on services and investment.

Transactions in external assets and liabilities

This is the second balance of payments account and consists of all purchases and sales of assets by UK households, businesses and government in foreign countries and by foreign households, businesses and government in the UK. It was formerly known as the capital account.

Table 11.5 The UK's balance of payments on current account, 1996–1998 (second quarter) £m.

Time	Visible trade (balance)	Services	Investment	Transfers Income	Current Balance
1996(1)	−3144	2326	1170	−970	−588
1996(2)	−4094	1636	3164	−1422	−1526
1996(3)	−3681	2059	2455	−1193	−360
1996(4)	−1387	2876	1322	−937	1874
1997(1)	−1925	2997	2108	−613	2567
1997(2)	−4056	2379	3327	−895	754
1997(3)	−3201	2685	4122	−1521	2085
1997(4)	−2610	3100	2611	−501	2600
1998(1)	−4303	3730	2028	−1491	−36
1998(2)	−5183	2778	2794	−1083	−694

Source: Government Statistical Service, Economic Trends: Annual Supplement 1999, the Office of National Statistics. © Crown Copyright 2000

Transactions in external assets is a net amount and relates to the purchase by UK households, businesses and government of assets in other countries minus the sale of any such assets. These transactions will include the purchase of office blocks, factories and land (foreign direct investment) as well as the purchase of shares in existing companies (portfolio investment).

It also includes depositing money in overseas banks, loaning money overseas and buying foreign currencies. Even though this is storing up future wealth for the UK the fact that money leaves the UK makes this a debit or minus item. When the money transferred abroad earns interest on the loans or dividends on the shares purchased, these payments of course show up as credits in the invisibles on the current account. Finally, when external assets are sold by UK households, businesses and government, then the money returning to the UK is a credit item.

Transactions in external liabilities are the converse of the above. They relate to assets bought in the UK by foreign households, businesses and governments – such as BMW's purchase of Rover or Thomson–CSF's purchase of Racal. Since money enters the UK these are credit items. When BMW sold Rover it then became a debit item. Again, interest and dividend payments on these external liabilities show up as debit invisible items in the current account.

Do the balance of payments balance?

The balance of payments accounts must balance. If the UK has a deficit on its current account then it has to find the money to cover this deficit; foreigners will not just give us goods and services, unfortunately. Therefore, the UK can either make payments from its foreign currency reserves (an external asset) or it can borrow from overseas with foreigners, in return, acquiring assets in the UK (an external liability).

The balancing item

The balance of payments accounts cover a myriad of different transactions and as a result, when government statisticians calculate the balance of payments figures, it is impossible to obtain total accuracy. Not all transactions are recorded, or recorded properly. For example, there are omissions in the value of imports and exports recorded and sampling errors in the estimations of investment flows. Therefore, the balancing item seeks to address the differences in the data for the current account and external assets and liabilities and make sure that the balance of payments actually balances. The balancing item can vary significantly over the years and swing from positive to negative and back again.

Does a balance of payments deficit matter?

The UK has more commonly run a deficit on its balance of trade in recent years, i.e. it has imported more goods than it has exported. In some years, such as the early 1980s, this has been more than offset by a surplus on invisibles, reflecting the de-industrialisation which the UK has increasingly experienced in the last twenty years, i.e. the move from a manufacturing to a services economy. However, more commonly, there has been an overall deficit on the UK's current account. This is regarded as undesirable since it has to be financed by a surplus on the transactions in external assets and liabilities. In other words, to finance its current or short term consumption the UK is relying on inward foreign investment which creates long term claims on it through dividends and profit payments and the possible future repatriation of that capital. Having said that, if foreign direct investment promotes greater efficiencies in production, as the Japanese have done with UK car production, then there can be real benefits to the recipient economy.

If there is also a deficit on the transactions in external assets and liabilities this is perceived as even more undesirable. Under those circumstances, the main remedies which the UK government might adopt are to raise interest rates to attract foreign capital (external liabilities) or use its foreign exchange reserves. Raising interest rates will make investing in the UK more attractive; however, this might have adverse effects on UK businesses and the macroeconomy, especially if the UK was near the bottom of the business cycle. If foreign exchange reserves are used there is a risk that foreign investors, worried that continuing deficits might cause the value of sterling to fall, will sell sterling to avoid this potential risk. This could put greater pressure on the government which may now also have to use its reserves to defend the exchange rate against other currencies.

The most important point is the medium term trend of the balance of payments figures and the effect this has on the expectations of investors.

Self testing questions

1 Why is free international trade important to businesses?

2 What protectionist measures could governments use to inhibit free trade?

3 What is the difference between the balance of payments on current account and transactions in external assets and liabilities?

4 Why does the balance of payments rarely balance?

5 If the UK has a persistent balance of payments deficit should this be of concern to British businesses involved in international trade?

11.3 Managing exchange rates as a policy tool. Implications of exchange rate fluctuations for trade and business

Market forces and the value of currencies

Synopsis
This case study illustrates some of the factors which can influence the value of a currency on the foreign exchange (Forex) market. These maybe economic, political or even psychological. The case study shows that:

1 what politicians or major financial people say can impact on a country's exchange rate;
2 foreign currency dealers' behaviour influences exchange rates;
3 economic and political events can cause exchange rates to vary.

Case Study

11 March 1999

The resignation of the German Finance Minister Oskar Lafontaine, nick-named 'Red Oskar' because of his political beliefs, and described by *The Sun* as 'the most dangerous man in Europe', caused the euro to under-take a remarkable recovery in its value, reflecting the delight which international currency markets felt at the news. Lafontaine had been seen as a prime reason for disputes between the German government and the European Central Bank (ECB), which have harmed the value of the euro. It had been trading at $1.0800 to the euro but, after the announcement of Lafontaine's resignation, the currency's value rose to $1.1000 to the euro, as foreign currency dealers bought it in preference to other curren-cies (hence the US dollar fell in value against the euro). It also rose in value against sterling from 66.45p = 1 euro to 67.2p = 1 euro (sterling therefore fell in value against the euro). This was in spite of announce-ments earlier that day by the billionaire speculator George Soros, that the value of the currency would remain low as long as there were political tensions between the ECB and member countries of the EU.

29 March 1999

The euro fell to a record low level against sterling and the dollar as a result of the worsening crisis in the Balkans and signs of economic weak-ness in Europe. The euro fell in value to $1.0683, almost ten per cent below its value when it was launched on 1 January 1999, before it steadied at $1.0720. Sterling also rose against the euro (therefore the euro fell in value), reaching 66.05p = 1 euro (almost nine per cent above its launch value), before falling back and closing the day only fractionally up at 66.19p = 1 euro. The pound also fell against the dollar from $1.6211 to $1.6188. Other European currencies close to the Balkans actions by NATO suffered even more than the euro; the Bank of Greece (Greece's central bank) had to intervene in the market to try and stem a run on the drachma. Analysts predicted that if the Kosovo crisis worsened still more the euro would fall to $1.05 or even $1.04. This would be a record ten year low against the dollar for the currencies that now constitute the euro. The dealers in the foreign currency markets argued that even if the Kosovo crisis were soon resolved, the euro would still be under pressure because the economy of Euroland/the Eurozone was slowing down.

The above case studies illustrate the volatility of exchange rates. The fact that these examples are not current does not matter. They demonstrate that the market forces of demand and supply, which in turn are influenced

Table 11.6 Sterling spot and forward rates at close of business.

Currency/rates	Spot	1 Month forward	3 Month forward
Danish Kroner	11.965–12.029	$\frac{3}{8}-\frac{1}{8}$ pm	$\frac{7}{8}-\frac{5}{8}$ pm
US Dollar	1.6350–1.6482	0.5 pm–4.5 dis	0.25 pm–5.25 dis
Euro	1.6145–1.6164	12–15 dis	39–43 dis
Japanese Yen	173.29–174.35	$\frac{7}{8}-\frac{3}{4}$ dis	$2\frac{5}{8}-2\frac{1}{2}$ pm
Swiss Franc	2.5912–2.6102	$1-\frac{3}{4}$ pm	$2\frac{7}{8}-2\frac{5}{8}$ pm

by political, economic and other factors, will constantly influence the price of each currency (the exchange rate) against all others causing it to rise or fall.

The rate of exchange

This may be defined as the rate at which one currency trades for another, e.g. FF 10 = £1: DM 2.9 = £1. This is how the rate is quoted for tourists. If one looks at the financial pages of one of the broadsheets one will see rates quoted as in Table 11.6.

The current or spot rate of exchange at close of business is the exchange rate which was prevailing at the close of trading in the Forex (Foreign Exchange) market the previous night. In actual fact there are two spot rates of exchange quoted. The first rate quoted is how much of the currency foreign exchange dealers, e.g. banks, will give to a business buying substantial amounts of currency; for the Danish Kroner this is DK 11.965 for £1. Conversely, a business selling Kroner would have to give DK 12.029 for each £1 it wished to buy on the Forex market. The Forex dealer always operates on the basis of 'buy high, sell low', i.e. always quotes the price which makes him/her the most profit. The difference between the two prices is known as the margin.

Businesses may also enter into a forward contract to buy or sell a foreign currency one month or three months in the future at a rate fixed now. This can be particularly attractive for it gives certainty in a world where exchange rates can change significantly. Let us assume a UK business has agreed to sell optical instruments to an American company but, to secure the contract, has had to give its customer one month's credit, i.e. payment in US dollars to the total of $100 000 is not due for one month. If the exchange rate stays exactly the same as in Table 11.6, then in one month the UK company will receive $100 000/$1.6482 (since the dealer buys $ high) = £60 672.48. In reality there will also be exchange commission to pay but we ignore that for this example.

Now suppose that, in one month, when payment is actually due, the rate of exchange is $1.7500 to £1. This will give the British exporting firm a sterling figure of £57 142.86. In other words, merely by the exchange rate moving against it in that month the business has lost £3529.62. This will clearly have a significant impact on its profit margin and will encourage it, in future, to enter into a forward contract, fixing the rate now for the sale or purchase of currency, say one month hence. It can then build the cost of the forward contract into its price quotation to the customer to ensure that it is borne by the latter.

Forward rates

A forward rate is the spot rate on the day a forward contract is entered into, plus or minus the interest differential for the duration of the contract. The interest differential is a mix of the interest rate if the money was deposited for the duration of the contract in the country of the trader's currency (the UK, in the example above) or in the other currency's country (the US). The spot rate will usually move during the period of the contract in the direction of the forward rate.

Forward rates are quoted at a premium (pm) or a discount (dis). If the Forex market thinks sterling will rise in value against the dollar (or whatever the currency is) over the next month, the forward rate will be higher or more expensive than the spot rate and will be quoted at a discount. This discount will be added to the spot rate. For example, if the spot rate is $1.60 = £1, and the forward rate is $1.65 = £1, then sterling will be worth more forward and the dollar less, compared with the spot rate. This means that a British business selling dollars will have to give its bank more per £ than it buys if it has entered into a one month forward contract, compared with the spot rate when it entered the contract.

Conversely, if the expectation is that sterling will fall against the dollar, from $1.60 = £1 to $1.55 = £1, the forward rate will be lower than the spot rate, i.e. it will be quoted at a premium. This premium will be deducted from the spot rate. This means that sterling is worth less forward and the dollar more forward, compared with the spot rate.

It is also possible, although not common, to get the forward rate quoted at a premium for (the dealer) buying and at a discount for (the dealer) selling. This happens with the dollar rates quoted one month forward in Table 11.6.

Forward rates also show sub-units of the currency. Therefore, in the case of the dollar, the one month forward rates are quoted as 0.5 cent premium to 4.5 cents discount. Without wishing to get too bogged down in calculations which are not appropriate to a year one business economics textbook, the calculation for our example is shown below.

The UK firm enters into a contract to sell $100 000 one month forward.

Spot dollar selling rate for firm
  (dealer buys dollars)   = $1.6482
One month forward   +   0.0450

                                             = $1.6932

The one month forward discount rate of 4.5 cents is added to the spot rate giving the final rate of $1.6932. This guarantees the UK exporter receipts of $100 000/$1.6932 = £59 059.77 one month after the export deal is completed. The higher forward rate for sterling against the dollar compared with spot means that the market anticipates sterling strengthening over the next month against the dollar.

The reader will note that there is a convention for quoting currencies, e.g. FF10 = £1; $1.60 = £1. We could quote it the other way, e.g. FF1 = 10p; $1 = 62.5p but this is not conventional. The only exception is the euro which is quoted as, for example, 1 euro = 61p.

Demand and supply curves

In the section above, we considered how each currency is quoted at both a buying and a selling price by Forex dealers. For convenience, we will assume there is only one price or exchange rate at which one currency trades against another which is an average of the buying and selling prices. Figure 11.2 illustrates this.

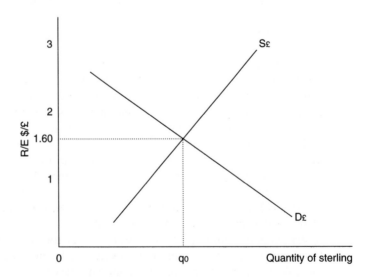

Figure 11.2 Demand and supply curves for sterling against the US dollar.

As can be seen, we have the familiar demand and supply curves encountered throughout this book. The vertical axis shows the price of sterling. It has to be measured against another currency, so the US dollar is being used. The vertical axis shows the quantity of sterling. In other words, sterling is a commodity just like any other good. At a high price little is demanded; at lower price more is demanded. Similarly, at a high rate of exchange, much sterling is supplied onto the market and as the price falls less is supplied. In Figure 11.2, the demand for and supply of sterling curves intersect at an equilibrium rate of $1.60 = £1. The demand and supply curves for sterling will shift in exactly the same way as in previous Figures.

Therefore, if there is a big increase in US demand for UK exports, the demand for sterling curve will shift to the right since US businesses will demand sterling to pay British exporters. It may be that some British firms will accept dollars, for example if they have to make other payments in dollars. In that case it is easiest just to maintain a dollar account. Otherwise British exporters will prefer payment in sterling since then the US customer bears the risk of any exchange rate movements in the period between when the contract is agreed and payment is made.

The reader should also note that we could draw another demand and supply curve, this time showing the demand for and supply of dollars against sterling. This would show events from the viewpoint of the dollar rather than sterling, as in Figure 11.2.

If the demand curve for sterling shifted to the right in Figure 11.2 (since people would be selling dollars to buy sterling, so more dollars would be supplied on the foreign exchange market), the price of sterling rises to, say $1.70 = £1, i.e. sterling is now more valuable since now people must give up an extra 10 cents to get £1, i.e. we move up the vertical axis on Figure 11.2. Conversely, as the price of sterling rises the price of dollars must fall.

What determines exchange rates?

As can be seen at the start of Section 11.3, exchange rates can be influenced by a variety of different factors. Space does not permit a detailed analysis so influences will be grouped with a brief discussion of each.

Trade imbalance

A trade imbalance on a country's balance of payments accounts may affect its exchange rate. For example, a persistent deficit on current account, not offset by a surplus on transactions in external assets and liabilities, will cause increased demand for foreign currencies relative to the domestic currency. Since the foreign currencies are paid for with the domestic currency, its supply will increase (supply curve shifts to the right) and its price/exchange rate will fall.

Economic policy

The economic policies which a government pursues may impact directly on the exchange rate of the domestic currency against other currencies. A government which tolerates high inflation will see the spot or current exchange rate fall as the value of the domestic currency falls. The inflation may be caused by any of the factors we considered in Chapter 9, Section 9.4. One policy option is for the government to reduce inflation through raising interest rates. If it operates tighter monetary policy this will help to achieve this; also, higher interest rates will make the domestic economy a more attractive place in which foreign investors will want to place their money. Since these investors will have to buy its currency to purchase stocks and shares, have new factories built etc., demand for it will rise and hence its price against other currencies will also rise.

Speculation

Large scale funds move around the world looking for short term profits by taking advantage of temporary differences in interest rates, or exchange rates. This is known as arbitrage and is a natural function of markets since the outcome is one price rather than a series of different prices for the same commodity (including currency), in different sub-markets, such as London, Tokyo and New York. However, with regard to currencies, if a country seeks to maintain a fixed exchange rate (discussed below) and forex dealers working for banks and multinational companies think the currency is overpriced and will fall in value, they will sell it. Their aim is to sell it at its current high price then if the exchange rate does fall, buy it back subsequently at the new lower rate; the difference is their profit. If sufficient speculators' expectations are that the currency is overpriced and they all sell, then their expectations become self-fulfilling since the very act of large scale selling will drive down the price.

Exogenous factors

An exchange rate can be hit by factors beyond its government's control, e.g. an economic crisis such as a major increase in crude oil prices, or an economic crisis in another part of the world which has implications for the first country's trade, or a political crisis such as a major regional conflict. In these cases there is little a government can do except to sit tight and wait for the storm to blow over.

Table 11.7 Sterling/deutschmark and sterling/dollar exchange rates, 1997–2000.

Year		ERI	DM/£	$/£
1997	6 May	99.7	2.81	1.62
	6 June	99.7	2.82	1.63
	10 July	104.1	2.97	1.69
	7 August	103.9	3.00	1.60
	6 November	102.4	2.89	1.68
1998	4 June	102.6	2.90	1.64
	8 October	100.6	2.76	1.72
	5 November	99.2	2.76	1.66
	10 December	99.6	2.76	1.66
1999	7 January	99.0	2.76	1.65
	4 February	100.6	2.84	1.64
	8 April	102.6	2.90	1.61
	10 June	104.4	2.99	1.60
	8 September	104.8	3.02	1.63
	4 November	106.0	3.07	1.64
	25 November	106.3	3.10	1.62
2000	13 January	108.1	3.14	1.65

Source: HM Treasury

The ERI is the exchange rate index. This is an average exchange rate made up of a number of different exchange rates, each weighted according to its relative importance. It is then expressed as an index with variations from a base year value of 100; for this index, that was 1990. The deutschmark/sterling and dollar/sterling exchange rates are nominal rates, i.e. the effects of inflation in the different countries are included in nominal rates. More commonly, business economists are concerned with real exchange rates, which measure the relative prices of goods in different countries when valued in a common currency. Changes in real exchange rates are a better measure of changes in the competitiveness of different countries through changes in prices.

Policy options to raise a currency's exchange rate

What policies might a government adopt to influence its country's exchange rate if it is falling? One option it has is to use monetary policy to boost the currency by raising interest rates. Alternatively, if the adverse expectations are due to a large and persistent trade deficit, it could seek to tighten fiscal policy (raise taxes and reduce expenditure) to dampen down the economy and hence imports. It might even use its currency reserves to buy the domestic currency to offset speculative selling. Or it might try to talk up the currency by government ministers or the chairperson of the central bank making positive statements about the currency's future.

Of course there have been times when government ministers have, thoughtlessly, said the wrong thing, and consequently worsened matters.

All of these assumptions are related to a falling or depreciating exchange rate, e.g. when the exchange rate for sterling falls from DM 2.80 = £1 to DM 2.60 = £1. In practice this can be beneficial to a country since a lower value of the domestic currency against foreign currencies means that exports will be cheaper and imports dearer. Depending on price elasticities of demand for these exports and imports this could lead to a reduction in any balance of trade deficit which the country has.

Conversely, when a currency rises or appreciates in value, exports will be become relatively more expensive and, depending on the price elasticity of demand for them, demand may fall. Conversely imports will be cheaper. Although this may cause an increase in the amount of them, their lower price may assist a government to keep down the rate of domestic inflation.

Exchange rate stability – the benefits for business

At this point the reader has probably reached two conclusions. Firstly, that exchange rates can be volatile and secondly that they can have a major impact on businesses. If exchange rates are stable then they offer businesses many advantages:

1 Most importantly, stable rates mean that there is certainty with regard to payments which businesses have to make and the revenues they receive when these are in foreign currencies. Profit margins will not be affected by sudden exchange rate changes nor will businesses suddenly find themselves incurring extra costs from purchasing foreign currency to make payments.

2 Using foreign currencies incurs other costs for businesses. Banks charge commission for buying and selling currency. If a business maintains bank accounts in different currencies this will incur further costs as will the invoicing and other documentation involved with business transactions in different currencies. If, additionally, a business has to hedge against a possible future exchange rate change, by taking out a forward contract, this will incur further costs. Stable exchange rates would remove this necessity.

3 Stable exchange rates mean that a business can quote prices in other countries and currencies without having to change them regularly (a factor which will deter sales). Stable prices also save the business the need to keep changing sales brochures and other documentation.

4   Stable exchange rates also require governments to exercise prudence with regard to macroeconomic policies which will provide a stable business environment and hence benefit firms. If a government chooses to operate an expansionary economic policy, this may well cause imports to increase and exports to contract, the latter because rising domestic demand is diverting exports from overseas. As the balance of payments worsens, the government will have to adopt more prudent economic policies or face speculative pressures on the currently stable exchange rate.

11.4 Different exchange rate regimes

So far we have not defined precisely the main types of exchange rate system or regime. This section seeks to briefly review the main types of exchange rate regime in terms of their relevance to business.

Fixed exchange rates

Here, the rate of exchange of a currency against others, or more likely a number of currencies against each other, is maintained at a fixed rate, without permitting variations due to market forces. In this extreme case, a government is forced to intervene in the Forex market, buying or selling to compensate for any changes in demand or supply. For example, if the country has a current account balance of payments deficit there will be an excess supply of the domestic currency since it has been supplied to buy the relevant foreign currencies to pay for the imports; the central bank will offset this by buying up the excess domestic currency. Appropriate internal macroeconomic policies will also need to be implemented to maintain the rate. For example, if there is strong economic growth, encouraging imports to meet rising domestic demand, this would need to be reduced by tighter monetary and fiscal policies.

The most effective way to operate a fixed exchange rate system is in conjunction with exchange controls. These are limits on how much foreign currency is made available to domestic importers or citizens travelling abroad. Employed now by many developing nations and, until 1987, by many European countries, these prevent large scale ouflows of capital from a country. The system is managed by a government department or central bank and their permission is needed before such flows of funds can take place, preventing their destabilising effects and helping, therefore, to maintain stable exchange rates. With the ending of UK exchange controls (in 1980), the supply of funds in the world which can easily and quickly move from country to country far outweighs central banks' reserves.

Taken to its extreme, the currency is not traded at all on the open or forex market so that only small amounts can be bought and sold with government permission. The rate is then fixed by the government, although at times with some acknowledgement of market pressures. In India, for example, it is illegal to take rupees into or from the country, no matter how small the amount.

In Figure 11.2, in our hypothetical example, the exchange rate would be fixed at $1.60 permanently, regardless of its true value if it were traded freely. Fixed exchange rates are not commonly used in free market economies, although the current transition of the EU to a single European currency required fixed exchange rates for members' currencies during the period 1999–2002.

Adjustable peg system of exchange rates

Between 1945 and 1971, the economies of the advanced non-communist countries operated a system of largely stable exchange rates known as the Bretton Woods system. This was an adjustable peg exchange rate system whereby the value of each currency was fixed in relation to gold and hence the US dollar, the price of gold being fixed at $38 per ounce. The currency was then allowed to vary by up to +/–1 per cent of its agreed or central rate, or parity, depending on demand and supply. Before the rate reached the limits of +/–1 per cent, the central bank of the currency under threat would intervene in the market, buying if the currency approached its – 1% limit, or selling if the currency approached its + 1% limit. The reader might like to compare this with the Exchange Rate Mechanism later in this chapter.

If pressures continued to drive the currency up or down then the government would need to adopt appropriate monetary or fiscal polices; if the value of the currency was falling the government would need to raise interest rates to make the currency more attractive. However, raising interest rates to defend sterling might have adverse effects on UK businesses and the macroeconomy, especially if the UK was near the bottom of the business cycle. It might also implement deflationary fiscal policies if the fall in the exchange rate were due to high demand for imports and also exports being sucked into satisfying domestic demand.

The problem with pegged exchange rates is if speculative pressures on the exchange rate become overpowering. As noted before, speculators' expectations become self-fulfilling and a central bank might exhaust its foreign currency reserves, seeking to defend its currency as speculators sell it. It can seek to borrow from other central banks but if that and appropriate monetary and fiscal policies have no effect it will be forced to devalue, i.e. lower the parity rate, for instance, from $2.80 = £1, to $2.40 = £1, as the UK did in 1967. If it has lowered the rate enough, speculative pressures will abate and the speculators take their profits. For governments under the Bretton Woods system, being forced to devalue was seen as a sign of political failure and economic ineptitude; in fact it should have been a recognition that as economic conditions change, pegged exchange rates agreed years before are no longer appropriate.

Managed floating

Also known as dirty floating, this system allows exchange rates to vary or float within wide margins. Section 11.5, which discusses the widening of ERM bands to +/–15 per cent in 1992 to accommodate speculative pressures, is a good example of dirty or managed floating, although at the time it was never described as such by the EU. Dirty floating gives greater opportunity for the currency to respond to market forces without central authorities having to intervene to defend its value. At times, governments do not even reveal what the theoretical limits are for their currency, hence inhibiting the ability of speculators to drive the rate up or down.

Managed floating is perceived as giving an element of stability without the disadvantages of being in a straightjacket such as imposed by the adjustable peg system.

Free floating exchange rates

It was Karl-Otto Pöhl, the former President of the Bundesbank, who argued 'interest rates should be set according to domestic monetary conditions and the exchange rate should be left to go where it will.'

Free floating or clean floating is, as its name suggests, the situation where the exchange rate can rise (known as appreciation) or fall (known as depreciation) as market forces wish, in theory without government interference or involvement of any sort, such as varying interest rates. As such, any balance of payments deficit which the country has will automatically correct; if imports exceed exports, for example, the exchange rate will fall until imports become so expensive and exports so cheap as to eliminate the imbalance. As Karl-Otto Pöhl suggests in the quotation above, the advantage of free floating rates is that the economy can be managed independently and the currency left to its own devices. Of course, in a very open economy like the UK, an exchange rate which fluctuates wildly can have a major impact on economic performance. If the economy is at full capacity, depreciation of the exchange rate will increase demand for exports. Since this is an injection into the circular flow of income, it will increase aggregate demand, output and employment. If the economy is working at less than full capacity, output should increase without significant price increases. However, if the economy is working at full capacity, this increase in demand will generate inflationary pressures which, in part, will offset the effects of the depreciation.

Of course, the best way to avoid exchange risks is for us all to share the same currency; this is discussed in Section 11.5 below.

Self testing questions

Self Testing Questions

1 Use your library to find recent examples of changes in the value of a currency. Why did these changes occur and did the government of the country whose currency was affected do anything to offset the changes?

2 Why are exchange rates not constant over time?

3 Discuss the activities of speculators in the international economy.

4 What are the main differences between dirty floating and a managed peg exchange rate system?

5 How might a government influence the exchange rates of its currency and why?

11.5 Economic and monetary union; the implications of the single currency for European business

The single European currency: when will the UK join?

Synopsis

This case study discusses UK government statements about readiness to join economic and monetary union (EMU). It also explores an IMF study, published in 2000, which identified sterling as overvalued against the euro and hence suggested that the UK could not yet join the single European currency. It explores a number of key characteristics which are:

1 The UK government believes that the UK economy is not yet ready to join the single currency.

2 The market exchange rate of sterling against the euro was, at the time of writing, far higher than the ideal rate at which the UK would be able to join the single currency. Sterling's value would therefore need to fall substantially before entry.

3 If a country joins when its currency is overvalued, or when the business cycle is out of sync with those of Continental Europe this will cause considerable economic problems for it.

Case Study

In October 1997 Gordon Brown, the UK's Chancellor of the Exchequer, stated that, in principle, the UK government supported membership of the single currency, but that it was not yet ready to join. He suggested that, subject to a satisfactory referendum, the UK could join after the next election (2002 at latest), provided certain conditions improved. He argued that the UK could not join, firstly, because the UK economy (or more precisely its business cycle) had not converged with those economies whose countries were committed to joining the single currency (known as Euroland or the Eurozone). Secondly, countries which opted for monetary union had to be flexible enough to cope with any internal or external shocks, such as German reunification, which would impact upon their economies. The UK had high levels of unemployment and a persistent lack of skills in its workforce which were inhibiting this flexibility; therefore it would find it difficult to cope with such shocks.

Thirdly, Brown argued, the single currency will have an effect on the level of investment which businesses undertake. It should boost investment but if countries are not properly prepared the effects could be adverse. The UK economy has a history of macroeconomic instability which has discouraged business investment levels in the past; joining the single currency too soon could create still further macroeconomic instability. Hence the UK economy needs to converge to the Euroland economies before it joins them in the single currency.

Brown also argued that the single currency will have a major impact on the UK's financial services sector, which needs a transition period before it can modify its ATMs, payments and settlement systems etc. Finally, to achieve business cycle convergence, a period of low inflation and and economic stability is needed. Hence to join too soon would be very detrimental.

In late 1999, this message was reinforced by the European Commission which, in its annual review, drew attention to stronger than expected economic growth in the UK. This, it argued, would force the Bank of England to raise interest rates rapidly, to offset rising inflationary pressures. In contrast, there was a much more benign outlook for inflation in the Eurozone, meaning that interest rate differentials between it and the UK would widen. As a result, the Commission argued, Britain's economy would not converge with that of the single currency area before the beginning of 2002.

This was further reinforced by an IMF working paper, authored by economists from the IMF, the World Bank, the Bank of Spain and Deutsche Bank and published in 2000, which argued that sterling was significantly and exceptionally overvalued against the euro and would need to fall in value by more than 20 per cent before the UK could join the single currency. The report argued that an ideal rate would be 81p to the euro, which is equivalent to DM2.41 to £1 (at the time of writing this case study sterling was trading at 61.21p equals 1 euro or DM 3.21). An earlier IMF report had claimed that the UK government would need to take 'specific actions' to make sterling weaker, i.e. fall in value, before the UK could join the euro.

The IMF working paper argued that sterling was also substantially over-valued against the dollar and the yen after a sustained appreciation during the mid and late 1990s; and that the euro was undervalued against the US dollar because of the strength of the US economy (causing the dollar to rise in value) and weaknesses in the European economy (causing the euro to fall on value). A fair exchange rate for the euro would, it claimed, be $1.26 to 1 euro, about 25 per cent higher than the prevailing exchange rate at the time of writing. The report argued that ' by end-1998, the pound and dollar were both overvalued against the euro, and the recent weakness of the latter has widened this misalignment.'

The report also asserted that Germany had joined the single currency at an exchange rate where the deutschmark was overvalued by about 3 per cent when the exchange rates of members of the single currency were locked at end 1998. This overvalued currency explained some of the problems that German exporters experienced during 1999 (an over-valued currency causes exports to be more expensive and imports to be cheaper). The Italian lira was a little undervalued when Italy joined, whilst France and Spain joined the single currency at about the correct rates.

The above case study emphasises the importance of countries' economies converging before membership of the single currency is acceptable. Clearly, in the case of the UK, it is not ready for membership for some time. Nonetheless, the single currency has major implications for business. This last section of Chapter 11 explores this.

Economic and monetary union

The Treaty of Maastricht

The Inter-Governmental Conference (IGC) held at Maastricht in 1991, provided the programme which would lead EU members to a single European currency.

There had been a report, issued in 1989 and known as the Delors Report after the President of the European Commission, Jacques Delors. This had envisaged that all EU countries would join the single currency and then subsequently adjust their business cycles to converge with Germany's, since this was the strongest. As seen from the previous case study, convergence of business cycles was seen as essential to avoid the problems already discussed, when countries had to adopt inappropriate monetary policies to keep their currencies in line with the deutschmark, because their business cycles were out of synch with Germany's. With converged business cycles, every country could use the same economic policies and benefit equally.

In contrast, the Treaty of Maastricht, which emerged from the 1991 IGC, argued that only those countries which had met certain conditions or criteria would be able to join the single European currency. The reason for this was that if convergence of business cycles occurred first, then there would be far less pressure on economies to adjust after joining the single currency. If, however, convergence was left until after single currency membership, economies would experience major and painful dislocations as they sought to co-ordinate their business cycles with Germany's. This in turn would impact severely on businesses and on the stability of the new European currency against other currencies.

For example, countries joining the single currency with high inflation rates would find that their goods would have higher prices against other EU countries when all were priced in euros. They could not allow their exchange rate to fall against other countries to offset this, since they no longer would have one against other EU countries. This would, therefore, mean falling demand for their products, consequent unemployment and extremely painful recession until inflation was squeezed out of the system and the country's goods and labour were again competitively priced.

The Maastricht convergence criteria

The rules which countries had to meet to qualify for single currency membership were:

1 Inflation to be no higher than 1.5 per cent above the average for the three EU countries with the lowest rates during the previous year.
2 Long term interest rates (the rates on 10 year government bonds) to be no higher than 2 per cent above the three EU countries with the lowest rates during the previous year.
3 The exchange rate to have been in the normal band of the ERM (± 2.25 per cent) for two years without devaluing.
4 The country's budget deficit not to exceed 3 per cent of its gross domestic product (GDP).
5 The national debt of the country should not exceed 60 per cent of GDP.

On the basis of these, in March 1998, eleven EU countries qualified for membership of the single currency. The UK, Denmark and Sweden were not ready to join whilst Greece was not able to join through not meeting the convergence criteria, but still expressed its desire to do so. To reinforce this it joined the ERM for the first time.

The way forward

In 1998 the European Central Bank was formed and this has the authority to set the interest rate which prevails across the eleven countries which have qualified for single currency membership – the so called Euroland or Eurozone.

In January 1999 the exchange rates of the eleven participating countries were fixed and the euro came into existence as a legal entity in its own right. Trading of the euro began against other currencies, although its persistent first year fall in value was as much due to the strength of the dollar as to the weakness of the euro. Additionally, participating governments, the European Commission and the European Investment Bank, began borrowing in euros. Preparation for the change-over to the exclusive use of the euro continues during 1999–2002 and, in January 2002, the euro circulates through Euroland as notes and coins, in parallel with domestic currencies. In July 2002 domestic currencies will cease to be legal tender.

Implications for business

For Euroland businesses, the single currency will bring all the advantages of a fixed exchange rate without any of the disadvantages, of particular importance since over 60 per cent of European Union countries' trade is with each other. In other words, there will be certainty regarding payments and income receipts without incurring the costs of undertaking foreign exchange transactions. There will, therefore, be no need to undertake forward contracts to hedge against possible exchange losses. For banks and other financial services providers this means the loss of an important source of income. However, tourism, which is a major European industry, will certainly benefit from the single currency, as will the transport industry.

The implementation of the euro means that consumers will be able to compare prices of similar goods and services produced in different countries, i.e. there will be transparency in terms of pricing. This will increase the pressures on businesses to keep prices down and improve quality to remain competitive, but it will also offer opportunities to businesses to sell in markets to which they previously had limited access because of the costs and risks of currency conversion. Of course, the euro will still fluctuate against other currencies such as sterling, the dollar and the yen, with all the risks that involves.

The single currency will contribute to harmonisation of wages across the eurozone, since labour will be able to see wage differences in different countries and will, increasingly, move to take advantage of them. This will put competitive pressures on low wage countries that will be forced to raise them. However, higher wages should lead to higher demand for goods and services, although with the single currency and the single market, expenditure may not be on domestically produced goods.

The size of the eurozone may well attract inward investment from other parts of the world, which will create increased competitive pressures for some domestic suppliers, but will benefit businesses receiving it. This increased investment is because movement of funds across borders within the EU will avoid unstable exchange rates. In the past these meant losses might be made by investors during the time before dividends, profits or capital were repatriated to the country of origin.

Countries which joined the single currency are required, under the 1996 Stability and Growth Pact, to maintain the Maastricht convergence criteria, with the exception of that concerning the exchange rate, which of course will be redundant. The requirement that a country's budget deficit does not exceed 3 per cent of its GDP is perceived to be particularly important. Hence a government will not be able to borrow heavily to finance extra expenditure; if it does it will be fined by the European Commission. Therefore, EU fiscal policy is anti-inflationary. Additionally, the European Central Bank is politically independent. It will set interest rates across the Eurozone and will seek to keep inflation low. Therefore, monetary and fiscal policy will both demonstrate prudence, which should create a favourable economic environment in which businesses can flourish.

The outsiders

For EU countries outside the Eurozone there are both costs and benefits from maintaining a separate currency. The main benefit is the ability to retain control or sovereignty over one's own economic policy. Whilst the UK stays outside the Eurozone, interest rates will be set by the Bank of England rather than the European Central Bank. Having said that, in anticipation of joining the single currency, the UK government gave operational independence to the Bank of England in 1997, which was a requirement for single currency membership. Additionally, UK interest rates are persistently higher than Eurozone rates, so single currency membership could be argued to benefit businesses through lower borrowing costs.

Similarly, a country outside the Eurozone is not constrained by the Maastricht convergence criteria, including the size of its internal or budget deficit. This means that a government can use fiscal policy to boost an economy by increasing its budget deficit. It also means that a government facing high inflation can allow the exchange rate of its currency against others to depreciate to keep its exports cheaper and so retain competitive advantage.

On the cost side, there is the problem that a country outside the Eurozone is excluded from central decision making which will affect it either immediately or when it subsequently does join the single currency. It has been said that those in a club make the rules to suit themselves; those joining later have to accept what has already been agreed even if it goes against their best interests. This is particularly relevant since the single currency is perceived as another step on the road to eventual political union, in other words, a United States of Europe. It is, therefore, a real cost to those outside the Eurozone.

There is also the issue that, certainly in the case of the UK, some foreign businesses such as Toyota have argued that if the UK does not adopt the euro instead of sterling, they will consider switching their productive plant to the Eurozone. The City (of London) has also expressed concerns that financial services could relocate to Frankfurt which, for some years, has been seeking to supplant the UK as the European financial centre, a quest helped by the location there of the European Central Bank.

Self testing questions

1. What are the current exchange rates of sterling against the euro and the deutschmark? How far do they need to change to achieve the 'ideal rates' identified in the case study in Chapter 1, Section 1.4?

2. Why is the UK not yet ready to join the single European currency? Should it?

3. What are the main benefits to business from the single currency?

4. Why was it necessary for economies to converge their business cycles before joining the single currency rather than afterwards?

5. Why do the Maastricht convergence criteria require tight limits for a country's budget deficit and national debt?

11.6 Summary of chapter

This chapter has explored the importance of an open economy to business. It began by examining some main theories of international trade, demonstrating the theoretical gains to be derived from trade. The terms of trade were examined for their impact on a country's trade performance and the issues of free trade and protectionism were explored and evaluated.

The value of trade flows are recorded in a country's balance of payments. The components of these were examined, including why the balance of payments must always balance. The implications of a deficit on current account and on transactions in external assets and liabilities were examined, including remedies for addressing such deficits.

The chapter then examined exchange rates, distinguishing between spot and forward rates and examining the factors influencing exchange rates. Policy options to change a country's exchange rates were discussed. The benefits of exchange rate stability for businesses were analysed; this then led on to an examination of different exchange rate regimes.

The chapter concluded by discussing the single European currency and its implications for business, including the benefits.

11.7 Further questions

1 What is the current state of the UK terms of trade? Explain what the figures mean.

2 In the past, countries have sought to be completely self-sufficient rather than engage in international trade. What are the advantages and disadvantages of this?

3 Does a balance of payments deficit matter? Explain your answer.

4 If businesses want certainty in international trade why don't all countries adopt fixed exchange rates?

5 Why is the EU adopting a single currency?

11.8 Further reading

Harris, N. (1999). *European Business*, 2nd edition. Basingstoke: Macmillan Business.

Kerr, W. A. and Perdikis, N. (1996). *The Economics of International Business*. London: Chapman and Hall.

Salvatore, D. (1995). *International Economics*, 5th edition. Hemel Hempstead: Prentice Hall International.

Sodersten, B. and Reed, G. (1999). *International Economics*, 3rd edition. Basingstoke: Macmillan.

The Economist

The *Financial Times*

The Times

IMF Yearbooks

The European Commission: http://www.cec.org.uk

The International Monetary Fund: http://www.imf.org

The Office of National Statistics: http://www.ons.gov.uk

The Treasury: http://www.hm-treasury.gov.uk

The World Trade Organisation: http://www.wto.org/

Index

Absolute advantage, law of, 339
Accelerator, 317–19
Adopter categories, 128–9
Aggregate demand, 277–80, 327, *see also* Demand
Aggregate supply, 277–80, 328–29, *see also* Supply
Airbus Industrie, *see* European defence industry
Amazon.co.uk, 212
Ansoff's product/market matrix, 132–33
Asda, 232

Balance of payments, 34, 345–50
Black markets, 158–61
Boeing Corporation, 182–3
Boston Consulting Group (BCG)'s product portfolio matrix, 133–5
Breaking even, 46–7
British Airways, 73–4
British Gas, 224–5
British Leyland, 83–4
BSkyB, 37–41
Budget (1999), 295–8
Business cycle, 34, 313, 319–21, 322–4
Business economics, 10–12
Business economic environment, 27–30
Business objectives, 3
Business operations, 54
Business organisations, 12–14
Business strategy, 3, 52, 205–6

Capital, 3, 7
Capital account, *see* Balance of payments
Capital (working), *see* Working capital
Car industry, 100–5, 243, *see also* British Leyland, Nissan
Cartel, *see* Oligopoly
Centrally planned economies, 21, 144–6
Circular flow of income, 275

Collusion, *see* Oligopoly
Comparative advantage, law of, 339–41
Competition Act, 2000, 213
Competition Commission, 230, 243, 248–50
Competitive scope, 209–10
Competitiveness, 242–3
Consumer durables, 6
Consumer goods, 5
Consumer sovereignty, 143
Consumption, 272–3
Cost plus, *see* Pricing policies
Costs:
　average, 78–9, 98–9
　(total) fixed, 75–6
　long run, 81, 84–5
　marginal, 78–9, 96–8
　marginal social, 188–9, *see also* Marginal social benefits
　(total) variable, 75–6
　total, 76
Cross elasticity of demand, *see* Elasticity of demand
Current account, *see* Balance of payments

Demand, 21–2, 23, 146–51, 354–5
Diminishing returns, the law of, 80–1
Diseconomies of scale, 83
Distribution channels, 118–20
Double counting, 268

E-commerce, 29, 129–31
Economic and monetary union (EMU), 364–69
Economic growth, 33–4, 325
Economics, definition, 5
Economies of scale, 81–3, 237
Economies of scope, 85–6
Egg Internet bank, 204–5

Elasticity of demand, 169–80, 226–7
Elasticity of supply, 180
Enterprise, *see* Entrepreneur
Entrepreneur, 3, 7
Entry barriers, 25, 209, 214, 220
Euro, *see* Single European currency
European defence industry, 236–7
European Union, 252–7
Exchange rates, 350–7
Exchange rate policy, 36, 293–4, 308, 357–8
Exchange rate regimes, 359–62
Externalities, 6, 187–8

Factors of production, 3, 7, 75
Fiscal policy, 35, 290–2, 308
Fixed factors (of production), 75
Flexible management systems, 63–8
Forecasting, *see* Market research
Foreign direct investment, 16–20
Forward rates, *see* Exchange rates
Four 'Ps', *see* Marketing, mix
Free trade, *see* Protectionism
Full employment, 305

Game theory, 216–18
Grey markets, 162–6
Gross domestic product, 265
Gross national product, 266

Halifax Plc, 91–2
Horizontal integration, 239–40
Households, 4

Income elasticity of demand, *see* Elasticity of
    demand
Increasing returns to scale, *see* Economies of scale
Industrial sectors (of the economy), 15–16
Inflation, 31–2, 280–94
    cost push, 286–7
    demand pull, 284–6, 287
Inflation–unemployment relationship, 309–13
Inputs, *see* Factors of production
Interest rate policy, 4
International trade, 276, 335–50
Investment, 273, 327
Invisible trade, 347

Japanisation, 67–8
Just in time (JIT) production, 66–7
Joint ventures, 243

Kinked demand curve, 218–19

Labour market, 192–202
Labour supply, 3, 7
Land, 3, 7
Limited liability company, *see* Business
    organisations
Lloyds-TSB, 258–61

Maastricht convergence criteria, *see* Treaty of
    Maastricht
Macroeconomics, 9, 263–334
Manchester United, 37–41
Marginal social benefits, 188–9
Market economies, 21
Market failure, 184–91
Market research, 57–61
Market segmentation, 111
Market structures, 23–6
Marketing, 106–39
    characteristics, 107–8
    communications, 117–18
    mix, 109–10, 114–20, 121–2
    strategy, 108–10, 131–5
Markets, 140–3
Marks & Spencer, 44–5, 106–7
Mergers and acquisitions, 238–9, 240–2
Microeconomics, 9
Minimum wage, 197–202
Mission (of a business), 51
Monetary policy, 36, 288–90, 307–8
Monetary Policy Committee, 281
Monopolies & Mergers Commission, 214,
    247–8
Monopolistic competition, 24–5, 221–3
Monopoly, 25, 224–6, 229–30
    discriminating, 226–8
Multiplier, 314–17

National expenditure, 267, 269–70
National income, 266, 267
National product, 265, 267
News Corporation, 16–17, 170
Nissan, 68–70

Office of Fair Trading (OFT), 170, 213, 244,
    245–7
Ofwat, 245–6, 250–1
Oligopoly, 24, 211–20
Opportunity cost, 8

Partnership, *see* Business organisations
Penetration pricing, *see* Pricing strategies
Perfect competition, 25–6, 228–30
PESTLE, 28–30
Phillips curve, 310–13
Price elasticity of demand, *see* Elasticity of demand
Privatised industry regulators, 250–1
Production possibility curve, 279, *see also* Ofwat
Porter's five forces model, 209–10
Porter's value chain, 49–51
Positioning (the product), 114
Price, 20, 23, 31–2, 116, 155–66
Price ceilings, 158–61
Pricing policies, 127–8
Pricing strategies, 126–7
Primary sector, *see* Industrial sectors
Producer goods, 5
Product life cycle, 123–6
Product mix, 115
Profit maximising, *see* Profitability
Profit satisfying, *see* Profitability
Profitability, 14, 45–6, 90, 100–4
Profits, normal, 93
   monopoly, 94
   supernormal, 93
Promotion, *see* Marketing, communications
Promotional pricing, *see* Pricing policies
Protectionism, 342–5
Psychological pricing, *see* Pricing policies
Public Sector Debt Repayment (PSDR), 290, 292
Public Sector Net Cash Requirement (PSNCR), 290, 304

Resources, *see* Factors of production
Revenue:
   average, 89–90, 98–9
   marginal, 90, 96–8
   total, 77, 87–9

Sales revenue maximisation, 47–8
Savings, 22, 273–4
Scarcity, 8
Scottish Widows, 258–61

Secondary sector, *see* Industrial sectors
Services, 6
Seven 'Ps', *see* Marketing, mix
Short term, 75
Single European currency, 362–4
Skimming the cream, *see* Pricing strategies
Small & medium sized enterprises, 223
Socio-economic groupings, 112
Sole trader, *see* Business organisations
Sony, 53
Strategy, *see* Business strategy
Structure–Conduct–Performance Paradigm, 207–9, 215–16
Subsidies, effects of, 255–6, 269
Supply, 22–3, 151–5, 354–5
Supply side policies, 292–3, 308
SWOT analysis, 55–7
Synergy, 241

Targeting strategies, 113–14
Terms of trade, 341–2
Tertiary sector, *see* Industrial sectors
Total quality management (TQM), 63–6
Transfer payments, 269
Treaty of Maastricht, 364–5

Unemployment, 32, 301–9
   classical, 305
   cyclical, 305
   frictional, 305
   natural rate of, 307
   seasonal, 305
   structural, 306

Variable factors (of production), 75
Vertical integration, 239–40
Visible trade, 346–7

Wal-Mart, 231–2
Wave 105.2FM, 61–2
What the market will bear, *see* Pricing policies
Working capital, 3

Yardley, 1–3

THE
BUSINESS CASES
WEB SITE

BUSINESS CASES

◢ **Quality case study materials from quality authors**

◢ **Instant access to cases & tutor support material**

◢ **'Quick view' summaries & author profiles**

◢ **Download PDFs and 'copy' for use on specified courses**

◢ **No registration fee**

◢ **Pay on-line or open an account**

Check out this excellent site today

www.businesscases.org